416

March Madness

The Story of High School Basketball in Illinois

Jim Enright

ILLINOIS HIGH SCHOOL ASSOCIATION
Bloomington

ACKNOWLEDGMENTS

The author and publisher wish to sincerely thank the following for their invaluable contribution to complete the work of "March Madness," particularly each of the IHSA member schools which supplied the photograph(s) of their outstanding state championship team(s).

Dave Arnold, National Federation of State High School Assns.
Jerry Ashby, Northwestern University
Curt Beamer, Urbana Courier
Charles Bellatti, Jacksonville
Jack Brickhouse, WGN-TV
Jim Dynan, Peoria Penny Press
Ron Ferguson, Normal
Charles E. Flynn, Champaign
Dave Frye, Joliet Herald-News
Bill Gleason, Chicago Sun-Times
Don Hazen, Joliet Herald-News
Wayne Hecht, Assembly Hall
Larry Henry, Kankakee Daily Journal
LeRoy Jirik, Chicago
Bob Jones, Centralia
Merle Jones, Carbondale Southern Illinoisan
Howie Judson, Hebron
Chuck Keefer, Rockford Newspapers
Paul King, Peoria Journal Star
Fory Kyle, Joliet Herald-News
Steven Jay Levine, National Basketball Hall of Fame

Joe Mooshil, Associated Press
Bill Niepoetter, Centralia Sentinel
Tom Parkinson, Assembly Hall
Mike Pearson, Univ. of Illinois Athletic Assn.
Larry Perryman, Shelbyville Daily Union
Frank Pitol, Collinsville
Leonard Primer, Chicago
Lowell Reidenbaugh, The Sporting News
James Reiter, Tolono
Chuck Rolinski, Toluca
John Rosenthal, Univ. of Illinois Athletic Assn.
Richard Scherer, Chicago
Les Sintay, United Press Photos
Milt Sprunger, Washington
Loren Tate, Champaign News-Gazette
Jenny Whitten, Normal
Lee Williams, National Basketball Hall of Fame
Al Willis, Florida
Fred "Brick" Young, Bloomington

IHSA OFFICE STAFF

June Ayers, Normal
Shirley Ballinger, Bloomington
Denise Beard, Bloomington
Ella Bethea, Bloomington
Marilyn Black, Bloomington
Joyce Boeckman, Bloomington
Helen Coffman, Normal
Debbie Crosson, Bloomington
Margaret Indlecoffer, Bloomington

Ruth Loane, Bloomington
Kay Lynch, Bloomington
Angie Myers, Bloomington
Suzie Nybert, Gridley
Judy Pinkston, Normal
Mark Rustemeyer, Bloomington
June Walters, Bloomington
Jan Wrigley, Normal
Mary Zeigler, Normal

*To the forgotten people
in basketball, the wives of the
coaches and the officials . . .*

Library of Congress Catalog Card Number: 77-70386
ISBN: 0-9601166-1-3

First Printing

PAIR OF LEADERS—Current IHSA Executive Secretary Harry Fitzhugh, left, and Former Centralia Star Athlete Dwight "Dike" Eddleman, right, meet at a most logical point—the Illini Union on the Campus of the University of Illinois, Urbana-Champaign—and the main topic of discussion obviously is *March Madness*. Fitzhugh, as well as the vast majority of sportwriters, broadcasters, coaches, and fans, label Eddleman, now head of the Fighting Illini Grants-In-Aid Office, the greatest athlete ever produced through IHSA interscholastic competition.

TABLE OF CONTENTS

CHAPTER 1   THE MEN WHO HAVE MADE THE IHSA WORK

CHAPTER 2   THE CHAMPIONS

CHAPTER 3   PUT ME IN, COACH!
The Coaches

CHAPTER 4   WE'RE NUMBER 1!
The Teams

CHAPTER 5   DRIBBLE! PASS! DRIVE! SCORE!
The Players

CHAPTER 6   THERE IS A LOT TO BE SAID ABOUT MARCH MADNESS

CHAPTER 7   THE STORY IN NUMBERS
from 1908 to the present

THE CHAMPIONS
From 1908 To The Present

Freeport ★

★ Rockford

★ Hebron

Evanston ★

Dundee ★

Chicago ★

CHICAGO
Marshall
Carver
Hirsch
Phillips
Morgan Park

Elgin ★

★ Maywood

★ Cicero

Batavia ★

★ La Grange

Dolton ★

★ Hinsdale

Harvey ★

Joliet ★

★ Galesburg

★ Peoria

Canton ★

★ Pekin

★ Bloomington

★ Champaign

★ Mt. Pulaski

★ Villa Grove

Springfield ★

★ Decatur

★ Quincy

★ Taylorville

Paris ★

★ Hillsboro

Lawrenceville ★

★ Granite City

★ Collinsville

★ Venice

★ Centralia

Mt. Carmel ★

★ Mt. Vernon

★ Pinckneyville

Herrin ★

★ Johnston City

★ Marion

★ Ridgway

STATE TOURNEY HISTORY
By JIM FLYNN
Assistant Executive Secretary

It's called "March Madness". It may be the most contagious ailment in Illinois since the common cold. It strikes everywhere—from Chicago to Cairo, from Galena to Paris—sometime during the third month of the year. It is accompanied by tears—of joy and sorrow—and a distinct increase in the heartbeat. It is not fatal, yet, everyone who catches it is infected for life.

Since 1908, when Peoria High School beat Rock Island, 48–29, at the Oak Park YMCA Gym in the first State Basketball Tournament, Illinois, in the vernacular of the times, is "up for grabs" until a new state champion is decided.

The late Lewis Omer, then athletic director at Oak Park High School, originated the idea of the State Tournament. Thirteen teams were invited to the tournament. The next year, following Mr. Omer's suggestion, the infant Illinois High School Athletic Association took over the venture, which has emerged as one of the most widely publicized and competitive state prep tournament series in the nation. The 1909 tournament was held in the Bloomington YMCA Gym. Two years later, Bradley University was the site for the State Tournament, and Rockford High School belted Mt. Carroll, 60–15, for the championship. (Rockford's 60-point effort would be a title game record for the next 34 years.)

For several years, then, the tournament was alternated between Bradley and Millikin University in Decatur. In 1918, Springfield High School's gym was the site of the tournament the only time it has been held in a high school facility—and the famed Arthur L. Trout guided his Centralia Orphans to the first of three titles they would win under his leadership. At the same time, much-respected Sports Editor Fred "Brick" Young of the Bloomington Pantagraph officiated in his first of a record 12 consecutive state tournaments.

Finally, in 1919, the state tournament found a home in Champaign on the campus of the University of Illinois. The first seven tournaments played on the home court of the "Fighting Illini" were in the Old Gym Annex. When Huff Gym was opened in 1926, the emotional appeal—as well as the demand for tickets—of the tournament mushroomed. Since 1963, the University's concrete "flying saucer"—the magnificent Assembly Hall, with a seating capacity of 15,877—has been the site of the State Tournament.

Changes in playing format of the tournament have generally

spawned increased fan interest and availability of tickets, since the first "Sweet Sixteen" in 1934. In 1936, the series of competition was established to include tournament play at the District, Regional, Sectional and "Sweet Sixteen" level. (In 1941, a one-year experiment with a four-team State Final was conducted.) Next significant change came in 1956, when the present system of eight Super-Sectional encounters produce an "Elite Eight" set of finalists who advance to Champaign for the state-wide televised State Tournament. The two-class system was initiated in 1972 with state-record-streak shattering Dolton (Thornridge) taking the Class AA (for schools with enrollments of 751 or more) title, and Lawrenceville claiming the Class A (for schools with enrollments of 750 or less) trophy—a beautiful prize that has become one of the most highly-sought schoolboy trophies in the nation.

Members of the first "Sweet Sixteen" field included champion Quincy, runnerup Thornton (Harvey), third-place Equality, fourth-place Moline, Champaign, Urbana, Streator, Peoria (H.S.), Springfield, Lawrenceville, Marion, Freeport, Charleston, Centralia, Chicago (Marshall) and Chicago (Lane Tech).

The 16-team field for the last single-class competition included: champion Thornridge, runnerup Oak Lawn, third-place Danville, fourth-place Springfield (Lanphier), Benton, Rockford (Boylan), Quincy (Catholic Boys), Granite City, Chicago (Harlan), Kewanee, Elgin (Larkin), Nashville, Winnetka (New Trier East), Paris, Normal (University High) and Peoria (Woodruff).

First state champion crowned in Champaign was Rockford, coached by Frank Winters, which bounced Springfield, 39–20. First champion in Huff Gym was Coach Glenn Holme's Freeport Pretzels, who edged Canton, 24–13. First champion in the Assembly Hall was Chicago (Carver), as Coach Larry Hawkins' Challengers, who took second the year before, beat Centralia, 53–52, on a fantastic shot from the corner at the horn by tiny guard Anthony Smedley.

Only district champion to win the title, after smaller schools were placed into district competition in 1938, was the famous 1952 Hebron team that boasted the tall and talented Judson twins, Phil and Paul, along with 6-7½ center Bill Schulz. Hebron, a school with an enrollment of only 99, outscored Quincy by a 6–1 margin in overtime to take the championship, 64–59. Other district teams to reach the final game were Braidwood in 1938 and the gigantic Cobden Appleknockers of 1964. Cobden, with a lineup that included the 6-6 Neal brothers, Chuck and Jim, and the equally big Smith cousins, Ken and Jim, lost to the Dave Golden-led Pekin Chinks, 50–45.

Perhaps the greatest game ever in the State Tournament History was the 1945 quarterfinal match between Decatur and Galesburg. The Runnin' Reds, finally captured a 73–72 overtime victory, but only after the score was tied or the lead changed hands an incredible 33—count em'—33 times. One of the most devastating performances by a team in a single game has to be Thornridge's 35-point (104–69) victory over Quincy in the first Class AA title game in 1972. That victory for the Boyd Batts-Quinn Buckner spearheaded Falcons was No. 54 in the school's 58-game state record winning streak.

Among the most memorable individual performances were those by Granite City's Andy Phillip in 1940; Dwight "Dike" Eddleman's single-handed victory for Centralia in 1942; Max Hooper's total of 57 points in back-to-back title games to give Mt. Vernon the 1949 and '50 championships; George Wilson's smooth as silk play at center for Chicago Marshall in 1958, and again in 1960; Collinsville's Bogie Redmon in the Kahoks' 32–0 season that concluded with an 84–50 win over Thornton (Harvey) in 1961; and the then all-time tournament scoring performance (152 points) of 6-9 Dave Robisch of Springfield in 1967.

In 1974, Lawrenceville became the first school since the origination of the two-class system to claim a second title in Class A competition. Coach Ron Felling's Indians, led by forward Rick Leighty, fought off Ottawa Marquette's comeback bid to win 54–53 in what was at the time the closest title game in Class A's brief history.

In 1976, when America celebrated its Bicentennial, fans in the Assembly Hall were treated to: 1) the greatest all-time individual scoring performance in the long history of the tournament series; 2) a pair of championship games that will long be remembered for their dramatic one-point conclusions.

Lawrenceville's senior guard Jay Shidler dazzled those in attendance and the statewide television audience with games of 37, 48 and 45 points. Those scoring outbursts, plus a 27-point effort in the Charleston Super-Sectional, brought the "Golden Gunner" or "Bionic Boy" as the press labeled him, the all-time tournament individual scoring record of 157 points. Needing 41 points to set the mark in the third place game, Shidler became the darling of the sellout crowd as each of his shots sailed toward the basket. When he scored tournament point No. 153, the building rocked with approval.

But Shidler's performance was only a prelude to a spine-tingling tilt between eventual champion Mt. Pulaski (a school that had grown in enrollment and cage talent through consolidation with nearby Elkhart) and Oneida (ROVA). ROVA lead 35–34 at half-time and 46–45 after three quarters. Mt. Pulaski moved ahead 55–54 with 2:35 to play and then the lead changed four times in the next 113 seconds. Finally, with 42 seconds to go, Mt. Pulaski's super sophomore Jeff Clements (who scored 10 of his team's last 10 points) fired through what proved to be the clincher. ROVA worked for one final shot, trying to get the ball into 6-8 center Dave Johnson, but could not master the Mt. Pulaski defense. Finally, with six seconds left, Dwight Peterson fired up a 16-foot jump shot and missed, and Johnson had the rebound slip off his fingertips and out of bounds underneath the basket as time ran out.

One week later, Chicago (Morgan Park), trailing the entire game, nipped Aurora (West), 45–44, when Laird Smith got the tip from teammate Levi Cobb on a jump ball situation and fired through a jump shot from the right of the free throw circle as the ball fell through the net as the scoreboard clock registed 0:00. Trailing 33–26 after three quarters, Morgan Park put on a fourth-quarter rally that ranks as one of the greatest in IHSA State Tournament history.

INTRODUCTION

Three sets of numbers I'll always remember: US 55-428-257, the 7 digits inbedded into the dog tags I wore for two years; 3,100, the constant population total on the Pinckneyville city limits signs; and 65-39, the score by which Pinckneyville, my hometown, defeated East Rockford in the 1948 state high school basketball championship game.

What does the state tournament mean to me? It means my youth. It means growing up with a dream and a basket hung on a telephone pole in the alley. It means shoveling snow away from the cinders and tar so the rubberized, pebble-grained ball would bounce.

The magic words of my youth were *Sweet 16*. They meant ribbons of sunlight which filtered past the shades at Huff Gym during afternoon games; the map hanging at the end of the gym with 16 lights first blinking, then being extinguished, one by one; the lobby of the Inman hotel, clogged with cigar smoke, crew-cut kids in letter-sweaters, scalpers, and coaches looking for jobs.

As an 8th grader, I watched Duster Thomas' slow-break machine roll up those 65 points (yes, it was a record then) in the state finals. And today, when people talk of 1948—the year Israel became a free state, Citation won the Triple Crown, and Truman beat Dewey—I always interject: "Yeah, and Pinckneyville won the state championship."

Three years later in 1951, and again in 1952, I played in the same tournament. We didn't win it. But as each year passes, it matters less. Then, it meant everything. That senior year, 1952, was the first for the tournament to be televised (fortunately, the cameras weren't on yet in the quarterfinals, when I accidentally ripped the shirt off Mose Stokes' back. Funny about that incident, though. I never felt guilty. My coach, Duster, told me not to worry because they never washed their uniforms in Mt. Vernon, anyhow.).

Duster was a miracle man. So were coaches like Dolph Stanley (give him a high school team, and he'd eventually take it to Champaign). But in 1952, a miracle team was champion. Hebron had the Judson twins, Spooner, Wilbrandt, and Schultz; coach Russ Ahearn had green socks; the Hebron subs never even bothered to go to the locker room at halftime; and I'll always remember the desolation of the Quincy bench in the state title game when Bruce Brothers fouled out in overtime.

A year later, sitting in the crowd, I watched another kid from Pinckneyville, Bob Quillman, sink a one-handed baseball throw from the OTHER foul line to end the 3rd quarter . . . but it didn't do much good. LaGrange had Ted Ciaizza and won anyhow.

The state tournament, too, means sending out boys to become men like Tom Millikin, who enjoys a rare position in prep record books. He played with a state championship team (Pinckneyville, 1948), coached another (Proviso East, 1969), and was principal when the Maywood school won again in 1974.

So much for Pinckneyville self-indulgence, but nostalgia is predictable. It always takes one back to roots. Perhaps, in this case, because life in those small, coal-mining communities of southern Illinois was tied ever so tightly to what happened in March at Champaign.

Millions of others in this state, I suspect, have similar memories . . . if not as participants, as spectators. That's the kind of hold this event enjoys. There was a magic with the *Sweet 16* . . . when every school, no matter the size, shared the same dream. And though some of that magic has diminished (or does it just seem that way with each new year?), the current tournament format is more functional and remains the best sports show in the midwest.

To me, it's still the memory of Dr. Gene Stotlar teaching me the rocking-chair fake in an alley game; it's Deacon Davis of Freeport looking one way and passing the other; it's hometown names like Pursell, Lazenby, Gladson, and Margenthaler.

Also, though, it's George Wilson and Marshall high school of Chicago finally breaking the championship barrier . . . then the undeniable city onslaught from Carver, Hirsch, Phillips, and Morgan Park . . . a ceaseless flow of talent, evidence that this tournament, once the showcase for rural basketball in Illinois, had been overpowered by the City League game.

My 13-year-old son now attends the state tournament. Magic words to him are *Elite Eight,* and most of his heroes are black. He hasn't missed a game in four years, and he's seen teenagers leap through the air and do things with a basketball that my heroes of the past never dreamed could be done (when I first tried to guard Bobby Joe Mason of Centralia, and he flipped a backward pass over his shoulder to a fastbreak trailer, I thought the ultimate had been reached).

Hopefully, whether he ever plays the game or not, my son will also gather memories of this great tournament.

Isn't it part of growing up in Illinois?

RICK TALLEY

MOLDERS OF MARCH MADNESS
—The Illinois High School Association was informally started in 1898 and hired the nation's first full-time chief administrator in 1922. From that date through 1976, only three men have served the students and the schools as Executive Secretary of the IHSA. The first was Charles W. Whitten, left,

who served from 1922 to 1942. He was followed by Albert Willis, center, who served from 1942 to 1968. Harry Fitzhugh, left, succeeded Willis in 1968 and is the present Chief Administrator for an association that employs a full-time staff of 19 in its Headquarters Building, 2715 McGraw Dr., Bloomington.

Chapter 1

The Men Who Have Made the IHSA Work

C.W. WHITTEN

Ever since the birth of organized high school athletics in Illinois, the executive end has been the hallmark of expert and progressive leadership. If ever one organization was tailored to the personality of its original leader, it is the Illinois High School Association (until 1940 Illinois High School Athletic Association). That leader was Charles W. Whitten, a stately and strong man who served as the association's first executive secretary. He moved with poise and dignity, looking more like the chairman of the board than the judge administering justice in Illinois high school interscholastic activities.

When Miss Jenny Whitten was advised that somebody once described her father as being "soft as putty on the outside and hard as iron on the inside," she declared it a perfect fit. And don't for one minute think that Miss Whitten didn't speak from experience.

"My sister Mable, my father, and I were taking our customary Sunday walk. When we passed a flower bed, Mable reached down and picked one. Sometime later I grabbed it out of her hand and crushed it. When Mable started to cry, my father said: 'Jenny, you have done that once too often. When we get home you will be punished.' Our walk continued, and my father was kind as usual. We talked and visited like we did before the incident."

"When we returned home he got a peach switch and wrapped it around my ankles a few times. Nothing more was said. Nothing more needed to be said, but that was the last time I ever snatched anything from Mable's possession."

Although he was the leader for literally thousands of high school boys in Illinois, Whitten never had any sons and only two daughters,

Jenny and Mable. "One time I asked him," Jenny recalled, "if he was sorry that he didn't have a son? He said, 'No I'm not, I'm very happy with my two girls.' "

It was 1922 when Whitten came upon the Illinois scene. Before he was to retire, Whitten enjoyed 20 years as the executive officer of the Illinois High School Athletic Association, 13 years as the executive secretary of the National Federation of State High School Athletic Associations, and seven years as commissioner of the Illinois Inter-collegiate (Little 19) Athletic Conference.

As he talked of retirement in the late 1930s, the Champaign News-Gazette carried a four part series on Whitten's work and achievements for the IHSAA. It was co-authored by Eddie Jacquin, the News-Gazette Sports Editor, and Bill Marsteller, one of the newspaper's sports staffers.

When the series was completed, Whitten sent the following letter to Jacquin: "Well, my dear Eddie, I have just completed reading the four articles published in the News-Gazette dealing with my administration of the IHSAA. These articles have succeeded in breaking down one of my lifelong resolutions, namely, that I would never write any letter of protest to any newspaper or sports editor because of anything that may have appeared in the paper's columns.

"I have occasionally written letters of approval of statements, but I give my word that as far as my memory serves me, this will be the first letter of protest I've ever written.

"And what is the basis of my present protest? It is simply this, Eddie, that you and Mr. Bill Marsteller have written in far too complimentary terms of me personally with respect to the achievements of the IHSAA during my administration.

"I shall have to confess to you that the articles which you have published make pleasant reading for me. I believe that they will be pleasant reading for my children and my grandchildren. Also, for others who may have some concern for the reputation of The Old Man. I want to say, however, that although the achievements you mention actually have taken place during my term in office, they couldn't have been brought about by me single-handedly.

"Many schoolmen, many members of various boards, many principals, and many coaches have rendered helpful and cordial assistance. It would be most ungracious of me if I failed to mention the one man who has stood by as my right hand and served with intelligence and vigor during the past 12 years: H.V. Porter. He has shouldered a large portion of the rather arduous burdens involved in the promotion of the programs so well described in your series of articles."

It's to be wondered how today's crop of rebellious leaders in sports would have reacted in the credit-sharing situation Whitten handled so expertly.

Whitten's career started as a teacher in 1887. It was in a one-room schoolhouse in Marshall County, 10 miles east of Lacon and 40 miles north of Peoria. Later he was elected to the Board of Directors from DeKalb High School. C.W. served on the board until 1922 when he resigned to become manager of the IHSAA as the association's first paid employee. Previously, this work had been handled by different principals around the state. After Whitten took office it was estimated there were 500 athletic contests a week during the school year.

Writing about Whitten's new role and the progress of the association 17 years later in the News-Gazette, Marsteller wrote: "When the IHSAA promoted Whitten from the board to manager in 1922, it launched its biggest advance in history. It was like a kid growing into his first pair of long pants."

While a student at the University of Illinois, Whitten spent some of his spare time teaching geometry and physics in the basement of the old University Hall to kids who were a bit short on college entrance credits.

When he took over as IHSAA manager, Whitten established the headquarters in DeKalb and became the first paid high school association administrator in the nation. In 1905 the association had 21 member schools. By 1922 the membership count was 665. In 1939 the count increased to 918, and most of the Chicago schools, among the last to fall in line, had signed up.

By now Whitten was called a "czar" in some quarters, but never by men who worked with him in connection with IHSAA projects. Always ready to save for a rainy day, one year Whitten discovered the association earned more money in interest ($3,000) than it banked from membership fees, two dollars from each of the 918 member schools for a total of $1,836.

Improved officiating in all forms of competition was another of his projects. Almost overnight the number of officials jumped from 200 to 1,400. Also, he was a foremost booster of the high school association's using their own playing codes instead of a blanket adoption of college rules. Whitten reasoned that frequently the college rules were harmful when used by younger athletes.

Back in his native Stark County, some folks knew Whitten as "Willie," and others as Charles William Whitten. Few young men ever traveled more than Whitten as he moved from Bradley to Varna to Normal to Urbana to DeKalb to Elmhurst to Joliet before moving to St. Petersburg, Florida to live out his retirement. "My father," Jenny claimed, "always enjoyed living and working in small towns. Never did he become a Metropolitanite. Even when the association office was moved to Chicago, he retained the family home in Elmhurst."

With his vast interest seeking to improve academic standards, what attracted Whitten to the athletic side of the high school ledger? Daughter Jenny, herself an outstanding student-teacher who majored in foreign languages and studied abroad, explained her father's stand saying, "Often I would hear him say he never wanted to see the athletic tail wag the educational dog. I've frequently wondered what his reaction would be to today's activity between schools and athletes."

In that direction, Miss Whitten noted, "I'm very glad I was teaching during a time when the classes were small enough to regard the students as individuals instead of a number in a computer. Today it's education on a mass production basis."

During the time when Whitten was a student at Bradford High School, the tuition was 11 dollars a year, eggs sold for five cents a dozen, and butter cost 15 cents a pound. The individual independence of the family surfaced when Miss Whitten recalled her sister Mable's decision to get her masters degree at the University of Arizona. "I'm going somewhere," Mable noted, "where I won't be known as Jenny Whitten's sister or C.W. Whitten's daughter."

Whitten completed a 272-page book in January of 1950 titled "Interscholastics." It is a primer of his observations and philosophies during a long and successful career as a national leader in high school athletics. It is the framework of the IHSAA. In his book Charles William Whitten lists such IHSAA staffers as Albert Willis, Helen Thomas Nelson, and Milton Sprunger for special credit along with principals Harry D. Anderson of Des Plaines; Fred L. Biester of Glen Ellyn; Oscar M. Corbell of Centralia; Silas Echols of Mount Vernon, and two collegiate representatives: Dr. William C. Reavis of the University of Chicago, and Dr. Robert B. Browne of the University of Illinois. Together they shaped the history of one of the greatest associations in America.

AL WILLIS

Anybody trading sports talk with Al Willis the first time would come away convinced he was a name dropper at the very highest level. When major league baseball had to be told the facts about signing future prospects before they finished high school, Willis, with a small committee of other executive secretaries, immediately set up a direct line of communication. He contacted the one man who could —and would—do something about the situation. That was Judge Kenesaw Mountain Landis.

Judge Landis, baseball's first commissioner, was in the process of pulling all the loose ends together when he died. Willis' next stop was the office of the new commissioner, Albert Benjamin "Happy" Chandler. Happy was a United States senator from Kentucky when he was drafted to become Landis' successor. Chandler's views on this particular brand of "cradle robbing" were as strong as his predecessors.

It wasn't too much later when professional football discovered the wonders of wealth and glory attached to television. Sunday was considered the pros' best day of the week in building schedules, but still some moguls had other ideas about how best to collect more television money.

Some thought Friday nights would be good television time because there would be a second dividend to clip. That would be the constant "selling" of all the upcoming games on the Sunday schedule. Again Al Willis became a man in motion, and yelled loud enough to be heard from Sacramento to Saginaw, and on to Schenectady:

"You can't do that. Friday night is high school football night."

In record time Willis was sharing the same conference table with Bert Bell, the Commissioner of the National Football League. Bell, buoyed with the opinions of such pro football titans as the Bears' George Halas, the Cardinals' Charles W. Bidwill, and the Steeler's Art Rooney agreed with Willis' claim.

The NFL absolutely would not compete with the nation's high schools on Friday nights during the football season. And Bell's word was law among the pros as the state high school associations across the country were to learn in a most authoritative manner. Willis now was two-for-two wrestling with professional baseball and football to protect the rights, as well as the future, of the high school programs and athletes.

Some years later Willis and the IHSA was involved in another winning scrimmage. This one in the United States Supreme Court concerning the eligibility dispute of Rockford's Jasper Robinson. This was one of sports' early day high court showdowns, a forerunner to present practices that make attorneys about as active as the pitcher or the quarterback in pro play.

Al Willis hasn't spent all his time with men like Judge Landis, Happy Chandler, and Bert Bell. As a youth he was as interested in the academic side of the ledger as he was the athletic program. This training served him well during his 26-year term as the second executive secretary in the history of the IHSA.

He was front and center when the association was a one man, one office, one chair, one desk operation with a single telephone in the hub of Chicago's financial district, LaSalle Street. These limited quarters were a long way from the wide open spaces around Eldorado, which Al enjoyed as a youth.

Harrison Willis, Al's father, wore as many as three hats providing a living for his family in the early 1900's. The senior Willis was a miner, farmer, and cattle buyer—not for himself, but for a friendly and wealthy rancher in the Eldorado area. Because trucks and wagons weren't available to move the livestock to their new home, Al used to walk the various purchases down dirt roads and across fields.

It was during these walkathons with his father that young Willis learned to love the outdoors, an excellent conditioner for his high school athletic career. He played both football and basketball at Eldorado High School, and frequently the football season ran longer than the basketball season.

"At that time," Willis began, "basketball was regarded as a sissy game played mainly by girls. Due to this rating, most schools concentrated more on football than basketball building their year-to-year schedules."

Nevertheless, Al was able to find something to do during basketball's short season. He had a part in the senior play during all four years he spent in high school. "It was during this time," Willis noted, "that I developed an interest in all activities including athletics. I've always felt that music, drama, and speech were as important to a school's total program as basketball, football, and other sports.

"I didn't realize the oddity of playing in four senior plays until my young grandson asked recently, 'Grandpa, how could you be in the senior play when you weren't a senior?' "

Al's school days appeared over following his high school graduation. The family lacked the funds to send him to college, and he went to work in the coal mines. He was equipped for this work inasmuch as he spent his last two summer vacations in the mines.

When he wasn't working, "Miner" Willis spent some of his free time visiting the train depot in Eldorado. This was easy to do because one of his father's best friends was a telegraph operator there. Frequently, as he sat listening to the clicking telegraph instruments trying to decode the many messages, Al envisioned himself becoming an operator.

This dreaming posed Al's own $64 question: how does one become an operator? Not too much later he learned that the Chillicothe (Ohio) Business School offered a course in telegraphy. Also, the school fielded teams in both football and basketball. Now, Willis had three reasons for wanting to enroll at Chillicothe. Shortly, ways and means were discovered to get him to Chillicothe, and the student-athlete was back in business to continue his education.

Willis lettered in both football and basketball and was making good progress in the telegraphy course when his bright future darkened. Friends had an important message for him. It concerned advance automation, and the toll it was taking in drying up the telegraph operator's job market. What to do? Al elected to accept the advice and returned to Eldorado, hoping for another new start.

Not too long afterwards Willis found a new benefactor who would provide some financial assistance if he could raise the tuition. This second start was finalized when Al picked McKendree College and was en route to the Lebanon campus the next fall. After his sophomore year Willis married Alice Creighton, a McKendree co-ed from Fairfield.

During his junior year, he was elected captain of the football team, and this particular honor produced a new avenue of income. Al became the head waiter in the school's dining room.

Before he was to finish his stint at McKendree, Willis was to become one of the college's first 13 players to win four varsity letters in a single season. Al earned this top level recognition in football, basketball, baseball, and track helping McKendree improve its athletic fortunes.

Following graduation from McKendree, Al set out to find a job. In this search he was aided by Dr. Cameron Harmon, the college president. Dr. Harmon provided the downfield blocking to assure Willis getting his first position. It was at Flat Rock, an oil town in southern Illinois with a three-year high school. The McKendree-trained Willis received an annual salary of $1,800 for coaching both football and basketball at Flat Rock.

After his two-season coach role, Willis was elevated to the school's combined coach and principal position. This promotion upped his salary six hundred dollars to $2,400. He retained this position for three years before moving from Flat Rock to Fairfield, where he coached football, basketball, and the school's limited track program. Four years later Willis became Fairfield's principal, a post he held for five years.

Minus the coaching chores and enjoying additional free time as principal, the door was opened for Willis to launch a new career in officiating. As a charter member of the Illinois Officials' Association, Willis worked football and basketball and judged track meets.

Willis' third move took him from Fairfield to Batavia, where he accepted the principalship. In Batavia Al's next door neighbor was Lyle "Dutch" Clarno, one of the midwest's topflight officials in both collegiate and high school competition. Willis and Clarno struck up an immediate friendship as they toured the northern half of Illinois on their officiating assignments.

Recalling his association with Clarno, Willis explained, "We traveled hundreds of miles together and officiated many, many games in both football and basketball. At that time Dutch probably was the busiest official in the Chicago area. He worked a full schedule in the Big Ten and the major independents like DePaul, Loyola, Marquette, and Notre Dame.''

Willis was in the process of closing out his second year as Batavia's principal when one telephone call added a brand new dimension to his life. The call was from C.W. Whitten, then the manager of the Illinois High School Athletic Association based in Chicago. Whitten had a job to offer and sought Al's reaction to becoming his assistant. H.V. Porter, who had held the position was moving from the Illinois organization to the National Federation. Now Whitten was scouting for somebody who would possibly become his successor after serving as an apprentice in the Chicago office.

It wasn't an easy decision for the man who had moved from Flat Rock to Fairfield to Batavia. Instead of working for just one school, Al would be associated with almost every high school within the state. He was qualified, having served as coach, principal, and official following his exit from McKendree College. Willis accepted Whitten's offer and was quick to adopt his new superior's philosophy.

"Whenever Mr. Whitten had a decision to make," Al recalled, "he would say, 'Working in athletics, one has to be soft as putty on the outside and hard as iron on the inside.' Once he made a decision, he refused to second guess himself—and the situation was closed."

Willis had an opportunity to apply this philosophy many times after he became the second executive secretary of the IHSA. Working with B. Floyd Smith, the principal of Benton High School, the association amended its rule barring all-black schools from participating in the boys' state basketball tournament. After several moves were made to solve this growing controversy, Smith offered to "accept the responsibility" of assigning the all-black Mounds-Douglas school to the Benton Regional.

Screams of protest became thunder-loud when Mounds-Douglas defeated West Frankfort, then one of the tournament favorites, in the opening round. Even Mounds-Douglas' loss in its next game failed to quiet the charges and counter-charges from fans on a statewide basis.

Now the black athlete is to the IHSA and its programs what Joe Morgan is to the two-time winning Cincinnati Reds in baseball's World Series.

Having learned first hand the value of on-the-job-training—the two years he spent as C.W. Whitten's assistant—Al Willis worked with an assistant named Harry Fitzhugh, the present executive secretary of the IHSA. There is a striking similarity within the lifestyles of Albert Willis and Harry Fitzhugh, the Nos. 2 and 3 executive secretaries of the Illinois association. Both are in total agreement that the state championship basketball tournament is one of the very best amateur events on the national sports calendar.

HARRY FITZHUGH

If Tom Gilbert kept a box score on the successful progress of four of his foremost athletes while coaching at tiny Auburn High School in the early 1930's, he would have a perfect four-for-four in baseball parlance. Taking advantage of a rule of the time, allowing him to coach and teach industrial arts at the high school level without a degree, Tom Gilbert helped send four athletes into the wonderful world of sports. First there was venerable Emil "Dutch" Leonard, whose baffling knuckleball enabled him to win 191 games during a 20 year major league career.

While Leonard was testing his talents for the Brooklyn Dodgers, Washington Senators, Philadelphia Phillies, and finally the Chicago Cubs, Tom Gilbert was back in Auburn molding three athletes for future intercollegiate competition. Jack Volc was the leader of this parade, finishing his high school eligibility two years ahead of two more amazing Auburnites, Harry Fitzhugh and Ernie Pricco.

Deciding time had come for him to get his degree, Gilbert entered Eastern Illinois Teachers College in Charleston. Making this Auburn to Charleston move, Tom didn't travel empty handed. He was accompanied by Jack Volc, who had just completed a two-year stint as a coal miner, and Fitzhugh and Pricco—newly graduated and accomplished Auburn athletes in football, basketball, and baseball.

In Fitzhugh's case Gilbert arranged for a job as well as lodging in Charleston. The job was the equivalent of a scholarship in those days to cover the $10.00 per quarter tuition, as well as book rental and an activities card. Harry's off-campus address was the rooming house Tom Gilbert's mother operated in Charleston.

Fitzhugh's job was most unusual. He was a daily three-hour breakfast chef in a Charleston restaurant, where the railroad train crews met for breakfast every morning from 4 to 7. Thereafter, it was Harry's day to do as he liked between his academic and athletic chores.

As a collegian he limited his athletic activity to varsity football and baseball. In connection with his association with Leonard, a senior at Auburn when he was a freshman, Harry recalled, "I told people that Dutch threw the knuckleball, Carl Hubbell the screwball, and I threw the rocket ball—it exploded as it sailed over the fence."

Fitzhugh is typical of most successful athletes in giving full credit to their high school coach for assertiveness and patience and leadership as career-builders. The man who was to become only the third executive secretary of the IHSA and one of the nation's foremost athletic administrators recalled, "I seriously doubt if I would have been able to attend college without Tom Gilbert's help. He opened all the doors, and I couldn't hazard a guess what might have happened to me without him. It was depression time then, and jobs were hard to come by, especially jobs for kids in college."

Following graduation from Eastern, Harry quickly discovered it was still difficult finding a job at the high school teaching and coaching levels. Because none were available, and he was without Tom Gilbert's important downfield blocking, Fitzhugh took an elementary school position in Bushton, a small community just north of Charleston.

It was a two-story building which housed the first four grades on the first floor and the fifth through eighth grades on the second. He taught the top four grades, earning $80.00 a month as teacher and another $10.00 each month for his duties as principal.

After three years at Bushton he moved on to Franklin, where he was to wear four different hats over a period of 29 years, from 1937 to 1966. In order he was a teacher, an assistant coach, principal, and finally superintendent. In fact, there was one period when Harry served as both principal and Mister Superintendent for 12 years.

It was during this period that Harry discovered new ways and means of finding additional income. He officiated in his spare time and well remembers his very first fee. "I worked two basketball games alone and was paid three dollars and fifty cents," Fitzhugh recalled.

During his tenure at Franklin, a school later consolidated with Alexander and Nortonville, Harry literally struck gold. He first served for two years on the IHSA Legislative Commission before beginning the first of six three-year terms as a member of the IHSA Board of Directors. He also served as president of the board during three of these terms, excellent on-the-job training for what was to become the biggest—and best—promotion of his life.

After 18 years on the board, Mister Fitzhugh moved to Chicago to become assistant secretary under Al Willis, then the Association's executive secretary. When Willis retired June 30, 1968, his successor was Harry Lee Fitzhugh. He took over the next day—in time to start working on some of the association's most meaningful and historic projects.

With a total of 20 years IHSA experience under his belt, the soft speaking, mild mannered Fitzhugh has one foremost goal: making the Illinois association the very best high school athletic body in the United States. The girl's interscholastic program has grown rapidly since 1968. At that time there were no state championships for girls in any sports. Today there are more programs for girls than boys.

Five years ago steps were taken to remove the David and Goliath pattern of the boys' state high school basketball tournament by a switch to divisions. Several plans were proposed and studied. When the high school principals were polled, they voted for two classes: Class A schools with an enrollment up to 750; Class AA schools with an enrollment of 751 or more students.

The two-class pattern was launched in 1972 and immediately proved as popular as Ernie Banks, the all-time Mister Cub, speaking at a Little League baseball banquet in Toluca. In connection with the nation's bicentennial birthday in 1976, the Class A tournaments attracted a total attendance of 351,795 along with a turnout of 421,665 for the Class AA competition—a grand total of 773,460.

Furthermore, the competition couldn't have been more pulse-pounding. Mt. Pulaski topped Oneida 59 to 58 for the Class A title, and Chicago (Morgan Park) edged Aurora (West) in a 45-44 cliffhanger for the Class AA championship.

Although he regarded himself as being better in baseball than football, a half hundred of Eastern's foremost athletes figured differently. During a reunion to honor Charlie Lantz, Eastern's esteemed coach for more than 40 years, the group elected two all-time All-Star teams in football. The first era spanned from 1911 to 1931, the second from 1932 to 1951.

In the all-player selections Fitzhugh was picked at end for the 1932 to 1951 team, an honor he holds in deep affection to this day.

After a long and successful officiating career, Harry missed assignment to the State Championship Basketball Tournament due to a rule he helped write as a member of the IHSA Board of Directors. The rule prohibited any current member of the board from working in the "Sweet Sixteen" for obvious reasons. First, it was installed to avoid any possible criticism along the lines of "Why shouldn't he work the tournament, he's a member of the board." Or, on the other hand, if trouble developed the board would be forced to take action one way or the other against one of its members.

With his fulltime fairness, Harry stressed, "I thought it was a good rule when it was made, and I still do."

Nevertheless, Harry's officiating tenure extended over 30 years, and he worked with such outstanding officials as Dwight Wilkey, Bob Brodbeck, Bill Filson, John "Red" Pace, Ron Gibbs and Russ Shields to name a few.

Then it was mainly the Little 19 Conference as well as the top high schools and smaller colleges within the state. "Fitz" had three planks in his officiating program: fellowship, physical conditioning, and the fees—a welcome addition to the family budget.

"Most times we would drive together to the various sites, and the fellowship was outstanding," Harry said recalling past events. "There wasn't nearly the pressure other officials encountered in the Big Ten, the Big 8, and the Missouri Valley conference. It truly was a (paid) fun project from start to finish."

In connection with the upcoming two shot technical foul in the search for improved bench decorum, Harry claimed, "Whatever it takes to achieve this point, I'm all for it. If two technical free throws will get the job done, fine. If I was permitted to write one rule, I would foul the coach every time he gets off the bench with the clock running."

"I realize the coach is out there to win, but he has other purposes. He must set an example of decorum on the bench."

When it comes to trivia memory tests, Fitzhugh can compete with Jimmy Durante, because he also has a million of them. Just like every basketball buff within the state, Fitzhugh leads off with Hebron's overtime triumph over Quincy in the 1952 state championship game. It was the first and only overtime test ever in the title game as Hebron stamped itself the greatest of all the Li'l David winners.

Harry well remembers tiny Cobden's magnificent stand against Pekin in 1964, giving credit to Dawdy Hawkins for an outstanding coaching job in behalf of his Chinks from the Peoria area. "Never have I heard more enthusiasm greet one team than when Cobden was introduced," Harry recalled. "There was Dawdy's team, standing first on one leg and then the other. Still he had it fired up for the tipoff, and the victory over another courageous district contender— the amazing Apple Knockers from Cobden."

Mister Secretary recalled Decatur's 73-72 classic overtime conquest of Galesburg in 1945 and Laird Smith's shot of more recent vintage as Morgan Park derailed Aurora (West) in the 1976 final. Smith's shot slipped through the net as the buzzer sounded.

In connection with the IHSA's shift to two divisions in 1972, Harry admits his original reaction was negative. "My reasoning, maybe not too sound," Fitzhugh claimed, "was a personal and philosophical thing. I like to think in America, regardless where you start out in life, you will have an opportunity to be Number One. In a class system you can only become Number One in your class when it's possible you might win the whole ball of wax.

"Since the shift in basketball, we now have divisions in football, golf, track, cross country, and wrestling in boys sports. I'm sure there will be more divisions in the future because I must admit it gives more communities and more people an opportunity to really excel.

"When the Class A winner and its prideful followers leave Champaign, they feel they are Number One in the state as well as the entire country. It's a matter of record that some of the Class A championship games were contested better than some of the Class AA finals before capacity crowds in the Assembly Hall."

After a five-year test of the Class A basketball tournament, Fitzhugh is convinced the two-class system has proved itself in Illinois. He fears, however, that the addition of any more new divisions would dilute the program and possibly lessen the interest. "It's much like the football coach who awards a letter to everybody who comes out for the squad," Harry began. "Then the award isn't nearly as meaningful to the 15 to 20 athletes who logged most of the playing time during the entire season."

The third executive secretary in the history of the IHSA didn't have to test his memory to stress the tremendous interest and appeal of the two-class system. He used the consolation game played between Lawrenceville and Buda-Sheffield (Western) in the 1976 Class A Tournament to prove his point. The appearance of just one player, Lawrenceville's Jay Shidler, filled the Assembly Hall for this secondary feature on the last night of the tournament.

The massive crowd turned out to see Shidler, and the crowd wasn't disappointed. It thrilled to Shidler's complete performance as a shooter, jumper, passer, rebounder, and play-maker. Playing a typical American role, the carrot-topped athlete saved the best for last to escalate the Lawrenceville command: Ride With Shide. He was the game's high scorer with 45 points to tie down a record-setting collection of 157 points in four tournament games.

There is overtime wonderment in Illinois, and in several other states, about the wisdom of playing the third-fourth place game. Frequently, the contestants are upset and weary over earlier losses and find it next to impossible to get "up" for this no-fun game.

"We've heard most of the pros and cons regarding the game for a long time," Harry explained, "but so far our people have seen fit to play it. Players and fans seldom forget a winner, and in the years ahead the immediate protests fade away with such claims as, 'That was a good night when we beat so and so for third place in this or that particular tournament.'

"Generally it has been suggested that we use a coin flip to decide the third and fourth place winners and present similar trophies to both teams. To me that would dilute the award just as the football coach did when he presented the entire squad with letters."

With or without a new crop of Jay Shidlers, it's apparent the consolation game will remain a fixture in both Class A and Class AA tournaments far into the future. Good game, bad game, the record has blossomed into many grand and glorious memories for later years.

Because he isn't quarrelsome by nature, the best Harry will yield in any comparison of the Illinois program with that of the rest of the nation is a down-the-middle split. "When Jack Drees, who played at Iowa, was part of our television program, he told me the three states he considered tops were Illinois, Indiana, and Kentucky," Eastern's illustrious alumnus volunteered. "I can't help but think that we are as good as Indiana, and they are as good as we are. If we played a series of games with Indiana, I'm sure we'd split about 50-50.

"In the overall picture when you take into account all the sports we have in this state for the boys and the girls, we would have to rank first or very near first in all-around performance compared to the rest of the nation. We are strong in gymnastics, and all this strength is concentrated in the northern part of the state."

"We are strong in swimming, track and field, and wrestling. We have a great football program. We're strong in basketball, and have a very good baseball program. All this progress is due to good school systems, outstanding coaches, and a public which will support our programs."

One of the oddities in Illinois competition surfaced some short years ago when Dixon High School won the state championship in girls' bowling. So far, so good. The title-winning team was comprised of one girl and four boys.

IHSA by-laws make it local option, leaving it up to the individual schools whether they wanted to permit boys and girls to compete in the same sports during the regular season. But, in state tournament competition, the Board of Directors ruled it will be strictly boys vs. boys and girls vs. girls. That is the way the situation stands at the present time.

Establishing the fact he favors ample action, especially in basketball, Fitzhugh would willingly champion a move to bring the 24 to 30 second clock into Illinois basketball. "If I had the opportunity to make one change in the basketball rules, I would go to the clocks to assure keeping the ball in play," Harry claimed. "I might be talking against myself now because I've seen slowed down games I've enjoyed. Especially some of Duster Thomas' teams at Pinckneyville. They possessed the expertise to keep the ball moving without stalling or running themselves to death. I do believe his teams were so capable and so well conditioned they could play six games a day without tiring."

Harry has been on the executive side of athletics long enough to know that the role of athletics is frequently abused, especially when a school board is attempting to push through a new tax referendum. Often the board members will threaten to eliminate all sports unless there is a favorable vote to raise more money for the overall operation of the school.

Many schoolmen are most vociferous in protesting such tactics because sports, for the most part, pay their own way. This is particularly true in football, basketball, and wrestling. During recent years, wrestling's growth in the popularity league has advanced to brand new dimensions—and is still growing.

The present membership of the IHSA stands at 826. At one time it was over 900. This reduction is the result of continuing consolidation of the smaller schools. Even in this era of bigger schools there are still some high schools in Illinois with enrollments spanning from 60 to 70 to 80 to 100. Fitzhugh, making an educated guess, estimated that the medium average enrollment at the opening of the 1976-77 school year was around 300.

Harry envisions more reductions in the future because there will be increased consolidations. "The time is coming." Fitzhugh explained, "when two or three communities will take advantage of improved roads and transportation methods to form one bigger high school. We have a good example of this in McLean County, where the Olympia school district once housed five high schools. Now these five schools have been consolidated into one high school—one beautiful high school. It is complete with a swimming pool and other improved facilities for an enrollment which is in excess of 1,000 students.

"There are both pros and cons to be weighed in these situations, but there are so many more things you can offer youth in a bigger school than a smaller school. It offers more competition for the students plus providing increased opportunities to get ahead. Just consider the swimming pool by itself. None of the original five schools would have one on an individual basis.

"They can play football where they couldn't before. They can offer more sports and more activities. They can publish a school newspaper. There is every opportunity for the student to excel—if he takes advantage of it."

Always a liberal thinker, Harry has no desire to put down or stamp out the benefits of a smaller school. He realizes there have been many great people who attended and later were graduated from these smaller high schools. He's confident they would have done equally as well in a bigger school. Possibly even better.

Fitzhugh is of the opinion that schools can become too big and students can get lost in the sea of enrollment when it soars to 4,000 to 5,000. Checking a study by a panel of university professors, Harry considers a reasonable enrollment best favors the student when it is limited to 1,000 to 1,200.

The man from Auburn who has lived his entire life within the state, is a big booster for televising IHSA programs—and his favorable stand doesn't spring from the added revenue the magic lantern produces. "Most people don't realize the association has to work with limited facilities from a seating standpoint." Harry noted. "Therefore, television is a service we can provide our fans when tickets aren't available. Some years we could double, maybe triple, our ticket sales for the basketball tournament in the Assembly Hall in Champaign. Once the nearly 16,000 seats are sold, that is it. Still our fans aren't shut out because television is available.

"At the outset of television some association executives around the country were concerned, claiming it would hurt in-person attendance. They reasoned people wouldn't pay to see an event if they could see it free on TV in the comfort of their homes. Our board never shared these views. For that reason we have expanded the coverage from the Class A and Class AA Basketball Tournaments and Football Playoffs to the Girls Basketball Tournament and the Girls Gymnastics Meet with Illinois Bell as the sponsor. Also, WGN will again carry the state championship boys gymnastics and swimming meets as it has for many years."

When the Association's first executive secretary took office in 1922, it was a one-man, one-office, one-desk operation out of a Joliet High School. Then, in 1926, the office was moved to LaSalle Street in downtown Chicago. Now, the newly-built headquarters on McGraw Drive in Bloomington rates with the very best in both amateur and professional sports across the entire country.

In launching this project with the Board's approval, Fitzhugh stamped himself as a very brave individual from a financial standpoint. The Association's coffers had a $75,000 balance when the building was originally proposed. When the project was completed for the opening July 1, 1974, the total cost, including everything from landscaping to the latest in modern equipment was $470,000.

During the United State's Bicentennial celebration, the IHSA had an extra event: a mortgage-burning party. The building debt was paid off within two years. Fitzhugh, who will never be accused of running to center stage seeking the spotlight, has his own special philosophy in the promotion of the Association's various sports. In his own modest way, Harry says, "I would rather have 1,000 happy persons watching an event for 50 cents than 500 unhappy people at one dollar."

There is good reason to sing the Notre Dame school song whenever the Fitzhughs gather for a family reunion. Harry and his wife, Vera, who also is an Auburn native, have two daughters, Mrs. Bill (Judy) Reichart and Mrs. Bill (Nancy) Zloch, and three grandchildren. Nancy met Bill, a former Notre Dame quarterback, in '65, when she attended St. Mary's College, South Bend.

H.V. PORTER

"Administering a national organization is a relay race without a finish line..." Henry Van Arsdale Porter (his friends called him H.V.), who devoted a lifetime of work and dedication to high school athletics and athletes, used these words making his swan song in 1958. Although he was successful in a combination teacher-coach-principal role early in life, Porter's foremost contributions came under the heading of three B's: books, basketballs, and backboards.

A meticulous worker who was forever striving for perfection, new

Illinois High School Athletic Association Administrator Porter set out to tackle problems most men didn't even realize existed as the editor of the IHSAA's publication devoted to high school athletics and athletes: "The Illinois Athlete"

In 1929, Porter devoted new effort to making the size of the basketball adoptable to the smaller hands of the schoolboy athlete. People at all levels of the game were convinced the project was on a dead end street. If he was fazed by all the negative reaction, Porter didn't show it outwardly. Instead he kept plugging away, and it wasn't too long before the allowable 32-inch circumference of the basketball was cut to the present 29½-inch ball.

Porter envisioned another change in the basketball, and his suggestion for the adoption of a molded and seamless ball produced screams of protest which rattled rafters in every fieldhouse and gym in the country. Traditionalists scoffed at the idea. Long years after the new ball became a fixture in prep play, the NCAA continued to vote down its acceptance.

Finally, the old-styled pumpkin-shaped ball disappeared from the collegians' view. Porter's molded ball, of course, took its place. And that wasn't all. The collegians reasoned, if the molded ball is good for basketball, why wouldn't it work in football? It would. It did, and another Porter discovery was promptly recorded in the win column of the astute innovator.

Working with the late Oswald Tower, then "Mister Rules" of basketball, H.V. was instrumental in codifying and simplifying the existing basketball rules. Maybe you remember some of the action-minded changes? The center jump was eliminated and such new thinking as the 10-second line was inserted into the rules. As the scoring increased, so did the interest in the game.

The year was 1933 when Porter tackled another new project. This time he launched work to re-design the backboard using his newly developed fan-shaped backboard to replace the aged rectangular type. While the new board was quickly adopted by the National Federation of State High School Athletic Associations, some of the collegians balked at making the switch. In fact the "old" board still is being used in all NCAA tournaments.

When Porter set out to revise and improve the high school football code, he was joined by the late Hugh Ray. Together they worked on rules which proved to be a startling departure from the collegiate code in general use at the time. These new rules in the Porter-Ray manner were systematic, simplified, and logical in arrangement.

Speaking of Porter's many contributions, Harry Fitzhugh, the third executive secretary of the IHSA, noted, "I never met a man as dedicated as Henry Porter. His astuteness was amazing, and when he analyzed a project or a problem he had every answer on the tip of his tongue. The molded ball and the fan shaped backboard were two milestones in his life," Harry Fitzhugh explained, "after much, much experimentation with the help of people. Henry was an authority on rules when it came to basketball and football. He was nationally acclaimed because he not only knew the rule, but the philosophy behind it and the reasons for its development.

"Mister Porter was the assistant to Mister C.W. Whitten in the IHSA I'd say for about 12 years—1928 to 1940—when he moved over to the National Federation as executive secretary. He also helped develop the athletic officials department for Mister Whitten and the IHSAA at that time. Originally, not all the states were members of the Federation, but slowly they joined up. Up until five or six years ago it was Texas against the world, but Texas eventually joined the federation.

"Another side of his life was serving as director of the high school band and orchestra when he already was the principal, teacher, and coach at Athens. H.V. was a different type of man. He had a world of talent, but he never sought the spotlight. He loved music, and he was an avid reader—a real innovator who never ran out of new ideas."

During his brief tenure as teacher-coach-principal, Porter made stops at Mount Zion, Keithsburg, Delavan, and Athens. His 1924 Athens basketball team advanced to the finals of the state tournament before losing to Elgin 28-17. Henry Porter's career spanned 40 years before he died in retirement October 27, 1975. He was 84 years young.

MILT SPRUNGER

It was a delightful autumn afternoon. Milt Sprunger was holding court in the yard of his farm home on Guth Road on the outskirts of Washington. He could point to acres and acres of golden corn stalks in every direction, a most unusual situation for a man who had devoted most of his life to athletics at the high school level.

Milt joined the IHSA in 1943 with the title of assistant secretary under the command of Al Willis. He worked mainly on the non-athletic programs, directing speech and music. Later his workload included the training and registration of athletic officials and getting out the association's monthly magazine. Not too much later, Sprunger was assigned to the state wrestling tournament program and the state track meet series.

"Frequently in my spare time," Milt recalled, "I would have an opportunity to get home before midnight."

After 13 years at this pace Milt convinced Willis the office staff needed a third man, and Sid Alkire came aboard from the Springfield branch of the Department of Public Instruction. Alkire was assigned to non-athletic activities and later was placed in charge of the swimming and tennis tournaments.

Operating on the theory that the association was no stronger than its weakest official, all the officials were required to register for football, basketball, baseball, and swimming. Each official paid a two dollar fee to register, and the number doubled during Sprunger's tenure. Milt started with an estimated 1,200 and was working with a state-wide staff of about 2,500 officials leading into 1964.

Although the ISHA refuses to hold hearings protesting an official's judgment, Milt laughed recalling an official's error of a rule definition. In this particular game the score was tied at the end of regulation time. The rule book called for a three-minute overtime period. One of the two officials assigned to the game claimed the rule had been changed to five-minute overtime periods in high school competition. After overtime bickering and debate, the five-minute period was agreed upon with one stipulation: that the score of the game after three minutes would be officially recorded for both coaches.

After three minutes of play, Team A was leading. After the full five minute overtime, Team B had taken the lead. When the ISHA held a hearing on the situation, the game was awarded to Team A, the leader at the three-minute mark.

The two coaches had a better idea; they would replay the game. When permission was sought and received, Milt told the two mentors: "I hope you have a good game and draw a big crowd." Sounding like two parrots, the coaches answered: "That is why we are replaying the game."

Sprunger well remembers three different bids to establish class basketball in IHSA tournament competition. "It was about 1950 when the demands really became serious," Milt recalled. "In fact, Al Willis and I worked out a schedule for Class A and Class B teams which we could live with just in case there was an immediate demand for it. Then Hebron came along in 1952, and the talk for divisions was quickly silenced. It fired up a second time early in the 1960s, when little Cobden—reacting much like Hebron—finished second after almost beating one of Dawdy Hawkins' very good Pekin teams. Once more the demands were silenced, but within a few years the issue was drawing steam again. It was now evident that most of the coaches wanted the change and were gaining support from their athletic directors."

Describing the personalities of C.W. Whitten and Al Willis, Milt noted, "They were as different as day and night. Mister Whitten always claimed there was just one way to say no. Mister Willis was different. He would hear everybody out. Especially the press and schools asking for hearings on eligibility rulings. Both were equally firm in their own ways."

A non-athlete during his entire life, Sprunger spent 23 years teaching and serving in principal roles at Buda (9) and Roseville (14) before launching his 21-year tenure with the IHSA in Chicago. "For 21 years with the Association, I had exactly the job I wanted all my life," Milt mused as he recalled his limited officiating assignments and his cross-country travel lecturing at rules' interpretation meetings.

A native of Berne, Indiana, where he attended high school, Sprunger went to college in Bluffton, Indiana before moving to Illinois. Now in retirement with ample time to check such items as corn averaging 147 bushels to the acre, Milt is like Will Rogers: all he knows about sports is what he reads in the newspapers. He's amazed at the growth of the girls' programs, and he's pleased with the state's soccer progress for the original 40 school program.

At the outset Sprunger opposed the shift to class basketball on the basis of "why spoil a good thing?" Presently he likes the Class A and Class AA format, but envisions a lack of fan interest if "we adopt any more classifications."

Milt remembers a "What Price Glory?" situation attached to Rockford West's winning the 1955 state basketball tournament. In making the presentation of the championship trophy to Coach Alex Saudargas, Fred Biester, a member of the IHSA board, called him "Coach Sauer-grass." When West repeated in 1956, Biester, presiding at the same ceremony, said: "Coach I'm glad you won because this time I'm going to pronounce your name correctly."

He did, and Saudargas accepted the trophy to herald West's success in becoming the third back-to-back winner in tournament history.

Officers of the Association

(Listed in Sequence)

PRESIDENT

C. P. Briggs, Aurora, 1903
James E. Armstrong, Chicago, 1904
E. U. Graff, Rockford, 1905–1907
C. L. Phelps, Aurora, 1908
Wm. Wallis, Bloomington, 1909
F. M. Giles, DeKalb, 1910–1916
C. P. Briggs, Rockford, 1917–1920
R. G. Beals, Decatur, 1921
G. J. Koons, Pontiac, 1922–1927
H. D. Anderson, Gilman, 1928–1932
E. S. Simmonds, Pittsfield, 1933
Silas Echols, Mount Vernon, 1934–1937
R. S. Wilson, Potomac, 1938
J. O. Austin, Athens, 1939
B. Floyd Smith, Benton, 1940–1951
B. Floyd Smith, Fairfield, 1952–1957
Harry L. Fitzhugh, Franklin, 1958–1966
Robert C. Grant, Watseka, 1967
Forrest L. Tabor, Rock Falls, 1968–1972
James Brim, Concord, 1973–1975
Hewey E. Tweedy, Anna-Jonesboro, 1975–1976
Joseph J. Sirchio, Chicago (Steinmetz), 1976—

VICE-PRESIDENT

Edward L. Boyer, Bloomington, 1903
J. O. Leslie, Ottawa, 1904
L. M. Castle, Springfield, 1905–1907
Wm. Wallis, Bloomington, 1908
S. W. Ehrman, Decatur, 1909–1910
Jesse H. Newlon, Decatur, 1913–1916
I. M. Allen, Springfield, 1917
A. J. Burton, Rock Island, 1918
W. L. Hagan, Monticello, 1919
Will C. Robb, Spring Valley, 1920–1921
C. W. Whitten, DeKalb, 1922
J. O. Marberry, Rockford, 1923–1924
W. C. Handlin, Lincoln, 1924
L. C. Fulwider, Freeport, 1925–1930
R. E. Stringer, Herrin, 1931
E. M. Peterson, Tolona, 1933–1934
E. H. Mellon, Winchester, 1935
R. S. Wilson, Potomac, 1936–1937
J. O. Austin, Athens, 1938
B. Floyd Smith, Benton, 1939
O. L. Rapp, Canton, 1940–1941
W. M. Runyon, Winchester, 1942
S. E. Alkire, Griggsville, 1943
Roy Clark, Gilman, 1944–1945
S. E. Alkire, Griggsville, 1946
E. D. Finley, Delavan, 1947–1949
Robert C. Grant, Watseka, 1950–1952
Harry L. Fitzhugh, Franklin, 1953–1957
Robert C. Grant, Watseka, 1958–1961
Joseph D. Dixon, Monmouth, 1962–1964

Robert C. Grant, Watseka,
1965–1966
Carl E. Nation, McLeansboro,
1967
A. Hunter Chapman, New Lenox
(Lincoln-Way), 1968–1969
James Brim, Concord, 1970–1972
Bernard A. Quish, Kelvyn Park
H.S. Chicago, 1973
Hewey E. Tweedy, Anna-Jones-
boro, 1974–1975
Roy E. Sheppard, Mattoon,
1975–1976
Nicholas Mannos, Skokie (Niles
West), 1976–

SECRETARY-TREASURER
H. E. Brown, Rock Island, 1903
Wm. E. Geiger, Aurora, 1904
H. E. Brown, Rock Island, Kenil-
worth, 1905–1906
L. W. Smith, Harvey, Joliet,
1917–1928
C. H. Kingman, Ottawa,
1929–1932
Fred L. Biester, Glen Ellyn,
1932–1961
Robert C. Grant, Watseka,
1962–1963

SECRETARY
Robert C. Grant, Watseka, 1964
Carl E. Nation, McLeansboro,
1965–1966
Forrest L. Tabor, Rock Falls,
1967
James Brim, Chapin, 1968–1969
Bernard A. Quish, Kelvyn Park
H.S., Chicago, 1970–1972
Hewey E. Tweedy, DuQuoin, 1973
Roy E. Sheppard, Mattoon,
1974–1975

Richard Mariani, Woodhull (Al-
wood), 1975–1976
Don Mellon, Pittsfield, 1976–

TREASURER
[Appointed by Board]
Lynn H. Gibbs, Rantoul,
1964–1970
Raymond E. Collier, Aurora,
1971–1975

BOARD MEMBERS
(Not Officers)
J. O. Marberry, 1917–1918
W. L. Hagan, Neoga, 1917–1918
H. B. Black, Mattoon, 1919–1921
J. F. Mabrey, Geneseo, 1919
H. C. Hopkins, Jacksonville, 1920
Silas Echols, Mount Vernon,
1921–1922
O. M. Swank, Anna, 1922–1924
L. W. Hanna, Centralia,
1923–1928
R. D. Brummett, Greenville,
1925–1927
S. E. Le Marr, Abingdon,
1928–1930
R. B. Browne, Casey, 1929
W. A. Goodier, Bloomington,
1931–1936
A. W. Evans, Chicago, 1932–1936
R. W. Damron, Elkville, 1933
C. M. Campbell, Fisher,
1935–1936
James Gaffney, Chicago,
1937–1939
R. V. Lindsey, Pekin, 1937–1938
J. B. Buckler, Casey, 1939
Olice Winter, Chicago, 1940–1948
Gerald W. Smith, Alexis, 1942

A. H. Chapman, Winchester,
1947–1948
James H. Smith, Chicago,
1949–1953
Harry L. Fitzhugh, Franklin,
1949–1952
James Hatcher, Morton,
1950–1952
Curtis Alexander, Tolono, 1953
Joseph D. Dixon, Monmouth,
1953–1961
Glenn D. Worst, Calumet H.S.,
Chicago, 1954
Robert C. Grant, Watseka,
1954–1957
Neal Duncan, Calumet H.S., Chicago, 1955
Neal Duncan, Hyde Park H.S.,
Chicago, 1956
Richard C. McVey, Harrison
H.S., Chicago, 1957
Wallace H. Fristoe, Morgan Park
H.S., Chicago, 1958
Carl E. Nation, McLeansboro,
1958–1964
William E. McBride, Farragut
H.S., Chicago, 1959–1961
Wallace H. Fristoe, Morgan Park
H.S., Chicago, 1962–1965
James W. Lewis, Argo, 1962–1965
Forrest L. Tabor, Rock Falls,
1965–1966
William E. McBride, Farragut
H.S., Chicago, 1966
A. Hunter Chapman, New Lenox,
(Lincoln-Way), 1966–1967
James Brim, Chapin, 1967
Bernard A. Quish, Kelvyn Park
H.S., Chicago, 1967–1969
Donald L. Pratt, Monticello,
1968–1970
Hewey E. Tweedy, DuQuoin,
1968–1972

William E. Rider, Lombard,
1970–1971
Gail L. Borton, Jr., Charleston,
1971
Roy E. Sheppard, Mattoon,
1972–1973
Bruno W. Waara, Arlington
Heights, 1972–1974
Richard Mariani, Toluca,
1973–1975
Joseph J. Sirchio, Steinmetz, Chicago, 1974–1976
Nicholas Mannos, Skokie (Niles
West), 1975–1976
Don Mellon, Pittsfield, 1976
John Dowling, Watseka, 1976 to
date
John Lavelle, Henry-Senachwine,
1976 to date
David McClintock, Nashville,
1976 to date

Association Administrators

EXECUTIVE SECRETARIES

Charles W. Whitten, 1922–1942
Albert Willis, 1942–1968
Harry Fitzhugh, 1968–present

ASST. EXEC. SECRETARIES

H. V. Porter, 1929–1940
Geraldine Rennert, 1936–1967
Albert Willis, 1940–1942
K. L. Letsinger, 1941–1942
Milton F. Spunger, 1943–1963
Sydney E. Alkire, 1956–1967
Thomas Frederick, 1963–1967
Harry Fitzhugh, 1966–1968
L. L. Astroth, 1968–present
Ola Bundy, 1968–present
H. David Fry, 1968–present
James P. Flynn, 1973–present
Cynthia B. Adams, 1975–present

Chapter 2
The Champions

1908
March 28-29
Oak Park Y.M.C.A.

Peoria Breaks on Top . . .

It all began with the late Lewis Omer's idea, a post-season high school basketball tournament. The Oak Park High School athletic director invited 13 teams to play in the Oak Park YMCA. Before Peoria swept to the championship, beating back Wheaton, Hinsdale, and Rock Island, two teams—Aurora and Joliet—forfeited to cut the charter field to 11 teams.

Omer's brainchild caught fire immediately, drawing large as well as enthusiastic crowds. This made it easy for the Oak Park administrator to sell the project to the Illinois High School Athletic Association, an organization of fewer than 200 schools. In this manner the tournament became an annual fixture, moving to Bloomington, Peoria, Decatur, and Springfield before it found a permanent home in Champaign.

The Peoria powerhouse averaged more than 40 points per game. In the championship game Lynch Conway and William Forrest scored 18 of the winning Lions' 20 field goals against runner-up Rock Island.

First Round

Peoria 41, Wheaton 26
Rock Island 50, LaSalle 9
Hinsdale 34, Mt. Carroll 29
Aurora (West) forfeited to Wheaton
Joliet forfeited to LaSalle
Mt. Carroll 47, Geneva 20
Rock Island 31, Evanston 23
Hinsdale 60, Riverside 9
Oak Park 58, St. Charles 27

Semifinals

Peoria 32, Hinsdale 25
Rock Island 38, Oak Park 28

Final

Peoria 48, Rock Island 29

Championship Game

COACH: Les Straeser

Peoria (48)	FG	FT	TP	Rock Island (29) *	FG	FT	TP
Frank Trefzger, rf	1	8	10	Andy Voss, rf	0	0	0
Lynch Conway, lf	11	0	22	Richard Litt, lf	0	8	8
William Forrest, c	7	0	14	Dan Brennan, c	4	0	8
Frank Worley, rg	1	0	2	John Streckfus, rg	0	0	0
Charles Drysdale, lg	0	0	0	Walter Young, lg	6	0	12
TOTALS	20	8	48	TOTALS	10	8	28

*Rock Island was awarded one point.

Officials: Norton and Harlow

ILLINOIS' FIRST STATE HIGH SCHOOL basketball champions—Peoria's 1908 LIONS Left to right, seated: Frank Worley, guard; Lynch Conway, forward; Bill Forrest, center. Standing; Frank Trefzger, forward; Jim Luke; Coach Les Straeser; Charles Drysdale, guard; Linton Turner, guard.

1909
March 19-20
Bloomington Y.M.C.A.

Hinsdale Happiness . . .

Bloomington was the tournament site when Hinsdale captured the 1909 championship. After an opening round rout of Mt. Carroll, the upstaters used balanced scoring to unseat Peoria as the reigning champions. Fred Cortis was high scorer with a 7-for-7 free throw record as Hinsdale defeated Washington 18-13 in the title game. Preston Davidson followed with six points, and Gilbert Keith had five. The two guards, Fred Bahlmann and Frank Dana, were scoreless as the two teams settled for a total of only nine field goals.

First Round

Bloomington 30, Centralia 19
Hinsdale 56, Mt. Carroll 7
Washington 42, Joliet 25
Rock Island 42, Mt. Vernon 11

Semifinals

Hinsdale 21, Bloomington 14
Washington 20, Rock Island 12

Finals

Mt. Carroll 26, Rock Island 9 (3rd Place)
Hinsdale 18, Washington 13 (Championship)

(Note: Centralia, Mt. Carroll, Joliet, Mt. Vernon, after first round losses, moved into a consolation bracket.)

Championship Game

COACH: John Snider

Hinsdale (18)	FG	FT	TP	Washington (13)	FG	FT	TP
Preston Davidson, f	3	0	6	Steele Zinser, f	1	0	2
Fred Cortis, f	0	7	7	Roy Risser, f	1	0	2
Gilbert Keith, c	1	3	5	Forest Moyer, c	3	0	6
Fred Bahlmann, g	0	0	0	Meinhardt Ryf, g	0	3	3
Frank Dana, g	0	0	0	Cullom Long, g	0	0	0
TOTALS	4	10	18	TOTALS	5	3	13

1909 CHAMPION HINSDALE RED DEVILS—Front row: Fred Bahlmann, Woodbury Melcher, Middle row: Fred Cortis, Gilbert Keith, Preston Davidson. Top row: Frank Dana, Coach Arthur Collins.

1910
March 11-12
Bloomington Y.M.C.A.

Home Court Triumph . . .

Bloomington, hosting the tournament a second straight time, became the first host winner. After impressive victories over Nokomis and Mt. Sterling, Bloomington upended Rock Island for the championship 32-25. Harold Hufford scored 14 points for the winners. Center Dick Litt was high scorer for Rock Island with 15. Hinsdale, the defending champion, finished third with a 26-21 win over Mt. Vernon. Bloomington scored 120 points for a 40-point average during its tournament sweep.

First Round

Bloomington 36, Nokomis 17
Rock Island 27, Mt. Vernon 24

Second Round

Bloomington 52, Mt. Sterling 10
Rock Island 37, Hinsdale 27

Finals

Hinsdale 26, Mt. Vernon 21 (3rd Place)
Bloomington 32, Rock Island 25 (Championship)

(Note: Nokomis, Mt. Vernon, Mt. Sterling, and Hinsdale, after first or second round losses, moved into consolation bracket.)

Championship Game

COACH: Tom O'Neill

Bloomington (32)	FG	FT	TP	Rock Island (25)	FG	FT	TP
Byron Darst, lf	1	0	2	John Streckfus, rf	2	0	4
Harold Hufford, rf	4	6	14	Harry			
Fred Wolrab, c	4	0	8	Behnamann, lf	2	0	4
Walter				Dick Litt, c	4	7	15
Sutherland, lg	0	0	0	Sidney			
Adlai Rust, rg	3	0	6	Steenburg, rg	0	0	0
TOTALS	12	6	*30	John McManus, lg	1	0	2
				TOTALS	9	7	25

* Bloomington was awarded 2 points.
  Halftime score: Bloomington 19, Rock Island 10
  Officials: G. O. Laustead (St. Louis); G. E. DeKriuf (Chicago)

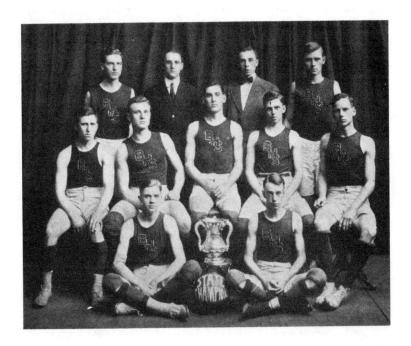

1910 CHAMPION BLOOMINGTON (H.S.) PURPLE RAIDERS—Front row: Byron Darst, Harold Hufford. Second row: Laurence Twomey, Fred Wollrab, Walter Sutherland, Adlai Rust, Lewis Kessler. Third row: Eugene Hamill, W. F. Schilling (Faculty Manager), Thomas O'Neil (Coach), Bruce Jarrett.

1911
March 10-11
Bradley Gym, Peoria

Campus Target Practice . . .

Bradley College of Peoria provided the tournament with its first campus stage, and Rockford became a runaway winner at a record pace. Rockford opened with a 39-23 win over Jacksonville and closed taking Mt. Carroll apart 60-15. In the championship game, two Franks — Thomas and Johnson — scored 38 points between them as Rockford rushed past rival defenders to collect 28 field goals. This topped, by eight, Peoria's 20 field goals when they won in 1908. In this manner Rockford became the first unbeaten champion at 22-0.

First Round

Rockford 39, Jacksonville 23
Paris 43, Washington 21
Rockford 44, Granite City 30
Mt. Carroll 58, Paris 30

Finals

Granite City 44, Paris 35 (3rd Place)
Rockford 60, Mt. Carroll 15 (Championship)

Championship Game

COACH: Ralph E. Venum

Rockford (60)	FG	FT	TP	Mt. Carroll (15)	FG	FT	TP
Frank Thomas, f	7	4	18	Lloyd Fox, f	1	0	2
Frank Johnson, f	10	0	20	Ralph Eskelson, f	0	0	0
Casson Squire, c	4	0	8	Walter Smith, c	2	7	11
Roger Welsh, g	5	0	10	Harry Ross, g	0	0	0
Roy Collentine, g	2	0	4	Dwight Bennett, g	1	0	2
Totals	28	4	60	Totals	4	7	15

Officials: Bruce Rutherford (Peoria); Earl Bridge (Galesburg)

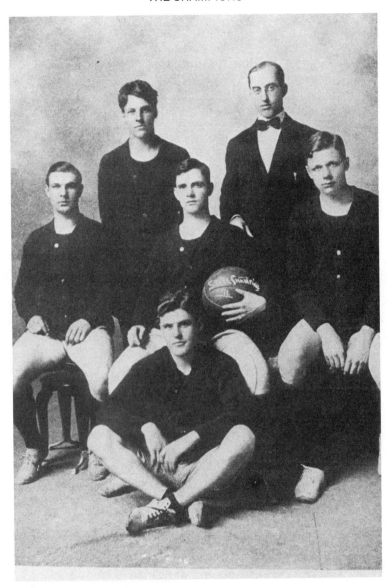

1911 CHAMPION ROCKFORD E-RABS—Front: Roy Collentine. Second row: "Bealy" Thomas, Frank "Eckie" Johnson (Capt.), "Cap" Squire. Third row: "Hod" Welsh, Coach Ralph Venum.

1912
March 8-9
Millikin Gym, Decatur

New Home: Millikin . . .

Three was the magic number as Batavia became the fifth winner and new champion when the super schoolboy shootout was waged on the Millikin campus in Decatur. Batavia led by three (14-11) at halftime; won by three 28-25 as three free throws made the difference in its title game conquest of Galesburg. There was a fourth three in Batavia's sweep: its three-point 29-26 win over Granite City in the semifinals. Incidentally, Galesburg was a three point winner 26-23 over host Decatur in the second semifinal showdown.

First Round

Batavia 32, Canton 23
Granite City 30, Hillsboro 27
Decatur 27, Galesburg 26
Hillsboro 32, Canton 31
Galesburg 27, Hillsboro 23

Semifinals

Batavia 29, Granite City 26
Galesburg 26, Decatur 23

Finals

Hillsboro 38, Decatur 31 (3rd Place)
Batavia 28, Galesburg 25 (Championship)

Championship Game

COACH: K. C. Merrick

Batavia (28)	FG	FT	TP
Parks Riley, lf	2	0	4
Raymond McDermott, rf	2	8	12
Walter Trantow, c	5	0	10
Dwight Emigh, lg	1	0	2
Charles Barr, lg	0	0	0
Horace Bone, rg	0	0	0
Totals	10	8	28

COACH: T. W. Callihan

Galesburg (25)	FG	FT	TP
Herbert Pihl, lf	4	4	12
Gordon Bridge, rf	2	1	5
Lawrence Ingersol, rf	1	0	2
Fred Phillips, c	0	0	0
Eric Erickson, rg	3	0	6
John Halladay, lg	0	0	0
Byron Scott, lg	0	0	0
Totals	10	5	25

Halftime score: Batavia 14, Galesburg 11
Officials: Rufus Gilbert (Peoria); Ted Roe

1912 CHAMPION BATAVIA BULLDOGS—Front row: Dwight Emigh, Bailey, Raymond McDermott, Charles Barr. Middle row: Horace Bone, Walter Trantow, Hanson. Top row: Coach K.C. Merrick.

1913
March 7-8
Bradley Gym, Peoria

Back to Bradley . . .

The tournament moved back to Peoria for its second stand on the Bradley campus, and this proved to be a good luck charm for Galesburg. The Silver Streaks won the championship, which escaped them the previous season, by edging Manual of Peoria 37-36. It was the first one-pointer in the tournament's title game history. Herbert Pihl proved a one-man gang offensively with 21 points, blending six field goals with nine freethrows.

First Round

Peoria (Manual) 47, Abingdon 20
Winnetka (New Trier) 33, Hillsboro 19
Galesburg 39, Mt. Vernon 33

Semifinals

Peoria (Manual) 29, Hillsboro 24
Galesburg 37, Winnetka (New Trier) 30

Final

Galesburg 37, Peoria (Manual) 36

Championship Game

COACH: E. W. Hayes

Galesburg (37)

	FG	FT	TP
Belford Van Pelt, f	4	0	8
Lawrence Ingersol, f	3	0	6
Herbert Pihl, c	6	9	21
Eric Erickson, g	1	0	2
Byron Scott, g	0	0	0
Totals	14	9	37

Peoria (Manual) (36)

	FG	FT	TP
William Angelsea, f	3	1	7
Gus Keupper, f	1	0	2
Dan Ewell, f	1	1	3
Lester De Trempe, c	8	1	17
Ralph Werner, g	0	1	1
Rodney Doering, g	3	0	6
Totals	16	4	36

Officials: Musselman; Davis

1913 CHAMPION GALESBURG ZEPHYRS—Front row: Lawrence Ingersol, Herbert Pihl, Belford Van Pelt. Back row: Mgr. Rose, Greer, Eric Erickson, Byron Scott, Coach E.W. Hayes.

1914
March 13-14
Millikin Gym, Decatur

Close at Half, Rout at Finish . . .

Hillsboro broke open a close game which was a tight 17-16 at halftime. They did it with a potent second-half surge to run down Freeport 42-19 for the championship as the tournament returned to Millikin in Decatur. Freeport made only three points in the second half as Eugene Seymour outscored the entire losing team with 20 points. Galesburg's bid for a second straight crown ended early in a 49-23 first-round loss to Evanston (Academy). Hillsboro then eliminated the upstart Evanstonians. The title loss snapped Freeport's 17-game winning streak.

First Round

Evanston (Academy) 49, Galesburg 23
Hillsboro 43, Granite City 40
Normal (University High) 29, Peoria (Manual) 27
Freeport 33, Centralia 30

Semifinals

Hillsboro 37, Evanston (Academy) 21
Freeport 32, Normal (University High) 20

Finals

Normal (University High) 31, Evanston (Acad.) 23 (3rd Place)
Hillsboro 42, Freeport 19 (Championship)

Championship Game

COACH: D. O. Kime

Hillsboro (42)	FG	FT	TP
Ira Henemeyer, lf	5	0	10
Eugene Seymour, rf	8	4	20
Chester Guthrie, c	4	0	8
Wilbur Kortkamp, lg	1	0	2
Edward Elledge, rg	1	0	2
Brenton Marland, rg	0	0	0
Totals	19	4	42

COACH: Dan Dougherty

Freeport (19)	FG	FT	TP
Russell Mullinix, lf	0	0	0
Leo Koehler, lf	2	0	4
Oscar Hill, rf	4	0	8
Chester Langenstine, c-g	0	0	0
John Hart, c	1	0	2
Torrey Foy, rg	1	3	5
Julius Guhl, rg	0	0	0
John Bonn, lg	0	0	0
Totals	8	3	19

Halftime score: Hillsboro 17, Freeport 16
Officials: Ralph Tenney (Decatur); C. E. Howell (Decatur)

1914 CHAMPION HILLSBORO HILLTOPPERS—Front row: Ira Hennemeyer, Edward Elledge, Brenton Marland, Back row: Wilbur Kortkamp, Chester Guthrie, Eugene Seymour, Coach D.O. Kime.

1915
March 11-12
Millikin Gym, Decatur

Foy's Foul Flips . . .

Thirteen freethrows, a tournament record, by Torrey Foy made it easy for Freeport to set back Springfield 27-11 in the championship game. The tourney was contested for the second straight March on the Millikin campus in Decatur. It attracted such potent newcomers as Carbondale and Shelbyville—both impressive first round winners before bowing out in the semifinals. Freeport, an 18-2 winner on the season, averaged 35 points per game to complete its sweep.

First Round

Springfield 21, Rock Island 19
Shelbyville 30, Naperville 20
Carbondale 22, Decatur 21
Freeport 41, Granite City 20

Semifinals

Springfield 27, Shelbyville 10
Freeport 38, Carbondale 14

Finals

Shelbyville 33, Carbondale 8 (3rd Place)
Freeport 27, Springfield 11 (Championship)

Championship Game

COACH: Dan Dougherty

Freeport (27)	FG	FT	TP
Oscar Hill, rf	3	0	6
Leo Koehler, lf	2	0	4
Chester Langenstine, c	0	0	0
Torrey Foy, rg	2	13	17
Glenn Holmes, lg	0	0	0
Totals	7	13	27

Springfield (11)	FG	FT	TP
Art Dawson, rf	1	7	9
Jerome Dunne, rf	0	0	0
Chester Bowles, lf	0	0	0
Harry Eielson, c	1	0	2
Clifford Turnbull, c	0	0	0
Edward Sternaman, lg	0	0	0
Amos Sawyer, lg	0	0	0
Raymond Wilson, rg	0	0	0
Totals	2	7	11

Halftime score: Freeport 11, Springfield 6
Officials: Gunn; Shipley

1915 CHAMPION FREEPORT PRETZELS—Front row: Russell Mulnix, Paul Gilbert, Herbert Biersach. Second row: Torrey Foy, Oscar Hill, Leo Koehler, Mgr. Gunl. Third row: Coach D. B. Dougherty, Chester Langenstein, Glen Holmes.

1916
March 10-11
Millikin Gym, Decatur

First Two-Time Winner . . .

Bloomington, a winner in 1910, became the first two-time champion with an impressive 25-17 decision over Robinson in the championship game. Balanced scoring produced the Bloomington triumph. Vern Greiner, Laird Mace, and Theodore Bean, the winners' front line, accounted for 23 of the winners' 25 points. Benton Springer led Robinson, making its tourney debut, with 13 points. DuQuoin beat Springfield 32-13 for third place.

First Round

Robinson 24, Aurora (East) 19
Springfield 18, Rockford 11
Bloomington 16, Joliet 11
DuQuoin 30, Moline 15

Semifinals

Robinson 14, DuQuoin 13
Bloomington 19, Springfield 13

Finals

DuQuoin 32, Springfield 13 (3rd Place)
Bloomington 25, Robinson 17 (Championship)

Championship Game

COACH: E. W. McClure

Bloomington (25)	FG	FT	TP
Vern Greiner, f	3	3	9
Laird Mace, f	4	0	8
Theodore Bean, c	3	0	6
Mevis Jennings, c	1	0	2
George Morrison, g	0	0	0
Francis McMurray, g	0	0	0
Delmar Gottschalk, g	0	0	0
Totals	11	3	25

COACH: William F. Livingston

Robinson (17)	FG	FT	TP
Chalon Titsworth, f	1	2	4
Douglas Dewey, f	0	0	0
Benton Springer, c	5	3	13
Paul Norris, g	0	0	0
Eddie Kirk, g	0	0	0
Totals	6	5	17

Halftime score: Bloomington 13, Robinson 6
Officials: William Duerr (Decatur); C. E. Howell (Decatur)

1916 CHAMPION BLOOMINGTON (H.S.) PURPLE RAIDERS—Front row: Norton Richardson, Russell Strange. Second row: Clarence Bean, Delmar Gottschalk, Vergne Greiner, Layard Mace, Mevise Jennings. Third row: Harry McMurry, Theodore Bean, George Morrison, Coach Earl McClure.

1917
March 9-10
Millikin Gym, Decatur

From Fourth to First . . .

Springfield, fourth the previous season, did a complete turnaround to win
its first championship in what was to prove the last meet contested at
Millikin in Decatur. The Senators steamrollered Rock Island,
Bloomington, and Belvidere in that order. Springfield was held to a 6-5
halftime edge against Belvidere in the title game but fused a 26-point spree
in the second half to win in a rout 32-11.

First Round

Springfield 34, Rock Island 23
Bloomington 15, DuQuoin 10
Peoria (Manual) 20, Lawrenceville 9
Belvidere 24, Sullivan 16

Semifinals

Springfield 14, Bloomington 9
Belvidere 16, Peoria (Manual) 6

Finals

Bloomington 20, Peoria (Manual) 9 (3rd Place)
Springfield 32, Belvidere 11 (Championship)

Championship Game

COACH: Roy A. Wentz

Springfield (32)	FG	FT	TP		Belvidere (11)	FG	FT	TP
Jerome Dunne, f	4	0	8		Myron Silvius, f	2	0	4
Max Poscover, f	3	0	6		Ben Lear, f	1	2	4
George Teasley, f	0	0	0		Herbert Comstock, c	0	0	0
Vernon Edwards, f	0	0	0		Allie Jukes, g	0	0	0
Harry Eielson, c	4	0	8		Harold Gilroy, g	0	3	3
Ben Clouser, g	3	4	10		Stan Wells, g	0	0	0
Nelson Jones, g	0	0	0		Totals	3	5	11
Harry Lock, g	0	0	0					
Totals	14	4	32					

Halftime score: Springfield 6, Belvidere 5
Officials: Charles P. Lantz (Charleston); Shipley

1917 CHAMPION SPRINGFIELD (H.S.) SENATORS—Front row: Vernon Edwards, Nelson Jones, Ben Clouser, Harry Eielson, Jerome Dunne, Max Poscover, Sternaman. Back row: Asst. Coach A.S. Nevins, George Teasley, Blanbelt, Mayor H.S. Betty, Portridge, Paoli, Coach Roy Wentz.

1918
March 14-15-16
Springfield High School Gym

Here Comes Centralia . . .

The second decade of the state tournament opened with Centralia sweeping to the championship played for the first and last time in Springfield. It was feast or famine for Centralia. Coach Arthur Trout's first title team won its first game from Galesburg 32-30; ran over Elgin 37-16; slipped past Shelbyville 25-23 and took home the winning trophy with a 35-29 derailing of University High of Normal.

Thursday

DuQuoin 21, Rockford 18
Elgin 26, Winnetka (New Trier) 25
Centralia 32, Galesburg 30
Normal (University High) 28, Champaign 18
Lawrenceville 23, Canton 18

Friday

Shelbyville 18, DuQuoin 17
Centralia 37, Elgin 16
Normal (University High) 30, Lawrenceville 26

Saturday Afternoon

Centralia 25, Shelbyville 23
Normal (University High) 20, Canton 19

Saturday Evening

Canton 20, Shelbyville 19 (3rd Place)
Centralia 35, Normal (University High) 29 (Championship)

Championship Game

COACH: Arthur L. Trout Centralia (35)	FG	FT	TP
Wade Storer, rf	0	0	0
Henry Hurd, lf	3	0	6
Telle Lederman, rf	3	0	6
Charles Maddox, c	4	0	8
Harry Blakeley, rg	6	0	12
Harold Hartley, lg	0	3	3
Totals	16	3	35

COACH: Francis James Normal (29) (University High)	FG	FT	TP
Clarence Westhoff, rf	6	0	12
Henry Capen, lf	5	0	10
Alvin Hoffman, c	0	0	0
Bane Pierce, rg	3	0	6
Arthur Buck, lg	0	1	1
Totals	14	1	29

Halftime score: Centralia 17, Normal (University High) 16

Officials: Fred "Brick" Young (Bloomington)
D. V. Shipley (Chicago)

1918 CHAMPION CENTRALIA ORPHANS—Front row: Henry Hurd, Harold Hartley, Wade Storer. Second row: Coach A. L. Trout, Telle Lederman, Stanley Thomas, Charles Maddox, Harry Blakely, T. W. Clarida.

1919
March 13-14-15
Gym Annex, University of Illinois

Rockford Rules Again . . .

Rockford climaxed a 23-1 record by winning the 1919 state tournament to join Bloomington as a two-time winner. It was the first tourney played in Champaign-Urbana at the Gym Annex at the University of Illinois and marked the debut of "Brick Young" officiating his first of nine straight title games. Rex Enright and Harry Englund scored 30 points between them as Rockford beat Springfield 39-20 for the championship. The champions out-scored four foes 125-54.

First Round

Champaign 23, Alton 19
Springfield 30, Morris 13
Shelbyville 28, Atwood 26
Herrin 18, Rock Island 16
Rockford 31, Flora 10

Second Round

Springfield 18, Champaign 9
Herrin 16, Shelbyville 15
Peoria (Central) 50, Barry 15
Rockford 37, Dundee 10

Semifinals

Springfield 20, Peoria (Central) 18
Rockford 19, Herrin 14

Finals

Peoria (Central) 24, Herrin 10 (3rd Place)
Rockford 39, Springfield 20 (Championship)

Championship Game

COACH: Frank J. Winters

COACH: Schale

Rockford (39)	FG	FT	TP
Rex Enright, f	8	0	16
Leslie Sodergren, f	2	3	7
Harry Englund, c	7	0	14
Joel Carlson, g	1	0	2
Hugh Powell, g	0	0	0
Totals	18	3	39

Springfield (20)	FG	FT	TP
Tom Greenan, f	0	0	0
Max Poscover, f	6	6	18
Lile Marland, c	0	0	0
Harry Hodde, g	1	0	2
Ira Johnson, g	0	0	0
Totals	7	6	20

Officials: Fred H. Young (Bloomington);
Charles P. Lantz (Charleston)

1919 CHAMPION ROCKFORD E-RABS—From left: Ralph Baker, Hugh Powell, Joel Carlson, Rex Enright, Harry Englund (Capt.).

1920
March 18-19-20
Gym Annex, University of Illinois

Records Don't Mean Much . . .

If ever one team was a prohibitive favorite in the championship game it was Canton opposing Mt. Vernon. Canton had won 30 of 33 games and scored 92 points winning three games to reach the finals. Mt. Vernon's record was a lackluster 16-8 with 65 points during the first three tourney tilts. In the showdown, Mt. Vernon won its first championship with an 18-14 upending of Canton with hothanded Russell Miller leading all scorers with 12 points.

First Round

Canton 16, Peoria (Manual) 14
Joliet 40, Streator 26
Olney 43, Champaign 24
Galesburg 25, Shelbyville 23
Marion 23, Decatur 17
Rockford 45, Centralia 21
Bloomington 35, Jerseyville 29
Mt. Vernon 25, Elgin 13

Quarter-Finals

Canton 35, Joliet 19
Olney 32, Galesburg 21
Marion 22, Rockford 20
Mt. Vernon 25, Bloomington 24

Semifinals

Canton 37, Olney 18
Mt. Vernon 15, Marion 13

Finals

Marion 29, Olney 20 (3rd Place)
Mt. Vernon 18, Canton 14 (Championship)

Championship Game

COACH: Floyd Stables Mt. Vernon (18)	FG	FT	TP
Russell Miller, f	4	4	12
Roy Miller, f	2	0	4
Chester Staley, c	0	0	0
Jimmy Johnson, g	0	0	0
Milton Forsyth, g	1	0	2
Totals	7	4	18

COACH: R. A. Deffenbaugh Canton (14)	FG	FT	TP
Marion Negley, f	2	0	4
Roger Perkins, f	1	0	2
Hubert Devault, f	0	0	0
Fred Johnson, f	0	0	0
Clyde Campbell, c	2	0	4
Claude Berry, g	0	4	4
Tophill Simon, g	0	0	0
Totals	5	4	14

Halftime score: Mt. Vernon 11, Canton 7
Officials: Fred H. Young (Bloomington);
Charles P. Lantz (Charleston)

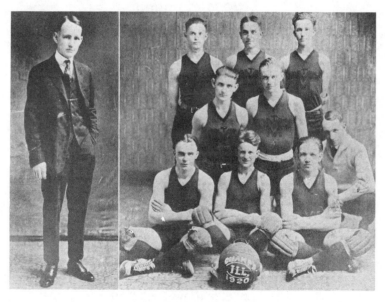

1920 CHAMPION MT. VERNON RAMS—Front Row: Milton Forsyth, Russell Miller, James Johnson, Asst. Coach. Second Row: Roy Miller, Staley. Third Row: Harris, Thomas Wells, Harel Ester. Left: F.F. Stables, Coach.

1921
March 17-18-19
Gym Annex, University of Illinois

When 24 Was Magic . . .

Marion followers were emotionally spent twice before their favorite team finally scored two one-point victories to earn the coveted crown. Marion edged New Trier of Winnetka 24-23 in overtime to survive the semifinals. A nine-point scoring spree in the last quarter carried Marion to another 24-23 triumph and the championship against Rockford. The winners used eight players, and six accounted for points in the tense battle as Ralph Baker scored 15 points for Rockford.

First Round

Batavia 27, Mt. Carmel 22
Collinsville 21, Fairbury 15
Flora 24, Moline 22
Galesburg 29, Charleston 7
Marion 15, Elgin 14 (ot)

Second Round

Streator 42, Trenton 13
Rockford 45, Pittsfield 13
Batavia 31, Peoria (Central) 16
Collinsville 19, Flora 17
Marion 19, Galesburg 15
Macomb 38, Springfield 19
Winnetka (New Trier) 34, Decatur 31
Champaign 27, Mt. Vernon 19

Quarterfinals

Rockford 29, Streator 28
Batavia 24, Collinsville 9
Marion 25, Macomb 9
Winnetka (New Trier) 29, Champaign 28

Semifinals

Rockford 32, Batavia 21
Marion 24, Winnetka (New Trier) 23 (ot)

Finals

Winnetka (New Trier) 33, Batavia 28 (3rd Place)
Marion 24, Rockford 23 (Championship)

Championship Game

COACH: E. H. Schreiber   COACH: Louis Erickson

Marion (24)	FG	FT	TP		Rockford (23)	FG	FT	TP
William Wallace, f	3	0	6		Warren Kasch, f	3	0	6
John Slater, f	1	1	3		Ralph Baker, f	7	1	15
Luke Johnson, f	1	0	2		Thomas Ledger, c	0	0	0
Willis Stone, f	1	0	2		Carl Miltmore, c	0	0	0
Norman Belford, c	2	5	9		Wesley Carlson, g	1	0	2
Raymond Biggs, g	0	0	0		Edward Pelgen, g	0	0	0
Owen Stotlar, g	0	0	0		George Fridley, g	0	0	0
Ray Robinson, g	1	0	2		Totals	11	1	23
Totals	9	6	24					

Score by quarters:

Marion	4	7	4	9	—	24
Rockford	8	10	4	1	—	23

Officials: Fred H. Young (Bloomington); Howard V. Millard (Decatur)

1921 CHAMPION MARION WILDCATS—Front Row: John Slater, Owen Stotlar, Raymond Biggs, Norman Belford, William Wallace. Second Row: Coach Edwin Schreiber, Willis Stone, Ray Robinson, Luke Johnson.

1922
March 17-18
Gym Annex, University of Illinois

Centralia is Back . . .

Atwood had hoped to keep a date with destiny but missed by 16 minutes. Centralia made sure of this by winning its 26th of 30 games leveling Atwood for the championship 24-16. Wiley Cox (12) and Marc Hughes (8) led the scoring to assure Centralia becoming the third two-time winner. After a 12-12 halftime standoff, Atwood faded to suffer its first loss in 22 games.

First Round

Centralia 31, Rockford 23
Atwood 17, Peoria (Central) 15

Finals

Rockford 45, Peoria (Central) 26 (3rd Place)
Centralia 24, Atwood 16 (Championship)

Championship Game

COACH: Arthur L. Trout

Centralia (24)	FG	FT	PF	TP
Marc Hughes, f	1	6	2	8
Leonard Parker, f	0	0	0	0
Clarence Barr, f	0	0	1	0
Harry Lender, c	2	0	2	4
Wiley Cox, g	6	0	2	12
John Lichtenfeld, g	0	0	0	0
Lloyd Keller, g	0	0	0	0
Totals	9	6	7	24

COACH: Lawrence Hamilton

Atwood (16)	FG	FT	PF	TP
Laverne Manaugh, f	1	0	1	2
Hugh Harshbarger, f	2	0	1	4
Claude Ware, c	3	2	2	8
Wayne Reeder, g	1	0	1	2
Stoughton Reeder, g	0	0	0	0
Totals	7	2	5	16

Score by quarters:

Centralia	5	7	7	5	—	24
Atwood	5	7	2	2	—	16

Officials: Fred H. Young (Bloomington); M. Driggs (Rock Island)

1922 CHAMPION CENTRALIA ORPHANS—Front row: Vernon Drenckpohl, Fred Holland. Second row: Lloyd Keller, Marc Hughes, Wiley Cox, Leonard Parker, Harry Lender. Third row: Clarence "Bud" Saul, John Lichtenfeld, Clarence Bar, L. N. Hanna, T. W. Clarida, Coach A. L. Trout.

1923
March 16-17
Gym Annex, University of Illinois

Brand New Maverick . . .

Rockford's hopes of becoming the first three-time winner in state tournament history missed by four points. Thus, Villa Grove became another new name on the title roster beating Rockford 32-29 as William Barmore scored 22 points. Harold Gleichman (14) and Louis Behr (13) paced Rockford as Villa Grove's 10-8 scoring edge in the last quarter made the difference. Canton finished third, beating Greenville 12-10.

First Round

Rockford 26, Greenville 23
Villa Grove 38, Canton 25

Finals

Canton 12, Greenville 10 (3rd Place)
Villa Grove 32, Rockford 29 (Championship)

Championship Game

COACH: Curtus Pulliam

Villa Grove (32)	FG	FT	TP
Wayne Hulse, f	1	0	2
William Barmore, f	8	6	22
Kenneth Reynolds, c	4	0	8
Ernest Combs, g	0	0	0
Harold Sanders, g	0	0	0
Totals	13	6	32

COACH: E. U. McDonald

Rockford (29)	FG	FT	TP
Louis Behr, f	4	5	13
Harold Gleichman, f	7	0	14
Anthony Roskie, f	1	0	2
Fred Kulberg, f	0	0	0
Robert Reitsch, c	0	0	0
Clifford Nelson, g	0	0	0
Ralph Johnson, g	0	0	0
Totals	12	5	29

Score by quarters:

Villa Grove	9	6	7	10	—	32
Rockford	8	6	7	8	—	29

Officials: Fred H. Young (Bloomington); Sam Barry (Galesburg)

1923 CHAMPION VILLA GROVE BLUE DEVILS—Team members included: Coach Curtus Pulliam, Wayne Hulse, William Barmore, Kenneth Reynolds, Ernest Combs, Harold Sanders.

1924
March 21-22
Gym Annex, University of Illinois

Elgin, Mills Make Their Mark . . .

Elgin warmed up for its first state championship by beating back Canton in a 16-14 pulse pounder. Then the upstate team pounced upon Athens for a 9-1 edge in the first quarter en route to a 28-17 title triumph. Louis Semeny led the winners with 12 points as Doug Mills and Herbert Hill, his fellow forwards, contributed five points apiece. Soon basketball buffs would know Mills as the basketball coach and athletic director of the University of Illinois.

First Round

Elgin 16, Canton 14
Athens 26, West Frankfort 19

Finals

Canton 30, West Frankfort 6 (3rd Place)
Elgin 28, Athens 17 (Championship)

Championship Game

COACH: Mark Wilson

Elgin (28)	FG	FT	FTM	PF	TP		Athens (17)	FG	FT	FTM	PF	TP
Douglas Mills, f	1	3	1	0	5		John Zalenas, f	0	2	1	1	2
Herbert Hill, f	2	1	1	1	5		Herman Hibbs, f	1	1	0	0	3
Harry Lang, c	2	2	1	2	6		Bruce Perkins, f	3	0	2	0	6
Louis Semenz, g	4	4	0	0	12		Henry Winterbauer, c	2	2	5	1	6
Andrew Solyom, g	0	0	0	4	0		Edward Winterbauer, g	0	0	0	2	0
Fred Lehmann, g	0	0	0	1	0		John Bokoski, g	0	0	0	3	0
Totals	9	10	3	8	28		Totals	6	5	8	7	17

Score by quarters:

Elgin	9	8	4	7	—	28
Athens	1	6	5	5	—	17

Officials: Fred H. Young (Bloomington);
Arthur Swedberg (Rock Island)

1924 CHAMPION ELGIN MAROONS—Front row: Ted Stern, Bates Stone, Doug Mills, Herb Hill, Haywood Biggers. Second row: Coach Mark Wilson, Elmer Johnson, Andy Solyom, Soup Semenz, Harry Lange, Fritz Lehman, E. C. Waggoner, Mgr.

1925
March 20-21
Gym Annex, University of Illinois

New Coach, Old Story . . .

Elgin switched coaches, Cliff Adams replacing Mark Wilson, and still became the first back-to-back winner in tournament history. Going all the way with just five players, Elgin toppled Champaign 25-17. This success gave the repeating champions a two-season total of 49 victories in 54 games. Mills, shifted from forward to guard by Adams, scored three baskets for six points—two fewer than pacemaker Chapman Wells.

First Round

Champaign 23, Marion 15
Elgin 31, Canton 16

Finals

Canton 30, Marion 17 (3rd Place)
Elgin 25, Champaign 17 (Championship)

Championship Game

COACH: Clifton E. Adams

Elgin (25)	FG	FT	TP
Chapman Wells, f	4	0	8
Herbert Hill, f	0	2	2
Andrew Solyom, c	1	0	2
Douglas Mills, g	3	0	6
Gerald Slavic, g	3	1	7
Totals	11	3	25

COACH: Less Moyer

Champaign (17)	FG	FT	TP
Frank McCallister, f	2	2	6
Hurem Derment, f	1	2	4
William Johnson, f	0	0	0
Fred Hyland, c	1	3	4
Raymond Fisher, g	0	0	0
Don Gamble, g	1	0	2
Totals	5	7	17

Officials: Fred H. Young (Bloomington);
Arthur Swedberg (Rock Island)

1925 CHAMPION ELGIN MAROONS—Front row from left: Doug Mills, Andy Solyom, Herb Hill, Jerry Slavik, Carl Ackmann. Second row: Coach Cliff Adams, Ozzie Hill, Chap Wells, Foy Flora, Haywood Biggers, E.C. Waggoner, Mgr.

1926
March 19-20
Huff Gym, University of Illinois

History and Huff . . .

The tournament found another new home, the George Huff Gymnasium on the University of Illinois campus and wrote history in the process. Glenn Holmes, who played for Freeport when it won the 1915 tournament title in Decatur, was the same Glenn Holmes who coached the Pretzels to a 24-13 rout of Canton to win the 1926 championship.

This dual role enabled Holmes to become the first player-coach to be involved in two state championships at the same school. Holmes later molded nationally ranked high school football teams at both Freeport and Oak Park High School.

In the 1926 final, Herbert Stimpert scored 15 points—two more than the entire Canton team—to assure Holmes his historic first.

Semifinals

Canton 20, Flora 18
Freeport 21, Athens 15

Finals

Flora 23, Athens 14 (3rd Place)
Freeport 24, Canton 13 (Championship)

Championship Game

COACH: Glen Holmes

Freeport (24)	FG	FT	FTM	PF	TP
Herbert Keith	3	0	4	2	6
Maurice McClanathan, f	1	1	1	2	3
Herbert Stimpert, c	6	3	1	2	15
Howard Broughton, g	0	0	0	1	0
Ralph Ruthe, g	0	0	0	1	0
Totals	10	4	6	8	24

COACH: Mark Peterman

Canton (13)	FG	FT	FTM	PF	TP
Eddie Lane, f	2	1	2	2	5
Nathan Deutch, f	1	1	0	1	3
Dave Vance, c	0	2	0	0	2
Dick Morgan, g	1	1	2	0	3
Russell Cardosi, g	0	0	0	2	0
Totals	4	5	4	5	13

Halftime score: Canton 10, Freeport 9

Officials: Fred H. Young (Bloomington); Art Swedberg (Rock Island)

1926 CHAMPION FREEPORT PRETZELS—Harold Shippee, Quinter Bere, Herbert Keith, Howard Broughton, Capt. Harold Neidigh, Ralph Johnston, Maurice McClanathan, Ralph Ruthe, Herbert Stimpert, Charles Stone, Coach Holmes.

1927
March 24-25-26
Huff Gym, University of Illinois

Photo Finish Time . . .

Mt. Carmel and Peoria (Central) tossed matching records on the line when they met for the 1927 championship. Reaching the finals, each team had won 30 games and lost two. In the all or nothing showdown, Mt. Carmel scored a most impressive 24-18 triumph. The Kamps, Babe and Bob, joined George Eaton to account for all of the winners' points. East St. Louis defeated Champaign 25-20 for third place.

First Round

East St. Louis 26, Rockford 12
Peoria (Central) 42, St. Charles 15
Champaign 34, Mt. Olive 21
Mt. Carmel 35, Athens 19

Semifinals

Peoria (Central) 33, East St. Louis 11
Mt. Carmel 35, Champaign 23

Finals

East St. Louis 25, Champaign 20 (3rd Place)
Mt. Carmel 24, Peoria (Central) 18 (Championship)

Championship Game

COACH: Cliff Garrett

Mt. Carmel (24)	FG	FT	FTM	PF	TP
Babe Kamp, f	4	0	0	1	8
George Eaton, f	4	3	2	1	11
Frank Henneberger, c	0	0	0	3	0
Robert Kamp, g	2	0	0	4	5
George Crum, g	0	0	0	1	0
Alfred Elzey, g	0	0	0	3	0
Totals	10	4	2	12	24

COACH: Salen Herke

Peoria (Central) (18)	FG	FT	FTM	PF	TP
Arthur Verner, f	1	1	2	1	3
George Soper, f	3	2	3	1	8
Robert Green, c	2	3	2	1	7
John Gimming, g	0	0	1	2	0
Lorenz Tower, g	0	0	1	0	0
Totals	6	6	9	5	18

Official: Leo T. Johnson (Decatur); Fred "Brick" Young (Bloomington)

1927 CHAMPION MT. CARMEL ACES—Front row: Coach Cliff Garret, Robert Kamp, George Eaton, Frank Henneberger, Babe Kamp, Alfred Elzey. Back row: Crawford, George Crum, Hawkins, Davidson, Wise.

1928
March 22-23-24
Huff Gym, University of Illinois

Slow, Slower, Slowest . . .

Offensive operations dipped to a new slow low in tournament competition when the championship game produced only 27 points. Canton scored 18 of them to beat Aurora (West) 18-9. Clarence Anderson scored all of Aurora's points as the game produced more history. It marked the first and only time in a tournament title game one player scored all of his team's points, and a team failed to reach double digits.

First Round

Witt 33, Streator 31 (ot)
Canton 23, Benton 11
Aurora (West) 28, Rochelle 14
Griggsville 22, Hutsonville 21

Semifinals

Canton 19, Witt 17
Aurora (West) 31, Griggsville 24

Finals

Witt 40, Griggsville 26 (3rd Place)
Canton 18, Aurora (West) 9 (Championship)

Championship Game

COACH: Mark A. Peterman

Canton (18)	FG	FT	FTM	PF	TP
Chester Eddy, f	3	2	0	0	8
Frederick Schnell, f	0	0	1	4	0
Charles Coleman, c	3	1	0	2	7
Frank Mace, g	0	2	1	3	2
Russell Cardosi, g	0	1	1	0	1
Fred Carmack, Jr., g	0	0	0	0	0
Totals	6	6	3	9	18

COACH: Ralph Fletcher

Aurora (West) (9)	FG	FT	FTM	PF	TP
Arthur Whitson, f	0	0	0	2	0
Elmer Alexander, f	0	0	0	1	0
Clarence Anderson, c	3	3	5	2	9
William Barnes, g	0	0	2	1	0
Phillip Hazlett, g	0	0	1	1	0
Ray Vorreis, g	0	0	0	0	0
Totals	3	3	8	6	9

Score by quarters:

Canton	2	6	2	8	— 18
West Aurora	3	0	3	3	— 9

Officials: Fred H. Young (Bloomington); Lyle Clarno (Batavia)

1928 CHAMPIONS CANTON LITTLE GIANTS—Front row: Chester Eddy, Fred Schnell, Edgar Brons, Russell Cardos, Frank Mace, Charles Coleman, Junior Carmack, Coach Mark Peterman. Second row: "Opie" Eshelman, Al Pschirrer, Harry Maxwell, Claude McMullin, Vernon Phillips, Joe Moore, Ray Smith, Morrow Schnell.

1929
March 21-22-23
Huff Gym, University of Illinois

One Touch of Football . . .

Tony Blazine, who was to become a football standout as a collegian and pro, centered Johnston City's successful climb to the heights of schoolboy basketball in Illinois. Blazine scored 7 points as Johnston City parlayed an 11-point fourth quarter into a 30-21 spanking of Champaign to take home the title trophy. Freeport, a first-round winner, settled for third place, under the leadership of Coach Adolph Rupp, with a 27-15 triumph over Peoria (Central). After moving on to the University of Kentucky, Rupp became one of the game's all-time winningest coaches.

First Round

Champaign 43, Mt. Carmel 30
Freeport 30, Wheaton 28
Peoria (Central) 27, Witt 18
Johnston City 14, Lincoln 9

Semifinals

Champaign 40, Freeport 24
Johnston City 19, Peoria (Central) 15

Finals

Freeport 27, Peoria (Central) 15 (3rd Place)
Johnston City 30, Champaign 21 (Championship)

Championship Game

COACH: Larue VanMeter

Johnston City (30)	FT	FT	FTM	PF	TP
Ralph Davison, f	2	4	1	1	8
Dwight Hafeli, f	0	1	0	0	1
Hubert Pearce, f	5	0	1	1	10
Tony Blazine, c	3	1	1	1	7
Albert Feduris, g	1	0	1	2	2
Hubert Groves, g	1	0	0	2	2
Totals	12	6	4	7	30

COACH: L. R. Moyer

Champaign (21)	FG	FT	FTM	PF	TP
William Hagerman, f	2	2	1	1	6
Archie McDonald, f	1	0	1	1	2
Roy Goudie, f	1	1	2	1	3
Albert Hall, c	4	2	1	1	10
Roger Cox, g	0	0	0	1	0
Emerson Dexter, g	0	0	0	1	0
Fred Armstrong, g	0	0	0	0	0
Totals	8	5	5	6	21

Score by quarters:
Johnston City   10 4 5 11— 30
Champaign   10 3 5   3— 21
Officials: Fred H. Young (Bloomington); Carl Johnson (Batavia)

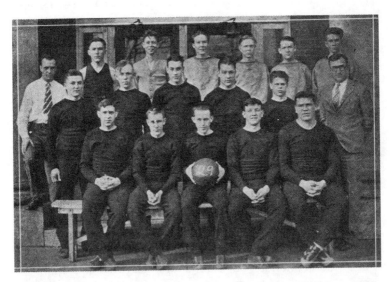

1929 CHAMPION JOHNSTON CITY INDIANS—Seated: Hubert Pearce, Ralph Davison, Hubert Groves, Tony Blazine, Albert Feduris, Middle Row: William Poliokiatis, Stanley Sudosky, Dwight Hafeli, Charles Hafeli, Marshall Ellis, LaRue Van Meter, Coach. Back Row: L.A. Alderman, Coach, John Podlesnik, Raymond Hobbs, Clyde Jobe, Ira Clark, Carl Williams and Cecil Fletcher.

1930
March 20-21-22
Huff Gym, University of Illinois

Record Four Overtimes . . .

The tournament launched the 1930's with one of the best contested first-round fields ever. Sandwiched around Beardstown's 28-27 win over Waterman in four overtimes were Bloomington's 20-19 tripping of Evanston, Olney's three point edge (21-18) over Carbondale, and Peoria's (Manual) 18-16 defeat of Atwood. Manual became Peoria's second champion beating back Bloomington 38-25 in the finals.

First Round

Bloomington 20, Evanston 19
Olney 21, Carbondale 18
Beardstown 28, Waterman 27 (4 ot's)
Peoria (Manual) 18, Atwood 16

Semifinals

Bloomington 33, Olney 23
Peoria (Manual) 31, Beardstown 25

Finals

Olney 27, Beardstown 18 (3rd Place)
Peoria (Manual) 38, Bloomington 25 (Championship)

Championship Game

COACH: Telford Mead   COACH: Eugene Harrison

Peoria (Manual) (38)	FG	FT	FTM	PF	TP
Robert Claus, f	5	0	0	2	10
Charles Wolgemuth, f	6	1	2	2	13
Kenny Shoup, f	1	0	0	0	2
Neve Harms, c	2	4	6	1	8
Ben Schwartz, g	1	0	0	2	2
Hervey Benson, g	0	3	0	2	3
Totals	15	8	8	9	38

Bloomington (25)	FG	FT	FTM	PF	TP
Gerald Cooke, f	4	1	1	2	9
Jay Hallett, f	0	0	3	2	0
Don Argo, c	4	4	0	3	12
Wilbur Auspurger, g	1	1	3	1	3
Clark Buescher, g	0	1	0	4	1
Woodruff Johnson, g	0	0	0	0	0
Totals	9	7	7	12	25

Score by quarters:
(Peoria) Manual   8   10   7   13   —   38
Bloomington   3   7   6   9   —   25

Officials: A. C. Serfling (Oak Park); Art Cox (Rushville)

1930 CHAMPION PEORIA (MANUAL) RAMS—Front row: Kenneth Shoup, Robert Clauss, Charles Wolgemuth, Nevious Harms, Hervey Benson, Ben Schwartz. Second row: Clarence Richarson, Harold Mongerson, Laverne Tjarks, Charles Reece, William Ritchie, Albert Mitzelfelt, Joe Blotner, Coach Mead.

1931
March 19-20-21
Huff Gym, University of Illinois

Rex is Galesburg's Hex ...

Sharpshooter Ray Rex led the way for Decatur's first championship, scoring a game high total of 12 points. This made it possible for Decatur to derail Galesburg in the title match 30-26 as the winners made it a fast finish with a 22-10 scoring edge in the second half. Harrison Tech finished third, providing Chicago with a new first in the schoolboy classic. It was the first time a Chicago school finished within the tournament's top four.

First Round

Chicago (Harrison Tech) 44, Mt. Vernon 33
Decatur 24, Collinsville 23
Galesburg 30, Peoria (Manual) 22
Johnston City 23, Rantoul 14

Semifinals

Decatur 27, Chicago (Harrison Tech) 20
Galesburg 28, Johnston City 27

Finals

Chicago (Harrison Tech) 28, Johnston City 26 (3rd Place)
Decatur 30, Galesburg 26 (Championship)

Championship Game

COACH: Gay A. Kintner   COACH: Gerald Phillips

Decatur (30)	FG	FT	TP
John Stuckey, f	0	5	5
Paul Hill, f	2	3	7
Al Schroeder, c	2	2	6
Ray Rex, g	5	2	12
Duane Garver, g	0	0	0
Kelly Martin, g	0	0	0
Totals	9	12	30

Galesburg (26)	FG	FT	TP
Culver Mills, f	4	3	11
Robert Anderson, f	1	1	3
Don Robinson, f	1	0	2
Harold Henderson, c	1	4	6
Howard Ashely, g	1	0	2
Joe Burford, g	0	0	0
Paul Mitchell, g	0	2	2
Totals	8	10	26

Score by quarters:

Decatur	2	6	12	10	—	30
Galesburg	6	10	2	8	—	26

Officials: Arthur Bergstrom (Casey); Milton Forsyth (Mt. Vernon)

1931 CHAMPION DECATUR (STEPHEN DECATUR) RUNNIN' REDS—Front row: Alfred Schroeder, Raymond Rex, John Stuckey, Paul Hill, Dwight Martin, Duane Garver. Top row: Wayne Schroeder, Eugene Heger, Martin McDaniel, George Keller, Russell Shafer, Mgr., Gay Kintner, Coach.

1932
March 24-25-26
Huff Gym, University of Illinois

The Earl of Cicero...

Erwin Earl was the main man as Morton of Cicero became the 1932 champion sweeping past Hillsboro, Kewanee, and finally Canton. Earl scored nine points in Morton's 30-16 mauling of Canton to gain the title. Morton, up by two (17-15) after the third quarter, salted away the game by outscoring Canton 13-1 in the final period. Ten players, five on each side, shared in the scoring.

First Round

Canton 19, Springfield 12
Lawrenceville 31, Rantoul 21
Kewanee 12, Benton 11
Cicero (Morton) 29, Hillsboro 12

Semifinals

Canton 24, Lawrenceville 20
Cicero (Morton) 28, Kewanee 20

Finals

Lawrenceville 27, Kewanee 19 (3rd Place)
Cicero (Morton) 30, Canton 16 (Championship)

Championship Game

COACH: Norman A. Ziebell

Cicero (Morton) (30)	FG	FT	TP
Charles Fendrich, f	1	0	2
William Dostal, f	0	0	0
Stanley Cech, f	0	0	0
Irwin Kopecky, f	2	4	8
James Vopicka, c	2	1	5
Charles Hermanek, g	0	0	0
William Kobes, g	2	2	6
Erwin Earl, g	4	1	9
Totals	11	8	30

COACH: Archie Chadd

Canton (16)	FG	FT	TP
Melvin Taylor, f	0	1	1
Virgil Pilcher f	0	0	0
Elmer Mettler, f	3	1	7
William Davis, f	0	0	0
Francis Vandermeer, c	1	1	3
Rolla McMullen, g	0	2	2
Grady Stanfel, g	1	1	3
Totals	5	6	16

Score by quarters:

(Cicero) Morton	6	7	4	13	—	30
Canton	4	7	4	1	—	16

Officials: Harlow Sutherland (Bloomington);
R. E. Ashley (Riverside)

1932 CHAMPION CICERO (MORTON) MUSTANGS—Front Row: Erwin Eral, William Kokes, Irwin Kopecky, Capt., James Vopicka, Charles Fendrych, Charles Hermanek, Back Row: Coach Ziebell, Lory, Mgr., Jania, William Dostal, Sirovy, Lang, Stanley Cech, Kayse, Tenk, Fencl, Mgr., Hynd, Trainer.

1933
March 23-24-25
Huff Gym, University of Illinois

Harvey's Hero: Tom Nisbet . . .

The tournament's second 27-point championship game produced the second one-point winner, Thornton of Harvey. Unable to use its famous run and gun offense, Thornton blended Tom Nisbet's eight points into a 14-13 win over Springfield. It launched what was to become a dynasty in schoolboy basketball. In slowing down the playing tempo, Springfield "won" the first and second quarters with 3-2 edges. Thornton scored the only points in the third period (2), and won the game with an 8-7 advantage in the last quarter.

First Round

Springfield 30, Hutsonville 15
Gillespie 25, Chicago (Lake View) 23
Harvey (Thornton) 39, Mahomet 28
Benton 23, Canton 21

Semifinals

Springfield 17, Gillespie 14
Harvey (Thornton) 28, Benton 19

Finals

Benton 36, Gillespie 18 (3rd Place)
Harvey (Thornton) 14, Springfield 13 (Championship)

Championship Game

COACH: Jack Lipe

Harvey (Thornton) (14)	FG	FT	TP
Lou Boudreau, f	1	0	2
Howard McMorris, f	0	0	0
Miles Klein, f	0	0	0
Ted Sliewinski, c	0	1	1
Darwin Hutchins, g	1	1	3
Tom Nisbet , g	1	6	8
Totals	3	8	14

COACH: Mark A. Peterman

Springfield (13)	FG	FT	TP
Chuck Frazee, f	2	0	4
Robert Cook, f	0	0	0
Bob Good, f	0	0	0
Leroy Halberg, c	2	1	5
Charles Warren, g	1	1	3
William Martin, g	0	1	1
Pete Urbanckas, g	0	0	0
Totals	5	3	13

Score by quarters:

Thornton (Harvey)	2	2	2	8	—	14
Springfield	3	3	0	7	—	13

Officials: R. L. Ashley (Riverside);
Harlow Sutherland (Bloomington)

1933 CHAMPION HARVEY (THORNTON) FLYING CLOUDS—Front Row: Lou Boudreau, Miles Klein, Darwin Hutchins, Ted Sliwinski, Howard McMorris, Tom Nisbet. Back Row, left to right: Cuspak, Mgr., Vogler, Hellman, Jenkins, Mc-Comb, Coach K.J. Lipe.

1934
March 22-23-24
Huff Gym, University of Illinois

Major League Distinction . . .

Two athletes who were destined to become famous baseball players participated in the 1934 tournament in the persons of Lou Boudreau and Phil Cavarretta. Boudreau's team, Thornton of Harvey, bowed to Quincy 39-27 in the championship game. Cavarretta's team, Lane Tech of Chicago, was eliminated in the quarterfinals by (you guessed it) Thornton. The big star of the title test was Quincy's Perry Barclift, who scored 11 field goals. The thrill theme was provided when Lane Tech beat Springfield 13-11 in triple overtime in round one.

First Round

Charleston 36, Freeport 16
Quincy 31, Centralia 23
Moline 26, Lawrenceville 21
Urbana 33, Peoria (Central) 30
Equality 21, Marion 20
Chicago (Marshall) 37, Champaign 17
Chicago (Lane Tech) 13, Springfield 11 (3 ot's)
Harvey (Thornton) 42, Streator 21

Quarterfinals

Quincy 29, Charleston 20
Moline 25, Urbana 20
Equality 33, Chicago (Marshall) 17
Harvey (Thornton) 40, Chicago (Lane Tech) 18

Semifinals

Quincy 39, Moline 18
Harvey (Thornton) 30, Equality 20

Finals

Equality 38, Moline 26 (3rd Place)
Quincy 39, Harvey (Thornton) 27 (Championship)

Championship Game

COACH: Selmar A. Storby

Qunicy (39)	FG	FT	FTM	PF	TP
Perry Barclift, f	11	0	2	2	22
George Evans, f	0	0	0	0	0
John Bingaman, f	2	0	1	0	4
Howard Roan, f-c	0	0	0	0	0
Joe Martin, f	0	0	0	0	0
Bill Reinberg, c	0	0	0	4	0
Harry Hall, g	6	0	1	0	12
Bob Reeves, g	0	0	2	3	0
John Zimmerman, g	0	1	0	0	1
Totals	19	1	6	9	39

COACH: Jack Lipe

Harvey (Thornton) (27)	FG	FT	FTM	PF	TP
Lou Boudreau, f	4	0	2	1	8
Gordon McComb, f	3	1	3	4	7
Howard McMorris, f	0	0	0	0	0
Kenneth Heilman, c	1	1	4	0	3
Tom Nisbet, g	4	1	1	0	9
Darwin Hutchins, g	0	0	0	2	0
Totals	12	3	10	7	27

Score by quarters:

Quincy	6	10	12	11	—	39
(Harvey) Thornton	8	7	2	10	—	27

Officials: R. L. Ashley (Riverside);
Wendell Williams (Mt. Vernon)

1934 CHAMPION QUINCY (H.S.) BLUE DEVILS—Front row: John Bingaman, Robert Reeves, William Rineberg, Harry Hall and Perry Barclift. Back row: Coach Selmer O. Storby, George Evans, Howard Roan, Everett Turner, Joe Martin, John Zimmerman, Asst. Coach Fred Barnes.

1935
March 21-22-23
Huff Gym, University of Illinois

Revenge, It's Wonderful . . .

Springfield, beaten by Thornton of Harvey in the 1933 championship game, turned the tables in the 1935 final. This trip, the Senators upended the Flying Clouds 24-19, leaving Thornton with a 1-2-2 log in three straight tournaments. Lou Boudreau's 10 points paced Thornton, giving him a total of 20 points in three straight tournaments. For Coach Mark Peterman of Springfield, it was his second championship. His first was Canton's climb to the top in 1928.

First Round

Moline 34, Joliet 15
Quincy 27, Rockford 24
Springfield 26, Mt. Carmel 21
Champaign 25, Highland Park 21
Harvey (Thornton) 43, Marion 30
Peoria (Central) 40, Danville 22
Hillsboro 45, Pinckneyville 24
Pekin 39, Galesburg 31

Quarterfinals

Moline 31, Quincy 30
Springfield 28, Champaign 16
Harvey (Thornton) 45, Peoria (Central) 28
Pekin 37, Hillsboro 19

Semifinals

Springfield 23, Moline 20
Harvey (Thornton) 35, Pekin 20

Finals

Pekin 22, Moline 16 (3rd Place)
Springfield 24, Harvey (Thornton) 19 (Championship)

Championship Game

COACH: Mark A. Peterman   COACH: Jack Lipe

Springfield (24)	FG	FT	TP	Harvey (Thornton) (19)	FG	FT	TP
Emerson Dailey, f	0	0	0	Lou Boudreau, f	5	0	10
Whitey Sapp, f	0	0	0	Gordon McComb, f	1	1	3
Herb Scheffler, c	6	1	13	Kenneth Heilman, c	1	0	2
Perry Feaman, g	4	1	9	Edward Beinor, g	0	1	1
Paul Nunes, g	1	0	2	William Shumpes, g	1	0	2
				Howard McMorris, g	0	1	1
Totals	11	2	24	Totals	8	3	19

Score by quarters:

Springfield	2	8	6	8	—	24
Harvey (Thornton)	0	10	3	6	—	19

Officials: J. B. Travincek (Chicago); J. C. Robb (Princeton)

1935 CHAMPION SPRINGFIELD (H.S.) SENATORS—Back Row: Farris, Perry Feaman, Paul Nunes, Emerson Dailey, Engel. Front Row: Fultz, Herb Scheffler, Miller, Whitney Sapp, Roff, Coach Mark Peterman.

1936
March 19-20-21
Huff Gym, University of Illinois

Eleven Time Loser Hits Bingo. . .

It was almost unbelievable, underdog Decatur giving Coach Gay Kintner his second championship within five years. The advance statistics showed Danville was undefeated in 22 consecutive games. Decatur, meanwhile, had managed only 23 victories in its first 34 games. Down 15-12 at halftime, Decatur turned on the adrenalin putting together a 14 point second half to anchor its 26-22 title triumph. Johnston City, a 20-19 loser to Decatur in the semifinals, captured third place with a 32-20 decision over Mt. Pulaski.

First Round

Fulton 25, Paris 19
Mt. Pulaski 22, Joliet 16
Danville 28, Centralia 26
Moline 32, Aurora (West) 19
Johnston City 24, Maywood (Proviso) 18
Vandalia 40, Zeigler 36
Decatur 17, Peoria (Manual) 13
Hull 35, Chicago (New Phillips) 23

Quarterfinals

Mt. Pulaski 32, Fulton 18
Danville 31, Moline 29
Johnston City 30, Vandalia 26
Decatur 30, Hull 27

Semifinals

Danville 36, Mt. Pulaski 33
Decatur 20, Johnston City 19

Finals

Johnston City 32, Mt. Pulaski 20 (3rd Place)
Decatur 26, Danville 22 (Championship)

Championship Game

COACH: Gay A. Kintner

Decatur (26)	FG	FT	FTM	PF	TP
Kenneth Park, f	2	2	2	1	6
Eddie Reynolds, f	0	1	1	3	1
William Dearth, f	0	0	1	0	0
Paul Weingand, c	4	2	0	2	10
Dale Minick, g	2	2	0	1	6
Harold Baker, g	0	3	1	2	3
Totals	8	10	5	9	26

COACH: Ned Whitesell

Danville (22)	FG	FT	FTM	PF	TP
Herman Owens, f	1	0	2	3	2
Bob Williams, f	2	0	2	4	4
John Payne, f	0	0	0	0	0
Jean Tuggle, c	2	1	1	1	5
Jack Owens, g	1	2	1	1	4
Dick Jones, g	2	3	1	3	7
Totals	8	6	7	12	22

Score by quarters:
Decatur	3	9	7	7	—	26
Danville	6	9	3	4	—	22

Officials: J. B. Travincek (Chicago); John Hall (Mt. Vernon)

1936 CHAMPION DECATUR (STEPHEN DECATUR) RUNNIN' REDS—Front row: Ken Park, Harold Baker, Paul Weingand, Dale Minick, Eddie Reynolds. Top row: Coach Gay Kinter, Wendy Bauman, Dean Butt, Robert Fisher, Victor Walters, William Dearth.

1937
March 18-19-20
Huff Gym, University of Illinois

New Team in Title Town . . .

Decatur came back to the tournament with 11 more losses in 1937, but its luck wasn't nearly as good. Joliet tossed a poised, balanced team at Decatur to win a 40-20 runaway. The winners' finishing kick, fused by Benny Macuk's accurate marksmanship, was amazing inasmuch as it put 18 points on the board for the last quarter. The victory was Joliet's 27th in 31 games, and the loss left Decatur with a 23-12 log.

First Round

Vandalia 28, Zeigler 26
Joliet 31, Athens 24
Chicago (Wells) 23, Galesburg 20
Collinsville 34, Carbondale 23
Woodstock 37, Oblong 31
Pekin 25, Rushville 24
Moline 24, Dundee 23
Decatur 21, LaSalle-Peru 10

Quarterfinals

Joliet 43, Vandalia 19
Collinsville 20, Chicago (Wells) 18
Pekin 27, Woodstock 26
Decatur 14, Moline 11

Semifinals

Joliet 28, Collinsville 26
Decatur 23, Pekin 15

Finals

Collinsville 31, Pekin 18 (3rd Place)
Joliet 40, Decatur 20 (Championship)

Championship Game

COACH: Herman Walser

Joliet (40)	FG	FT	FTM	PF	TP
LeRoy Hagan, f	3	0	0	2	6
Benny Macuk, f	7	2	2	0	16
Harold Starr, f	0	1	1	0	1
Don Moore, f	0	0	2	2	0
Charles Winston, c	1	1	0	1	3
George Macuk, g	0	0	0	0	0
Harold Ashenbrenner, g	1	3	1	2	5
Louis Ginnetti, g	1	0	0	1	2
Mike Savich, g	3	1	2	2	7
Frank Wardley, g	0	0	0	0	0
Totals	16	8	8	10	40

COACH: Gay A. Kintner

Decatur (20)	FG	FT	FTM	PF	TP
Ken Park, f	2	1	0	2	5
Bob Campbell, f	0	0	0	1	0
Pete Williams, f	0	0	0	0	0
William White, f	1	0	0	1	2
Ham Schiene, f	0	1	1	0	1
Dale Minick, c	3	0	3	3	6
George Smith, g	1	1	1	4	3
Lee Cook, g	1	1	2	1	3
Joe Shellabarger, g	0	0	0	0	0
Elza Kirby, g	0	0	1	0	0
Totals	8	4	8	12	20

Score by quarters:

Joliet   9   4   9   18 — 40
Decatur   3   5   5   7 — 20

Officials: John Hall (Mt. Vernon); Ernest Lieberson (Chicago)

1937 CHAMPION JOLIET (H.S.) STEELMEN—Top Row: Willard Aschenbrenner, Benjamin Macuk, Captain Michael Savich, Charles Winston, and LeRoy Hagen. Bottom row: George Macuk, Louis Ginnetti, William Moore, Frank Wardley, and Harold Starr.

1938
March 14-15-16
Huff Gym, University of Illinois

It's 36 Going and Coming . . .

Dundee put it together to win its first state championship to launch the fourth decade of boys' basketball in Illinois. The contenders from the northern part of the season hit a magic number of 36 twice. Dundee scored 36 points to win its first round test against Pekin. It repeated with 36 points, gaining the title in a 36-29 conquest of Braidwood. Chicago, always a bridesmaid in the tourney, picked off a spot in the trophy brigade when Von Steuben finished fourth.

First Round

Johnston City 32, Champaign 26
Chicago (Von Steuben) 32, Granite City 31
Galesburg 23, Rock Island 21
Braidwood 27, Glen Ellyn (Glenbard) 19
Carbondale 36, Rockford 30
Paris 33, Decatur 20
Harrisburg 36, Milton 25
Dundee 36, Pekin 29

Quarterfinals

Chicago (Von Steuben) 29, Johnston City 27
Braidwood 35, Galesburg 30
Paris 24, Carbondale 22
Dundee 38, Harrisburg 26

Semifinals

Braidwood 38, Chicago (Von Steuben) 24
Dundee 51, Paris 36

Finals

Paris 30, Chicago (Von Steuben) 20 (3rd Place)
Dundee 36, Braidwood 29 (Championship)

Championship Game

COACH: Eugene de Lacey   **COACH:** Charles Pinnick

Dundee (36)	FG	FT	TP
Chris Hansen, f	3	4	10
Don Blanken, f	7	1	15
Arthur Melahn, c	1	0	2
Donald Adams, g	1	1	3
John Shumacher, g	3	0	6
Totals	15	6	36

Braidwood (29)	FG	FT	TP
Edward Viglia, f	4	0	8
Frank Bohac, f	0	1	1
Lawrence Crichton, f	3	0	6
Stan Simpson, c	0	1	1
William Hocking, g	6	1	13
Robert Patterson, g	0	0	0
Totals	13	3	29

Score by quarters:

Dundee	9	8	7	12	—	36
Braidwood	10	7	4	8	—	29

Officials: Ernest Lieberson (Chicago); Ronald Gibbs (Springfield)

1938 CHAMPION DUNDEE (COMMUNITY) CARDUNALS—Front Row: Julius Simonini, Clarence Massier, Bruce Eichler, Walan Fitzsimmons, Frederick Younghans. Back Row: John Schumacher, Donald Adams, Donald Blanken, Christian Hansen, Arthur Melahn, Richard Heidinger.

1939
March 16-17-18
Huff Gym, University of Illinois

Points Key Rockford's Third Win . . .

Balanced scoring tied to a 50-point-per-game average keyed another first for Rockford: its third championship. Rockford rushed past Canton, Zeigler, and Wood River to qualify for the title tilt against Paris. A 53-44 conquest of Paris enabled Rockford to close out the season with a 27-2 record.

First Round

Wood River 34, Moline 22
Cicero (Morton) 42, Chicago (Lane Tech) 37
Rockford 50, Canton 24
Zeigler 21, Roodhouse 11
Champaign 41, Dwight 30
Centralia 37, Bradley 31
Paris 25, Flora 22
Peoria (Woodruff) 45, Gillespie 39

Quarterfinals

Wood River 32, Cicero (Morton) 19
Rockford 47, Zeigler 34
Centralia 49, Champaign 35
Paris 51, Peoria (Woodruff) 42

Semifinals

Rockford 43, Wood River 27
Paris 39, Centralia 30

Finals

Wood River 34, Centralia 28 (3rd Place)
Rockford 53, Paris 44 (Championship)

Championship Game

COACH: James Laude

Rockford (53)	FG	FT	FTM	PF	TP
Norman Anderson, f	4	2	1	1	10
Stanley Stasica, f	6	2	1	1	14
Harlan Anderson, f	0	0	0	0	0
Paul McDaniels, f	0	0	0	0	0
Robert Wallin, c	4	5	2	1	13
Frank Alonzo, g	2	2	1	2	6
Eugene Speck, g	4	2	0	2	10
Totals	20	13	5	7	53

COACH: E. W. Eveland

Paris (44)	FG	FT	FTM	PF	TP
Floyd Henson, f	7	1	0	1	15
Ralph Hooker, f	6	3	0	2	15
Harold Anderson, f-g	2	1	0	1	5
Lawrence Humerickhouse, c	1	1	0	3	3
Thomas Burton, g	0	1	0	2	1
Robert Calinese, g	2	1	1	3	5
Totals	18	8	1	12	44

Score by quarters:

Rockford	11	21	13	8	—	53
Paris	9	10	14	11	—	44

Officials: Ronald Gibbs (Springfield); A. C. Daugherty (Palestine)

1939 CHAMPION ROCKFORD E-RABS—Front row: Robert Wallin, Eugene Speck, Stanley Stasica, Frank Alonzo, Normal Anderson. Second row: Harlan Anderson, George Champion, Keith Mulford, Coach Jim Laude, Albert Volsch, Paul McDaniels.

1940
March 14-15-16
Huff Gym, University of Illinois

Clap Hands, Here Comes Andy . . .
Many athletes have had much to do about the success and progress of high
school basketball in Illinois, but few have contributed more than Andy
Phillip. After closing out his career at Granite City, Andy moved to the
University of Illinois to become the hub of the famous Whiz Kids. He
played just such a role in the 1940 final. His 15 points and astute play-
making keyed Granite City's 24-22 shading of Herrin.

First Round

Champaign 44, Chicago
   (Crane) 25
Salem 55, Beardstown 29
Herrin 30, Chicago Heights
   (Bloom) 25
Paris 36, Taylorville 35
Moline 28, Casey 23
Lewiston 31, Hebron 30
Dundee 72, Rushville 47
Granite City 45, Streator 31

Semifinals

Herrin 21, Champaign 17
Granite City 41, Moline 38

Quarterfinals

Champaign 34, Salem 30
Herrin 29, Paris 22
Moline 49, Lewiston 32
Granite City 35, Dundee 30

Finals

Moline 51, Champaign 33 (3rd Place)
Granite City 24, Herrin 22 (Championship)

Championship Game

COACH: Byron Bozarth

Granite City (24)	FG	FT	FTM	PF	TP
Evan Parsaghian, f	2	1	1	2	5
Dan Eftimoff, f	0	0	0	2	0
John Markarian, f	0	0	0	0	0
George Gages, f	2	0	0	0	4
Everett Daniels, c	0	0	0	0	0
Andy Hagopian, g	0	0	1	0	0
Andy Phillip, g	6	3	2	3	15
Edward Mueller, g	0	0	0	0	0
Edward Hoff, g	0	0	0	0	0
Totals	10	4	6	7	24

COACH: Russell Emery

Herrin (22)	FG	FT	FTM	PF	TP
Fred Campbell, f	6	1	2	1	13
Junior Newlin, f	0	0	1	1	0
Leon Davis, c	0	0	0	2	0
Dallas Lillich, g	3	1	1	2	7
Edward Parsons, g	1	0	2	3	2
Totals	10	2	6	9	22

Score by quarters:
Granite City   5   6   4   9   —   24
Herrin   10   6   0   6   —   22
Officials: Stuart Legault (Chicago); Ralph Elliott (Danville)

1940 CHAMPION GRANITE CITY WARRIORS—Coach Byron Bozarth, John Markarian, Sam Mouradian, Ed Hoff, Evon Parsaghian, George Gages, Andy Phillip, Andy Hagopian, Danny Eftimoff, Ebbie Mueller, Harold Brown, Everett Daniels, Coach Leonard Davis.

THE CHAMPIONS

1941
March 21-22
Huff Gym, University of Illinois

Points, Power, Poise . . .

Basketball buffs well remember the 1941 tournament as tops in fingernail biting and emotion—and with good reason! The four finalists played three of the most magnificent one-pointers in the meet's history. Morton of Cicero assured a second title for Norm Ziebell winning the semifinal 30-29 from Centralia and then tipped Urbana 32-31 to claim the championship. Fred Green, who later played with the Whiz Kids, helped Urbana hurdle its semifinal test with a 39-38 conquest of Canton.

Semifinals

Cicero (Morton) 30, Centralia 29
Urbana 39, Canton 38

Finals

Centralia 67, Canton 37 (3rd Place)
Cicero (Morton) 32, Urbana 31 (Championship)

Championship Game

COACH: Normal A. Ziebell

Cicero (Morton) (32)	FG	FT	FTM	PF	TP
Arnold Laver, f	1	2	1	2	4
Fred Ploegman, f	0	1	0	0	1
Joseph Demkovich, f	2	2	2	1	6
Charles Tourek, f	0	0	0	0	0
Ray Leitner, c	2	3	3	3	7
Robert Hoffman, g	2	2	2	1	6
Chester Strumillo, g	3	2	1	0	8
Totals	10	12	9	7	32

COACH: Lou Stephens

Urbana (31)	FG	FT	FTM	PF	TP
Clyde Rusk, f	1	0	0	2	2
George Widing, f-c	0	0	0	0	0
Bob Gibson, f	1	2	0	4	4
Fred Green, c	6	2	2	4	14
Walt Franklin, g	1	0	3	3	2
Nelson Walden, g	0	0	0	0	0
Leal Nelson, g	4	1	0	2	9
Totals	13	5	5	15	31

Score by quarters:
Cicero (Morton)   7 9 8 8 — 32
Urbana   9 6 13 3 — 31

Officials: M. S. Vaughn (Rockford); Edward Marfell (Springfield)

1941 CHAMPION CICERO (MORTON) MUSTANGS—Front Row: Mgr. Robert Yonko, Charles Cuda, Fred Ploegman, Chester Strumillo, Ray Leitner, Robert Hoffman, Robert Soucek. Back Row: Ben Shack, Trainer: Frank Hulka, Edward Vosyka, Joe Demkovich, Arnold Laver, Joe Grove, Joe Novotny, Charles Tourek, Norman A. Ziebell, Coach.

1942
March 19-20-21
Huff Gym, University of Illinois

Eddleman's Expertise Escalates . . .

Centralia and Coach Arthur Trout became a three-time winner, riding the all-around finesse of a super athlete, Dwight Eddleman. Centralia arrived in Champaign with a 30-6 record and left with a 34-6 log attached to the title trophy. In rapid order, Centralia brushed past West Frankfort, Wood River, Freeport, and Paris. Eddleman scored 16 points to blueprint his team's 35-33 victory in the championship showdown. Freeport's bid for a third title ended with a 31-30 win over Morton of Cicero, another three-time bidder, in the semifinals.

First Round

Paris 64, Urbana 40
Streator 45, Normal 34
Decatur 53, Dixon 37
Cicero (Morton) 42, Springfield (Cathedral) 32
Centralia 42, West Frankfort 28
Wood River 35, Chicago (Lindbloom) 19
Freeport 42, Moline 24
Olney 47, Quincy 40

Quarterfinals

Paris 43, Streator 32
Cicero (Morton) 49, Decatur 45
Centralia 31, Wood River 29
Freeport 29, Olney 24

Semifinals

Paris 28, Cicero (Morton) 21
Centralia 45, Freeport 42

Finals

Freeport 31, Cicero (Morton) 30 (3rd Place)
Centralia 35, Paris 33 (Championship)

Championship Game

COACH: Arthur L. Trout

Centralia (35)	FG	FT	FTM	PF	TP
Tarrell Robinson, f	0	2	1	4	2
Dwight Eddleman, f	6	4	2	1	16
Bernard Schifferdecker, f	1	0	0	2	2
Robert Wham, c	0	0	1	0	0
Jim Seyler, g	3	3	2	1	9
Fred Pearson, g	2	2	1	1	6
Totals	12	11	7	9	35

COACH: E. W. Eveland

Paris (33)	FG	FT	FTM	PF	TP
Max Norman, f	1	4	1	4	6
Nate Middleton, f	5	0	2	4	10
Paul Pederson, f	0	0	0	0	0
Dave Humerickhouse, c	1	3	1	2	5
Dick Foley, g	3	0	1	2	6
Warren Collier, g	3	0	1	1	6
Gene Hancock, g	0	0	0	0	0
Totals	13	7	6	13	33

Score by quarters:

Centralia	4	10	2	19	—	35
Paris	8	6	11	8	—	33

Officials: Carl Johns (Batavia); B. C. Beck (Danville)

1942 CHAMPION CENTRALIA ORPHANS—Front row: Bernard Schifferdecker, Bob Wham, Fred Pearson, Dwight Eddleman, Farrell Robinson, Jim Seyler. Top row: Bill Davis, Farrell Benefiel, Coach A. L. Trout, Harry Lutz, Mgr., Harry Fortney, Jim Edgar, Virgil Krutsinger.

1943
March 18-19-20
Huff Gym, University of Illinois

Paris In Power Drive Early . . .

It was evident at the outset that Paris hadn't forgotten its unhappiness over losing the championship to Centralia in 1942. The champions-to-be slugged Joliet 74-40 in a first round rout and continued to win in impressive manner against Chicago's Kelvyn Park and Salem. Playing Moline for all the marbles, Paris took a 21-16 lead in the first half and dominated the game to the finish. Gordon Taylor paced the scoring with 12 points as all of the winners' six players made contributions. Salem outlasted Elgin 69-58 to take third place.

First Round

Elgin 60, West Rockford 56
Wood River 55, Pekin 49
Moline 45, Anna-Jonesboro 30
West Frankfort 55, Decatur 39
Salem 49, Canton 47
Champaign 33, Quincy 32
Paris 74, Joliet 40
Chicago (Kelvyn Park) 45, Kewanee 30

Quarterfinals

Elgin 44, Wood River 40
Moline 39, West Frankfort 37
Salem 49, Champaign 46
Paris 45, Chicago (Kelvyn Park) 34

Semifinals

Moline 45, Elgin 39
Paris 53, Salem 50

Finals

Salem 69, Elgin 58 (3rd Place)
Paris 46, Moline 37 (Championship)

Championship Game

COACH: Ernest W. Eveland   COACH: Roger Potter

Paris (46)	FG	FT	FTM	PF	TP
Max Norman, f	1	5	0	4	7
Delbert Glover, f	4	0	0	3	8
Dave Humerickhouse, c	1	1	1	2	3
Richard Foley, g	3	2	1	3	8
Gordon Taylor, g	6	0	0	0	12
Paul Pederson, g	3	2	2	0	8
Totals	18	10	4	12	46

Moline (37)	FG	FT	FTM	PF	TP
Frank De Meyer, f	5	2	2	4	12
Albert VanLanduyt, f	2	1	2	1	5
Cal Anders, c	3	2	3	0	8
William Hall, g	2	1	0	1	5
Jim Grafton, g	2	1	0	4	5
LeRoy Skantz, g-f	1	0	1	0	2
Porter Bennett, g	0	0	0	3	0
Harold Heiland, g	0	0	0	0	0
Jim Schell, g	0	0	0	0	0
Totals	15	7	8	13	37

Score by quarters:

Paris	8	13	14	11	—	46
Moline	6	10	10	11	—	37

Officials: Carl Johnson (Batavia); Gregory Shoaff (Springfield)

1943 CHAMPION PARIS TIGERS—Front row: Bob Cochran, John Cychol, Chester Dahlgren, Leo "Nick" Swinford, Don Blair. Second row: Paul Pederson, Gordon Taylor, Dick Foley, Del Glover, Max Norman, Dave Humrickhouse, Coach Ernie W. Eveland.

1944
March 16-17-18
Huff Gym, University of Illinois

Super Charged Powerhouse . . .

Some buffs rated it the best team in the history of schoolboy basketball in Illinois. Whether it was or wasn't probably will be debated as long as the state tournament is played. This much is definite: no one team will fashion a better single season record with present rules in vogue. When Taylorville, paced by Ron Bontemps and Johnny Orr, beat Elgin 56-33 in the 1944 championship game, it concluded a perfect season of 45 consecutive victories. Between them, Bontemps and Orr scored 35 points—two more than Elgin's entire total.

First Round

Anna-Jonesboro 55, Marseilles 34
Elgin 39, Pekin 38
Rockford (West) 71, Kankakee 22
Chicago (South Shore) 62, Quincy 38
Canton 47, West Frankfort 39
Champaign 44, Mount Carmel 32
Taylorville 52, East St. Louis 34
Kewanee 36, Paris 34
Douglass (Mounds) 49, Dunbar (Madison) 34 (Game to determine championship of colored conference)

Quarterfinals

Elgin 65, Anna-Jonesboro 38
Chicago (South Shore) 39, Rockford (West) 33
Champaign 57, Canton 42
Taylorville 51, Kewanee 30

Semifinals

Elgin 48, (Chicago) South Shore 47
Taylorville 40, Champaign 36

Finals

(Chicago) South Shore 52, Champaign 34 (3rd Place)
Taylorville 56, Elgin 33 (Championship)

Championship Game

COACH: Dolph Stanley

Taylorville (56)	FG	FT	FTM	PF	TP
John Orr, f	7	3	2	2	17
Don Janssen, f	1	0	1	2	2
Dean Duncan, f	0	0	0	1	0
Ronald Bontemps, c	8	2	1	1	18
Dave Jones, g	3	2	2	4	8
Schulte Bishop, g	2	1	1	4	5
Jack Richards, g	0	0	0	0	0
Charles Riester, g	2	0	1	1	4
Joe McAdam	0	1	0	0	1
Dale Brown, g	0	1	0	0	1
Totals	23	10	8	15	56

COACH: E. R. Ahearn

Elgin (33)	FG	FT	FTM	PF	TP
Karl Plath, f	2	2	6	4	6
James Rager, f	1	2	0	2	4
Howard Kugath, c	2	1	0	1	5
Eugene Manley, c	0	0	0	0	0
William Myers, c	0	1	0	1	1
Sam Sauceda, g	4	6	1	2	14
Jack Burmaster, g	1	1	0	5	3
William Goedert, g	0	0	0	1	0
Tom Parker, g	0	0	1	1	0
Totals	10	13	8	17	33

Score by quarters:

Taylorville	8	16	13	19	—	56
Elgin	10	9	10	4	—	33

Officials: Carl Johnson (Batavia); R. C. Kaegel (Belleville)

1944 CHAMPION TAYLORVILLE TORNADOES—Front Row: Joe McAdam, David Jones, John Orr, Ronald Bontemps, Donald Janssen, Jack Richards. Second row: Dean Duncan, Schultte Bishop, Francis Stahr, Dale Brown, Charles Noren, Bob Slaybaugh, Richard Wilson. Third row: Ralph Willison, Michael Ganey, Harold Parrish. Upper right—Coach Dolph Stanley. Upper Left—Manager

1945
March 15-16-17
Huff Gym, University of Illinois

Decatur Deals Disaster . . .

Decatur's preview of adding machine basketball surfaced when the Big Red averaged 68.5 points per game to win a third state title with Coach Gay Kintner at the controls. Decatur was building toward an eventual 39-2 record when it gunned down such powerhouses as Collinsville, Galesburg, Moline, and Champaign. In the championship showdown, Decatur beat Champaign 62-54 as four players scored in double digits. Bob Doster was the leader with 18. Jesse Clements led Champaign with 19.

First Round

Somonauk 45, Carbondale 35
Champaign 47, Cicero (Morton) 46
Quincy 46, Springfield 38
Peoria (Central) 38, Flora 36
Galesburg 45, West Frankfort 42
Decatur 77, Collinsville 45
Elgin 44, Rockford (East) 39
Moline 35, Chicago (Senn) 32

Quarterfinals

Champaign 77, Somonauk 28
Quincy 54, Peoria (Central) 46
Decatur 73, Galesburg 72 (ot)
Moline 41, Elgin 39

Semifinals

Champaign 50, Quincy 32
Decatur 62, Moline 46

Finals

Quincy 49, Moline 47 (3rd Place)
Decatur 62, Champaign 54 (Championship)

Championship Game

COACH: Gay A. Kintner

Decatur (62)	FG	FT	FTM	PF	TP
Ralph Rutherford, f	5	1	1	3	11
John Malerich, f	5	4	2	1	14
Robert Hoyt, f	0	0	1	0	0
Robert Kurek, f	0	0	0	0	0
George Riley, c	8	0	1	5	16
Robert Stauber, c	0	0	0	0	0
Robert Doster, g	6	6	3	3	18
Tom Krigbaum, g	0	2	3	4	2
Robert Neuendorf, g	0	1	0	1	1
James Arnold, g	0	0	0	0	0
Totals	24	14	11	17	62

COACH: Harry Combes

Champaign (54)	FG	FT	FTM	PF	TP
Ted Beach, f	5	3	0	1	13
Earl Harrison, f	1	1	0	4	3
Rodney Fletcher, f	1	1	1	1	3
Fred Major, f	0	2	1	2	2
Dick Kelly, c	2	4	2	3	8
Dick Paterson, g	3	0	0	5	6
Jesse Clements, g	9	1	0	2	19
Jim Cottrell, g	0	0	0	2	0
Totals	21	12	4	20	54

Score by quarters:

Decatur	14	12	17	19	—	62
Champaign	9	10	16	19	—	54

Officials: Eddie Murphy (Peoria); Ernest Driggers (Mt. Vernon)

1945 CHAMPION DECATUR (STEPHEN DECATUR) RUNNIN' REDS—Front row: Ralph Rutherford, Bob Doster, George Riley, Bob Neuendorf, John Malerich, Tom Krigbaum. Top row: Bob Stauber, Bob Hoyt, Gay Kintner, Coach, Jim Arnold, Bob Kurek.

1946
March 14-15-16
Huff Gym, University of Illinois

Ted Helps Beach Centralia . . .

Champaign made its second straight appearance in the championship game and walked away a 54-48 winner over Centralia. Ted Beach put 22 points on the board to cushion the Maroons' first title success under the direction of Coach Harry Combes. Centralia qualified for its fourth final by inching past Dundee 45-44 in a tense semi-final game. In the championship struggle, Champaign built a 10-point edge in the first half and coasted home.

First Round

Decatur 59, Pana 41
Dundee 56, Quincy 49
Centralia 50, Kewanee 36
Robinson 47, Pontiac 44
Rockford (East) 74, Chicago (Tilden) 57
Collinsville 50, Springfield (Cathedral) 28
Marion 42, Calumet City 38 (ot)
Champaign 49, Galesburg 40

Quarterfinals

Dundee 55, Decatur 48
Centralia 63, Robinson 50
Rockford (East) 43, Collinsville 37
Champaign 55, Marion 43

Semifinals

Centralia 45, Dundee 44
Champaign 53, Rockford (East) 47

Finals

Dundee 59, Rockford (East) 53 (3rd Place)
Champaign 54, Centralia 48 (Championship)

Championship Game

COACH: Harry Combes

Champaign (54)	FG	FT	FTM	PF	TP
Ted Beach, f	9	4	0	1	22
Earl Harrison, f	3	0	1	2	6
William Johnston, f	0	0	0	0	0
Rodney Fletcher, c	3	0	1	3	6
John McDermott, c	2	1	3	1	5
Jim Cottrell, g	6	2	0	5	14
Fred Major, g	0	1	0	1	1
Totals	23	8	5	13	54

COACH: Arthur Trout

Centralia (48)	FG	FT	FTM	PF	TP
Colin Anderson, f	7	0	1	1	14
Kenneth McBride, f	2	2	1	4	6
Charles Oland, c	3	1	0	1	7
Don Schnake, g	3	0	1	3	6
Harold Rush, g	4	7	0	2	15
Totals	19	10	3	11	48

Score by quarters:

Champaign	7	16	13	18	—	54
Centralia	8	5	11	24	—	48

Officials: William Downes (Chicago); Walter Johnson (Cambridge)

1946 CHAMPION CHAMPAIGN (H.S.) MAROONS—Front Row: Ted Beach, Capt., Jim Cottrell, Earl Harrison, Fred Major, Rodney Fletcher. Back Row, left to right: Asst. Coach Harold Jester, Kirby Knox, Bobby Clark, John McDermott, Dick Petry, Bill Johnston, Coach Harry Combes.

1947
March 20-21-22
Huff Gym, University of Illinois

Champaign's Dynasty Ends . . .

It was shades of Thornton of Harvey in the 1930s when Champaign advanced to the championship game a third straight time. Where Thornton had put together a 1-2-2 string, the home town Maroons were forced to settle for a 2-1-2 finish. Paris had too many guns for Champaign and won the title game 58-37. Bob Owens scored 22 points to help seal Paris' second successful championship bid. Pinckneyville's 47-42 beating of Pekin in the third place battle provided hints of the future.

First Round

Collinsville 48, Flora 37
Pekin 54, Marseilles 47
Dundee 69, Springfield 47
Champaign 52, Murphysboro 39
Paris 70, Beardstown 33
Chicago (South Shore) 43, Galesburg 37
Kewanee 56, Rockford (East) 53
Pinckneyville 45, Aurora (East) 34

Quarterfinals

Pekin 42, Collinsville 41
Champaign 47, Dundee 45
Paris 49, Chicago (South Shore) 37
Pinckneyville 47, Kewanee 26

Semifinals

Champaign 73, Pekin 53
Paris 57, Pinckneyville 50

Finals

Pinckneyville 47, Pekin 42 (3rd Place)
Paris 58, Champaign 37 (Championship)

Championship Game

COACH: Ernest W. Eveland

Paris (58)	FG	FT	FTM	PF	TP
Glen Vietor, f	6	2	1	2	14
John Wilson, f	3	2	1	2	8
Richard Henson, f	1	1	0	0	3
Robert Owens, c	9	4	0	4	22
Dow Morris, g	1	2	1	3	4
Don Glover, g	2	3	0	1	7
Totals	22	14	3	12	58

COACH: Harry Combes

Champaign (37)	FG	FT	FTM	PF	TP
Ted Beach, f	5	1	0	0	11
Richard Petry, f	0	0	1	3	0
Wayne Wells, f	0	0	0	1	0
Bernard Bryant, f	0	0	0	0	0
Bobby Clark, f	0	0	2	1	0
Rodney Fletcher, c	4	3	4	4	11
John McDermott, c	2	0	0	3	4
Ray Walters, g	1	4	0	2	6
Fred Major, g	2	1	0	1	5
Kenneth Wilk, g	0	0	0	0	0
Totals	14	9	7	15	37

Score by quarters:

Paris	10	17	20	11	—	58
Champaign	7	13	13	4	—	37

Officials: Sam Gillespie (St. Elmo); Ted Search (Chester)

1947 CHAMPION PARIS TIGERS—Front row: Don Glover, Dow Morris, Bob Owens, Duane "Bucky" Eveland, Glen Vietor, John Wilson, Coach Ernie W. Eveland. Second row: Floyd Garrett, Mgr., Max Wilson, Fred Blair, Ronnie Beeson, Ronnie Cummins, Dick Henson.

1948
March 18-19-20
Huff Gym, University of Illinois

It's The Johnson-Gladson Show . . .

Pinckneyville's strong finish in 1947 established it as the team to beat in 1948, and the downstaters didn't falter. With Bob Johnson and Frank Gladson scoring 21 points apiece, Pinckneyville coasted to a 65-39 rout of Rockford (East) in the championship game. It was the winners' first title as Pekin, eventually winner of the tournament's third place, proved the most troublesome going down the tournament trail.

First Round

Springfield (Cathedral) 57, Harvey (Thornton) 50
Pinckneyville 45, Moline 35
Pekin 50, LaSalle-Peru 46
Marion 65, Collinsville 60
LaGrange 61, Hillsboro 44
Canton 41, Quincy 37
Rockford (East) 54, Champaign 53 (ot)
Chicago (Marshall) 54, Robinson 49

Quarterfinals

Pinckneyville 58, Springfield (Cathedral) 36
Pekin 53, Marion 45
LaGrange 45, Canton 41
Rockford (East) 51, Chicago (Marshall) 49

Semifinals

Pinckneyville 36, Pekin 31
Rockford (East) 61, LaGrange 54

Finals

Pekin 45, LaGrange 38 (3rd Place)
Pinckneyville 65, Rockford (East) 39 (Championship)

Championship Game

COACH: Merrill Thomas

Pinckneyville (65)	FG	FT	FTM	PF	TP
Robert Johnson, f	7	7	2	3	21
Thomas Millikin, f	4	0	2	3	8
William McCrary, f	0	0	0	0	0
William Williams, f	0	0	0	0	0
David Davis, c	3	3	1	0	9
Richard Craig, c	0	0	0	0	0
Percy Clippard, g	1	3	4	3	5
Frank Gladson, g	8	5	1	1	21
Richard Luke, g	0	1	0	1	1
Charles Gruner, g	0	0	0	0	0
Totals	23	19	10	11	65

COACH: Jim Laude

Rockford (East) (39)	FG	FT	FTM	PF	TP
William Weaver, f	3	1	1	3	7
Donald Harris, f	0	0	0	0	0
Eugene Lenz, f	0	0	0	3	0
Harold Samorian, f	1	0	0	0	2
George Sheatz, f	0	2	0	0	2
Peter Anderson, c	4	3	1	3	11
Walter Johnson, c	2	3	1	5	7
Eugene Tarabilda, g	3	0	0	2	6
Frank Calacurcio, g	2	0	2	4	4
Gordon Stang, g	0	0	0	0	0
Totals	15	9	5	20	39

Score by quarters:

Pinckneyville	18	17	16	14	— 65
East Rockford	6	13	10	10	— 39

Officials: Ted Search (Chester); William Carlin (Peoria)

1948 CHAMPION PINCKNEYVILLE PANTHERS—Front row: Percy Clippard, Tom Millikin, Bob Johnson, Dave Davis, Frank Gladson. Back row: Bill Nesbitt, Mgr. Dick Luke, Dick Craig, Bill Williams, Bill McCrary, Charles Gruner, Coach Merrill "Duster" Thomas.

1949
March 17-18-19
Huff Gym, University of Illinois

History In The Making . . .

Not too many basketball buffs took Mt. Vernon's bid for its first title since 1920 too seriously during the first-round games. The team opened with a lackluster 54-52 conquest of Johnston City. Everything changed when play advanced to the quarter-finals, and Max Hooper & Company blasted Decatur 71-51. After a 37-31 ouster of Aurora (West), Mt. Vernon shot down Hillsboro 45-39 to win the championship. Hooper scored 21 points as 12 of the 13 players in the game for both teams put points on the board.

First Round

Decatur 82, Pittsfield 48
Mt. Vernon 54, Johnston City 52
Chicago (Tilden) 58, Oneida (ROVA) 41
Aurora (West) 45, Elgin 42
Moline 64, Rockford (West) 38
Nashville 43, Ottawa 39
Pekin 60, Robinson 52
Hillsboro 45, Champaign 42 (ot)

Quarterfinals

Mt. Vernon 71, Decatur 51
Aurora (West) 34, Chicago (Tilden) 33
Nashville 33, Moline 31
Hillsboro 45, Pekin 39

Semifinals

Mt. Vernon 37, Aurora (West) 31
Hillsboro 50, Nashville 33

Finals

Aurora (West) 49, Nashville 39 (3rd Place)
Mt. Vernon 45, Hillsboro 39 (Championship)

Championship Game

COACH: Stanley A. Changnon   **COACH:** Fred Ewald

Mt. Vernon (45)	FG	FT	FTM	PF	TP
Wiley Mays, f	3	3	3	3	9
Eddie King, f	2	1	1	3	5
John Riley, f	0	1	0	1	1
Max Hooper, c	9	3	3	1	21
Bobby Lee, g	1	0	0	4	2
Walter Moore, g	2	3	3	0	7
Totals	17	11	10	12	45

Hillsboro (39)	FG	FT	FTM	PF	TP
Stanley Wallace, f	3	4	1	4	10
George Demas, f	1	0	2	5	2
William Heifer, f	1	0	0	2	2
Roscoe Sydnor, f	0	0	0	1	0
Richard Sturgeon, c	4	3	2	4	11
Charles Boston, g	1	1	0	3	3
Leroy Ott, g	5	1	1	5	11
Totals	15	9	6	24	39

Score by quarters:

Mt. Vernon	12	7	13	13	—	45
Hillsboro	12	8	11	8	—	39

Officials: Gordon Kickels (Lemont); Robert Young (Maywood)

1949 CHAMPION MT. VERNON RAMS—Front row: Eddie King, Bobby Brown, Sam Kirk, James Wilson, Bob Wood, John Riley. Top row: Willie Mays, Max Hooper, Bob Lee, Walter Moore.

1950
March 16-17-18
Huff Gym, University of Illinois

Call Out The Bomb Squad . . .

It sounded like the Fourth of July in March as Mt. Vernon became only the second team in tournament history to win back-to-back championships. The winners' tournament-long explosion was deafening as Mt. Vernon used a 65-86-57-85 scoring spree to become an undefeated champion. Max Hooper scored a record 36 points as Mt. Vernon tumbled Danville 85-61 to clinch the crown with its 33rd consecutive triumph. Elgin also pulled out all the stops, manhandling Collinsville 81-65 to finish third.

First Round

Chicago (Tilden) 46, Sterling 35
Elgin 75, Lawrenceville 40
Freeport 69, Paris 56
Mt. Vernon 65, Peoria (Spalding) 48
Quincy 62, Taylorville 42
Collinsville 69, Kewanee 52
Danville 69, Monmouth 48
Bradley 67, Johnston City 55

Quarterfinals

Elgin 59, Chicago (Tilden) 50
Mt. Vernon 86, Freeport 61
Collinsville 54, Quincy 46
Danville 59, Bradley 52

Semifinals

Mt. Vernon 57, Elgin 49
Danville 62, Collinsville 60

Finals

Elgin 81, Collinsville 65 (3rd Place)
Mt. Vernon 85, Danville 61 (Championship)

Championship Game

COACH: Stanley A. Changnon

Mt. Vernon (85)	FG	FT	FTM	PF	TP
John Riley, f	7	1	0	5	15
Eddie King, f	4	0	4	1	8
Bobby Wood, f	0	0	0	0	0
James Stokes, f	0	0	0	0	0
Max Hooper, c	16	4	1	1	36
Charles Owens, c	0	0	0	0	0
Bobby Brown, g	4	1	0	1	9
Walter Moore, g	8	1	2	2	17
James McMain, g	0	0	0	1	0
Mose Stokes, g	0	0	0	1	0
Totals	39	7	7	12	85

COACH: Laurence Newtson

Danville (61)	FG	FT	FTM	PF	TP
William Spangler, f	11	0	0	0	22
Ronald Rigoni, f	2	2	2	3	6
William Quam, f	0	0	1	1	0
Gene Michaelson, f	0	0	0	1	0
Gene Loercher, c	6	2	2	2	14
Walter Jackowski, c	0	0	0	0	0
Sammy Sams, g	4	0	1	2	8
Robert Wright, g	5	1	5	4	11
Pete Werner, g	0	0	0	0	0
Robert Pacot, g	0	0	1	0	0
Totals	28	5	12	13	61

Score by quarters:

Mt. Vernon	18	22	25	20	—	85
Danville	17	16	11	17	—	61

Officials: Harold Inman (Champaign); Lynn Gibbs (Rantoul)

1950 CHAMPION MT. VERNON RAMS—Front row: Bob Brown, John Riley, Max Hooper, Walter Moore, Eddie King. Back row: Coach Stanley Changnon, James McMain, M. Stokes, Charles Owens, J. Stokes, Bob Wood.

1951
March 15-16-17-18
Huff Gym, University of Illinois

Meet Freeport's Mr. Points . . .

Freeport became a three-time winner in the state classic with a four-game sweep. The Pretzels reached the pinnacle with a 71-51 triumph over Moline to close out the season with 31 victories in 33 games. McKinley Davis, the Pretzels' season-long leading individual scorer, canned 24 points in the title match. Quincy, in the midst of building another powerhouse, edged Decatur 60-58 in the battle for third place.

First Round

Marion 70, Macomb (Western) 65
Freeport 67, Edwardsville 64
Peoria (Woodruff) 76, Odell (St. Paul) 62
Decatur 68, Danville 58
Moline 59, Pinckneyville 55
Robinson 60, Chicago (Parker) 46
Lincoln 54, Oak Park 41
Quincy 58, Hinsdale 46

Quarterfinals

Freeport 65, Marion 51
Decatur 73, Peoria (Woodruff) 50
Moline 59, Robinson 44
Quincy 65, Lincoln 63

Semifinals

Freeport 88, Decatur 60
Moline 64, Quincy 63 (ot)

Finals

Quincy 60, Decatur 58 (3rd Place)
Freeport 71, Moline 51 (Championship)

Championship Game

COACH: Harry Kinert

Freeport (71)	FG	FT	FTM	PF	TP
Gene Schmitt, f	2	3	1	1	7
Harlan Fritz, f	5	0	3	3	10
Roger Meads, f	0	1	0	0	1
Carl Cain, f	0	0	0	0	0
McKinley Davis, c	10	4	4	4	24
James Hill, c	0	0	0	0	0
Thomas Williams, g	6	4	1	5	16
Ben Dorsey, g	6	1	0	0	13
Eugene Ingold, g	0	0	1	1	0
William Spahn, g	0	0	0	0	0
Totals	29	13	10	14	71

COACH: Norman Ziebell

Moline (51)	FG	FT	FTM	PF	TP
Ray Pearson, f	1	0	0	0	2
Robert Anders, f	2	2	0	2	6
William Seaberg, f	2	0	0	0	4
Mark Engdahl, f	1	1	4	1	3
Ted Simpson, f	1	1	1	0	3
George Hoke, c	4	1	3	2	9
Don Carothers, c-g	5	0	0	1	10
Robert Van Vooren, g	5	2	0	2	12
Austin Duke, g	1	0	1	5	2
Totals	22	7	9	13	51

Score by quarters:

Freeport	22	20	10	19	—	71
Moline	15	13	15	8	—	51

Officials: L. J. Hackett (Peoria); Burdell Smith (Peoria)

1951 CHAMPION FREEPORT PRETZELS—Front row: Thomas Williams, Eugene Schmidt, Harlan Fritz, McKinley "Deacon" Davis, Ben Dorsey. Second row: Mgr. William Trunk, Eugene Ingold, Carl Cain, Jim Hill, Coach Harry Kinert, William Spahn, Roger Meads, Mgr. Douglas Smith.

1952
March 19-22-1952
Huff Gym, University of Illinois

Jolly Green Giants Court Cinderella . . .

Famous firsts fell on Champaign as rapidly as stars fell on Alabama when Hebron, everybody's favorite team outside of its opponents, won it all in 1952. Hebron was the first district winner to take the Illinois championship. The Green Giants were the first twin-powered champions to win in overtime en route to a 64-59 conquest of Quincy.

Assuring Coach Russ Ahearn's greatest hour of glory, Hebron, a one-time loser going into the tournament, came out flying high with its 35th victory. The Green Giants tipped Champaign by nine; Lawrenceville by 10; Rock Island by eight before finding themselves locked in a 58-58 standoff after regulation time in the title test.

In the overtime, Hebron's first of the season, Bill Schulz dunked a high lob from Don Wilbrandt; Phil Judson turned brother Paul's belt high pass into an easy layup, and Wilbrandt's fielder finalized the new champions' 6-1 edge in the extra period.

First Round

Mt. Vernon 57, Kankakee 56
Pinckneyville 56, Chicago (Roosevelt) 44
Taylorville 82, Peoria (Manual) 64
Quincy 74, Freeport 68
Hebron 55, Champaign 46
Lawrenceville 63, Madison 61
Jacksonville 57, Ottawa 47
Rock Island 56, Harvey (Thornton) 35

Quarterfinals

Mt. Vernon 55, Pinckneyville 51
Quincy 69, Taylorville 64
Hebron 65, Lawrenceville 55
Rock Island 61, Jacksonville 49

Semifinals

Quincy 54, Mt. Vernon 51
Hebron 64, Rock Island 56

Finals

Mt. Vernon 71, Rock Island 70 (3rd Place)
Hebron 64, Quincy 59 (ot) (Championship)

Championship Game

COACH: Russ Ahearn

Hebron (64)	FG-FGA		FT-FTA		PF	TP
Don Wilbrandt, f	3	16	4	7	4	10
Phillip Judson, f	3	8	6	7	3	12
William Schulz, c	12	16	0	1	2	24
Paul Judson, g	6	12	1	4	3	13
Kenley Spooner, g	2	7	1	1	3	5
Totals	26	59	12	20	15	64

COACH: George Latham

Quincy (59)	FG-FGA		FT-FTA		PF	TP
Charles Fast, f	3	10	4	5	4	10
Jack Gower, f	5	10	1	2	2	11
Bruce Brothers, c	8	12	4	6	5	20
Thomas Payne, c	1	5	0	0	1	2
Phillip Harvey, g	2	12	4	4	2	8
Richard Thompson, g	2	14	4	4	0	8
Totals	21	63	17	21	14	59

Score by quarters:

Hebron	14	20	14	10	6	—	64
Quincy	16	19	13	10	1	—	59

Officials: Clyde McQueen (Springfield); J. Russell Shields (Greenfield)

1952 CHAMPION HEBRON GREEN GIANTS—Front row: Coach Russ Ahearn, Ken Spooner, Paul Judson, Bill Schulz, Phil Judson and Don Wilbrandt. Second row: Jim Bergin, Jim Wilbrandt, Joe Schmidt, Bill Thayer, Clayton Ihrke.

1953
March 18-21-1953
Huff Gym, University of Illinois

Another Undefeated Champion . . .

Hebron, the Cinderella team, was a tough act to follow, but LaGrange (Lyons) was up to the challenge. With Ted Caiazza scoring 25 points, LaGrange defeated Peoria Central 72-60 in the championship game to climax a flawless string of 29 consecutive victories. The muscular machine from Lyons opened its successful drive by eliminating DuSable, the Chicago representative, in the first round 85-68. Between the first and last games, LaGrange first took out St. Teresa of Decatur and then defeated Pinckneyville.

First Round

LaGrange 85, Chicago (DuSable) 68
Decatur (St. Teresa) 54, Canton 52
Pinckneyville 48, DeKalb 42
Jacksonville 57, Hillsboro 52
West Frankfort 67, Elgin 64
Peoria (Central) 81, Highland 53
Ottawa 80, Rock Island 66
Danville (Schlarman) 78, Lawrenceville 65

Quarterfinals

LaGrange 75, Decatur (St. Teresa) 48
Pinckneyville 58, Jacksonville 57
Peoria (Central) 70, West Frankfort 68
Danville (Schlarman) 56, Ottawa 43

Semifinals

LaGrange 78, Pinckneyville 65
Peoria (Central) 66, Danville (Schlarman) 58

Finals

Pinckneyville 71, Danville (Schlarman) 42 (3rd Place)
LaGrange 72, Peoria (Central) 60 (Championship)

Championship Game

COACH: Greg Sloan

LaGrange (72)	FG-FGA		FT-FTA		PF	TP
Leon McRae, f	3	6	0	0	4	6
Joel McRae, f	4	10	4	5	3	12
Robert Caffee, f	4	10	2	4	4	10
Willard Johnson, f	0	0	0	0	0	0
Ted Caiazza, c	11	23	3	6	2	25
Dave McKeig, c	0	0	0	0	0	0
Charles Sedgwick, g	3	10	2	2	5	8
Nate Smith, g	1	9	2	2	3	4
Joe Lawlor, g	0	0	7	8	4	7
Totals	26	68	20	27	25	72

COACH: Dawson Hawkins

Peoria (Central) (60)	FG-FGA		FT-FTA		PF	TP
Harold Douglas, f	5	10	6	9	4	16
Alan Swanson, f	3	7	1	2	1	7
Jim Ashby, f	0	3	1	1	0	1
Nick Panos, f	0	2	0	0	0	0
Hiles Stout, c	10	25	7	9	2	27
Jerry Lewis, g	1	2	3	3	5	5
Dave Lancaster, g	0	1	1	1	1	1
Jerry Green, g	0	1	1	4	3	1
Chet Ziegler, g	0	2	2	6	2	2
Leon Hurst, g	0	0	0	0	0	0
Totals	19	53	22	35	18	60

Score by Quarters:

LaGrange	20	22	13	17	—	72
Peoria (Cent.)	17	18	10	15	—	60

Officials: Art Bouxsein (Princeton); Frank Falzone (Rockford)

1953 CHAMPION LAGRANGE (LYONS) LIONS—Front row: Leon McRae, Joel McRae, Ted Caiazza, Robert Caffey, D. Williams, Harold Caffey. Second row: S. Heeter, J. Pendexter, R. DeSantis, R. Blake, W. Kennedy, J. Groeser, Coach Sloan. Third row: Nate Smith, P. Brooks, Charles Sedgwick, Joe Lawlor, Willard Johnston, J. O'Donnell, Mgr.

1954
March 17-20-1954
Huff Gym, University of Illinois

Eight-Minute Season . . .

The 1954 tournament will forever be remembered as jubilation for Mt. Vernon and massive heartbreak for DuSable of Chicago. Actually, it boiled down to an eight-minute season for both teams. DuSable, unbeaten in 31 straight games, and three-time loser Mt. Vernon were tied 57-57 after three quarters of the championship game. After three DuSable players fouled out, Mt. Vernon outscored the Chicago team 19-13 in the final period to finalize a 76-70 triumph. It was without question one of the most controversial finishes in the meet's long history.

First Round

Mt. Vernon 61, Danville 54
Moline 70, Rockford (East) 53
Harvey (Thornton) 83, Cumberland 59
Pinckneyville 43, Springfield 37
Quincy 64, Princeton 60
Chicago (DuSable) 87, Bowen 64
Barrington 57, Litchfield 38
Edwardsville 60, Peoria (Central) 54

Quarterfinals

Mt. Vernon 73, Moline 59
Pinckneyville 61, Harvey (Thornton) 47
Chicago (DuSable) 80, Quincy 66
Edwardsville 59, Barrington 57

Semifinals

Mt. Vernon 70, Pinckneyville 44
Chicago (DuSable) 89, Edwardsville 73

Finals

Pinckneyville 54, Edwardsville 42 (3rd Place)
Mt. Vernon 76, Chicago (DuSable) 70 (Championship)

Championship Game

COACH: Harold Hutchins

Mt. Vernon (76)	FG-FGA		FT-FTA		PF	TP
Fred Deichman, f	1	4	1	2	1	3
Goff Thompson, f	3	8	5	7	2	11
Jerry Clark, f	1	4	1	1	3	3
Larry Whitlock, c	5	11	1	1	2	11
Albert Avant, g	9	22	5	6	2	23
Don Richards, g	9	19	7	8	2	25
Totals	28	68	20	25	12	76

COACH: Jim Brown

Chicago (DuSable) (70)	FG-FGA		FT-FTA		PF	TP
Charlie Brown, f	11	20	1	1	5	23
McKinley Cowsen, f	3	7	1	1	1	7
Sterling Webb, f	0	0	0	0	0	0
Shellie McMillon, c	10	15	4	9	3	24
Paxton Lumpkin, g	5	21	3	5	5	13
Karl Dennis, g	1	4	0	0	5	2
Brian Dennis, g	0	1	1	1	0	1
Eugene Howard, g	0	0	0	0	0	0
Totals	30	68	10	17	19	70

Score by Quarters:
Mt. Vernon   18 17 22 19 — 76
Chicago (DuSable)   20 15 22 13 — 70
Officials: Joe Przada (East St. Louis); John K. Frazer (Alton)

1954 CHAMPION MT. VERNON RAMS—Front row: Al Avant, Don Richards, Larry Whitlock, Fred Deichman, Goff Thompson. Coach Harold Hutchins, Kim Driggers, Gale Gruend, George Mendenall, Jerry Clark, Gene Brookman.

1955
March 16-19, 1955
Huff Gym, University of Illinois

Rockford Turns West to Title Town . . .

One timely field goal marked the return of Rockford (West) to top rating in Illinois high school basketball. Playing long-time rival Elgin, West won 61-59 as Rockford scored 19 baskets to the losers' 18 in the championship showdown. The highspot of this torrid barn-burner came when Rockford scored six points in one second to help overcome Elgin's 40-27 halftime edge. Six players, three on each team, scored in double digits as Elgin's Gary Smith led with 18.

First Round

Princeton 60, Moline 58
Shawneetown 61, Park Forest (Rich) 56
Elgin 63, Georgetown 40
Galesburg 77, Paris 66
Rockford (West) 58, Decatur 54
Lincoln 54, Peoria (Spalding) 52
Quincy 70, Chicago (Marshall) 59
Pinckneyville 66, Alton 60

Quarterfinals

Princeton 66, Shawneetown 48
Elgin 66, Galesburg 60
Rockford (West) 75, Lincoln 65
Pinckneyville 53, Quincy 51

Semifinals

Elgin 71, Princeton 66
Rockford (West) 54, Pinckneyville 46

Finals

Pinckneyville 58, Princeton 53 (3rd Place)
Rockford (West) 61, Elgin 59 (Championship)

Championship Game

COACH: Alex Saudargas

Rockford West (61)	FG-FGA		FT-FTA		PF	TP
Fred Boshelo, f	5	11	7	12	3	17
Nolden Gentry, f	4	13	6	8	3	14
John Wessels, c	2	13	0	0	2	4
Donald Grabow, c	0	1	2	2	0	2
Rex Parker, g	2	8	5	6	4	9
Rodney Coffman, g	6	9	3	4	4	15
Robert Washington, g	0	0	0	0	0	0
Totals	19	55	23	32	16	61

COACH: Bill Chesbrough

Elgin (59)	FG-FGA		FT-FTA		PF	TP
Gary Seigmeier, f	1	4	5	6	5	7
Charles Rachow, f	1	1	1	2	4	3
Earl Lamp, f	0	1	2	3	1	2
Tom Aley, c	5	10	3	4	2	13
Paul Hudgens, g	5	12	6	7	3	16
Gary Smith, g	6	15	6	7	3	18
Totals	18	43	23	29	18	59

Score by Quarters:

Rockford (West) 10 17 20 14 — 61
Elgin   24 16   8 11 — 59

Officials: Jim Patterson (Crete); Tom Kuzmanoff (Arlington Heights)

1955 CHAMPION ROCKFORD (WEST) WARRIORS—Front row: Max Warner, Rex Parker, John Wessels, Nolden Gentry, Fred Boshella, Rod Coffman, Alex Saudargas. Second row: Doug Reed, Bob Washington, Tom Olson, Don Grabow, Joe Digiovanni, Sam Patton.

1956
March 13, 16 and 17, 1956
Huff Gym, University of Illinois

Point Titans Have Field Day . . .

Four outstanding marksmen, all of whom were to become topflight players in Big Ten competition, provided most of the heroics as Rockford (West) became the tournament's third back-to-back champion. In the process of becoming another two-point winner, West hung on for a 67-65 derailing of Edwardsville. Governor Vaughn (28) and Manny Jackson (21) kept Edwardsville in contention to the wire. Johnny Wessels (29) and Nolden Gentry (17) were tops for West as it finished with a second straight 28-1 record.

Super-Sectional

At Springfield	— Quincy 52, Springfield (Lanphier) 48
At Salem	— Edwardsville 73, Effingham (St. Anthony) 68
At Peoria	— Peoria (Central) 66, LaSalle-Peru 58
At Hinsdale	— Oak Park 62, Chicago Hts. (Bloom) 57
At Moline	— Rockford (West) 66, Galesburg 64
At W. Frankfort	— W. Frankfort 45, Pinckneyville 42
At Evanston	— Chicago (Dunbar) 88, Winnetka (New Trier) 56
At Decatur	— Rantoul 79, Taylorville 74

Quarterfinals

Edwardsville 68, Quincy 44
Oak Park 63, Peoria (Central) 48
Rockford (West) 82, West Frankfort 70
Chicago (Dunbar) 78, Rantoul 58

Semifinals

Edwardsville 88, Oak Park 61
Rockford (West) 61, Chicago (Dunbar) 48

Finals

Chicago (Dunbar) 73, Oak Park 56 (3rd Place)
Rockford (West) 67, Edwardsville 65 (Championship)

Championship Game

COACH: Alex Saudargas

Rockford West (67)	FG-FGA	FT-FTA	PF	TP
Nolden Gentry, f	5 10	7 8	2	17
Donald Slaughter, f	1 6	2 2	1	4
John Wessels, c	11 24	7 10	2	29
Robert Washington, g	6 12	5 6	2	17
Thomas Blake, g	0 1	0 0	0	0
Totals	23 53	21 26	8	67

COACH: Joe Lucco

Edwardsville (65)	FG-FGA	FT-FTA	PF	TP
Mannie Jackson, f	10 21	1 3	2	21
Harold Patton, f	2 5	0 1	5	4
Governor Vaughn, c	13 19	2 5	2	28
James Chandler, g	0 1	2 3	3	2
Kenneth Shaw, g	3 5	2 2	2	8
Richard Pulliam, f	1 2	0 0	0	2
Gordon Mallory, g	0 0	0 0	0	0
Totals	29 53	7 14	14	65

Score by Quarters:

Rockford (West)	18	15	21	13	—	67
Edwardsville	14	18	16	17	—	65

Officials: J. McCoskey (Murphysboro); Claude Rhodes (Benton)

1956 CHAMPION ROCKFORD (WEST) WARRIORS—Front row: Alex Saudargas, Bob Washington, John Wessels, Nolden Gentry, Don Slaughter, Tom Blake. Second row: Jack Flynn, Craig Peeples, Roger Peacock, Jay Heath, Chad Coffman, Max Warner.

1957
March 22-23, 1957
Huff Gym, University of Illinois

Unsung Hero: Meet John Tidwell . . .

Many stars, especially outstanding shooters, have surfaced during the long years of the Illinois State Tournament. There have been countless all-around standouts but few to match the total skills of Herrin's John Tidwell. He scored just six points, but his topflight floor play and generalship were most important in Herrin's 45-42 win over previously all-winning Collinsville in the championship match. It was Herrin's first title and Collinsville's first runner-up finish.

Super-Sectionals

At Decatur	— Champaign 57, Maroa 56
At Peoria	— Ottawa 58, Pekin 56 (2 ot)
At Moline	— Galesburg 60, Freeport 47
At Salem	— Collinsville 76, Charleston 57
At W. Frankfort	— Herrin 57, Mt. Vernon 44
At Hinsdale	— Elgin 53, Chicago Hts. (Bloom) 52
At Evanston	— Chicago (Crane) 60, Evanston 46
At Springfield	— Quincy (Notre Dame) 65, Springfield 53

Quarterfinals

Ottawa 54, Champaign 51
Collinsville 61, Galesburg 59
Herrin 66, Elgin 60
Quincy (Notre Dame) 70, Evanston 63

Semifinals

Collinsville 69, Ottawa 61
Herrin 68, Quincy (Notre Dame) 47

Finals

Ottawa 65, Quincy (Notre Dame) 64 (ot) (3rd Place)
Herrin 45, Collinsville 42 (Championship Game)

Championship Game

COACH: Earl Lee

Herrin (45)	FG-FGA		FT-FTA		PF	TP
Jim Gualdoni, f	3	7	4	14	2	10
Ivan Jefferson, f	2	8	4	11	5	8
John Tidwell, c	2	5	2	7	2	6
Willie Williams, g	2	6	0	0	0	4
Richard Box, g	6	11	5	12	1	17
Terry Miller, g	0	0	0	0	0	0
Totals	15	37	15	44	10	45

COACH: Vergil Fletcher

Collinsville (42)	FG-FGA		FT-FTA		PF	TP
Tom Jackson, f	5	14	2	5	2	12
Tracy Wilhoit, f	0	3	0	2	5	0
Terry Bethel, c	7	16	4	9	5	18
Bart Basola, c	1	2	0	0	1	2
Ernie Wilhoit, g	1	9	0	2	3	2
Jim Soehlke, g	2	2	2	4	1	6
Bob Vetter, g	1	1	0	0	0	2
Totals	17	47	8	22	17	42

Score by Quarters:

Herrin	10	12	10	13	—	45
Collinsville	14	6	12	10	—	42

Officials: William Cox (Charleston); Dwight Wilkey (Monticello)

1957 CHAMPION HERRIN TIGERS—Front row: Willie Williams, Bart Lindsey, J. Hendricks, Richard Box, Jerry Miller, Coach Earl Lee. Second row: Asst. Coach Hutchison, Steve Heard, Ivan Jefferson, John Tidwell, Kenneth Finney, Jim Gualdoni.

1958
March 21-22, 1958
Huff Gym, University of Illinois

Finally—A Chicago Winner . . .

A 50-year famine ended for Chicago teams in State Basketball Tournament play when Marshall took home the championship. Marshall's road show success started with a 63-43 conquest of Elgin in the Super-Sectional at Evanston. Thereafter, the Chicagoans mowed down Herrin, Aurora (West) and Rock Falls 70-64 in the title game. Steve Thomas was the winners' scoring leader with 26 points as Bob Jones (18), M. C. Thompson (17), and George Wilson (9) put all of Marshall's 70 points on the board. The win spotlighted 30 consecutive victories enabling Marshall to become another rare unbeaten champion.

Super-Sectionals

At Decatur	— Danville (Schlarman) 75, Arcola 57
At Moline	— Rock Falls 74, Fulton 62
At Salem	— Jerseyville 56, Highland 49
At Peoria	— Peoria (Spalding) 49, Ottawa 44
At Springfield (Feitshans)	— Springfield 46, Quincy 37
At Aurora (East)	— Aurora (West) 57, Bradley 54
At Evanston	— Chicago (Marshall) 63, Elgin 43
At West Frankfort	— Herrin 76, West Frankfort 75

Quarterfinals

Rock Falls 101, Danville (Schlarman) 76
Peoria (Spalding) 58, Highland 49
Aurora (West) 59, Springfield 48
Chicago (Marshall) 72, Herrin 59

Semifinals

Rock Falls 66, Peoria (Spalding) 59
Chicago (Marshall) 74, Aurora (West) 62

Finals

Peoria (Spalding) 59, Aurora (West) 53 (3rd Place)
Chicago (Marshall) 70, Rock Falls 64 (Championship Game)

Championship Game

COACH: Isadore "Spin" Salario

Chicago (Marshall) (70)

	FG-FGA	FT-FTA	PF	TP
Steve Thomas, f	9 17	8 10	1	26
M. C. Thompson, f	6 14	5 7	3	17
George Wilson, c	4 10	1 6	4	9
Robert Jones, g	9 20	0 2	3	18
Tyrone Johnson, g	0 2	0 0	3	0
Jimmy Jones, g	0 0	0 0	1	0
Paul Brown, g	0 0	0 0	1	0
Totals	28 63	14 25	16	70

COACH: Richard Haselton

Rock Falls (64)

	FG-FGA	FT-FTA	PF	TP
Kenneth Siebel, f	6 18	8 11	4	20
Douglas Martin, f	0 2	3 4	4	3
James Coin, c	5 13	0 1	4	10
Gary Kolb, g	2 9	4 4	1	8
Paul Gallentine, g	7 13	2 3	4	16
Frank Simester	2 8	3 4	2	7
Totals	22 63	20 27	19	64

Score by Quarters:

Chicago (Marshall)	17	15	20	18	—	70
Rock Falls	20	18	15	11	—	64

Officials: Ed Bronson (Evergreen Park); Robert A. Young (Maywood)

1958 CHAMPION CHICAGO (MARSHALL) COMMANDOES: Front Row: Coach Isadore Salario, Mgr. Alvin Harvey, Bobby Jones, Tyrone Johnson, George Wilson, Steve Thomas, M. C. Thompson, Mgr. Charles Bowen. Second Row: Isaac Patterson, Morris Mathews, Lonnie Elliott, Bob Smith, Jerome Faulkner, Ben Stevenson, Ron Banks, Paul Brown, Jim Jones, Gordon Lemons, Asst. Coach Will Gaines.

1959
March 20-21, 1959
Huff Gym, University of Illinois

Springfield Bags Third Title . . .

The Super-Sectionals followed a "Beat the Champs" theme as the likes of Rockford (West), Marshall of Chicago, Centralia, and Taylorville were eliminated before packing their suitcases for the trip to Champaign. Springfield (H.S.) took advantage of this opening and moved swiftly through the field to win its third championship—but first since 1935. The Senators closed out a 33-1 season by beating Aurora (West) in the finals 60-52. Tom Cole led the winners with 26 points.

Super-Sectionals

At Salem	— Madison 83, Centralia 69
At Evanston	— Waukegan 63, Chicago (Marshall) 62
At Springfield	— Springfield 73, Macomb 39
At Peoria	— Peoria (Central) 70, Ottawa 47
At Hinsdale	— Aurora (West) 71, Harvey (Thornton) 58
At Decatur	— Rantoul 66, Taylorville 61
At West Frankfort	— Herrin 62, Benton 50
At Moline	— Galesburg 65, Rockford (West) 49

Quarterfinals

Waukegan 62, Madison 50
Springfield 60, Peoria (Central) 53
Aurora (West) 71, Rantoul 62
Galesburg 73, Herrin 69

Semifinals

Springfield 64, Waukegan 40
Aurora (West) 74, Galesburg 61

Finals

Galesburg 78, Waukegan 66 (3rd Place)
Springfield 60, Aurora (West) 52 (Championship)

Championship Game

COACH: Ray Page

Springfield (60)	FG-FGA		FT-FTA		PF	TP
Charles						
Shauger, f	3	10	4	6	4	10
George Mathis, f	7	15	5	5	5	19
Tom Cole, c	11	21	4	7	2	26
Lynn Neff, g	1	4	1	1	1	3
Jim Wieties, g	0	1	0	1	4	0
Lee Pelham, f	1	1	0	0	0	2
TOTALS	23	52	14	20	16	60

COACH: Richard Dorsey

Aurora (West) (52)	FG-FGA		FT-FTA		PF	TP
Jim Konrod, f	3	7	0	0	2	6
Larry Secor, f	1	4	2	2	5	4
John Schwenk, c	3	8	7	11	3	13
Bill Small, g	7	18	4	7	5	18
Ed Potteiger, g	1	4	2	3	1	4
Tom Young, g	2	4	0	0	0	4
Jim Cronin, g	1	1	1	2	0	3
TOTALS	18	46	16	25	16	52

Score by Quarters:

Springfield	17	14	14	15	—	60
Aurora (West)	14	10	9	19	—	52

Officials: Wayne Nohren (Longview); Alvin Gebhardt (Peoria)

1959 CHAMPION SPRINGFIELD (H.S.) SENATORS—Left to right: Nils Olson, Stan Merrick, Tom Frick, George Mathis, Bob Plohr, Tom Cole, Coach Ray Page, Charles Shauger, Lee Pelham, Ed Markert, Eddie Greenberg, Lynn Neff, Bob Farris, Jim Wieties.

1960
March 18-19, 1960
Huff Gym, University of Illinois

Dial M For Marshall's Magic . . .

After a single season sabbatical away from the State Final Tournament following their loss in the 1959 Super-Sectional, Marshall's courtwise Commandoes bounced back to win a second title within three years. With George Wilson receiving ample help from newcomers like Eddie Jakes and Ken Moses, Marshall ripped past Elgin, Monmouth, Decatur, and Bridgeport. The Chicagoans hit Bridgeport with a 28-point explosion in the title game's first quarter, and Marshall was never in trouble as it rolled to a 79-55 rout.

Super-Sectionals

At Evanston	— Chicago (Marshall) 71, Elgin 55
At Springfield	— Monmouth 49, Springfield 48
At Aurora	— Maywood (Proviso East) 65, Kankakee 62
At Decatur	— Decatur 52, Danville (Schlarman) 46
At Peoria	— Ottawa 78, Pekin 66
At Olney	— Bridgeport 85, Greenville 73
At Rock Island	— Galesburg 77, DeKalb 71
At East St. Louis	— West Frankfort 64, Granite City 62

Quarterfinals

Chicago (Marshall) 55, Monmouth 35
Decatur 53, Maywood (Proviso East) 52
Bridgeport 61, Ottawa 55
West Frankfort 66, Galesburg 65

Semifinals

Chicago (Marshall) 74, Decatur 62
Bridgeport 74, West Frankfort 60

Finals

West Frankfort 75, Decatur 53 (3rd Place)
Chicago (Marshall) 79, Bridgeport 55 (Championship)

Championship Game

COACH: Isadore "Spin" Salario   **COACH:** Ray Estes

Chicago (79)	FG-FGA		FT-FTA		PF	TP
(Marshall)						
George Wilson, f	5	9	7	8	1	17
Charles Jones, f	6	9	0	1	2	12
Edward Franklin, c	5	10	1	2	1	11
Eddie Jakes, g	8	13	2	3	2	18
Kenneth Moses, g	7	16	1	1	1	15
James Pitts, f	0	1	0	2	0	0
Donald Jackson, f	1	2	0	0	1	2
James Giglio, g	2	2	0	0	3	4
Lenwood Flint, f	0	0	0	0	0	0
Ronald Knight, g	0	1	0	0	1	0
TOTALS	34	63	11	17	12	79

Bridgeport (55)	FG-FGA		FT-FTA		PF	TP
Richard Martin, f	5	12	0	0	3	10
Bernie Gray, f	7	17	2	5	3	16
Steve Cunningham, c	6	23	1	2	1	13
Dennis Magee, g	5	13	1	1	2	11
Jim Brown, g	1	7	0	0	4	2
Clifton Joiner, g	0	2	0	1	0	0
Mike Shuppert, g	0	1	3	5	0	3
Dennis Oney, g	0	0	0	0	0	0
TOTALS	24	75	7	14	13	55

Score by Quarters:

Chicago (Marshall) 28   16   19   16   —   79
Bridgeport   18   12   9   16   —   55

Officials: Robert Young (Maywood); Frank Falzone (Rockford)

1960 CHAMPION CHICAGO (MARSHALL) COMMANDOS—Front row: Coach Isadore "Spin" Salario, George Wilson, Ken Moses, Eddie Jakes, Charley Jones, Ed Franklin, Athletic Director Bosco Levine. Back row: James Pitts, Donald Jackson, Wayne Stingley, Donald King, James Giglio, Lenwood Flint, Lon Knight, Lavele Swanagain.

1961
March 16-17, 1961
Huff Gym, University of Illinois

It's the Bogie & Fred Show . . .
Collinsville didn't need any additional pep talks coming into the 1961 tournament. Four years earlier the school lost the championship and a 34-game winning streak in the season's last game. Now, there were some "wrongs" to be righted. After edging Centralia 66-64 in the Super-Sectional, Bogie Redmon and Fred Riddle ignited scoring sprees that enabled Collinsville to win by successive edges of 23, 37, and 34 points and climaxed a 32 game winning streak by routing Thornton of Harvey 84-50 in the title game.

Super-Sectionals

At West Frankfort — Benton 65, Belleville 59
At Peoria   — Peoria (Manual) 61, Ottawa 45
At Salem   — Collinsville 66, Centralia 64
At Rock Island — Rockford (East) 60, Moline 53
At Evanston   — Chicago (Marshall) 56, Waukegan 55
At Decatur   — Danville (Schlarman) 76, Clinton 75
At Springfield — Springfield 58, Monmouth 48
At Hinsdale   — Harvey (Thornton) 48, Cicero (Morton) 36

Quarterfinals

Peoria (Manual) 54, Benton 51
Collinsville 71, Rockford (East) 48
Chicago (Marshall) 61, Danville (Schlarman) 36
Harvey (Thornton) 54, Springfield 52

Semifinals

Collinsville 76, Peoria (Manual) 39
Harvey (Thornton) 49, Chicago (Marshall) 47

Finals

Chicago (Marshall) 73, Peoria (Manual) 58 (3rd Place)
Collinsville 84, Harvey (Thornton) 50 (Championship)

Championship Game

COACH: Vergil Fletcher

Collinsville (84)	FG-FGA		FT-FTA		PF	TP
Bob Bosola, f	4	10	4	5	2	12
Fred Riddle, f	8	11	8	9	3	24
Bogie Redmon, c	12	17	7	12	2	31
Bob Simpson, g	3	6	3	3	4	9
Bob Meadows, g	2	3	0	0	4	4
Ronnie Mottin, f	0	1	0	0	1	0
Harry Hildreth, g	1	1	0	0	0	2
Joe Brennon, f	0	1	0	0	0	0
Than Byrkit, g	0	0	2	4	0	2
Ronnie Matikitis, c	0	0	0	0	0	0
TOTALS	30	50	24	33	16	84

COACH: William Purden

Harvey (50) (Thornton)	FG-FGA		FT-FTA		PF	TP
Renault Banks, f	4	8	1	2	4	9
Wilfred Henry, f	1	4	1	3	3	3
Leon Clark, c	2	6	1	1	3	5
Jack Dabon, g	4	8	3	3	4	11
Bob Caress, g	3	7	2	2	2	8
Al Dehnert, f	0	1	3	3	1	3
Fred Lindsay, g	1	3	3	4	0	5
John McKibben, g	1	3	2	2	1	4
Reuben Poindexter, f	0	0	2	2	1	2
Marvin Keeling, g	0	0	0	0	2	0
TOTALS	16	40	18	22	21	50

Score by Quarters:

Collinsville	14	23	20	27	—	84
Harvey (Thornton)	14	9	9	18	—	50

Officials: Herb Scheffler (Springfield); Ernest Reynolds (Carterville)

1961 CHAMPION COLLINSVILLE KAHOKS—Front row: Robert Meadows, Ron Mottin, Fred Riddle, Coach Vergil Fletcher, Marc Fletcher, Bogie Redmon, Bob Basola, Bob Simpson. Second row: Asst. Coach Bill Hellyer, Than Byrkit, Ronald Matikitis, Joe Brennan, Harry Hildreth, Asst. Coach Bert Weber.

1962
March 23-24, 1962
Huff Gym, University of Illinois

Story Book Start and Finish . . .

Two guys named Jim, one named Jerry, another named Ken, and a fifth named Prentis encountered one of the toughest starts and finishes in tournament history to assure Decatur its fourth title. In the Super-Sectional, Decatur advanced by shading Urbana 41-40. After wins over Rock Island and Quincy, the Runnin' Reds tackled Chicago (Carver) led by Cazzie Russell and Joe Allen. Down by 10 after the first quarter, Decatur rallied to nip Carver 49-48 to turn its 31st victory into the championship. Fabulous Cazzie scored 24 points, half of Carver's total, in a losing cause.

Super-Sectionals

At Eldorado   — McLeansboro 53, Marion 52
At Aurora (East)   — Elmhurst (York) 84, Harvey (Thornton) 63
At East St. Louis — Centralia 78, Belleville 66
At Evanston   — Chicago (Carver) 48, Chicago (St. Patrick) 42
At Rock Island   — Rock Island 64, Rockford (Auburn) 44
At Decatur   — Decatur 41, Urbana 40
At Quincy   — Quincy 72, Springfield 53
At Peoria   — Washington 58, Pontiac 57

Quarterfinals

McLeansboro 84, Elmhurst (York) 58
Chicago (Carver) 56, Centralia 50
Decatur 61, Rock Island 56
Quincy 45, Washington 37

Semifinals

Chicago (Carver) 54, McLeansboro 41
Decatur 47, Quincy 44

Finals

Quincy 85, McLeansboro 45 (3rd Place)
Decatur 49, Chicago (Carver) 48 (Championship)

Championship Game

COACH: John Schneiter

Decatur (49)	FG-FGA		FT-FTA		PF	REB	TP
Jim Johnson, f	7	11	3	6	2	9	17
Prentis Jones, f	5	13	1	4	2	4	11
Ken Barnes, c	3	11	4	10	1	6	10
Jerry Hill, g	3	11	1	2	3	3	7
Jim Hallihan, g	2	5	0	0	1	1	4
TOTALS	20	51	9	22	9		49

COACH: Larry Hawkins

Chicago (Carver) (48)	FG-FGA		FT-FTA		PF	REB	TP
Gerry Jones, f	3	6	0	0	2	2	6
Harold Dade, f	1	2	0	1	0	0	2
Joe Allen, c	2	6	0	0	1	8	4
Cazzie Russell, g	11	24	2	6	3	15	24
Bruce Raickett, g	1	4	1	4	2	0	3
Curtis Kirk, f	2	4	1	3	2	3	5
Joe McEwen, g	0	0	0	0	1	0	0
Robert Cifax, f	0	1	0	0	0	0	0
Marlbert Pradd, g	2	3	0	0	0	0	4
TOTALS	22	50	4	14	11		48

Score by Quarters:

Decatur	10	15	14	10	—	49
Chicago (Carver)	20	7	7	14	—	48

Officials: Joe Starcevic (Peoria); Alvin Gebhardt (Peoria)

1962 CHAMPION DECATUR (STEPHEN DECATUR) RUNNIN' REDS—Front row: Gary Stewart, Prentis Jones, James "Bulldog" Johnson, Ken Barnes. Top row: Asst. Coach Jack Kenny, Dave Hayes, Lee Endsley, Jack Sunderlik, Bruce Gray, Jim Hallihan, Jerry Hill, Coach John Schneiter.

1963
March 22-23, 1963
Assembly Hall, University of Illinois

Smedley's Medley: The Possible Dream . . .

Anthony Smedley was the eighth man in the lineup, but he definitely was Number One in the hearts of fans following Chicago's Carver High School. With time running down to mere seconds in the championship game, Smedley took one shot and scored one basket for two points. That was all Carver needed to top Centralia 53-52 and earn its first state championship in the first tournament played in the Assembly Hall on the University of Illinois campus in Champaign. Had Hollywood written the Smedley script the pandemonium couldn't have been more exciting.

Super-Sectionals

At Salem — Centralia 59, Collinsville 48
At West Frankfort — Metropolis 53, Herrin 52
At Quincy — Springfield (Lanphier) 91, Galesburg 67
At Moline — Rockford (Auburn) 62, Aledo 51
At Peoria — Peoria (Central) 35, Braidwood 34
At Decatur — Decatur 93, Watseka 73
At Evanston — Chicago (Carver) 54, Waukegan 41
At Hinsdale — Chicago Hts. (Bloom) 62, Geneva 60

Quarterfinals

Centralia 74, Metropolis 45
Springfield (Lanphier) 58, Rockford (Auburn) 56
Peoria (Central) 60, Decatur 45
Chicago (Carver) 57, Geneva 50

Semifinals

Centralia 50, Springfield (Lanphier) 46
Chicago (Carver) 40, Peoria (Central) 37

Finals

Springfield (Lanphier) 60, Peoria (Central) 47 (3rd Place)
Chicago (Carver) 53, Centralia 52 (Championship)

Championship Game

COACH: Larry Hawkins

COACH: Robert Jones

Chicago Carver (53)	FG-FGA		FT-FTA		PF	REB	TP
Joe Allen, f	8	12	2	4	2	17	18
Curtis Kirk, f	1	6	0	1	3	3	2
Robert Cifax, c	4	15	2	2	1	8	10
Charles Glen, g	1	4	1	1	1	1	3
Kenneth Maxey, g	7	13	4	6	3	5	18
Gerry Jones, f	0	0	0	0	1	4	0
Michele Page, g	0	0	0	0	0	0	0
Anthony Smedley, g	1	1	0	0	0	0	2
TOTALS	22	51	9	14	11		53

Centralia (52)	FG-FGA		FT-FTA		PF	REB	TP
Carl							
Heinrichsmeyer, f	4	9	0	1	3	2	8
Herb Williams, f	1	2	3	5	1	8	5
Cliff Berger, c	2	12	2	2	2	8	6
Don Duncan, g	5	11	2	2	3	4	12
Ron Johnson, g	8	20	2	4	0	4	18
Rich Zgol, f	1	2	1	2	0	2	3
Merritt Pulley, c	0	0	0	0	1	0	0
TOTALS	21	56	10	16	10		52

Score by Quarters:

Chicago (Carver) 15 15 13 10 — 53

Centralia 12 14 13 13 — 52

Officials: Tony Sacco (Oak Park); Tony Tortorello (Chicago)

1963 CHAMPION CHICAGO (CARVER) CHALLENGERS—Front Row: Kenneth Maxey, Ricardo Armstrong, Robert Cifax, Elree Cox, Carter Gilmer, Anthony Smedley, Manager Tyrone Parker. Second row: Coach Larry Hawkins, Fred Hickman, William Hornsby, Gerry Jones, Edward Kendall, Curtis Kirk, Adolph Lawrence, Asst. Coach Horace Howard. Back row: Joseph Allen, Peter Norfeleet, Michele Page, Leslie Patmon, Charles Glenn.

1964
March 20-21, 1964
Assembly Hall, University of Illinois

Colorful Cobden Comes Close . . .

It was shades of 1952 when Hebron became the only district champion school ever to win the state championship. Now it was Cobden, the best show in town with the second-best basketball team. Becoming a 32-game winner on the season, the big team from the little school shot past Pinckneyville, Galesburg, and Decatur. Now Cobden was 32 minutes away from becoming the "new" Hebron. Time, like Cinderella, ran out as Pekin outgeneraled the daring Apple Knockers from way down south in Illinois. Pekin parlayed a 50-45 victory into its first title under crafty coach Dawson Hawkins. Still, 95 percent of the fans cheered for the loser.

Super-Sectionals

At Evanston — Evanston 55, Chicago (Crane) 53
At Normal — Decatur 53, Arcola 37
At West Frankfort — Cobden 68, Pinckneyville 66
At Springfield — Galesburg 79, Springfield (Lanphier) 66
At Salem — Centralia 55, Collinsville 50
At Rock Island — Rock Island (Alleman) 57, Rockford (Auburn) 56
At Peoria — Pekin 61, Streator 46
At Aurora (East) — Lombard (Glenbard East) 42, Bradley-Bourbonnais, 37

Quarterfinals

Decatur 73, Evanston 59
Cobden 60, Galesburg 57
Rock Island (Alleman) 57, Centralia 56
Pekin 84, Lombard (Glenbard East) 43

Semifinals

Cobden 44, Decatur 38
Pekin 69, Rock Island (Alleman) 36

Finals

Decatur 73, Rock Island (Alleman) 54 (3rd Place)
Pekin 50, Cobden 45 (Championship)

Championship Game

COACH: Dawson Hawkins   COACH: Dick Ruggles

Pekin (50)	FG-FGA		FT-FTA		PF	REB	TP
Amel Massa, f	0	4	2	3	2	6	2
Jim Couch, f	4	10	4	4	0	2	12
Jim Sommer, c	3	9	3	3	2	8	9
Ron Rhoades, g	4	7	1	3	3	2	9
Dave Golden, g	6	10	6	6	5	4	18
Toney Buzick, f	0	0	0	0	0	1	0
Rick Venturi, g	0	0	0	0	0	0	0
TOTALS	17	40	16	19	12		50

Cobden (45)	FG-FGA		FT-FTA		PF	REB	TP
Jim Neal, f	4	7	1	3	3	5	9
Ken Flick, f	2	6	0	0	0	5	4
Chuck Neal, g	3	7	1	3	4	8	7
Ken Smith, g	8	15	1	1	3	5	17
Jim Smith, g	4	8	0	1	2	2	8
Bob Smith, g	0	2	0	2	4	1	0
Rodney Clutts, f	0	3	0	0	1	0	0
Roy Witthoff, f	0	0	0	0	1	1	0
Roger Garner, g	0	0	0	0	0	0	0
Darrell Crimmins, g	0	0	0	0	0	0	0
TOTALS	21	40	3	10	18		45

Score by Quarters:

Pekin	15	16	5	14	—	50
Cobden	8	16	7	14	—	45

Officials: Robert Brodbeck (Peoria); Joe Starcevic (Peoria)

1964 CHAMPION PEKIN CHINKS—Front row: Trainer Jimmie "Doc" Lee, Asst. Coach Duncan Reed, Mgr. Richard Pitsek, Mike Gilliam, Ron Ahten, Tom Waskowski, Dave Golden, Steve Noriuel, Tony Buzeck, Jim Sommer, Arnel Masso, Jim Couch, Fred Quade, Dan McDonald, Rick Venturi, Ron Rhoades, Mgr. Terry Vogel, Asst. Coach Joe Venturi, Head Coach, Dawson Hawkins.

1965
March 19-20, 1965
Assembly Hall, University of Illinois

Collinsville Makes Up Time . . .

Collinsville hadn't won one tournament in the first 53 years of the Illinois boys' statewide classic. Suddenly, Coach Vergil Fletcher had the team on the track, and it won two in four years. Pulling out all the offensive plugs, Collinsville remained in power drive to win four games. In the title test against Quincy, Fletcher started and finished with just five players. Jack Darlington led the scoring parade with 17 points as Collinsville closed out the tourney winning a 55-52 barn-burner.

Super-Sectionals

At Evanston   — Chicago (Marshall) 69, Winnetka (New Trier) 52
At Moline   — Moline 64, Freeport 47
At Peoria   — Lockport (Central) 67, Pekin 61
At Olney   — Collinsville 82, Lawrenceville 58
At Normal   — Decatur 54, Danville 52
At Macomb   — Qunicy 56, Jacksonville 52
At Aurora   — Harvey (Thornton) 64, Franklin Park (East Leyden) 57
At Carbondale — Marion 65, Mt. Vernon 57

Quarterfinals

Chicago (Marshall) 75, Moline 72
Collinsville 70, Lockport (Central) 45
Quincy 71, Decatur 62
Harvey (Thornton) 64, Marion 60

Semifinals

Collinsville 76, Chicago (Marshall) 64
Quincy 64, Harvey (Thornton) 59

Finals

Chicago (Marshall) 66, Harvey (Thornton) 59 (3rd Place)
Collinsville 55, Quincy 52 (Championship)

Championship Game

COACH: Vergil Fletcher

Collinsville (55)	FG-FGA		FT-FTA		PF	REB	TP
Harry Parker, f	4	10	0	0	2	2	8
Don Birger, f	4	9	3	4	3	7	11
Dennis Pace, c	5	13	5	7	4	10	15
Jack Darlington, g	7	12	3	3	2	5	17
Steve Couen, g	0	3	4	4	3	0	4
TOTALS	20	47	15	18	14		55

COACH: Sherrill Hanks

Quincy (52)	FG-FGA		FT-FTA		PF	REB	TP
Bob McMahan, f	6	7	4	4	2	7	16
Gary Rottman, f	0	2	1	2	0	2	1
John Bucdh, c	2	3	1	2	1	7	5
Gary Thompson, g	4	7	5	8	1	3	13
Kurt Genteman, g	4	10	1	2	3	2	9
Marvin Sprague, g	3	11	0	1	3	2	6
Jim Jenkins, f	0	1	0	0	1	1	0
Harry Shair, c	0	1	2	3	1	4	2
Tim Miles, f	0	0	0	0	0	0	0
TOTALS	19	42	14	22	12		52

Score by Quarters:

Quincy	11	9	14	18	—	55
Collinsville	10	14	17	14	—	52

Officials: August Jacobs (Elmhurst); Tom Frangella (Chicago)

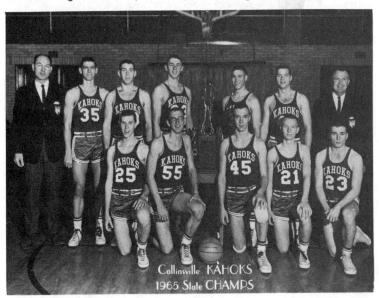

1965 CHAMPION COLLINSVILLE KAHOKS—Front row: Bruce Evans, Mike Vincent, Dennis Arnold, Keith Ziezel, Mike Belobraydic. Second row: Asst. Coach Frank Pitol, Harry Parker, Donald Birger, Dennis Pace, Jack Darlington, Steve Gauen, Coach Vergil Fletcher.

1966
March 18-19, 1966
Assembly Hall, University of Illinois

Thornton Is Back In Town . . .

It was a 33-year wait between Thornton's first and second state championships. Thornton won in 1933, beating Springfield in the final 14-13. Now
it's 1966, and Thornton wins again. This time Thornton scored more
points in the title test's first quarter (20) than the 1933 team scored in its
entire game. This fast start ignited the team from the Chicago suburb as it
out-raced and also out-played Galesburg 74-60. Rich Rateree (24) and
LaMarr Thomas (16) scored a total of 40 points between them for Thornton.

Super-Sectionals

At East St. Louis — Belleville 92, Lawrenceville 88
At Peoria   — Joliet (Central) 63, Pekin 50
At Macomb   — Galesburg 69, Springfield 65
At Carbondale   — Benton 46, Centralia 43
At Hinsdale   — Harvey (Thornton) 61, Wheaton (Central) 57
At Evanston   — Winnetka (New Trier) 78, Chicago (Marshall) 60
At Rock Island   — Rockford (West) 54, Rock Island 51
At Normal   — Decatur 68, Urbana 56

Quarterfinals

Belleville 74, Joliet (Central) 72
Galesburg 73, Benton 71
Harvey (Thornton) 59, Winnetka (New Trier) 44
Decatur 57, Rockford (West) 44

Semifinals

Galesburg 65, Belleville 64
Harvey (Thornton) 67, Decatur 45

Finals

Belleville 84, Decatur 57 (3rd Place)
Harvey (Thornton) 74, Galesburg 60 (Championship)

Championship Game

COACH: Bob Anderson

Harvey (74) (Thornton)	FG	FGA	FT	FTA	PF	REB	TP
Bob Landowski, f	1	5	4	5	5	9	6
Paul Gilliam, f	4	13	3	6	1	6	11
Jim Ard, c	6	7	1	2	5	10	13
Rich Rateree, g	10	15	4	5	3	2	24
LaMarr Thomas, g	6	14	4	5	5	4	16
Garland Mays, g	1	3	1	2	0	1	3
Estes Ross, f	0	2	1	2	1	1	1
Leonard Solomon, g	0	0	0	0	0	0	0
Hershel Lewis, f	0	0	0	0	0	0	0
Garry Carter, c	0	0	0	0	0	0	0
TOTALS	28	59	18	27	19	33	74

COACH: John Thiel

Galesburg (60)	FG	FGA	FT	FTA	PF	REB	TP
Barry Swanson, f	5	6	3	5	3	5	13
Bob Jasperson, f	2	7	1	2	5	3	5
Terry Childers, c	1	2	0	0	0	2	2
Roland McDougald	3	9	4	4	1	1	10
Dale Kelley, g	3	13	6	8	1	1	12
Bruce LaViolette, g	4	7	3	3	4	3	11
Mike Drasites, f	2	2	3	5	4	10	7
Steve Marshall, f	0	1	0	0	0	0	0
Leon Luckett, g	0	0	0	0	0	0	0
Lugene Finley, f	0	0	0	0	0	0	0
TOTALS	20	47	20	27	18	31	60

Score by Quarters:

Harvey (Thornton)	20	27	13	14	— 74
Galesburg	12	13	18	17	— 60

Officials: Tom Alexander (East Peoria); Jean DesMarteau (Kankakee)

1966 CHAMPIONS HARVEY (THORNTON) WILDCATS—Front Row: Estes Ross, Rich Rateree, Garland Mays, Leonard Solomon. Back Row, Ass't Coach Tom Hanrahan, LaMarr Thomas, Bob Landowski, Hershel Lewis, Paul Gilliam, Jim Ard, Larry Tanter, Garry Carter, Kevin Roberson, Coach Bob Anderson.

1967
March 17-18, 1967
Assembly Hall, University of Illinois

It's Miller Time—for Pekin . . .

Dawson Hawkins has always claimed that Fred Miller rated high among the very best players he had ever coached. If any more proof is desired to support Hawkins' opinion, it will be found in the summary of Pekin's 75-59 championship conquest of Carbondale in 1967. All Fred did in this game was score 16 field goals on 20 shots, convert 4 of 7 free throws, and pull in 7 rebounds while putting 36 points on the board. Springfield, eliminated by Pekin in the semifinals, claimed third place after outgunning Rockford (West) 81-65.

Super-Sectionals

At Peoria	— Pekin 77, Toluca 64
At Aurora	— Elmhurst (York) 72, Chicago (Harlan) 70
At Macomb	— Springfield 70, Quincy 68
At Normal	— Champaign 36, Decatur 35
At Evanston	— Flossmoor (Homewood-F.) 69, North Chicago 65
At Moline	— Rockford (West) 62, Moline 61
At Carbondale	— Carbondale 59, Benton 53
At Charleston	— Collinsville 59, Effingham 48

Quarterfinals

Pekin 94, Elmhurst (York) 70
Springfield 64, Champaign 61
Rockford (West) 79, Flossmoor (Homewood-F.) 60
Carbondale 53, Collinsville 47

Semifinals

Pekin 77, Springfield 61
Carbondale 67, Rockford (West) 66

Finals

Springfield 81, Rockford (West) 65 (3rd place)
Pekin 75, Carbondale 59 (Championship)

Championship Game

COACH: Dawson Hawkins

Pekin (75)	FG	-FGA	FT	-FTA	PF	REB	TP
Barry Moran, f	4	9	3	4	3	9	11
Dave Martin, f	0	5	0	0	1	4	0
Fred Miller, c	16	20	4	7	2	7	36
Doug Jones, g	3	9	0	2	1	2	6
Mark Freidinger, g	6	12	1	2	1	2	13
Rich Hawkins, g	0	0	0	0	1	0	0
Tom Vucich, g	2	3	3	4	0	1	7
Steve Kingdon, f	0	0	0	0	1	0	0
Scott Lange, c	1	4	0	0	1	2	2
John Venturi, g	0	0	0	0	0	0	0
TOTALS	32	62	11	19	11	27	75

COACH: John Cherry

Carbondale (59)	FG	-FGA	FT	-FTA	PF	REB	TP
L.C. Brasfield, f	8	12	3	3	2	7	19
Early Laster, f	5	6	0	3	5	2	10
Bill Perkins, c	7	10	0	1	4	11	14
Ken Lewis, g	3	4	1	1	0	0	7
Phil Gilbert, g	3	8	0	0	3	1	6
Terry Wallace, g	0	3	0	0	2	1	0
Geoff Partlow, g	0	0	0	0	0	0	0
Bob Crane, g	0	0	0	0	0	0	0
Dave Walls, f	0	0	0	0	0	0	0
Chuck Taylor, c	1	1	1	3	0	1	3
TOTALS	27	44	5	11	16	24	59

Score by Quarters:

Pekin	16	18	21	20 — 75
Carbondale	17	6	17	19 — 59

Officials: Tom Alexander (East Peoria); Paul Blakeman (Pontiac)

1967 CHAMPION PEKIN CHINKS—Front row: Trainer Jimmie "Doc" Lee, Jerry Normal, Tom Vuceck, Mark Friedinger, Dick Marshall, John Venturi, Rich Hawkins. Second row: Head Coach Dawson Hawkins, Mgr. Clark Joesting, Dave Martin, Doug Jones, Ken Higham, Kim Seeber, Randy Brienan, Mgr. Third row: Asst. Coach Bob Ontegal, Asst. Coach Joe Venturi, Fred Miller, Steve Kingdon, Scott Lange, Barry Moran, Mgr.Barry Soffietti.

1968
March 22-23, 1968
Assembly Hall, University of Illinois

Evanston Finally Victorious . . .

After 60 years Evanston discovered the winners' circle of the Illinois High School Basketball Tournament. The Wildkits' success was so convincing that a stranger couldn't be blamed for thinking it was a regular happening. The muscular and explosive Evanston powerhouse hit an even 70 points three times and 79 once to win the classic. Galesburg was the victim in the title game 70-51 to give the Evanston champions a seasonal reading of 30 victories in 31 games.

Super-Sectionals

At Carbondale — Carbondale 68, Mt. Vernon 66
At Hinsdale — Chicago (Crane Tech) 73, LaGrange (Lyons) 61
At Evanston — Evanston 79, Lockport (Central) 58
At Peoria — Peoria (Central) 83, Springfield (Lanphier) 72
At Normal — LaSalle (L.-Peru) 77, Danville (Schlarman) 68
At DeKalb — DeKalb 73, Rockford (Auburn) 53
At Macomb — Galesburg 68, Quincy 60 (ot)
At Charleston — Effingham 54, Belleville (West) 49 (ot)

Quarterfinals

Chicago (Crane Tech) 64, Carbondale 63
Evanston 70, Peoria (Central) 48
DeKalb 82, LaSalle (L.-Peru) 77
Galesburg 85, Effingham 52

Semifinals

Evanston 70, Chicago (Crane Tech) 54
Galesburg 63, DeKalb 60

Finals

Chicago (Crane Tech) 82, DeKalb 62 (3rd place)
Evanston 70, Galesburg 51 (Championship)

Championship Game

COACH: Jack Burmaster   COACH: John Thiel

Evanston (70)	FG-FGA	FT-FTA	PF	REB	TP
Robert Lackey, f	6 13	3 4	5	8	15
Bill Battinus, f	5 12	1 2	2	6	11
Farrell Jones, c	5 13	0 0	1	7	10
Walter Perrin, g	4 13	2 6	3	3	10
Ronald Cooper, g	5 8	11 14	1	8	21
Alvin Keith, f	0 1	1 2	1	1	1
Odell Johnson, g	0 0	0 0	0	0	0
Michael Hart, c	0 0	0 1	0	1	0
Alton Hill, f	0 1	0 0	0	1	0
Orestes Arrieta, g	1 1	0 0	0	1	2
TOTALS	26 22	18 29	13	36	70

Galesburg (51)	FG-FGA	FT-FTA	PF	REB	TP
Dave Wood, f	2 6	1 2	2	2	5
James Reinebach, f	3 5	1 2	4	2	7
Ruben Triplett, c	3 11	4 4	5	9	10
Leon Luckett, g	4 9	0 0	1	5	8
Fred Mims, g	6 10	1 3	1	6	13
Roland McDougald, g	0 1	0 1	2	1	0
Steve Olson, f	2 7	2 4	1	3	6
Lugene Finley, f	0 3	0 0	0	4	0
Zack Thiel, g	1 1	0 0	1	0	2
Michael Doyle, f	0 1	0 0	0	0	0
	21 54	9 16	17	32	51

Score by Quarters:

Evanston	18	24	15	13	—	70
Galesburg	16	9	14	12	—	51

Officials: Fred L. Gibson (Carlyle); Ernest L. Reynolds (Carterville)

1968 CHAMPION EVANSTON WILDKITS—Front row: Alvin Keith, Mike Hart, Odell Johnson, Orestes Arrieta, Alton Hill, Bill Battinus. Back row: Asst. Coach Steve Power, Ron Cooper, Farrell Jones, Bob Lackey, Walt Perrin, Coach Jack Burmaster.

1969
March 21-22, 1969
Assembly Hall, University of Illinois

Thirty and One A Repeater . . .

Only the name changed in the posting of the state tournament's new champion: Proviso East of Maywood. When Proviso East pinned Peoria (Spalding) 58-51 for the title, The Pirates posted a 30-1 record. In this manner, Maywood matched the record Evanston parlayed into the 1968 title. Proviso East's coach, Tom Milliken, thus joined the select few who have been associated with state champions both as player and as coach. Milliken played for Pinckneyville when they won the title in 1948.

Super-Sectionals

At Carbondale	— Mt. Vernon 71, Carbondale 63
At DeKalb	— Aurora (East) 67, Dixon 50
At Peoria	— Peoria (Spalding) 47, Lincoln 41
At Charleston	— Belleville (East) 47, Mattoon 45
At Macomb	— Galesburg 77, Quincy 64
At Normal	— Champaign (Central) 55, Normal (Community) 63, (3 ot)
At Evanston	— Waukegan 63, Harvey (Thornton) 61
At Hinsdale	— Maywood (Proviso East) 47, Chicago (Hirsch) 46

Quarterfinals

Aurora (East) 52, Mt. Vernon 46
Peoria (Spalding) 80, Belleville (East) 61
Champaign (Central) 62, Galesburg 57
Maywood (Proviso East) 52, Waukegan 44

Semifinals

Peoria (Spalding) 66, Aurora (East) 53
Maywood (Proviso East) 37, Champaign (Central) 36

Finals

Champaign (Central) 56, Aurora (East) 49 (3rd place)
Maywood (Proviso East) 58,
Peoria (Spalding) 51 (Championship)

Championship Game

COACH: Tom Millikin

Maywood (58) (Prov. East)	FG-FGA		FT-FTA		PF	REB	TP
Peter Bouzeos, f	3	5	0	0	3	7	6
Harvey Roberts, f	2	7	1	2	2	8	5
Jim Brewer, c	5	9	7	10	3	9	17
Walter Williams, f	5	10	2	4	3	7	12
William Allen, g	3	9	10	12	3	4	16
Ralph Sykes, c	0	1	0	0	0	1	0
Ira Carswell, f	1	3	0	2	1	3	2
John Munchoff, f	0	1	0	0	0	0	0
Keith Rash, g	0	0	0	0	0	0	0
TOTALS	19	45	20	30	15	39	58

COACH: Ron Patterson

Peoria (51) (Spalding)	FG-FGA		FT-FTA		PF	REB	TP
Charles Thorell, f	3	7	7	8	4	2	13
L. Barksdale, f	4	15	3	4	0	11	11
Lavin O'Neal, c	3	13	3	3	2	9	11
Art Jenkins, g	0	6	0	0	3	0	0
Marty McGann, g	1	2	0	0	1	2	2
Jim Moore, f	2	3	0	2	4	1	4
Rick Schaidle, g	0	0	0	0	4	0	0
Rich Lavin, f	1	1	0	0	0	0	2
Ken Wolbeck, c	2	6	0	0	3	9	4
Steve Schrader, g	2	3	0	1	0	1	4
	19	56	13	18	21	35	51

Score by Quarters:

Maywood (Proviso East)	4	11	14	22	—	58
Peoria (Spalding)	9	19	12	19	—	51

Officials: Jean W. DesMarteau (Kankakee)
Glen VanProyen (Glen Ellyn)

1969 CHAMPION MAYWOOD (PROVISO EAST) PIRATES—Front row: Walt Williams, Harvey Roberts, Jim Brewer, Pete Bouzeos, Bill Allen. Second row: Howard Godfrey, John Munchoff, Ralph Sykes, Ira Carswell, Keith Rash. Third row: Asst. Coach William Ebenezer, Steve Glos, Ted Pelikan, Ernest Lewis, Kirk Shearburn, Head Coach Tom Millikin.

1970
March 20-21, 1970
Assembly Hall, University of Illinois

St. Anthony Comes Close . . .

Effingham's effervescent representative, St. Anthony, came within mere seconds of pulling the major upset of the 1970 tourney. Playing in the quarterfinals, St. Anthony carried Lyons' LaGrange to the wire before losing 89-88. Surviving this pulse-pounder, LaGrange went on to win its second title in 17 years by rolling over East Moline 71-52. Owen Brown did outstanding double duty for Lyons, scoring 24 points and sweeping the boards for 24 rebounds. Brown's finesse helped LaGrange become the first undefeated champion since Collinsville in 1961.

Super-Sectionals

At Charleston — Effingham (St. Anthony) 85, Collinsville 79
At DeKalb — LaGrange (Lyons) 60, Sterling 42
At Carbondale — Okawville 66, Mt. Vernon 64
At Evanston — Joliet (Central) 71,
                Park Ridge (Maine South) 68
At Aurora — Aurora (East) 68, Chicago (Harlan) 61
At Peoria — Peoria (Spalding) 41, Lincoln 37
At Normal — LaSalle (L.-Peru) 81, Danville (H.S.) 63
At Macomb — East Moline (United) 75, Pittsfield 54

Quarterfinals

LaGrange (Lyons) 89, Effingham (St. Anthony) 88
Joliet (Central) 56, Okawville 43
Peoria (Spalding) 73, Aurora (East) 56
East Moline (United) 68, LaSalle (L.-Peru) 66

Semifinals

LaGrange (Lyons) 63, Joliet (Central) 52
East Moline (United) 77, Peoria (Spalding) 59

Finals

Joliet (Central) 82, Peoria (Spalding) 75 (3rd place)
LaGrange (Lyons) 71, East Moline (United) 52

Championship Game

COACH: Ron Nickevich

LaGrange (71) (Lyons)	FG	FGA	FT	FTA	PF	REB	TP
Dave VanSkike, f	8	14	2	2	2	4	18
S. Heinzelman, f	0	5	1	2	1	10	1
Owen Brown, c	11	24	2	5	3	24	24
Scott Shaw, g	6	10	2	2	1	5	14
Marc Washington, g	3	10	4	5	2	4	1
D. Wehrmeister, f	0	1	0	1	1	0	0
Jim Dethmer, g	1	1	0	0	0	0	2
Larry Lindberg, g	0	0	0	0	0	0	0
Paul Makris, g	0	0	0	0	1	0	0
Alex Christ, c	1	1	0	0	0	0	2
TOTALS	30	66	11	17	11	47	71

COACH: Cliff Talley

E. Moline (52) (United)	FG	FGA	FT	FTA	PF	REB	TP
Craig Davis, f	8	18	0	0	2	10	16
Daryl Griffin, f	1	7	2	3	2	1	4
T. Haliburton, c	2	10	2	3	4	3	6
Bob Hunter, g	6	12	2	2	2	5	14
Malcom Samuels, g	3	6	0	1	1	2	6
Bob Officer, f	0	7	6	7	1	2	6
Bob Gardner, f	0	1	0	0	1	1	0
Willie Dyer, g	0	2	0	0	0	0	0
	20	63	12	16	13	24	52

Score by Quarters:

LaGrange (Lyons)	16	14	17	24	—	71
East Moline (United)	16	12	14	10	—	52

Officials: Richard Henley (Herrin); Ted Search, Jr. (Chester)

1970 CHAMPION LAGRANGE (LYONS) LIONS—Front row: Rick Skoda, mgr., Mark Neer, Larry Lindberg, Bob Whitelaw, Jeff Hill, Scott Shaw, co-capt., Marcus Washington, co-capt., Paul Makris, Tom Wickham, Dan Przewoznik, Chuck Pribyl, Al Tucek, mgr. Third row: Kevin Dwyer, mgr., Jim Hilborn, mgr., Kevin Cummings, Mike Danner, Dave Wehrmeister, Steve Heinzelmann, Owen Brown, Alex Christ, Greg Szatko, Dave VanSkike, Jim Dethmer, Tom Vogele, Craig Meyer, Mr. Ron Nikcevich, Mr. Delton Stamp.

1971
March 19-20, 1971
Assembly Hall, University of Illinois

Welcome Aboard Quinn Buckner . . .

A new dimension was added to the 1971 championship game when it paired Thornridge of Dolton against Oak Lawn (Community) to make Chicagoland a can't-miss winner. And so it was — Thornridge winning a 52-50 thriller for the 21st link in a win streak which was to grow to a state record 58 consecutive victories. Quinn Buckner, who was to become everybody's Mister Everything, scored 18 points, four fewer than Oak Lawn sharpshooter C. J. Kupec.

Super-Sectionals

At Carbondale — Nashville 52, Benton 60
At Evanston — Oak Lawn (Comm.) 66,
Winnetka (New Trier East) 54
At Peoria — Springfield (Lanphier) 81,
Peoria (Woodruff) 68
At DeKalb — Rockford (Boylan) 64, Elgin (Larkin) 54
At Macomb — Kewanee 60, Quincy (Catholic Boys) 59
At Crete — Dolton (Thornridge) 63,
Chicago (Harlan) 63
At Charleston — Paris 74, Granite City 48
At Normal — Danville (H.S.) 62, Normal (University) 61

Quarterfinals

Oak Lawn (Comm.) 71, Benton 58
Springfield (Lanphier) 92, Rockford (Boylan) 78
Dolton (Thornridge) 63, Kewanee 58
Danville (H.S.) 63, Paris 61

Semifinals

Oak Lawn (Comm.) 69, Springfield (Lanphier) 65
Dolton (Thornridge) 57, Danville (H.S.) 47

Finals

Danville (H.S.) 77, Springfield (Lanphier) 57 (3rd place)
Dolton (Thornridge) 52, Oak Lawn (Comm.) 50 (Championship)

Championship Game

COACH: Ron Ferguson

Dolton (52) (Thornridge)	FG-FGA	FT-FTA	PF	REB	TP
Greg Rose, f	2 10	0 0	1	2	4
Boyd Batts, f	3 8	0 1	3	4	6
Mark McClain, c	2 2	0 0	2	3	4
Quinn Buckner, g	8 18	2 3	2	8	18
Mike Bonczyk, g	3 6	1 1	3	0	7
Mike Henry, f	5 11	1 1	3	0	7
TOTALS	23 55	6 9	12	27	52

COACH: Len Scaduto

Oak Lawn (50) (Community)	FG-FGA	FT-FTA	PF	REB	TP
Bob Carr, f	H 7	5 8	1	9	7
Brett Arnold, f	2 4	0 1	3	10	4
C. J. Kupec, c	9 15	4 4	2	8	22
Tom Dubetz, g	0 3	2 2	1	1	2
Jim Bocinsky, g	6 11	3 3	0	2	15
	18 40	14 18	7	30	50

Score by Quarters:

Dolton (Thornridge)	17	11	13	11	—	52
Oak Lawn (Comm.)	10	13	15	12	—	50

Officials: Harry Forrester (Champaign); Pat McGann (Peoria)

1971 CHAMPION DOLTON (THORNRIDGE) FALCONS—Front row: Mgr. Jeff Groger, Greg Rose, Tony Jackson, Coach Ron Ferguson, Mike Bonczyk, Jim Loggins and Mgr. Rick Remmert. Top row: Coach Ferguson's son, Gary, Asst. Coach Frank Nardi, Quinn Buckner, Chuck Hogan, Mark McClain, Boyd Batts, Al Vest, Mike Henry, Asst. Coach Al Holverson.

CLASS A
1972
March 10-11, 1972
Assembly Hall, University of Illinois

Big A Goes to Little L . . .

After 64 years, classification came to the state basketball tournament. Class A was comprised of schools with an enrollment of under 750 students. Coach Ron Felling brought his Lawrenceville Indians into this first-ever tournament with a 21-8 record. At the tournament's end, Lawrenceville left with a 25-8 record and the first trophy ever presented to a Class A winner. The clincher was Lawrenceville's 63-57 triumph over Mounds of Meridian as Mike Lockhard sparked the victory with 32 points.

Super-Sectionals

At Carbondale	— Mounds (Meridian) 56, DuQuoin 55
At DeKalb	— Elgin (St. Edward) 56, Shabbona 54
At Pontiac	— Streator (Woodland) 52, Chicago (Christian) 51
At East Moline	— Thomson 84, Farmington (East) 73
At Decatur	— Raymond (Lincolnwood) 83, Chrisman 78
At Normal	— Gibson City 69, Normal (University) 61
At Charleston	— Lawrenceville 71, Lovejoy 63
At Macomb	— Quincy (Catholic) 78, Piasa (Southwestern) 66

Quarterfinals

Mounds (Meridian) 54, Elgin (St. Edward) 52
Thomson 72, Streator (Woodland) 56
Raymond (Lincolnwood) 68, Gibson City 66
Lawrenceville 57, Quincy (Catholic) 56

Semifinals

Mounds (Meridian) 81, Thomson 74
Lawrenceville 75, Raymond (Lincolnwood) 68

Finals

Raymond (Lincolnwood) 90, Thomson 69 (3rd place)
Lawrenceville 63, Mounds (Meridian 57) (Championship)

Championship Game

COACH: Ron Felling

Lawrenceville (63)	FG	-FGA	FT	-FTA	PF	REB	TP
Rick Leighty, f	3	12	3	5	3	11	9
Tom Wolfe, f	0	1	1	2	5	5	1
Joe Leighty, c	2	8	2	3	4	4	6
Mike Lockhard, g	15	28	2	2	1	5	32
B. Heidbreder, g	2	8	2	3	0	2	6
Mike Miller, f	4	5	1	2	1	7	9
Walt Simmons, g	0	0	0	0	0	0	0
Tom Kirkwood, f	0	2	0	0	2	0	0
TOTALS	26	64	11	17	16	43	63

COACH: Jim Byassee

Mounds (57) (Meridian)	FG	-FGA	FT	-FTA	PF	REB	TP
Jackie Howard, f	4	15	2	4	2	4	10
C. Fitzgerald, f	2	7	2	3	4	9	6
Curtis Bogan, c	4	4	6	11	3	10	14
Tally Hawkins, g	6	10	0	3	3	7	12
Calvin Johnson, g	7	16	1	2	3	2	15
Jerry Meeks, c	0	0	0	0	1	1	0
Darrell Hudson, f	0	1	0	0	1	0	0
	23	53	11	23	17	43	57

Score by Quarters:

Lawrenceville	16	15	12	20 —	63
Mounds (Meridian)	15	14	10	18 —	57

Officials: Paul Brooks (Rock Island); Ken Rodermel (Freeport)

1972 CLASS A CHAMPION LAWRENCEVILLE INDIANS—Front row: Jeff Richardson, Mgr. Bob Seber, Mark Moore. Second row: Tom Wolfe, Mike Lockhart, Walt Simmons, Bill Heidbreder, Jeff Chansler. Third row: Rick Leighty, Joe Leighty, Chuck McGaughlay, Tom Kirkwood, Mike Miller.

CLASS AA
1972
March 17-18, 1972
Assembly Hall, University of Illinois

Buckner Is Back, So Is Batts . . .

"Super Star" Quinn Buckner came back to the tournament for a second stand, but he had to share the spotlight with an unknown in the "Who He?" bracket. In the championship game, the Dolton powerhouse destroyed Quincy 104-69 for back-to-back titles hinged to a flawless 33-0 seasonal record and a string of 54 consecutive victories. Buckner contributed 28 points, but teammate Boyd Batts had the hot hand. The unheralded Batts scored 14 field goals on 18 shots and hit 9 of 10 free throws for 37 points. Busy Boyd also led both teams with 15 rebounds.

Super-Sectionals

At Crete — Dolton (Thornridge) 74, Lockport (Central) 46
At Carbondale — Collinsville 78, Mascoutah 69
At Evanston — Evanston 62, North Chicago 60
At Peoria — Peoria (Manual) 61, Rock Island (Alleman) 51
At Aurora — Hinsdale (Central) 66, LaGrange (Lyons) 59
At Dekalb — Aurora (East) 93, Hoffman Estates (Conant) 53
At Chicago
    City Playoffs — Chicago (Crane) 75, Chicago (Marshall) 63
At Normal — Quincy (Sr.) 76, Kankakee (Eastridge) 70

Quarterfinals

Dolton (Thornridge) 95, Collinsville 66
Peoria (Manual) 82, Evanston 53
Aurora (East) 83, Hinsdale (Central) 81
Quincy (Sr.) 87, Chicago (Crane) 71

Semifinals

Dolton (Thornridge) 71, Peoria (Manual) 52
Quincy (Sr.) 107, Aurora (East) 96

Finals

Aurora (East) 74, Peoria (Manual) 66 (3rd place)
Dolton (Thornridge) 104, Quincy (Sr.) 69 (Championship)

Championship Game

COACH: Ron Ferguson

Dolton (104) (Thornridge)	FG-FGA		FT-FTA		PF	REB	TP
Greg Rose, f	13	21	0	2	4	8	26
Ernie Dunn, f	2	5	1	2	2	6	5
Boyd Batts, c	14	18	9	10	3	15	37
Quinn Buckner, g	11	17	6	6	4	11	28
Mike Bonczyk, g	1	4	2	2	4	0	4
Bill Gatlin, g	1	2	0	0	2	1	2
Bill Redman, f	1	1	0	0	2	1	2
K. Hutchinson,	0	0	0	0	0	1	0
Dave Anderson	0	1	0	0	0	0	0
Joe King	0	0	0	0	0	0	0
Fred Knutsen	0	0	0	0	0	0	0
TOTALS	43	69	18	23	22	49	104

COACH: Sherrill Hanks

Quincy (Sr.) (69)	FG-FGA		FT-FTA		PF	REB	TP
Don Sorenson, f	3	8	10	10	3	4	16
Robert Spear, f	4	5	4	6	1	5	12
Kel Cott, c	2	5	1	2	5	6	5
Jim Wisman, g	6	16	2	2	1	3	14
Larry Moore, g	5	22	5	5	3	1	15
Rick Ely, f	2	4	1	4	3	3	5
Mike Sellers	0	1	0	0	0	2	0
Bart Bergman	1	1	0	0	0	0	2
Dan Long	0	0	0	0	0	0	0
TOTALS	23	63	23	29	16	28	69

Score by Quarters:

Dolton (Thornridge)	25	32	21	26	—	104
Quincy (Sr.)	15	11	26	17	—	69

Officials: Robert Burson (Western Springs); Otho Kortz (Oak Lawn)

1972 CLASS AA CHAMPION DOLTON (THORNRIDGE) FALCONS—Front Row: Ernie Dunn, Quinn Buckner, Boyd Batts, Greg Rose, Mike Bonczyk. Second Row: Head Coach Ron Ferguson, Ken Rose, Fred Knutsen, Joe King, Sidney Lewis, Keith Hutchinson, Nee Gatlin, Bill Redman, Dave Anderson, Asst. Coach Dave Lezeau.

CLASS A
1973
March 16-17, 1973
Assembly Hall, University of Illinois

Ridgway, Team To Beat . . .

After watching Ridgway zing Pinckneyville in a 57-56 thriller in the Super-Sectional, basketball buffs were convinced that Ridgway was the team to beat in the Class A division of the tournament. This appraisal proved accurate. Ridgway ran away from its next three opponents, including Maple Park (Kaneland) in the final 54-51. In this manner Ridgway won the second Class A crown climaxed with a 32-1 record thanks to the sharpshooting of Mike Dixon (20) and Brent Browning (18).

Super-Sectionals

At Decatur	—Morrisonville 49, Cerro Gordo 59
At Pontiac	—St. Anne 81, Toluca 62
At Carbondale	—Ridgway 57, Pinckneyville 56
At Macomb	—Petersburg (Porta) 77, Mendon 72
At DeKalb	—Maple Park (Kaneland) 37, Ottawa (Marquette) 35
At Rock Island	—Fulton 38, Bushnell (B.-Prairie City) 37
At Normal	—Bloomington (Central Cath.) 68, Danville (Schlarman) 58
At Charleston	—Venice 71, Marshall 66

Quarterfinals

St. Anne 88, Cerro Gordo 70
Ridgway 85, Petersburg (Porta) 79
Maple Park (Kaneland) 42, Fulton 35
Venice 55, Bloomington (Central Catholic) 53

Semifinals

Ridgway 73, St. Anne 51
Maple Park (Kaneland) 46, Venice 34

Finals

Venice 73, St. Anne 66 (3rd Place)
Ridgway 54, Maple Park (Kaneland) 51 (Championship)

Championship Game

COACH: Bob Dallas

Ridgway (54)	FG-FGA		FT-FTA		PF	REB	TP
Mike Dixon, f	10	19	0	0	0	7	20
Mike Fromm, f	1	1	0	0	4	0	2
Dennis Pearce, c	3	8	0	1	4	9	6
Brent Browning, g	9	15	0	2	3	4	18
Danny Stevens, g	2	6	2	3	1	3	6
Jeff Drone, g	1	4	0	0	1	0	2
TOTALS	26	53	2	6	13	23	54

COACH: George Birkett

Maple Park (51) (Kaneland)	FG-FGA		FT-FTA		PF	REB	TP
Kirk Kreese, f	1	5	2	2	1	8	4
Steve Lynch, f	12	20	3	4	5	6	27
B. Sambrookes, c	4	15	6	7	3	14	14
Ackerman, g	0	2	0	0	1	3	0
Kevin Peterson, g	2	6	0	0	1	2	4
Paul Johnson, f	1	2	0	0	1	1	2
	20	50	11	13	12	34	51

Score by Quarters:

Ridgway	16	18	12	8	—	54
Maple Park (Kaneland)	8	16	13	14	—	51

Officials: Paul Brooks (Rock Island); Don Frits (Port Byron)

1973 CLASS A CHAMPION RIDGWAY EAGLES—Front row: Mike Fromm, Brent Browning, Dennis Pearce, Mike Dixon, Danny Stevens. Top row: Coach Bob Dallas, John Cross, Tony Cox, Jeff Drone, Jim Doyle, Don Wathen, Martin Duffy, Asst. Coach John Schmitt.

CLASS AA
1973
March 23-24, 1973
Assembly Hall, University of Illinois

One Win, Two Dividends . . .

When Hirsch outlasted Parker 55-53 to win the Chicago city playoff, the Huskies used this opening to go on and become the combined city-state champion. At the finish, Hirsch chopped down a suburban rival, New Trier East of Winnetka 65-51 for the state title—the fourth captured by a Chicago school. Hirsch got 33 points out of its two top scorers: John Robinson (17) and Ricky Green (16). East's two top gunners settled for 30 points as Chris Wall got 18 and Jim Cassady added 12.

Super-Sectionals

At Peoria	— Moline 67, Pekin 46
At Chicago City Playoffs	— Chicago (Hirsch) 55, Chicago (Parker) 53
At Normal	— Lincoln 61, Bradley (B.-Bourbonnais) 49
At Crete	— Lockport (Central) 62, Chicago Hts. (Bloom) 47
At Aurora	— Elgin (H.S.) 67, Maywood (Proviso East) 66
At DeKalb	— Aurora (West) 60, Rockford 52
At Carbondale	— Collinsville 77, Murphysboro 68
At Evanston	— Skokie (Niles West) 50, Winnetka (New Trier East) 54

Quarterfinals

Chicago (Hirsch) 57, Moline 50
Lockport (Central) 62, Lincoln 54
Aurora (West) 54, Elgin (H.S.) 49
Collinsville 61, Winnetka (New Trier East) 59

Semifinals

Chicago (Hirsch) 83, Lockport (Central) 67
Winnetka (New Trier East) 39, Aurora (West) 33

Finals

Aurora (West) 67, Lockport (Central) 45 (3rd Place)
Chicago (Hirsch) 65, Winnetka (New Trier East) 51 (Championship)

Championship Game

COACH: Charles Stimpson

Chicago (65) (Hirsch)	FG	FGA	FT	FTA	PF	REB	TP
Joshua Smith, f	7	14	0	0	0	4	14
John Robinson, f	6	14	5	7	2	8	17
Michael Mathews, c	4	6	0	0	3	3	8
Gregory Allen, g	1	2	2	2	2	4	4
Ricky Green, g	7	10	2	2	2	1	16
Robert Brooks, g	2	8	0	0	0	1	4
Carl Henderson, f	0	0	0	0	0	0	0
Cook	0	0	0	0	0	1	0
Alfred Bowen	0	1	0	0	0	0	0
Gregory Jones	1	1	0	0	0	0	2
Frank Byrd	0	0	0	0	0	0	0
Gordon Smith	0	0	0	0	0	0	0
TOTALS	28	56	9	11	9	22	65

COACH: John Schneiter

Winnetka (51) (New Trier East)	FG	FGA	FT	FTA	PF	REB	TP
Derek Kilmnik, f	3	11	0	0	3	12	6
Frank Moran, f	1	5	0	0	1	2	2
Chris Wall, c	9	17	0	0	0	13	18
Mike Allen, g	1	3	0	0	2	1	2
John Castino, g	4	8	1	4	1	2	9
Jim Cassady, f	6	16	0	2	2	7	12
Stu Ordman, f	1	2	0	0	1	0	2
Jeff Welch	0	0	0	0	0	0	0
David Harvey	0	1	0	0	0	0	0
Jim Fuhrman	0	0	0	0	0	0	0
David Holton	0	1	0	0	0	1	0
Tom Ureill	0	0	0	0	0	0	0
TOTALS	25	64	1	6	10	38	51

Score by Quarters:

Chicago (Hirsch)	14	20	12	19 —	65
Winnetka (New Trier East)	16	18	2	15 —	51

Officials: Raymond Brooks (Oak Park); Dan Davey (Elgin)

1973 CLASS AA CHAMPION CHICAGO (HIRSCH) HUSKIES—Alfred Bowens, Reece Morgan, Robert Brooks, Gordon Smith, Morris Ross, Joshua Smith, John Robinson, Michael Mathews, Gregory Jones, Michael Turner, Frank Byrd, Rickey Green, Carl Henderson, Gregory Allen, Roderick Cook.

CLASS A
1974
March 15-16, 1974
Assembly Hall, University of Illinois

What's New? Two Overtime Games . . .

One of the oddities associated with the Illinois state basketball tournament down through the years has been the scarcity of overtime games. During the quarterfinals of the third Class A phase of the competition, extra periods were required to decide two games. Lawrenceville tripped Cerro Gordo 77-72 in two overtimes, and Chicago Christian of Palos Heights got past Lexington 60-57 in a single overtime. Lawrenceville continued on to win its second championship in three years nipping Ottawa (Marquette) in a 54-53 thriller.

Super-Sectionals

At Decatur   — Cerro Gordo 75, Stewardson (S.-Strasburg) 67
At Charleston — Lawrenceville 63, Venice 57
At Normal   — Lexington 64, Watseka 63
At Streator   — Palos Hts. (Chg. Christian) 49, Spring Valley (Hall) 40
At Macomb   — Quincy (Catholic Boys) 70, Franklin 66
At Moline   — Prophetstown 77, Monmouth (H.S.) 60
At DeKalb   — Ottawa (Marquette) 58, South Beloit 39
At Carbondale — Ridgway 79, Ullin (Century) 49

Quarterfinals

Lawrenceville 77, Cerro Gordo 72 (2 ot)
Palos Hts. (Chicago Christian) 60, Lexington 57 (ot)
Quincy (Catholic Boys) 55, Prophetstown 44
Ottawa (Marquette) 50, Ridgway 47

Semifinals

Lawrenceville 56, Palos Hts. (Chicago Christian) 43
Ottawa (Marquette) 65, Quincy (Catholic Boys) 52

Finals

Palos Hts. (Chicago Christian) 71, Quincy (Catholic Boys) 62 (3rd Place)
Lawrenceville 54, Ottawa (Marquette) 53 (Championship Game)

Championship Game

| COACH: Ron Felling | | | | | | | |
Lawrenceville (54)	FG-	FGA	FT-	FTA	PF	REB	TP
Rick Leighty, f	10	19	4	6	4	11	24
Tom Wolfe, f	2	6	0	0	4	3	4
Stan Dickirson, c	1	2	0	0	1	6	2
B. Heidbreder, g	5	8	0	1	2	3	10
Jay Shidler, g	6	13	2	2	4	4	14
Roger Kull, g	0	2	0	0	1	1	0
TOTALS	24	50	6	9	16	31	54

| COACH: Bob Strickland | | | | | | | |
Ottawa (53) (Marquette)	FG-	FGA	FT-	FTA	PF	REB	TP
K. Conness, f	2	7	0	1	4	9	4
Jim Schaibley, f	0	3	0	0	2	8	0
Keith Renkosik, c	10	17	3	9	2	11	23
Marty Brown, g	6	19	1	1	3	4	13
Nick Tabor, g	5	8	3	4	1	1	13
	23	54	7	15	12	37	53

Score by Quarters:

Lawrenceville	14	16	14	10	— 54
Ottawa (Marquette)	13	17	14	9	— 53

Officials: William Dickson (Batavia); William England (Peoria)

1974 CLASS A CHAMPION LAWRENCEVILLE INDIANS—Front row Mgr. Mike Klein, Asst. Coach Jim Reedy, Coach Ron Felling, Asst. Coach Ken Trickett, Mgr. Wayne Pickering. Second row: Dave Hesher, Mark Joiner, Bill Heidbreder, Joe Cooper. Third row: Mike Argo, Jay Shidler, Roger Kull, Mike Myers. Back row: Stan Dickirson, Rick Leighty, Brent Pace, Tim Wolfe.

CLASS AA
1974
March 22-23, 1974
Assembly Hall, University of Illinois

Rebounding Is Name of the Game . . .

The muscular tempo of basketball played in the suburban schools of the Chicago area surfaced into full view when Proviso East of Maywood took out Bloom of Chicago Heights in the Class AA finals. En route to a 61-56 triumph, Proviso scored 27 baskets and gathered in 47 rebounds. Bloom remained in contention until the last quarter when Maywood posted a 21-13 edge. Bloom was credited with 46 rebounds as the rugged match produced 93 rebounds compared to 49 field goals.

Super-Sectionals

At Joliet	— Chicago Hts. (Bloom) 83, Olympia Fields (Rich Central) 69
At Evanston	— Arlington Hts. (Hersey) 39, Waukegan 31
At Normal	— Danville (H.S.) 66, Quincy (Sr.) 60
At Peoria	— Peoria (Central) 54, Freeport (Sr.) 51
At Aurora	— Maywood (Proviso East) 67, Elgin (H.S.) 57
At Chicago City Playoffs	— Chicago (Morgan Park) 84, Chicago (Phillips) 73
At DeKalb	— Oswego 64, Crystal Lake 47
At Carbondale	— Breese (Mater Dei) 66, Belleville (West) 60

Quarterfinals

Chicago Hts. (Bloom) 56, Arlington Hts. (Hersey) 51
Peoria (Central) 68, Danville (H.S.) 67
Maywood (Proviso East) 75, Chicago (Morgan Park) 55
Breese (Mater Dei) 42, Oswego 49

Semifinals

Chicago Hts. (Bloom) 67, Peoria (Central) 66
Maywood (Proviso East) 64, Breese (Mater Dei) 42

Finals

Peoria (Central) 80, Breese (Mater Dei) 55 (3rd Place)
Chicago Hts. (Bloom) 56, Maywood (Proviso East) 61 (Championship)

Championship Game

COACH: Glenn Wittenberg

COACH: Wes Mason

Maywood (61) (Proviso East)	FG	FGA	FT	FTA	PF	REB	TP
Joe Ponsetto, f	9	17	2	2	3	14	20
Roderick Floyd, f	4	6	0	1	4	10	8
Michael Stockdale, c	1	5	2	2	5	7	4
Jerry Montgomery, g	8	12	0	0	4	1	16
Doron Dobbins, g	4	8	3	8	2	5	11
Eugene Davis, g	1	3	0	2	2	2	2
Briant Johnson, f	0	0	0	0	0	0	0
Jack Karsents, f	0	0	0	0	1	0	0
TOTALS	27	51	7	15	21	47	61

Chicago Hts. (56) (Bloom)	FG	FGA	FT	FTA	PF	REB	TP
Audie Matthews, f	6	23	7	10	4	11	19
Robert McCoy, f	5	23	2	2	1	5	12
Emir Hardy, c	5	13	2	6	3	15	12
Derrick Smith, g	3	6	0	0	3	5	6
Alvin Higgins, g	2	7	1	3	2	2	5
Kelvin Small, c	0	1	0	0	2	2	0
Larry Thomas, f	1	1	0	0	1	1	2
Alan Lee, g	0	0	0	0	0	0	0
	22	74	12	21	16	46	56

Score by Quarters:

Maywood (Proviso East)	19	11	10	21 —	61
Chicago Hts. (Bloom)	16	17	10	13 —	56

Officials: Richard Deitz (McLeansboro); James Meyer (New Athens)

1974 CLASS AA CHAMPION MAYWOOD (PROVISO EAST) PIRATES—Front row: Rich Westbrook, Dan Williams, Gene Davis, Dave Ekstrom. Second row: Jerry Montgomery, Michael Stockdale, Joe Ponsetto, Roderick Floyd, Doron Dobbins. Third row: Coach John Blomquist, Briant Johnson, Marlon Thomas, Terry Williams, Ron Hodges, Jack Karstens, Coach Glenn Whittenberg.

CLASS A
1975
March 14-15, 1975
Assembly Hall, University of Illinois

Marathon Spurs Venice . . .

Venice played three overtimes to overcome Carmi in the Class A quarter-finals and then went on to win the championship. It was the third of four extra period games in two years and a rerun of Lawrenceville's success in 1974. Venice won a North-South final, upending Timothy Christian of Elmhurst 65-46 to win their fourth Class A championship. Venice's front-line produced 36 points in the title game with Jim Crowder scoring 11 points, Mike Henry 12, and Reggie Gardner 13.

Super-Sectionals

At Decatur   — Morrisonville 64, Hume (Shiloh) 59
At Charleston   — Venice 59, Carmi 58 (3 ot)
At Streator   — Buda-Sheffield (Western) 51, Lemont (Twp.) 46
At Normal   — Watseka 65, Normal (University) 59
At Carbondale   — Eldorado 58, Cairo 53
At Macomb   — Chatham (Glenwood) 54, Quincy (Catholic Boys) 51 (ot)
At East Moline   — Port Byron (Riverdale) 42, Bushnell (B.-Prairie City) 33
At Dekalb   — Elmhurst (Timothy Christian) 58, South Beloit 34

Quarterfinals

Venice 47, Morrisonville 41
Watseka 63, Buda-Sheffield (Western) 57
Eldorado 65, Chatham (Glenwood) 60
Elmhurst (Timothy Christian) 48, Port Byron (Riverdale) 18

Semifinals

Venice 57, Watseka 49
Elmhurst (Timothy Christian) 52, Eldorado 42

Finals

Watseka 74, Eldorado 65 (3rd Place)
Venice 65, Elmhurst (Timothy Christian) 46 (Championship)

Championship Game

COACH: Richard Essington

Venice (65)	FG-FGA	FT-FTA	PF	REB	TP
Reggie Gardner, f	4 6	5 5	0	8	13
James Crowder, f	4 8	3 4	3	5	11
Mike Henry, c	6 11	0 0	1	3	12
Jeff Corrie, g	3 10	0 0	2	3	6
James Turner, g	6 10	5 6	1	6	17
Mike Logan, f	0 0	2 2	0	0	2
Algie Crawford, f	0 0	4 4	0	0	4
Larry Arnold, f	0 0	0 0	0	1	0
Bernie Woodrome, c	0 0	0 0	0	0	0
Ricky Salmond, g	0 0	0 0	0	0	0
Tim Walker, c	0 0	0 0	0	0	0
TOTALS	23 45	19 21	7	30	65

COACH: Donald Greenfield

Elmhurst (46) (Timothy Christian)	FG-FGA	FT-FTA	PF	REB	TP
Tony Ratliff, f	6 10	2 2	4	6	14
B. VanderSchaaf, f	5 17	0 0	4	7	10
Jim Folgers, c	2 11	0 0	1	3	4
Howard Hoff, g	4 10	0 0	3	6	8
David Woldman, g	4 5	0 0	3	3	8
Bob Voss, f	0 0	0 0	0	0	0
Tim Bolt, c	0 0	0 0	0	0	0
Doug Slinkman, f	0 0	0 0	0	0	0
Van Seilstra, g	0 1	0 0	1	0	0
Rich Buikema, f	1 1	0 0	0	0	2
Randy VanDahm, g	0 0	0 0	0	0	0
Ted VanderNaald, g	0 0	0 0	0	0	0
	22 55	2 2	16	27	46

Score by Quarters:

Venice	17	10	19	19	— 65
Elmhurst (Timothy Christian)	6	4	14	22	— 46

Officials: Stan Decker (Normal); Mel Klitzing (Champaign)

1975 CLASS A CHAMPION VENICE RED DEVILS—Front row: Clark Ray, Lance Austin. Second row: Jeff Corrie, Mike Logan, Mike Henry, James Crowder, James Turner, Reggie Gardner. Third row: Asst. Coach Clarence Hand, Venice Govan, Tim Walker, Algie Crawford, Larrick Arnold, Rich Salmond, Coach Richard Essington.

CLASS AA
1975
March 21-22, 1975
Assembly Hall, University of Illinois

How Times Have Changed . . .

During Buddy Young's era, Chicago (Wendell Phillips) was labeled a football power due to Young's sensational ability to run with the ball. This billing underwent a major change in the 1975 Class AA tournament. Phillips rushed past Morgan Park in the Chicago playoff and bowled over Waukegan, Peoria (Richwoods), and Chicago Heights (Bloom). In Phillips' march to fame, center Larry Williams was the team's leader in scoring and rebounding.

Super-Sectionals

At Chicago	— Chicago (Phillips) 65, Chicago (Morgan Prk.) 60
At Evanston	— Waukegan 50, Park Ridge (Maine South) 41
At DeKalb	— Rockford (Auburn) 58, Aurora (West) 45
At Peoria	— Peoria (Richwoods) 94, Sterling (H.S.) 63
At Carbondale	— East St. Louis (Sr.) 89, Olney (E. Richland) 77
At Normal	— Bloomington (H.S.) 71, Decatur (Eisenhower) 63
At Aurora (East)	— Maywood (Proviso East) 72, Franklin Prk. (E. Leyden) 60
At Joliet (Central)	— Chicago Hts. (Bloom) 57, New Lenox (Lincoln-Way) 30

Quarterfinals

Chicago (Phillips) 67, Waukegan 61
Peoria (Richwoods) 65, Rockford (Auburn) 52
East St. Louis (Sr.) 73, Bloomington (H.S.) 66
Chicago Hts. (Bloom) 57, Maywood (Proviso East) 56

Semifinals

Chicago (Phillips) 86, Peoria (Richwoods) 69
Chicago Hts. (Bloom) 68, East St. Louis (Sr.) 55

Finals

East St. Louis (Sr.) 83, Peoria (Richwoods) 75 (3rd Place)
Chicago (Phillips) 76, Chicago Hts. (Bloom) 48 (Championship)

Championship Game

COACH: Herb Brown

Chicago (76) (Phillips)	FG	FGA	FT	FTA	PF	REB	TP
Robert Byrd, f	5	13	2	3	1	8	12
Norman Perry, f	5	10	3	5	1	7	13
Larry Williams, c	12	20	4	6	0	14	28
Vincent Robinson, g	2	10	3	6	1	4	7
Marty Murray, g	1	3	0	0	5	0	2
Herman Hoskins, g-f	0	2	0	0	2	0	0
Teddy James, f-c	2	4	1	1	1	3	5
Levon Richmond, g	1	1	1	2	2	0	3
Darius Cleamons, g-f	0	1	0	0	0	1	0
Ike Deal, f-c	1	2	0	0	1	2	2
Louis Reymond, g	2	7	0	3	3	1	4
TOTALS	31	73	14	26	17	52	76

COACH: Wes Mason

Chicago Hts. (48) (Bloom)	FG	FGA	FT	FTA	PF	REB	TP
Larry Lowe, f	4	9	0	0	1	10	8
Robert McCoy, f	1	13	5	6	2	15	7
Kelvin Small, c	4	11	0	0	4	4	8
Ernest Harper, g	1	2	0	0	3	0	2
David Barba, g	0	1	2	3	2	4	2
Alan Lee, g	5	13	0	0	2	2	10
Anthony Kennedy, f	0	2	0	0	1	4	0
Joe Hagemaster, g	1	2	3	5	2	2	5
Jeff Segert, g	3	5	0	0	2	0	6
Columbus Terell, c	0	0	0	0	0	0	0
Kevin Carrabine, f	0	1	0	0	0	1	0
	19	59	10	14	19	46	48

Score by Quarters:

Chicago (Phillips)	19	9	18	30	— 76
Chicago Hts. (Bloom)	10	10	12	16	— 48

Officials: Wilton Crotz (West Peoria); Wayne Meece (Normal)

1975 CLASS AA CHAMPION CHICAGO (WENDELL PHILLIPS) WILDCATS—
Front row: Herman Hoskins, Ike Deal, Norman Perry, Teddy James, Vincent Robinson, Levon Richmond, Larry Williams, Louis Reymond, Darius Cleamons, Robert Byrd, Marty Murray. Managers, C. Martin, G. Wilkes, Coach Herb Brown.

CLASS A
1976
March 12-13, 1976
Assembly Hall, University of Illinois

Moving Up From Fourth To First . . .

When Decatur defeated Danville for the championship in 1936, Mt. Pulaski finished fourth. The school wasn't heard from again until the Class A tournament was contested a fifth time. After dominating its first three opponents, Mt. Pulaski went home with the championship. This success resulted from Mt. Pulaski's 59-58 conquest of Oneida (ROVA) to finalize a 29-2 record. Lawrenceville, riding Jay Shidler's collection of 49 points, won the third place game. Shidler captured the tournament scoring record with 157 points in four games.

Super-Sectionals

At Rock Island — Oneida (ROVA) 58, Port Byron (Riverdale) 52
At Normal   — Bloomington (Central Catholic) 59, Watseka 57
At DeKalb   — Aurora (Marmion) 71, Winnebago 61
At Charleston — Lawrenceville 59, Lebanon 50
At Macomb   — Havana 64, Pleasant Plains 59
At Pontiac   — Buda-Sheffield (Western) 48, Palos Hts. (Chicago Christian) 46
At Carbondale — Eldorado 71, Cairo 56
At Decatur   — Mt. Pulaski 67, Westville 56

Quarterfinals

Oneida (ROVA) 49, Bloomington (Central Catholic) 46
Lawrenceville 66, Aurora (Marmion) 61
Buda-Sheffield (Western) 64, Havana 54
Mt. Pulaski 76, Eldorado 66

Semifinals

Oneida (ROVA) 77, Lawrenceville 70
Mt. Pulaski 74, Buda-Sheffield (Western) 56

Finals

Lawrenceville 65, Buda-Sheffield (Western) 57 (3rd Place)
Mt. Pulaski 59, Oneida (ROVA) 58 (Championship)

Championship Game

COACH: Edward Butkovich

COACH: Bob Merdedith

Mt. Pulaski (59)	FG-FGA		FT-FTA		PF	REB	TP
Jeff Clements, f	9	21	0	0	0	4	18
David Thompson, f	6	11	0	1	0	6	12
Jeff Anderson, c	9	19	1	1	2	16	19
David Welch, g	1	7	2	3	1	2	4
Brad Gibbs, c	2	6	0	0	0	5	4
Scott Moore, g	1	4	0	1	1	1	2
TOTALS	28	68	3	6	4	40	59

Oneida (ROVA) (58)	FG-FGA		FT-FTA		PF	REB	TP
Steve Holmes, f	0	2	0	0	3	2	0
John Bloss, f	0	2	0	0	1	2	0
Dave Johnson, c	13	22	2	3	3	12	28
Roger Saline, g	6	11	0	0	3	2	12
Dwight Peterson, g	4	7	0	0	1	4	8
Randy Dooley, g	2	4	0	0	0	2	4
Mike Shepherd, f	0	1	0	0	1	0	0
Steve Johnson, f	3	3	0	0	1	0	6
	28	52	2	3	13	28	58

Score by Quarters:

Mt. Pulaski	14	20	11	14 —	59
Oneida (ROVA)	12	23	11	12 —	58

Officials: Dave Dwyer (Peoria); William England (Peoria)

1976 CLASS A CHAMPION MT. PULASKI HILLTOPPERS—Front row: Bob Behle, Gary Helton, Danny Durchholz, Pat Przykopanski, Brad Gibbs, Scott Moore. Second row: Asst. James Copper, Asst. Joe Zimmerman, Gayle Cyrulik, David Welch, David Thompson, John Olson, Jeff Anderson, Jeff Clements, Head Coach Ed Butkovich.

CLASS AA
1976
March 19-20, 1976
Assembly Hall, University of Illinois

Shot Heard 'Round The State . . .

It was simultaneous—the buzzer sounding with the ball in the air. The shot funneled through the basket and the Class AA championship went to Morgan Park of Chicago instead of Aurora (West). Laird Smith was the youngster who provided the sensational breath-taking finish. It looked like Aurora was a winner going into the fourth quarter with a 33-26 edge. Not so. The Morgan Parkers responded with a 19-point spree in the last period to take a 45-44 thriller. Smith's game-winning shot came after teammate Levi Cobb controlled a jump ball with 5 seconds to go.

Super-Sectionals

At Joliet	— Dolton (Thornridge) 66, Homewood (H.-Flossmoor) 64 (ot)
At DeKalb	— Aurora (West) 53, McHenry 40
At Carbondale	— Marion 76, Edwardsville 74
At Normal	— Decatur (Eisenhower) 75, Normal (Comm.) 65 (ot)
At Chicago	— Chicago (Morgan Park) 75, Chicago (Vocational) 60
At Peoria	— Galesburg 52, Moline 47
At Evanston	— Wilmette (Loyola) 50, Skokie (Niles West) 44
At Aurora (West)	— Oak Park (O.P.-River Forest) 71, Elgin (H.S.) 55

Quarterfinals

Aurora (West) 82, Dolton (Thornridge) 52
Decatur (Eisenhower) 81, Marion 66
Chicago (Morgan Park) 53, Galesburg 48
Oak Park (O.P.-River Forest) 56, Wilmette (Loyola) 53 (OT)

Semifinals

Aurora (West) 63, Decatur (Eisenhower) 51
Chicago (Morgan Park) 59, Oak Park (O.P.-River Forest) 58

Finals

Oak Park (O.P.-River Forest) 73, Decatur (Eisenhower) 61 (3rd Place)
Chicago (Morgan Park) 45, Aurora (West) 44 (Championship)

Championship Game

COACH: William Warden

Chicago (45) (Morgan Park)	FG-FGA	FT-FTA	PF	REB	TP
Laird Smith, f	5 10	4 7	1	5	14
Eric Bowman, f	5 12	0 0	2	7	10
Levi Cobb, c	8 15	3 4	4	7	19
Jeffrey Berry, g	0 6	0 0	4	1	0
David Johnson, g	1 5	0 0	3	2	2
Anthony Ferguson, f	0 2	0 0	2	1	0
TOTALS	19 50	7 11	16	31	45

COACH: John McDougal

Aurora (44) (West)	FG-FGA	FT-FTA	PF	REB	TP
Jay Bryant, f	3 16	8 9	5	8	14
Ron Hicks, f	4 5	5 8	4	8	13
Bruce Johnson, c	2 3	1 2	2	7	5
Joe Michels, g	1 4	0 0	0	1	2
Larry Hatchett, g	1 9	2 3	2	6	4
Randy Schulz, f	0 0	0 0	1	0	0
Jerry Harris, g	3 5	0 0	1	4	6
	14 42	16 22	15	38	44

Score by Quarters:

Chicago (Morgan Park)	12	6	8	19 —	45
Aurora (West)	12	9	12	11 —	44

Officials: Ron Fahnestock (Canton); Larry Leitner (Pekin)

1976 CLASS AA CHAMPION CHICAGO (MORGAN PARK) MUSTANGS—Top row: Coach Bill Warden, Laird Smith, Eric Bowman, Levi Cobb, Everett Bell, Tony Ferguson. Second row: Kevin Glover, Greg Harris, David Johnson, Warren Morgan. Bottom row: Morris Griffin, Cornell Smith, Jeff Berry.

Chapter 3

Put Me in, Coach!
The Coaches

SHERRILL HANKS

When Sherrill Hanks left the Illinois high school coaching ranks he moved his office from Quincy High School to Quincy College, and he kept right on doing when he does best, winning. Under Sherrill's direction, the high school Blue Devils won 514 games in 24 seasons and linked together 17 consecutive 20-game winning seasons. Moving up to the collegiate ranks, Quincy's Hawks won 23 of 32 first season games for the school's best ever record.

Sherrill considered it a good break when he didn't have to leave Quincy in moving from high school to collegiate competition. "Quincy is a great basketball city, definitely one of the very best in the country," Hanks noted as he described an oddity. That would be the 3,500 seat capacity of Quincy's high school gym compared to 2,500 seats at Quincy College.

The man, who was an outstanding athlete for Shurtleff as a collegian, doesn't expect any trouble filling the college gym because of the vast interest in the Hawks. The man who fuels this interest is Sherrill Hanks, a super salesman as well as a winning coach. During the basketball season Hanks has a Saturday morning radio show and a Sunday night television program. Both shows are devoted strictly to the American game Doctor James Naismith invented by nailing a couple of bottomless peach baskets to the wall in the 1860s.

Boosting basketball wasn't always one of Sherrill's favorite pastimes. During his teen times in the Wood River area, baseball was his first love. Actually it was a parlay of baseball and the St. Louis Cardinals which shared Sherrill's loyalty. Hanks recalls the times when a dime would buy a roundtrip bus-trolley ticket from Wood River to St. Louis. What about the price of a ticket to get inside old Sportsman's Park once he reached Saint Louis?

"Never was that a worry. I was a member of the Cardinals' Knot Hole Gang, and that assured gratis admission," Hanks explained as he talked about such famous former day heroes as Pepper Martin, the brothers Cooper, Mort and Walker, and Marty Marion.

Between family and friends, Sherrill has put together a pretty good scouting system. Mike, his son, moved from Indiana University with the rank of graduate assistant under Bobby Knight, to fulltime assistant status working with Bob Weltich at the University of Mississippi. Krisna, the Hanks' daughter, is a cheerleader at Indiana. George Gaunder, a former teammate at Shurtleff, is a highly successful coach at St. Joseph, Michigan, High School. Purdue's Tom Scheffler, a 6-foot-10 center, is one of Gaunder's more recent discoveries.

If Hanks had the authority to make one change in the basketball rules, what move would he make?

"I think," Sherrill began, "we have to do something about the play under the boards. A kid goes in, leaps high straight up trying to score. A defensive man takes the spot the offensive player has just vacated. If he stands still he's going to the free throw line if the offensive man hits him on the way down.

"We stress shooting. We want increased scoring. I don't think that rule is fair, and something should be done about changing it. The shooter has to have a landing place, and he can't change his course at the last second to avoid hitting the defensive player."

Many coaches agree with Hanks' concern, but still nothing has been done about what is called "muscular play under the boards."

Meanwhile, it sounds like roll call when Sherrill reads his list of personal standouts. It starts with Rick Rineberg in 1962, and continues through in this manner:

Larry Gross, 1963;	Larry Moore, 1972;
Gary Thompson, 1965;	Bob Spear, 1973;
Billy Gay, 1967;	Bob Wisman, 1974;
Richard Hickman, 1969;	Darrell Douglas, 1975;
Tony Ball, 1971;	Terry Laaker, 1975.

Gone are the days when special trains carried fans to and from the storied series between Galesburg and Quincy. Then it was said, and with good reason, that 51 percent of the fans were attracted to the play between the Blue Devils and the Silver Streaks, and the other 49 percent showed up for the good theater starring Hanks and his Galesburg counterpart, John Thiel. Too bad Ed Sullivan didn't live long enough to book the Hanks-Thiel act on his national network variety show for television.

DAWDY HAWKINS

There was absolutely no evidence that this was the house where the winningest basketball coach in Pekin's majestic basketball history lived. No trophies. No pennants. No autographed basketballs. No yellowing programs. No fading team pictures. It was just a homey home on Sheridan Road in the city's white collar district.

The head of the house, Mayor William L. Waldmeier's administrative assistant, cushioned himself into his easy chair. Aleene, his wife, busied herself checking the food store shopping lists. Mindy, the friendly silver poodle, piled her toys at her master's feet and dared him to play, pitch and catch.

Finally, the talk shifted to basketball, and the man who led his beloved Pekin Chinks to two state championships within four years, never was in better voice. "I've been out of coaching and teaching long enough now to know age isn't a factor in anybody's life as far as new opportunities are concerned," an articulate Dawson Hawkins said with the same firmness he used to express himself during a pregame pep talk to his team.

"It's a brand new ball game now," the man both friend and foe called Dawdy continued, "because all you have to do is stay healthy and never lose your desire. Especially in athletics. It was a player-coach communication factor when I started. It was still the same factor when I retired. Never did I feel I wasn't within total communication with all of my players all the time.

This wasn't any short term relationship. Dawdy coached for 37 years, minus a two-year stint in the Navy. It all started for him in Eagle, Nebraska, in 1937. He touched down at three other schools in Cornhusker country before moving into Illinois, chalking up new dimensions in the Peoria-Pekin area for a quarter of a century. He spent 11 years at Peoria (Central) before moving across the river to launch a 14-year tenure in Pekin.

Hawkins envisions all athletics, both amateur and professional, continuing to escalate to new and greater heights. "Society has changed, but I haven't seen too many changes in the attitude of athletes," Dawdy claimed. "The public often makes greater demands, but I don't feel that sports are endangered. The players are bigger, better, faster, and more intelligent. At the very top level of pro sports I'm concerned about the future. The staggering salaries they are being paid, I feel, are way out of line. This could deter progress in the future."

When Pekin's popular professor of basketball launched his coaching career in Eagle, Nebraska, the game was regarded as a second rate sport there. Then, as now, Nebraska was a football state and everything else was second fiddle. Very little was done to emphasize the sport at the high school level because enrollments were low and teams had to travel great distances to find equal competition. Due to these handicaps, the public's early enthusiasm was slow in building.

Dawdy was quick to learn the situation was just reversed when he arrived at Peoria (Central). The emphasis in central and downstate Illinois was on excelling, and this progress fused enormous enthusiasm with improved coaching and facilities.

When he moved to Pekin, Hawkins was spared the job of developing his own feeder system—so important to every program at any level. "When I arrived here, Pekin had a junior high school program that went down to the sixth grade," Dawdy recalled. "The city had three junior high schools, and all of them competed at the state level. Actually, there is a total of five, because the high school draws from both North and South Pekin within the corporate limits."

Hawkins believes in strong assistants and has the track record to prove it. Joe Stowell, longtime coach at Bradley University, was one of Dawdy's assistants at Peoria (Central); Bob Ortegel, presently head coach at Drake University, spent three years working with Hawkins in Pekin, and another of Dawdy's aides, Duncan Reid, is one of Ted Owens' assistants at Kansas. Harry Whitaker, who also worked under Hawkins, took a different trail. He became the superintendent of schools in Peoria, while a namesake, Dick Whitaker, moved into the Naperville school system.

Inasmuch as Chicago and its suburbs have captured nine straight Class AA championships since Pekin won its second jewel in the state crown in 1967, has this dominance taken something away from the Elite Eight competition?

"That, I think, depends on the person watching the game," Dawdy reasoned. "As far as I'm concerned, the caliber of basketball is great. It doesn't matter to me whether the teams are from Chicago or wherever. The game we are seeing at the high school level these days is completely fantastic."

While the balance of power has shifted northward during recent seasons, Hawkins has noted a general growth on a state wide basis with more good teams and many more good players. Originally, Dawdy was opposed to the two-class system. Now he's very much in favor of it—branding it a tremendous asset to the overall picture.

"Now we have good players, statewide, regardless of the size of the school they come from," Hawkins stressed, "or the size of the community they represent." Dawdy used the 1976 North-South All-Star game as the best example of the situation.

"I was fortunate to be the head coach of the South squad," the former Pekin mentor began, "and on paper the North squad possessed most of the superior players. To combat this claim I told our players

I didn't believe there were any boundary lines for good basketball talent. A good player could come from any community. Apparently they agreed with me because the South won the Class AA game 86-72."

While his main concern was coaching and winning the Class AA game, Hawkins nevertheless found time to watch the sensational shooting antics of Lawrenceville's Jay Shidler in the Class A game and practice sessions. "The boy is unbelievable," Dawdy claimed. "I've never seen anything like him. He's definitely in the same category with two pure shooters I watched in the Big Ten some seasons back: Jimmy Rayl at Indiana and Rick Mount at Purdue.

"Shidler is so exciting he will fill the fieldhouse every game he plays. Inasmuch as I've lived in Illinois long enough to become a native, I really hoped the boy would enroll at Illinois.

"I have no direct ties with the university, but Shidler would have been a natural for the Illini. I was hoping both Jay Shidler and Levi Cobb would attend Illinois. Cobb, I hear, is there, and recently I read where Shidler was enrolled at the University of Kentucky."

Hawkins blames the geared-up recruiting of high school players, mainly the blue chippers, on the athletic directors at the college and university level. Dawdy thinks they are out to make basketball a big pay sport near the football plateau. Proving his own I.Q. is always higher than the Dow Jones' daily averages, the Pekin coach credited Cazzie Russell for turning the basketball program right around at a football orientated university, the University of Michigan.

"Winning attracts kids, as Bobby Knight is proving at Indiana right now," Dawdy claimed.

They didn't have to run any bingo parties for Pekin basketball during recent seasons. The Chinks grossed $40,000 a year, and this income paid for all the other sports' programs except football. The Pekin gym seats 4,500. After the visiting team is allotted 400 tickets, the remaining 4,100 are assigned to students and season ticket holders—and there are very few noshows.

After voting "no" on talk that the installation of the 30-second time clock is just up the road for high school basketball in Illinois, Hawkins explained: "I've always felt that squads with less material can overcome this deficit with strategy. We've won games just like other coaches have won games by using the clock during the game. It's part of strategy.

"I'll always be opposed to any rule or change that minimizes a coach's philosophy. It isn't fair to take away any of his incentive and weapons. The pros have a no-zone defense rule, but I've never seen it enforced. The pivot man is always zoning, and they are switching all the time in what is strictly a match-up zone."

Speaking of the pros, Hawkins doesn't object when his players attempt to mimic plays and patterns in the play-for-pay game. "If the kids don't over do it, and the coach can regulate that, I think this mimicking develops imagination and desire," he said.

During Pekin's two championship seasons, the Chinks won 61 games and lost five. "Our 1964 team," Dawdy explained, "was very small and quick. Also very smart and intelligent. The 1967 team was much bigger, physically. Maybe as much as 100 percent stronger. Also we had a Fred Miller and a Barry Moran—both very excellent players.

"Miller came along as a sophomore in 1965. We went 28 and 2 on the season, but that isn't all the story. We played in the annual holiday tournament in Pontiac that season, meeting Lockport (Central). We won the game by 27 points. Now we played Lockport (Central) again in the Super-Sectional, and they end up beating us by eight.

"How and why do these things happen? If somebody would detail all the intangibles involved in sports, maybe I could provide an answer or some insight. There are as many intangibles in high school basketball as there are in a World Series or a Super Bowl game. Sometimes coaches or managers can cope with 'em. Sometimes they can't, and that is the difference between winning and losing."

There is a heap of basketball savvy tucked away in the mind of Dawson Hawkins even if his name sounds more like that of an orchestra leader than a coach. Win or lose—and he didn't lose too many—Dawdy is a fascinating gentleman. Also the molder of state championship teams in both Illinois and Nebraska.

THE HERRIN BROTHERS
Homer Herrin, a Methodist minister in Bridgeport, had a set schedule for his two sons: Ron and Rich. They would go to church Sunday and Wednesday nights, and they could play basketball Tuesday, Friday and Saturday nights. Just like most small towns in the 1930s, one of Bridgeport's main attractions was a pool hall—a mecca for most youngsters, although it was out-of-bounds.

Nevertheless, Rich Herrin never turned down an opportunity to visit the hall to accept or issue a challenge. "Many times Rich would be lining up an important shot," Brother Ron recalled, "and somebody would yell: 'Hey Rich, here comes your father!' He would rush out the back door at incredible speeds, and I do believe that is how he developed his quickness."

Whatever the reason, Rich, three years younger than Ron, joined his brother as the Herrins won 15 varsity letters between them at Bridgeport High School, and a total of 21 more at McKendree College in Lebanon. While the likes of Ken and George Brett, and Gaylord and Jim Perry were putting their famous brother acts together, the Herrins were turning high school rivalries in Illinois into family feuds.

This was true when Ron launched his coaching career at Freeburg, and brother Rich was stationed at Okawville. Three times Freeburg and Okawville met in head-to-head combat, and Okawville won two of these showdowns. Seeking to add status in their climb up the ladder, Ron moved to Olney, and Rich to Benton. Twice Benton and Olney have met in tournament play, and each has scored a victory.

Now Rich has a 3-2 edge, and Ron is completely void of any ideas when he will have an opportunity to square this family competition at three games apiece. Maybe it will come in the next sectional tournament involving Benton and Olney. Maybe it won't, but this much is certain: the brothers would dislike eliminating each other in tournament traffic.

At the outset of their careers it appeared there would never be a family rivalry as coaches. When Rich entered McKendree, he planned on a pre-dentistry course. Then he changed his mind and decided to become a coach. Who is to say he made a bad decision inasmuch as the Brothers Herrin had won 72 games between them going into the 1976–1977 season? Rich's record was 428-133, Ron's 344-210.

Ron, who grew up seeing and cheering for the St. Louis Cardinals, was looking for a job after he finished a two-year service stint in June of 1954. His first stop was the office of Superintendent Leslie Purdy in Lebanon, where he had done some pre-war practice teaching. Purdy had one opening, a seventh-eighth grade teacher-coach. "I was discharged from the army one week, and in the class room the next," Ron explained, "because I was so happy to have a job."

One year later Ron was advised of an opening at Freeburg for a basketball coach. He applied. He was given the job. Freeburg won 93 games and lost only 43 during his five-season stay. The next stop was Olney (East Richland), in 1960.

Ron's list of achievements at Olney is as long as his arm. He was honored by two different newspapers. The Decatur Herald & Review named him Southern Illinois' Coach of the Year in 1972, and the Evansville (Indiana) Courier & Press encored this tribute in 1975.

Always one to take a stand and voice an opinion regarding anything which will build basketball, Ron originally wasn't in favor of Illinois' shift to class competition—and said so. "With just one class," the elder of the Herrin brothers claimed, "I thought Illinois had something very special. Also I was hoping the IHSA would return to the "Sweet Sixteen" format. When I'm coaching we have this present setup with the Super-Sectional. When I was playing we had the "Sweet Sixteen", and I liked it best of all.

"Now I can see where class basketball has been very good for the smaller schools, and that is most helpful. When 14,000 people turn out for the Class A tournament, that's real interest. Maybe a few more persons will attend the Class AA tournament, but the help for the smaller schools already has been established.

"I still say it will be difficult for a southern school to win in double A against the north, but maybe it will happen. As I see it, the southern schools are battling numbers, and that will be tough to top."

Just like so many players-turned-coach, Ron is grateful for the influence of his Bridgeport High School coach, Frank "Doc" Hunsaker. "He played football at the University of Illinois with Red Grange," Ron remembered, "and he had a most impressive background. Hunsaker coached all sports during my junior and senior years."

Later Hunsaker moved on to Robinson, where he turned out some outstanding teams.

Have Ron and Rich ever given any thought to sharing a combined head coachship?

"Never outside of the talking stage," the Olney coach answered, "and we're still not sure if it's workable. Maybe more so at the college level when the kids are more mature and have had additional experience."

There is one thing certain with Ron Herrin: he has no timetable for the future outside of the job he enjoys the most: working with kids. "I'm not sure I have any desire to be in administration outside of an athletic directorship," Ron mused, and it was evident he wasn't trying to fool anybody including himself.

While the State Tournament is the name of the game in Illinois, Rich owns a milestone every coach in the land would be happy to have. He's developed three undefeated teams in regular season play: 1966, 1967, and 1975.

During the decade of the 1960s Rich Herrin-coached Benton teams have won eight South Seven Conference championships, and finished second twice. Three Ranger machines have advanced to the Elite Eight, and four others lost out in a photo finish. Proving nobody wins without the horses, Rich has coached several standout players like Doug Collins, everybody's All-American, at Illinois State University, before turning pro to play in the NBA. The rest of the line forms on the right: Rich Yunkus, Georgia Tech; Dan Johnson, Western Kentucky; Bill Smith, Georgia Tech; Robert Corn,

Memphis State; Paul Dinkins, Creighton, and Rob Dunbar, Western Kentucky.

In 1967 the Dapper Dan Club of Pittsburgh picked Rich as the co-coach of its United States All-Star High School team. Due to IHSA rules concerning All-Star games, the former day pool player from Bridgeport was forced to decline the honor. Ron and Rich aren't twins, but they could be considering of closeness of their outstanding achievements:

RON

High School

- Eight varsity letters
- All-Conference in basketball

College

- Ten varsity letters
- All-Conference in football
- Basketball captain twice

Coaching

- Record (thru 1976) 344-210
- Three conference championships
- One "Sweet Sixteen" team
- Five regional tournament winners
- Southern Illinois Coach of the Year (2)

RICH

High School

- Seven varsity letters
- All-Conference in basketball

College

- Eleven varsity letters
- All-Conference Basketball twice

- Record (thru 1976) 428-133
- Eight conference championships
- Four state tournament teams
- Thirteen regional tournament winners
- Southern Illinois Coach of the Year (4)

Small wonder Freddie Klein, writing a Hoopster Hoopla story in the Wall Street Journal, covered almost everything in Benton from blazers, bags, and basketballs popping out of a mechanized hoop after a successful tip-in has been completed in practice. When 1,300 people show up for a grade school game, Rich Herrin isn't the only excited person in Benton's coal-mining community.

TONY MAFFIA

One of the best fast breaks in the history of basketball at Chicago's South Shore High School, oddly enough, involved the principal, Marie Voy Brewster. The year was 1944, and the event was the Illinois High School Boys' State Basketball Tournament in Champaign.

The South Shore team arrived the day before the opening of the "Sweet Sixteen" and was housed in the back end of a restaurant. Carpets were hung over a wire stretched from wall to wall and beds were moved in behind the carpets.

The players were assigned two to a bed, one of which collapsed during the night. During the scurrying to use the limited toilet facilities the next morning, somebody asked, "What is Miss Brewster going to say when she sees our home away from home?"

Reacting with the speed of lightning, Coach Tony Maffia claimed: "That can't happen. If she sees this place, she will order the team back to Chicago on the first available train."

Within a short time, Maffia assigned a courier to meet the train in the Champaign depot and tell the principal that advance plans had been changed. Everybody would meet in Huff gym before South Shore's first game.

"She was our number one fan," Maffia recalled, "but she never would stand for the boys spending another minute in such dingy quarters. No way would she have been blamed for ordering the team back home under the circumstances."

Later, everything ended "all's well" based on one of the oldest laws of sports—the spoils go to the winner! South Shore won its first round test, beating Quincy 62-38. After its loss, the Quincy team decided to return home. How did this help South Shore? The Chicago team moved into the improved hotel quarters the Quincy team vacated—and managed to sleep well for the rest of the tournament.

South Shore also played well during the rest of the tournament, ending in third place to become only the second Chicago representative to finish among the first four in the tournament's history. Harrison did it first, taking third in 1931. Small wonder some tournament critics used to call the Sweet Sixteen field "Fifteen teams and Chicago."

At the outset of the school year in 1941, Maffia was pretty much a

Maverick settling into a gym teacher's role at Crane with nary a single thought about South Shore or coaching basketball. Suddenly, South Shore needed a basketball coach, and Nat Wasserman, the school's football coach, nominated Maffia for the job.

Wasserman's recommendation was strong enough to assure Maffia the new assignment, and Tony moved into the new school where the enrollment was a blend of youths from the homes of blue and white collar workers on Chicago's southeast side. The first two years under Maffia, South Shore qualified for the city league playoffs. Then his third season proved a charm: the city championship and automatic entry into the "Sweet Sixteen."

"There was some snickering," the mild mannered Italian began, "when I said I figured we could win our first two games. After that I wasn't sure because I didn't know how the kids would respond to the busy finish, two games on the last day of the tournament.

"After winning from Quincy and then Rockford (West) 39-33 we lost a one pointer 48-47 to Elgin and defeated Champaign 52-34 for third place. That was the year Taylorville went unbeaten in 45 straight games to win it all. Trying to offset our lack of height we used a flexible zone defense, and it was our best weapon because some teams just didn't know how to react against it."

At the start of his tenure at South Shore—90 victories in 107 games for a .841 percentage spanning eight seasons—most of Maffia's experience had been gained as a player. "Maff" played in the long-ago national high school tournament at the University of Chicago and later in the Knights of Columbus League.

Salesmanship, Tony admits, was his first important job after he arrived at South Shore. Many of the players he envisioned as members of his senior team had different ideas about the class of competition they desired to tackle.

"We had the five-foot-seven rule at the time," Maffia remembered, "and almost all of our shorter players favored the junior division. I was convinced they had the skills to play on the senior team. Now it was my job to sell them my thinking. It wasn't easy, but one by one they finally came around to the senior squad.

"During that first season I made a mistake. I was working with 15 and frequently 17 kids, and that was too many, especially from an equal-time standpoint for both practice and playing. During the nightly scrimmages I would try to work around to the 10 players I wanted in building the seniors' varsity team."

After South Shore repeated as city champion in 1947, Tony credited Jake Fendley with making it possible for him to compare it most favorably with the third place finishers three seasons earlier. Whereas the 1944 Chicago representative was eliminated in the semifinals, the 1947 team's first loss came in the quarterfinals. Paris, the eventual winner, took out South Shore 49-37 after Maffia's crew upended Galesburg 43-37.

At the tournament's end Fendley was named to the all-tournament team to keep pace with Paul Schnackenberg, who was an all-tourney selection in 1944.

In putting together an .804 career percentage spanning 20 seasons, Tony is most proud of the fact that not one of his teams at South Shore or Dunbar ever missed making the post-season playoffs. "That, to me," Maffia mused, "is the idea of the game—go as far as you can!"

Offensively, Maffia never was an advocate of pattern play, favoring quickness and pet maneuvers instead. "We'd stress set plays in out-of-bounds situations," Tony noted, "trying for four or five extra baskets. Frequently, this emphasis would be the difference in the outcome of the game."

Another factor in South Shore's success was the feeder system the coach used in picking future players. "We had a High Y program, and I would officiate these games—the better to follow each individual's progress in prepping for the varsity," Maffia remembered.

Although he's retired from coaching, Tony has some definite opinions about basketball. He's opposed to the return of the dunk shot, billing it as "something spectacular the pros can use strictly for show." He hopes the two-shot technical foul will help improve coach conduct on the bench, but he refuses to believe it until it happens.

He is completely convinced that the best of the Illinois boys' basketball teams can play anybody anywhere—and win!

SPIN SALARIO

Basketball buffs called Coach Isadore "Spin" Salario's wide open and running offense at Chicago (Marshall) "Organized Bedlam". During a five-season span with Spin, the Commandos followed their own "Marshall Plan" to win four Public League championships, the same number of all-Chicago titles, and two State Tournament Crowns. Equally as amazing was Marshall's record of 86 victories in 92 games, discovering prep paradise by capturing the State's super showdown in Champaign in 1958 and 1960. What happened to the Commandos in 1959? Marshall was eliminated in the Super-Sectional by Waukegan in Northwestern University's McGaw Hall in Evanston.

Marshall became the first Chicago Public League Representative to win the State Tournament history in 1958 when the Commandos gunned down Rock Falls 70-64 to climax a perfect 30-0 record. Re-

FIRST IN ASSEMBLY HALL—The first championship game played in the Assembly Hall was in 1963 when Chicago (Carver) nipped Centralia, 53-52, in one of the greatest championship games in State Tournament history. A total crowd of 106,201 for the four sessions jammed the new hardwood mushroom, and 16,183 saw the championship battle. In this photo, Carver's Curtis Kirk (43) snares a rebound over Centralia's Carl Heinrichsmeyer late in the contest. Other Carver players pictured are Joe Allen (35), Van Bell (15) and Kenneth Maxey (55). Other orphans shown are Herb Williams (33 and behind Bell) and Cliff Berger. Carver won when reserve Anthony Smedley fired home a rebound jump shot from the far right corner at the final horn. (Photo By Champaign News-Gazette)

peating this success in 1960, Marshall routed Bridgeport 79-55 for victory No. 30 in 32 games.

Despite the derailment in the 1959 Super-Sectional, ace George Wilson joined some very select company—remember the fabulous Whiz Kids, Lou Boudreau, and Dike Eddleman?—when he was selected to the All-State team three straight seasons.

Salario agrees with Hollywood's claims that movies are your best entertainment buy. "I've always considered our 1958 team the best example of my coaching philosophy," Spin said, "and rerun the films of our win over Rock Falls when I study basketball. I've always said give me three key players, and I'll have a winning season geared to a goal of 100 points per game. Why 100 points? Because I feel you'll always win a lot more than you lose with 100 points on the board.

"I don't believe in running up the score, but I'm just as adamant about telling kids not to pass up opportunities for points. I've never had much of a record winning or losing one-point games because my teams don't play that close. I remember a Marshall-Dunbar meeting some seasons ago.

"We had a five-point lead with about a minute and a half to play. We didn't sit on the ball, and quickly Dunbar tied it up with 30 seconds still remaining. With 22 seconds showing on the board—I'll never forget that sight—Dunbar had a shot and three taps at the basket. I felt like I was sitting at the bottom of the barrel waiting for the ball to drop when George Wilson came through heavy traffic with the ball.

"I don't know how he managed it, but suddenly there he was alone with the ball and the clock ran out with the score tied. In our huddle before the overtime, I told the kids to forget caution. I wanted them to play the overtime the same way they would the first or forth quarter. Don't bother to watch the clock. Just play the only way you know how. We won the game by nine, outscoring Dunbar 10 to 1 in the extra period.

"The next day some of the newspapers and people in basketball criticized me for not protecting the lead when we could have won in regulation time. That is their privilege, but it was opposed to my philosophy. I coached one way for close to 25 years, and I wasn't going to change for 90 seconds."

Salario is a native Chicagoan who grew up on the west side. He was a frequent visitor to the American Boys Commonwealth Club where basketball is the game of the day every day. Spin remembers when the black youngsters followed the Jewish kids into the neighborhood, and the popularity of basketball continued. Then his name was "Spinach" Salario, and he ran as an entry with "Turkey" Stillman.

Who sliced the Spinach to cut his nickname to Spin? "Really I can't answer that. Maybe one of the kids who tired of calling me Spinach," Salario chortled.

Following the customary frank party line practiced by 99.9 percent of basketball coaches from Maine to Washington, and Minnesota to Texas, Spin explained: "I had hoped for bigger things in the game. Maybe a chance to coach pro basketball. I've always used a structured offense. Also I believe in spot shooting—the same way the pros spot shoot. Since 1950 I've held four different coaching jobs, and I'm happy to say I've enjoyed good communication with every athlete who ever played for me."

Moving along the coach trail, Spin stopped first at Tilden Tech for three years. He spent the next five at Marshall before shifting to college at Chicago State for 10, and Chicago Northeastern for six.

When Salario talks about individual players he reminisces glowingly as he recounts the achievements of George Wilson, M.C. Thompson, Steve Thomas, Bobby Jones, Tyrone Johnson, and Ralph Wells, who graduated at mid-term and missed the Commandos' successful invasion of Champaign in 1958. "I do believe Thomas, who shot from the corner, and Jones, who worked on the right guard side of our offense, were two of the best shooters I've ever seen in high school competition," the man enthused.

Although he's been involved in almost as many great games as any winning coach in the craft, Spin can spin many interesting tales about Marshall's 67-63 defeat of DeLaSalle in the Chicago city championship game before a record crowd of 15,642 in the Chicago Stadium. "It was whirlwind basketball at its very best," Salario concluded.

The Crane graduate received his BA at Chicago Teachers' college, picking up a year's credits when he was assigned to Louisiana State University in the Army's Specialist Training program. Spin attended Northwestern to get his Masters, and spent 10 consecutive summers at the University of Wisconsin to earn his Doctorate.

Of the countless compliments he's received during his win-packed career, Spin enjoys recalling Forddy Anderson's observation when he scouted Marshall checking recruits for Michigan State in the late 1950s. "Based on what I saw in this game today, Marshall should be playing in the NCAA Tournament," Anderson quipped.

Visitors to the Salario home are treated to some most unusual entertainment. Everytime the telephone rings, Spin's dwarf Parakeet flies atop his shoulder to join in the conversation. "I call the parakeet 'Oscar', and I'm 'Felix' because we call our little act 'The Odd Couple'. Oscar really can talk up a storm."

Spin admits he would vote early and often for the return of the

Sweet Sixteen format at the State Tournament, sending all 16 teams to Champaign. "There is something special about the *Sweet Sixteen* Salario claimed, "because the fans get to see all the teams in the same setting. We played three games within 24 hours, and none of our kids complained. Marshall met Herrin, the defending champion, in the 1958 tournament at 9 P.M. on Friday. We played Aurora (West) at 3 P.M. on Saturday, and were back for the 9 P.M. game Saturday night against Rock Falls. It was a rugged schedule, but an enjoyable one."

Spin neglected to say whether the three victories, 72-59 over Herrin, 74-62 over Aurora (West) and finally a 70-64 conquest of Rock Falls keyed his and his team's joy.

Speaking of calling the turn on a prospect, Spin hit a bullseye in connection with Carver's Cazzie Russell, later an all-American at the University of Michigan who is still going strong in the NBA. "Cazzie was only a sophomore when he came into our dressing room to congratulate us after a tough tournament victory," Salario noted. "That is real class. Especially for a kid who is only a sophomore in high school. I knew right then Cazzie would reach stardom because class is the trademark of a champion."

ALEX SAUDARGAS

Basketball is a crazy game!

Why?

Because you can commit a foul, and make it work to your advantage.

Who says so?

Alex Saudargas, who devoted 35 years to the game and loved every second of it. Especially in 1955 and 1956 when he led Rockford (West) to back-to-back state championships. At the time only two other schools had accomplished this achievement: Elgin in 1924 and 1925, and Mt. Vernon, 25 years later in 1949 and 1950. Then Thornridge of Dolton won a double dip in 1971 and 1972.

Saudargas knows all about fouling for profit. He coached the play. He used it. He won with it. "Check out all the sports," Alex commanded, "and only one can come close to comparing with basketball. It's baseball. A team can intentionally walk a batter, and make it work to its advantage by getting the next batter to hit into a double play.

"That's what I mean. Many basketball teams and some baseball teams can and will foul and end up with the advantage."

Saudargas celebrated his 60th birthday July 31, 1976. At the time it was apparent the Rockford Board of Education couldn't muster funds to continue the city's athletic program at the high school level.

Alex pondered his future until the following October when he announced his retirement.

His decision wasn't nearly as rapid as one of West's sensational feats in beating Elgin for the first championship in 1955. With two minutes and 19 seconds remaining in the game, Elgin owned a 57-51 lead. With two minutes and 18 second remaining, the game was tied at 57 all. Six points in one second! It sounds incredible, but Alex remembers all the magnificent details as if the dramatic rally was unfolded yesterday.

Reacting like a play-by-play sports announcer, Saudargas recalled the rally that will never be forgotten in Rockford—or in Elgin:

"Nolden Gentry, one of the finest athletes I ever coached, shoots. After the ball left his hands, he was fouled. The shot went in, and so did the two free throws he was awarded in the one-and-one situation.

"Now they throw the ball in. Two players, one from Rockford and one from Elgin, leap high for the throw-in. They collide in mid-air as the ball bounces off their hands.

"The clock ticks off one second and stops when the referee blows his whistle. The two players fall to the floor, and the Elgin player is called for a foul. My man, Rex Barker, gets a one-and-one, and makes both free throws.

"That's our six points, but it isn't the end of the story. One of the Elgin players booted the ball as he was sweeping down the court after Rex's two free throws. We get the ball. We score to go ahead. How much time remained now?

"I was so busy watching the score I forgot to look at the clock. There couldn't have been too much time because we won it by two— 61-59.

"Let me say something. We beat a real good Elgin team. Truly an outstanding team. It lost four games all season, and two of them to us. We beat them in Elgin, and I feel that game might have made the difference in the championship game. Our kids were up mentally. They knew they could win. I wasn't so sure when we fell behind in the first quarter and didn't make too much progress in the second.

"At halftime I told the kids; 'We've tried everything, and nothing works. Now we're going to try something new. We'll play man to man, and maybe we can surprise them with a new weapon.'

"It was a gamble because two of my kids had four fouls, but we had to risk the change because we were so far behind. During our big spurt in the third quarter we didn't make a single foul that the officials saw. Whenever I play back the film which I do frequently, I see some contact which the officials didn't call.

"As I say, these are the breaks required for a team to win the state championship. Breaks, luck, and confidence are all important factors to blend with finesse and skill."

Two titles in two years. Four hundred and 35 victories in 26 years with the Warriors to offset 198 losses, and one of the most colorful careers in the state's history. These are the plus marks on Alex's side of the ledger—not bad for somebody who by-passed basketball in college. While earning his degree at Northern Illinois University, Saudargas competed in varsity football and wrestling.

Nevertheless, Alex was a basketball fan, viewing games or practice when he wasn't wrestling. During a game between Illinois Wesleyan and Northern Illinois in DeKalb, the aggressive, stocky Lithuanian athlete was impressed with Wesleyan's defense. It was a zone press, the likes of which he had never seen before.

"I made a note of it," Alex began, "and told myself I would use it if I ever had an opportunity to coach basketball. As a book basketball coach I was looking for things to pass on to the kids besides fundamentals. I also remember seeing Hank Luisette when he introduced the one-handed jump shot. Not in person, but on film—and his accuracy was amazing."

All of these items proved very handy when Alex landed his first basketball coaching job—the new mentor at the Morris-Kennedy grade school in Rockford. "We had some kids who were pretty good using these new ideas," Saudargas recalled, "and we finished that first season 19 and zero. In fact, the school got some extra publicity because people wanted to know how grade school kids could run up 70, 80, or 90 points. Then the one-handed push shot was as popular as the dunk shot was to become later.

"The combination of the jump shot and the zone press bewildered some of our opponents."

Alex's decision to retire ended one of Rockford's foremost rivalries in the coach colony within the area. That would be the matchups between Saudargas and Dolph Stanley, the Silver Fox who kicked the props out from under early retirement by coaching after reaching the 70's. When Stanley was building powerhouse teams at Beloit (Wisconsin) College, he and Alex became fast friends as well as featured coaches conducting annual summer clinics at Beloit.

"We would put the coaches on the floor and show them every trick we knew," Alex opted. "When Dolph returned to the Rockford area we played it like Muhammad Ali does now. We used the same publicity philosophy. He would say he was annoyed at me, and I'd say that I was going to tear him apart. It made a lot of copy for the sports writers, and added a lot of new interest to our basketball programs.

"Actually we are very dear friends, and I regard Dolph as both a great coach and a very outstanding man."

Alex has "retired" twice. After he won his second state champion-ship in 1956, he went into the investment field for three years. The salary was better. The hours were shorter. Still he wasn't happy, al-though he could envision greater earning power for what he calls "My Woolworth family—ten children and five grandchildren."

In the fall of 1959 he was back at West, happy to be working with kids again. His last standout team advanced to the state semifinals in 1967 before losing to Carbondale in overtime. The 1967 club fin-ished 28-1—the same record West compiled to win in 1955 and 1956.

En route to his first championship the man who gets long mileage out of a bow tie and a crew haircut, admitted he aged a year during one 10 to 12 minute span. "Before our game with Lincoln," Alex began, "the media people were in our dressing room getting stories and taking pictures. I always had time for the sports writers and broadcasters because I realized they had their job to do just like I did.

"Before the game my assistants and managers took care of the players' needs, and I was the coach of the guy who kept the statistics. Now it's time to take the floor, and the big policeman orders all visi-tors out. Everybody left without delay because they knew I would al-ways cooperate. Quickly the door is locked, and I start out giving individual instruction from player to player.

"Finally I get around to Johnny Vessels, and I'm talking to myself. Vessels is nowhere in sight. One of the assistants said, 'I know he's here because he drove over with me.' Managers are running all over trying to find him—and still they can't track him down. I can't play him if he isn't available. His gear is there, but no Vessels. So I turn to our sixth man, 6-5 Don Grabow, and say, 'I guess you're starting, and this is what I want you to do.'

"We take the floor with a nine player squad, and within a few minutes the writers are around our bench and everybody asks the same question: 'Where's Vessels?'

"I can't tell 'em because I didn't know. I start to perspire and worry about what happened to John. Pretty soon one of the manag-ers spot him running down an aisle toward our dressing room. Had the place been on fire, he couldn't have dressed any faster.

"I walk onto the court as he's taking his warm-up shots and ask out of one corner of my mouth: 'Where in hell have you been?' Just like nothing ever happened, he answered: 'I have a date with one of the cheer leaders from East, and I had to get her a ticket.'

"Then he tells her to run over to the armory to buy a ticket from a scalper. While he's talking I can think of only one thing. Maybe East, our arch rival, was attempting to sabotage us. Nevertheless we play the game, win it with Vessels starting in place of Grabow."

In this manner West continued en route to Rockford's first state championship since 1939 when coach Jim Laude's machine bumped Paris 53-44 in the title game. Also it marked the last time any of Saudargas' players were tardy because they were buying a ticket for their date.

JOHN SCHNEITER

George Washington Harper never made it to the baseball Hall of Fame, but he knows why Walter Johnson is there. During a spring exhibition game between the Cincinnati Reds and the then Washington Senators, Harper came to the plate to face the Great Johnson. Walter threw two side arm blazing fastballs that Harper hasn't seen yet. After the second strike Harper walked away from the plate and returned to the Reds' dugout.

In his most articulate manner Bill Klem, the plate umpire, followed after Harper and said not too loudly: "Come back here. You have one strike left."

Answering Klem's command, the irritated Harper growled, "The heck with it. I don't want it. You can have it."

After some delay the Reds sent a pinch batter to the plate for Harper. He took one called strike, sat down and the game continued without Harper and the pinch batter.

There is a basketball coach in Illinois who recently updated Harper's story. In the process of molding 12 state tournament teams, seven in the *Sweet Sixteen* and five in the Elite Eight, this particular coach has finished first, second, and fourth. He needs a third place finish in the future to complete a 1-2-3-4 streak.

Just like George Washington Harper, Coach John Schneiter of Winnetka (New Trier East) doesn't want the third place finish. "Once I get that close, I want to finish first and forget about third place," Schneiter quipped with his customary frankness after learning how Harper passed up the third strike against the Big Train.

Schneiter has one of the most unique coaching setups in the entire state. John is the basketball coach at New Trier East. He's also the tennis coach at New Trier West—a relatively new school in Northfield, some three miles removed from East. Inasmuch as the total enrollment of the two schools is in excess of 6,000, Schneiter doesn't lack for numbers teaching the fine points of his two favorite sports.

There was a time when Schneiter said he would never coach again. That was the night he was sitting next to Coach Gay Kintner when Kintner died on the Stephen Decatur bench while a game was in progress. John was Kintner's assistant, and he was completely crushed by the incident.

"Right then I said I would never coach again," Schneiter began. "Then I realized what a happy mood Gay was in at the time of his death. Now I have promised myself I will never quit coaching."

Considering the fact he was only 27 years old when he led Decatur to the championship in 1962—one of the youngest winning coaches in *Sweet Sixteen* history—John really doesn't have to rush to register for Medicare and Social Security immediately.

Somewhere along the line John has compiled a good book on Pete Rose's lifestyle: hustle and pride. He's a stickler for detail in his search for perfection. His practice sessions are geared to Double O —Operation and Organization. When there was mention about the astutely organized drills of a man named Paul Brown and another named Johnny Wooden, Schneiter pulled a time schedule out of his pocket, saying: "This is the way I plan my workouts."

There it was, a dozen itemized different types of drills for the more than two dozen athletes taking part in the workout on an alternating basis. These drills were in high gear when John took a seat on the sidelines and explained,

"My kids have to do a lot of thinking. Because we aren't as big or as physical as some of the teams in our conference (the Old Suburban League), we have to win with brains instead of brawn. We don't follow any particular play patterns. It's my philosophy to use styles and types of play best fitted to the kid's skills.

"We stress defense ahead of everything else because I regard it as the most important phase of basketball. In the 1973 semifinals of the Elite Eight, our defense shut out Aurora (West) for nine minutes. Aurora didn't score a point during the full eight minutes of the third quarter, and a minute into the fourth period. We won the game 39-33. Without that tremendous defense it is difficult to think what might have happened."

Schneiter could field an outstanding team with the collegians he's coached in high school. This sixsome includes Kenny Barnes, Wisconsin; John Castino, Rollins; Larry Cohen, Illinois; Jim Hallihan, Miami of Ohio; Larry Rosenzweig, Stanford, and Chris Wall, Northwestern.

Following graduation from Olney High School, Schneiter enrolled at Millikin University in Decatur. John was a freshman at Millikin when Scotty Steagall was a senior-shooter for the Big Blue.

Typical of his craft—long on free speech and short on no comment—John is happy over the return of the controversial dunk shot to basketball's playing code. "I love it because it ignites spectator interest, and I'm for anything which is helpful to our game. Also I think it's okay to legislate against its use in the pre-game and half-time warmups.

"Players with the skills to use the dunk shot won't need the additional practice, and that means more excitement for the game itself."

Although he's still a member of the young coach group, Schneiter was asked if he had any special advice for rookie coaches just starting out.

"I would tell them the same thing I try to do: 'Get out in front and keep trying to improve your position.' That has always been my philosophy."

A bridge buff, who enjoys bidding and trying to make seven no trump during his noontime timeouts in the faculty recreation room, John is doing his utmost to cooperate with the energy program. He's a bike rider going to and from his basketball and tennis drills, assisting in his own conditioning program when the weather is conducive to it.

Persons meeting John for the first time couldn't be sure if they were being introduced to Coach Schneiter or a daily commuter going to and from his office because he's a major in assertiveness win or lose. And twelve tournament teams isn't bad for openers.

DOLPH STANLEY

When Taylorville won the 1944 state championship with a perfect 45-0 record, Coach Dolph Stanley said for both friend and foe to hear: "Teams like this one come along only once every 100 years."

Now, more than 33 years later, the silver-thatched Stanley continues his search for "another" powerhouse at his fifth Illinois high school. Now it's Rockford (Boylan) after stops at Equality and Mt. Pulaski ahead of Taylorville, and Rockford (Auburn) before Boylan. The man many buffs call "The Silver Fox," developed tournament teams at each school before and after a 14-year timeout: the first 12 to coach at Beloit (Wis.) College and the next two as athletic director at Drake University in Des Moines.

As a master tactician Stanley took a routine slip and roll offense and parlayed it into something close to 900 career victories. There are many men who deserve consideration as "Mister Basketball" in Illinois, but few come even close to matching Dolph's credentials. If there are any questions about Stanley's lifestyle being unusual, so, too, is the fact he won two sets of freshman basketball numerals at the University of Illinois. This is something the fabulous Whiz Kids didn't come close to matching.

He earned the first set as a legitimate freshman. Then he left the Fightin' Illini ranks for two years, and when he returned Dolph earned the second set as a junior playing with the freshmen.

Dolph can remember when the game almost died. Service calls for World War I were so big not too many young men remained at home to play the game. Then basketball was considered mainly a girl's game—not a particularly pleasant rating for a rugged youth named Stanley who adopted basketball after suffering a busted nose three different times playing football.

Nevertheless, the game survived, and so did Stanley. It was 1931 when Dolph took his first job at Equality. In four years, he developed a third place team and moved to Mt. Pulaski. During a three-season tenure, he led Mt. Pulaski to fourth place in 1936.

Then it was on to Taylorville for the native of Marion. After two years some of the Tornadoes' fans let their feelings be known that Dolph might be happier elsewhere in his search for "the good Christian boy" blessed with extraordinary skills on the basketball court.

"They didn't know I was from the same type of mine operations in Marion that they had in Taylorville," Dolph mused. "Also, I was being recognized as a coach—a goal we all strive for. Whereas I worked mainly with reserved farm boys in Equality and Mt. Pulaski, I had an entirely different group in Taylorville. They were rougher-speaking youths, and while I was making some changes I knew there was talk that I would be fired."

"In the process of elimination, we came up with some outstanding boys. They were leaders in the classroom as well as on the basketball court. We were well on our way during my third year, and for the next five seasons we had some almost unbeatable teams. We used the slip and roll offense, a technique I picked up scouting a game in Nokomis. Also, we used the tipping zone defense, a tactic I learned from Cam Henderson, longtime coach at Marshall College in Huntington, W. Va.

"Often I've been given credit for discovering these two tactics, but I don't deserve it. I made some basic changes in putting them to use, but a player I never met in Nokomis and Cam Henderson really deserve the credit for coming up with these two completely new and different ideas."

Molding his kind of team at Taylorville, Dolph worked mainly with a seven-player squad en route to the Stellar 45-0 campaign. Besides Johnny Orr and Ron Bontemps, who later gained All-American recognition under his direction at Beloit, Stanley discovered Don Jansen in a gym class. All he did was promote Jansen to the varsity squad. The 1944 team fused an eight-year record which produced 217 victories and 49 losses for an amazing .816 percentage.

Besides the devastation provided by Bontemps and Orr to blend with Jansen's surprising contributions, Shulte Bishop, Dean Duncan, Davey Joes, and Ben Wilhelm rounded out what history some day may acclaim as one of the best squads in the history of Illinois basketball.

"I've never coached an overly tall team," Dolph explained, "for two reasons. Never did I have the big boy in high school, and we never recruited one during my time at Beloit. To me basketball is speed, skill, finesse, polish, poise and pattern play. No, I don't discount the big man's place in the game, I just like speed and finesse more than height when we play our three-guard game. I've always felt there is a place for the good little man in basketball.

"I had three exceptional small players when Taylorville rolled through four seasons winning 126 games while losing only 13. My last year with the Tornadoes we won 29 of 34 games."

This sensational finish enabled Dolph to fashion a five-year record of 155-18 and a percentage reading of .896 before taking his new job trail to Beloit. Small wonder he called his Taylorville teams "almost unbeatable."

The only time Beloit played in the NIT it lost to Seton Hall and tree-tall Walter Dukes. "The program," Dolph chortled, "listed Dukes at six something—probably his height when he played in grade school. If he wasn't seven feet tall when we played him, he didn't miss by much. I'm sorry to see power basketball drifting into the game with so many tall players. Especially the seven footers."

"When I played in college I was considered a giant at 6-1. Now, I'd be lucky to make the first team let alone the squad. Power basketball is taking a toll in another direction. Some of our younger coaches are fouled up seeking the big man. They are pawning their souls to get him. That is bad. Very bad. Give me the player who wants to play, and I'll produce a winner.

"One of my Beloit teams ended a 21-game winning streak for Evansville College on its home floor. Also, we beat Indiana State when Johnny Wooden was coaching the team. Wooden apparently was impressed the way we played the game. During an interview on national television with Johnny Orr, the University of Michigan coach, Wooden said: 'John your Michigan team's (runner-up to national champion Indiana in 1976) quickness and timing reminded me of when you played at Beloit.' That was a tremendous thrill hearing a great coach like Wooden comparing Johnny Orr's two teams— the one he played for at Beloit, and the one he coached at Michigan."

The man who calls work the world's best medicine, has no thought of retiring. He was retired from Auburn after the 1969-1970 season after he reached 65—the automatic retirement age in the Rockford public school system. Then Stanley packed his gear and moved to Boylan, the No. 5 entry on his high school coaching record.

"Why should I retire?," Dolph asked: "I've had years and years of pleasure-filled association with many marvelous coaches. Arthur Trout, who developed so many great teams at Centralia, was one of my favorites. Trout taught me my first delayed offense. It was an excellent tactic to offset a lack of manpower trying to cope with or outmaneuver an opponent. That is why I was unhappy to read about Dean Smith, the coach of the winning American team in the 1976 Olympics, arming his team with a so called new tactic: the four corner offense. The stories I read said it was a brand new addition to basketball.

"Do you know just how old the four corner offense is? I used it when I started to coach at Equality in 1930, and I'm certain other coaches were using it at the same time or even earlier. Just check the records of the many successful coaches in Illinois to prove how much coaching has improved within the state.

"That is the way many of our younger coaches planned it. They are aggressive and use their imagination. They go to clinics. They ask questions. They digest the answers. Their interest and enthusiasm is healthy for the growth of the game."

Never one to lack for an opinion or build concern where the chips will fall, Dolph continued: "I'd like to tell all young basketball coaches that a college athletic directorship no longer is a mecca for the future. The two years I spent at Drake were the most unhappy years of my life. The athletic director's main two jobs are fund raising and working with the school's booster club to keep the various programs afloat. It wasn't my kind of work, and I moved back to the high school plateau."

Stanley is a stickler for details, and proved he did ample homework updating his knowledge on subjects other than strategy and philosophy. "How many sport fans," Dolph asked, "realize how the ball has been changed in baseball, basketball, and football? The circumference of a basketball used to be 33 inches. Now it's 30 inches. The old style ball seldom bounced true due to the laces. Now the ball is molded, much easier to handle passing or shooting.

"Baseball hopped up the ball. This is evident when some batters drive the ball out of the park taking a half swing. The football is smaller, no longer an odd-size pumpkin. It is easier to throw because a 50-yard pass on the fly no longer is a rarity. Also, the field goal kickers are reaching even greater distance, and these two things account for more scoring."

Ever loyal to his native Marion in downstate Illinois, the Boylan mentor is confident the south will rise again in the state's tournament series. In view of teams from northern urban areas dominating the Class AA competition from a numbers standpoint, Dolph stressed: "I said it, and I mean it. The switch to two classes has primed a lot of new basketball interest in the South. I've noticed this progress at three levels of competition: during the regular season, the state tournament series and the All-Star games matching the North against the South. The amount of competition has doubled, and the interest has increased at least 10 fold in some sections of the state which were considered dead. The smaller schools have bounced back, and I'm just as confident the bigger schools will enjoy the same type revival. Basketball games are won on the court, not on paper, as our winning south teams in the All-Star games have proved."

Stanley regards the return of the dunk shot as pitiful. He considers the present charge-block rule as the most atrocious rule in all sports. Dolph envisions serious trouble ahead if the present tempo of roughness isn't toned down.

"It thrilled me to see the United States win back the Olympic basketball championship," Stanley explained, "but the rough play disturbed me very much. That isn't the way the game should be played."

If given the opportunity Stanley would raise the basket to 12 feet. Why 12 feet? He answered:

"That way the dunking would be left to the taller players better equipped to do it. The little guy who is always trying to dunk the ball reminds me of the guy who can't sing. Nevertheless he's always trying—and so is the little dunker trying to attract attention at the expense of forfeiting team play."

Dolph Stanley is a fascinating personality. He says what he thinks and secretly he's hoping to retain his health to revise his claim in behalf of the 1944 Taylorville team. Then he said: "Teams like this one come along only once every 100 years." Instead of once he would very much like to amend his claim to "twice every 100 years."

HARRY COMBES

There is a home that basketball helped build at 611 West Green Street in Champaign. It's the home of Harry Combes, a class gentleman, whose magic number was three in becoming one of the state's most successful coaches.

Combes' first three surfaced when he led Champaign High School to consecutive 2-1-2 finishes in the State Basketball Tournament. There was a second three attached to Harry's record when the University of Illinois won three Big Ten championships during a four-season span after he became Doug Mills' successor at the Illini helm. Combes' third three blossomed when Illinois finished third three times in the NCAA Tournament.

The basketball woods is full of outstanding coaches, but few possess the humility and dignity that Harry added to the game. Win or

lose he literally was a ton of class. If he couldn't say something good
about an individual or team, he wouldn't say anything.

There was the night when Indiana won a 102-101 barn-burner
from Illinois in Champaign, and a critic asked, "How can a team
score 101 points and still lose?" In his customary adroit manner,
Combes' explained:

"Sir, we made just one mistake. We failed to get possession of the
ball for the last shot in the waning seconds."

En route to earning his sheepskin at Illinois, Combes earned all-
conference basketball status twice. Also he won two awards, the
Western Conference (Big 10) Honor Award for proficiency in athletics, and the Ralf Woods Memorial Trophy for his team's highest
free throw percentage in Big Ten Competition.

This success eventually triggered a move, about the distance of a
par five hole in golf, from Huff Gym to nearby Monticello to Champaign High School to become Les Moyer's assistant in both football
and basketball and head coach in baseball. Harry credits Moyer's
outstanding organization in helping Champaign continue its winning
tradition.

Les organized a feeder system in grade school and followed these
kids right through junior and senior high school. After Combes replaced Moyer as head coach in basketball, he had the opportunity to
work with the "best bunch of sophomores I've ever seen on one high
school squad."

"These kids, Ted Beach and Johnny McDermott to name just two,
were outstanding students and athletes," Harry explained. "Their
record proved how quickly they inherited the Champaign type of
tradition. In three years they won 106 and lost only seven games."

Unlike most exceptional young teams, the Maroons peaked as
juniors. When they toppled Centralia for the title in 1946, it was
their Number 37 victory in 38 games. Probably the biggest oddity
attached to Champaign's climb to the championship was the fact the
Maroons handed Centralia its tenth loss of the season in the title test.
This was an almost unbelievable achievement.

The 1945 Maroons bowed to Decatur, and the 1947 club was derailed by Paris—each time with the championship on the line.

Combes had just one chance to reach the tournament as a player
and was tripped up in the stretch. Playing for his native Monticello
as a senior, Harry and his teammates did a lot of dreaming and with
good reason. Monticello stamped itself one of the state's stronger
teams when it upended Champaign, Urbana, and Mattoon during the
regular season.

Then came the sectional finals against Hillsboro, and the Monticello season ended quickly. "Had we made it to state," Combes re-

called, "we would have played Morton of Cicero next and this could
have been extra interesting. I would have played against Jim Vopicka, the same Jim Vopicka who was both a classmate and teammate at the University of Illinois in later years."

Combes coached a running game, frequently proving that a team's
best defense was its offense geared to eagle-eyed marksmanship. "I
liked to have my boys run and beat the other fellow to the basket. To
me running was fun and a very important weapon. I don't mean race-
horse running. I mean a well-planned running game with the center
in the middle to take the best advantage of a pass or shoot opportunity," Harry explained.

"Watch the pros. They are running and I think it's a much better
game for the spectators from an action and finesse standpoint. Some
coaches play a slowed down game, and that is their prerogative. In
high school a coach has to play the game best suited to his personnel, but I can't buy talk that there is much more skill and science
playing the slow game compared to the running style.

"Whenever this situation came up at clinics or just a free-lance discussion about basketball, I had only one question to ask: 'Does it require greater art to handle the basketball on the dead run than it
does at half or quarter speed?' I know there will be some turnovers
running at top speed, but there will be a lot more spectacular play
for the fans—and they are the people who are buying our game."

Unlike some coaches and administrators who foresee the south
rising again in Illinois, Harry isn't all that confident. In the wake of
the north winning nine straight tournaments for the Chicago and
suburban areas, it's his opinion that this advantage was built on competition. "There is more good competition up north than there is
downstate," Combes claimed, "and I can't envision this situation
changing that rapidly.

"Almost every game a Chicago or suburban team plays is a rugged
test within the area. Downstate schools don't have as many opportunities. They can't be assured a rugged game everytime they play because there aren't that many topflight foes available. Also, travel is a
factor trying to schedule top teams for every game.

"By tournament time these northern teams are ready because they
have been through the mill. I've long felt that we often overlook the
one thing that is most important to all tournament teams. It's endurance. When my Champaign team lost to Paris in 1947, endurance
was a factor. After the semifinal game we were spent, unable to
bounce back as Paris did—playing as hard at the finish as it did at
the start.

"It proved what most of us had known for a long time. Coach
(Ernie) Eveland stressed conditioning to build endurance in the

same manner he taught fundamentals. Coach Eveland, I've got to think, was one of the pioneer coaches who required his players go out for cross country in the fall and track in the spring to assure building this endurance."

In connection with this two-game, day-night competition to close out the Illinois tournament each March, some of the state's coaches favor the adoption of a plank in the NCAA tournament pattern. For the good of the four finalists as well as providing prime-time television for the championship game, the NCAA plays semifinal games on Saturday afternoon and the finals the following Monday night.

The insight, which Combes provided this suggestion, sprung from the administrators' claim that the players as well as the students would miss too much time from school. "When a team reaches the Super-sectional level, the entire school is caught up in the mass hysteria that surely doesn't produce any overtime study. I can't believe that the students would suffer too much in the class room or study hall if the schedule was shifted to a Tuesday-Saturday-Monday format.

"It would be a much better break for the players involved in the championship and consolation games after almost two full days of rest."

Combes rides along with the *Sweet Sixteen* in the Super-Sectionals and the *Elite Eight* wind up in the Assembly Hall, in Champaign. He disliked the four-team final, claiming: "I just didn't feel it was a true state tournament because so few communities were involved," Harry noted.

After his second University of Illinois team won a Big Ten championship, the Illini mentor had reason to wonder what might have happened during his freshman season had Walt "Junior" Kirk not turned pro. Following a review of his team's 7-5 Big Ten record and 15-5 log overall, the man from Monticello said simply:

"We knew Walt was an exceptional player, or the pros wouldn't have signed him when they did. In all fairness to him I didn't or wouldn't say, 'Wait until next year.' Sometimes athletes don't get a second chance with the pros. I feel that's a decision the boy and his parents can best resolve."

His toughest game ever? In Combes' case it involved coaching plus a short stint as a dietician. "During the time when all 16 teams came to Champaign," Harry explained, "we drew one of those mid-morning games. It was tough to know when to feed, how much to feed, and what to feed our players. Finally I had the boys bring their mothers to school, and with their help I was able to set up a proper menu for them."

Just like so many of his counterparts, Combes opposed the Illinois shift to two divisions when it was made originally. Now he feels the Class A champion has the right to strut just like the Class AA winner. Also he feels the two classes have evened up the competition. Especially for the smaller Class A teams.

Combes rates Lawrenceville's Jay Shidler the "very best shooter" he's ever seen anywhere, adding, "And this young man is a total player. He can go get the ball as well as shoot it." He rates alley basketball as excellent training for athletes during the off-season. Harry can recall 10 to 12 years ago when his athletes played no holds barred alley basketball and didn't stand around waiting to have fouls called and a chance to shoot free throws in non-stop lively action.

Regarding recruiting, which he brands a coach's nightmare, Harry is convinced the present system works a hardship on the player—and should be revised. Real pressure develops when some of the so-called "can't miss" prospects miss, and some of the doubtful walk-ons make it big. At best, Harry claims, a "best yet" rating of a blue chip athlete is judgment at its best, and frequently judgment backfires.

The man, who wore socks as his trademark, was Illinois' tenth basketball coach following the likes of Ralph Jones, Craig Ruby, and Doug Mills. When it comes to musing about his "boys," Harry can talk far into the night. One of his more interesting stories concerns Johnny "Red" Kerr, a 6-foot-9 center, who came to Illinois from Chicago's Tilden Tech with less than two years of basketball experience. At Tilden Kerr was a soccer player before coach Bill Postl talked him into reporting for basketball. Big John was an immediate success, and the many achievements he enjoyed at Illinois were topped only during his career as a pro player.

During 12 seasons of play-for-pay basketball, the Tilden-Illini-trained Kerr put together such awesome statistics as 2,005 assists; 10,092 rebounds; 12,480 points, playing a total of 27,772 minutes in 905 games. Among Harry's favorite stories are those that concern the promotions of Bill Erickson and Van Johnson to bank presidents in Rockford. Also the election of Fred Green to a judgeship in Urbana; Dave Downey wearing two hats as an insurance broker and lawyer, and the explosive antics of Dike Eddleman—the choice of some Illinois loyalists as the best all-around high school athlete in the state's history.

ERNIE EVELAND

'Tis said Ernie Eveland got more mileage out of a basketball and a bow tie than any other coach in the incredible history of the boys' high school tournament in Illinois. Altogether he tutored 11 tournament teams, seven of them in a row, to anchor a prestigious parlay of two championships, two seconds, and a singleton third place finish.

Proving he'd never be a candidate for the Dummy of the Year award, Ernie coached Paris' cross-country team to four straight state championships. Where did the endurance runners come from? Coach Eveland's basketball squad. In this manner the Paris athletes wrote Harrier history while conditioning themselves for basketball —and more history under the frank speaking and free thinking Eveland.

Ernie coached for 41 years. This total includes a 24-season stint at Paris, and eight years in Alaska. Moving into the 49th state after finishing his Paris tenure, Ernie coached two years at Ketchikan, and the final six in Fairbanks. How and why does a coach move from the Land of Lincoln to Alaska?

"I had a friend, Jack Finch, who used to be a boxer and quit to become the superintendent at Ketchikan," Ernie began, "and he asked me to coach his basketball team. I stayed in Ketchikan two years, and moved to Fairbanks for six seasons."

After accounting for seven years at Waterman and 24 more at Paris, Ernie mused: "It's hell having to get along with different school boards that long."

The Eveland home is a mile south of Canton, where six different lakes are spread over 106 acres that Ernie calls the "little farm." What's little about 106 acres? "It's a little farm compared to the big fenced-in farm I use to own," Ernie explained.

Altogether he was a regular week-end hunter or fisherman—depending what was in season at the time—during his time in Alaska. Another favorite pastime for Mister E.E. is talking about "my boys who played for me in Paris." He starts with the Glover brothers, Del and Don, switches to Dick Foley, and John Wilson, and concludes with Dave Humrickhouse, who earned All-America mention at Bradley.

"I had an outstanding boy, Duane Swanson, at Waterman," Ernie noted, "and my coach at Bradley, A.J. Robertson, wanted him. Duane was all set to go to Bradley when Brick Young, the sports writer-referee in Bloomington, managed to detour him to Illinos Wesleyan. I never did find out how Brick managed to pull that one."

Recalling Dick Foley's important role as resident engineer when the Assembly Hall was built on the University of Illinois campus in Champaign, Ernie remembered another former day recruiting story:

"When Branch McCracken was coaching at Indiana, he called up Dick and asked him how he would like to spend a week-end in Chicago with one of his teammates? Dick accepted, and met McCracken in Chicago on schedule. Mac took both boys out to a big dinner, and later they went to see a couple of shows.

INDIANS' CHIEF—The Lawrenceville Indians coached by Ron Felling, shown here making his point at halftime of the 1974 Class A title game against Ottawa (Marquette), were a dominant force in the small-school series during the first five years of its existence. Lawrenceville won the first Class A title in 1972, repeated in 1974 and finished third in 1976 when Jay Shidler set the all-time tournament individual scoring record. (Photo By Curt Beamer, Urbana Courier)

HALL OF FAMERS—Two men who got their athletic career starts in State Tournament competition ended with spots in the Baseball Hall of Fame. They are Lou Boudreau, who was a standout for the Flying Clouds of Harvey (Thornton) in the 1930s, and Robin Roberts, who was a standout for Springfield (Lanphier) in the 1940s. (Photo By National Baseball Hall of Fame and Museum, Inc.)

"It was about midnight, as Dick tells it, when they returned to the hotel. When he asked for his key at the desk, there was a message. It read: 'Don't pay any attention to McCracken. We want you at Illinois.' It was signed: Doug Mills. I've often wondered if Dick would have been the resident executive on the Assembly Hall project if Doug hadn't left that note."

Gene Smithson, the coach at Illinois State, is another of Eveland's boys. "Gene's team was good enough to earn tournament team status," Eveland claimed, "but darned if we didn't get nudged in the sectional."

Ernie Eveland has come a long ways since he won four letters in track, and the same number of silver-gold miniature track shoes for cross-country at Bradley. "Robby always said I was too small for basketball," Ernie chortled. "I wasn't too small to scrimmage against the varsity all week—and then rest on game nights."

RON FELLING

Interested in an extra ticket for the next rock and roll concert? Got time to drop into Indianapolis for the annual Indy 500 automobile race? How about a fishing junket where you catch the limit in the first hour, and fry 'em the next? Could you be talked into going AWOL from your job to attend the finals of the NCAA Basketball Tournament?

Ask these questions of Ron Felling, the coach at Lawrenceville High School, and he will answer "yes", on all four counts. A native Hoosier, the colorful Felling made national headlines when he was asked what they did for recreation in Lawrenceville? He answered: "We play basketball, and watch the traffic lights change."

After nine years in the town on the banks of the Wabash river, Felling entered the 1976-77 campaign in what he calls his WASK season. Translated from Fellingese, it means: Without A Shidler Kid.

In the process of winning 211 of 256 games, Ron has had the good fortune of having two Shidlers. First there was Dennis, Ron's first All-Stater in 1970. Then came Jay, an outstanding marksman who earned All-State billing in 1976. "These kids are natural All-Staters," Ron mused, "because their father, Richard, was an All-Stater when he played."

Felling has organized the basketball program at Lawrenceville right down to the very last dribble of the daily workouts. "We have 39 players: five seniors, four juniors, 10 sophomores and 20 freshmen. Everybody gets equal time, and I have three assistants. One works with me, and the other two direct the junior varsity, and freshmen squads."

Lawrenceville plays in the North Egypt Conference, and had won seven of the last nine championships after 1976. While Ron finds pleasure talking about this particular 7 out of 9 ratio, there is a two-for-two statistic in his team's past which he enjoys reviewing. "It was a big school against little school format in Carbondale's annual holiday tournament," Felling stressed, "and we beat both Collinsville and Thornridge of Dolton on the same day. That was something."

When consideration of Illinois' shifting to class basketball got serious, Felling was just lukewarm on the idea. "I could detect watered-down basketball in the making," Ron observed, "and I didn't want any part of it. Still, the two-class system has been Utopia for the smaller schools. New fans. New interest. The rekindling of old rivalries.

"Nevertheless, I don't think Jay Shidler never received the recognition he deserved. Thousands saw him in person, but not many saw him on the tube."

Lawrenceville managed to win two of the first three Class A championships. Felling's team missed a bid when enrollment rolled over the 750 Class A cutoff in 1975.

Hometown Terre Haute, a toddlin' Indiana town on both the amateur and professional sports beat, was the capital of Ron's basketball world. He went to high school in Glenn, a seven-mile suburban stop east of Terre Haute. The school's enrollment generally remained around 200 during Felling's time, and he was one of 28 members of the senior class when he graduated. Ron's next stop was the campus of Indiana State University, where he played basketball for the Sycamores under the leadership of Coach Duane Klueh. "I wasn't the most complete player the game has ever known," Ron reasoned, "but I could shoot that ball through the hoop in the clutch."

Felling always was an aggressive youth, and today he claims "I'm probably the only basketball coach in the land who sold peanuts in the ball park when Terre Haute was a member of the Three I League in baseball."

Ron's favorite music is rock and roll. He's also an automobile buff, and has a perfect attendance record spanning the past 14 Indy 500-mile races to prove it. Whenever he feels the urge for rest and relaxation, Ron will call up Bobby Knight, the basketball coach at Indiana University, and arrange a meeting at a favorite fishing site.

If there was a turning point in Felling's career it came in March of 1963. Then Ron was the seventh grade teacher and coach at Merrillville, just outside of Gary, Indiana.

"A friend of mine called and said he had two tickets to the NCAA finals in Louisville, and wanted to know if I was interested in making the trip," Ron explained. "Within an hour we were on the road driving south. I saw one of the greatest basketball games ever played, Loyola of Chicago's overtime victory over Cincinnati in the finals.

When I returned to Merrillville I was fired on the spot for being absent from school. At the time I figured it was a tough price to pay, and then I realized I learned more about coaching watching Loyola, Cincinnati, Duke, and Oregon State than I would coaching a seventh grade team.

Nearing a 10-year association with Lawrenceville, Ron has found a new home for his family: his wife, Irene, two sons, and a daughter. "I met Irene at Indiana State, and we were married a short time later," Ron explained.

When asked how many legitimate scholarship offers the second sharpshooting son of the Shidlers actually received, Ron answered:

"First of all the letters filled three different shoe boxes. As for actual offers, I would guess the number was right around 30—and there was a reason for that. Jay told all the recruiters he wanted to go to college close to home, and most of the far away schools respected his wishes."

Shidler selected Kentucky, and started the Wildcats' opener as a freshman.

RON FERGUSON

Curt Gowdy said it best . . .

"This United States team is playing with the enthusiasm and spirit of a high school team playing in its first state championship tournament. Its quickness and unselfishness is awesome."

At the time, Curt Gowdy was talking on national television to report the United States' return to gold and glory in Olympic basketball. It was during the stretch run when devastation prevailed in the Americans' 95-74 rout of Yugoslavia in the championship showdown in Montreal July 27, 1976.

It remained for a young American from Illinois to dribble out the clock for what had to be the United States' most cherished conquest in its rich basketball heritage. His name? Quinn Buckner. The same Quinn Buckner who helped Thornridge of Dolton win back-to-back state championships in 1971 and 1972. The first time Thornridge reigned over the entire state. The second time Thornridge was the Class AA kingpin following a shift to division competition within the borders of the Land of Lincoln.

Uncounted millions viewed the action while listening to Gowdy's accurate and interesting comments as the Americans routed the team which earlier eliminated the defending champion, Russia. This elimination of Russia was an opportunity the Americans had hoped to have inasmuch as Russia's win in 1972 frequently has been regarded as a super heist to be compared only with Brinks' robbery in Boston some years ago.

Ron Ferguson followed every word and every second of the Americans' twenty-one point triumph; Ron Ferguson, the man who coached the brilliant Buckner during his formative years at Thornridge. That Ferguson did an outstanding job is best proved by the fact that the Dolton school won an Illinois record of 58 consecutive games before, during, and after its two successful title tests.

Then Ferguson, Buckner, and Mike Bonczyk were to high school basketball in Illinois what the legendary trio of Joe Tinker, Johnny Evers, and Frank Chance were to the Chicago Cubs in the early 1900s. They killed the opposition with outstanding defensive finesse —the Cubs in baseball, Thornridge in basketball.

Ferguson's tremendous success at Dolton was the springboard to promotion to Illinois State University in the tall corn country of McLean county. When it comes to titles, Ron is unique. He's both the assistant basketball coach and assistant athletic director at ISU.

"At the outset we had to struggle for so many victories," Ron recalled, "that the streak was merely a by-product of our two championship seasons. It's impossible for a team to build an extended streak unless it wins at least one state championship to continue the string into a second season."

It first happened in 1944 when Coach Dolph Stanley's Taylorville team went through the season and "Sweet Sixteen" with 45 straight victories. Taylorville won its first three games during the next season to set the record at 48 before Thornridge tossed it into the discards. Was pressure involved in the streak?

"It didn't appear to bother the kids," Ferguson answered, "but I don't mind saying it concerned me. Most high school teams reach their peak as seniors. After we won the first time when the team was forming as juniors, I wanted to make sure that I didn't make any mistakes during its senior year."

If Ron made any mistakes they most certainly didn't show up in the loss column. Thornridge won in 1971, tipping Oak Lawn in a 52-50 thriller to finish with thirty victories in 31 games. As seniors, Buckner, and Bonczyk, Boyd Batts, Greg Rose and Ernie Dunn put on a show Quincy (Sr.) won't soon forget. In anchoring a second title trophy, Thornridge became the first Illinois winner to top a hundred points. The Falcons' 104-69 upending of Quincy was its 33rd victory without loss.

Ferguson, built like an extra-large watch-charm guard for football duty, can take the weekly wire service rating polls or leave them alone. "The polls can be helpful although there are times when they look like a popularity contest," Ron reasoned. "Kids on teams rated

A GREAT AMONG THE GREATEST—Greg Rose (44) of the Falcons scores a pair of his 26 against the Blue Devils as teammates Boyd Batts (31), and Quinn Buckner (25), battle for position under the boards. (Photo By Les Sintay, United Press International)

SEEING RED—Against Rockford (West) center Dennis Hippe (41) taps in a rebound basket as teammate Larry Downs (51) watches. Rockford (West) players are Calvin Glover (32) and Greg Austin (34). Decatur won the game 57-44. (Photo By United Press International)

among the top 10 or 20 are always fighting to retain or improve their position. Kids on teams on the fringe generally are plugging away to be included.

"Nobody can see all the teams, and I suppose there is a loyalty attachment to a pollster's particular area. It's only natural that he would vote for a team close to home over one that is in another section of the state.

"I feel pretty much the same way about All-State teams. They aren't always representative, but they are nevertheless building and publicity factors in promoting a school's program. I enjoy working with the media because it has been a big help to me."

(In Illinois the wire services conduct their high school ratings in the same manner as at the university and small college levels. The UPI polls coaches while sports writers do the balloting in the AP weekly ratings.)

Ferguson regards Buckner, who was drafted by the Milwaukee Bucks in the NBA, as a complete player. "Quinn can pass, rebound, play sound defense, and score. Also he's an excellent leader, the type who can help an average player improve and help good players become great. He's coachable, and he can help coach because other players have such outstanding respect for him," Ron explained.

Ron claims he wasn't surprised when Buckner picked basketball over football for his last two years at Indiana saying, "Quinn likes football, but he enjoys basketball more." Then the mentor paid tribute to the gifted athlete when he said,

"During his four years at Thornridge I don't think there was ever a time when he shrugged off an academic assignment. Quinn worked just as hard at Indiana. He played two years of football, four seasons of basketball, and toured Europe one summer. Still he earned his degree in Business Education in four years. This is what I call total dedication."

Ferguson likened Buckner with K.C. Jones, former all-American at the University of San Francisco before he gained stardom with the pros. "I have reason to believe the Boston Celtics would have drafted Quinn on the second round," Ron began, "but he wasn't available. His style of play is the same style which provided the Celtics with their outstanding success down through the years."

Ron follows an amicable route when it comes to comparing Illinois' high school basketball with arch-rival Indiana's schoolboy competition. "I've always felt Indiana stressed offense while Illinois' game was stronger defensively," Ferguson noted. "Also I feel Illinois has more good players and good teams because it's bigger. No, I won't say it's better. Maybe just as good, but definitely not better.

"I remember Washington of East Chicago in 1971. Considering

the development and success of its players in college competition, I've always rated Washington one of the great all-time high school teams."

Although he opposed the shift to classification at the outset, he's all for it now, claiming, "With one class of competition, the North dominated statewide. The South now has an opportunity to rise again because some Class A towns were dead. It's different now. These towns are enjoying a re-birth of the Hebron spirit and most of them are getting great fan support.

"The southern towns take great pride in the fact that they are the father of high school basketball in Illinois, and it's impossible to dispute this claim."

Inasmuch as Ferguson is both an administrator and coach now, there is good reason to listen when he speaks. Especially when he stresses assertiveness saying, "Our next order of business is getting back to rating education first, and athletics second."

Ferguson's coaching career hasn't always included the Buckners and all-winning seasons. Ron was an assistant at Thornton in Harvey when the district was split with the opening of Thornridge. He applied for the head coaching job in basketball and was signed by his new superiors to the new Dolton setup.

While there is frequent talk in sports about five year plans before a particular program becomes successful, it's a fact Thornridge had to wait five years before basketball turned the corner with a winning record. Improving with each new season, Thornridge's first season record was a dismal 2-21. Twenty-one losses for a rookie coach aren't easy to accept, but Ron continued to laugh on the outside while crying on the inside looking for better days ahead.

His optimism clipped a dividend with a second season record of 9-13. The team's third year produced 10 victories in 22 games, and the Dolton machine moved pretty close to .500 with 11 victories and 12 defeats during the fourth season.

The excitement Ferguson had hoped for at the very outset finally was forthcoming during Thornridge's fifth season of basketball competition. The team played 25 games, and won 16 of them. Ron's confidence became reality as that first winning record set the tempo for future 20 game winning seasons.

Ferguson, who had been a five-year assistant at Harvey under the late Tommy Nesbet for one season and Bill Purden for four, welcomed a skilled freshman by the name of Quinn Buckner into the Thornridge fold in 1968. This was something akin to having a leading home run hitter for your designated hitter in baseball. Thornridge's fortunes spurted to new heights, and reached the climax with back-to-back state titles in 1971 and 1972.

One superstar won't assure a team becoming a winner, but he can be a tremendous assist—and nobody knows this better than Ron Ferguson. It's a long, long road from 2 and 21 to 58 consecutive victories.

THE FREEPORT SYSTEM

Should television ever decide to revive its "What's My Line?" national network show, Freeport has enough interesting items in basketball to keep the panel guessing overtime. Before the first guest would be introduced, it's entirely possible the panel would strike out trying to establish the high school teams' nickname. It's the Pretzels.

Once it is established that Freeport formerly housed a brewery, it isn't too difficult to determine the fact pretzels were a popular product within the German-based community. Also, it was an excellent way to perpetuate the name.

Now for the $64 questions:

1-Name the athlete-coach who helped make Freeport's state championship teams in 1915 and 1926 historic as well as unusual?

2-Who is the nationally famous coach who used Freeport as a springboard to everlasting fame and glory in both NCAA and Olympic competition?

3-After the Pretzels won the championship in 1951, who were the two players who moved outside the state to obtain their higher education, and where did they enroll?

4-Name the 6-foot-3 center in Freeport basketball who became a walk-on at the University of Illinois before shifting to play professional football with the Baltimore Colts, the Pittsburgh Steelers, and later with the Dallas Cowboys?

5-True or false: The high school has had 18 basketball coaches since 1907, and never fired one?

6-Did Freeport field a pair of twins who later played international basketball in Italy?

7-Of Freeport's 12 state tournament teams, how many survived first round competition?

8-Has Freeport ever had a basketball coach who was a teammate of Dike Eddlemen at Centralia?

9-True or false: One of Freeport's state championship teams was a nine-time loser during the regular season?

10-How many games did the Pretzels win posting the school's only undefeated season in 1919?

Now for the answers:

1-Glenn Holmes played for Freeport's title team in 1915 and coached its 1926 state champions. Holmes is the only coach to achieve this first at his own school. Tom Millikin played for

Pinckneyville's winners in 1948 and was the coach when Maywood (Proviso East) won in 1969.

2-Adolph Rupp, who coached championship teams at the University of Kentucky and in Olympic competition, was Freeport's coach for four years starting in 1927. His Freeport teams compiled a record of 58 victories in 75 games, and the Pretzels finished third in the state tourney of 1929.

3-Carl Cain and McKinley "Deacon" Davis were regulars when Freeport won in 1951, and both enrolled at the University of Iowa to play for Coach Bucky O'Connor.

4-Speedster Preston Pearson was a standout in basketball at both Freeport and the University of Illinois before finding fame and fortune switching to professional football as a running back for three of the NFL's foremost teams.

5-It is true Freeport has never fired a basketball coach.

6-Kerry and Kim Hughes, a pair of 6-foot-7 twins, played some varsity basketball as sophomores; almost none at all as juniors, and blossomed as seniors. They moved from Freeport to the University of Wisconsin and spent a season in Italy before Kim joined the New York Nets.

7-Six. Three won titles; the 1929 and 1942 teams finished third, and the 1950 team was eliminated in the second round.

8-Yes. The Pretzels' present mentor, Farrell Benefiel, was one of Dike Eddlemen's teammates at Centralia in 1941 and 1942.

9-Yes. The 1926 team won 19 and lost nine before upending Canton in the championship game.

10-Freeport played six games in 1919 and won all of them under Coach Charles Maples.

Rupp, who was to become the famous Baron of Bluegrass at the University of Kentucky, stopped in Freeport following graduation from the University of Kansas. Adolph learned his lessons well under Phog Allen and had four straight winning seasons with the Pretzels. Improving with each new season, Rupp's teams started with 8-3 in 1927 and advanced to 11-5, 19-5, and finally a 20-game winning year in 1929-1930.

When the Kentucky job opened, Adolph became an immediate candidate with impressive credentials topped by a .773 winning percentage during his Freeport tenure. What followed adds up to one of sports' most incredible stories.

Under Rupp's leadership, the Wildcats of Kentucky turned the Southeastern Conference into an annual one-team race. Each season the big hardwood fight was to determine who was going to finish second behind Kentucky. In 1948 and 1949 Rupp's team won back-to-back NCAA titles, and copped two more in the 1950s.

The rich Freeport tradition continued when both Cain and Davis made valuable contributions as Iowa marched to successive Big Ten championships in 1954 and 1955. Although it didn't develop as rapidly, the Preston Pearson story was equally as fascinating. The Freeport native, a slim, fleet basketball player made the big switch to pro football as Michigan State's Pete Gent had done earlier. Preston was a key player for both the Baltimore Colts and Pittsburgh Steelers. Then the unbelievable happended: Pearson was claimed by the Dallas Cowboys for NFL waiver price of $100.

Dallas Coach Tom Landry billboarded Pearson as the pros' best running back executing the screen pass.

Presently Freeport's basketball program is directed by Farrell Benefiel, who first decided to play Big Ten football and basketball at the University of Illinois, then, following a service stint, accepted Abe Stuber's offer of a scholarship at Southeast Missouri.

After coaching stops in Kincaid and Hoopeston, Farrell moved up to Freeport. During his first eight years as head coach of the Pretzels, Benefiel has had seven winning seasons. The lone loser was 1969 when Freeport won 11 and lost 13. In 1974 the Pretzels were 28-2 to help bolster Farrell's .678 percentage.

Probably no coach ever had an odder reason for quitting one job and taking another. During his fourth year at Hoopeston, the school built a new gymnasium without seats. Unable to adjust to this unprecedented move, Farrell transferred to Freeport as Coach Ron Norman's assistant.

During his high school competition at Centralia, Farrell was aboard in 1941 when the team Dike Eddlemen anchored lost to Marion and finished third. The next season it was a different story. Centralia went all the way, beating Paris in the title game.

"I do believe Dike was the best high school athlete in Illinois," Farrell said. "He was All-State in both football and basketball despite some troublesome injuries. During a track meet one day in Mt. Vernon they allowed him to enter as many events as he desired. He picked seven events; won six of them, and finished second in the shotput.

"My main event was the discus throw, and the single throw he made that day would have earned him fifth place in the state meet. I do believe that was the only time he ever threw the discus in his entire career. Our coach, Arthur Trout, used to say, 'If you are good enough you don't have to wear your name on the back of your shirt because they will know who you are.' I'm here to say right now that Coach Trout was right: everybody knew Dwight Eddlemen."

Coach Benefiel is a stickler for academic advancement and uses the blackboard in the Pretzels' dressing room to prove it. He posts each athlete's grades in the same manner box scores and statistics are posted.

"Our sophomores will average about 2.8, the juniors a shade over 3, and our seniors right around 3.5," Farrell claimed. "Every senior who played for me and graduated, has gone on to college. When our kids' grades are up, we know we're going to have a pretty good basketball team because class goes to class. There isn't any substitute for it."

Because he was graduated from Southeast Missouri in less than 33 months, Farrell had to sacrifice his senior year of competition.

Benefiel really is the publicity director of Freeport, in particular, and the Big Nine conference, in general, without official portfolio.

"At the end of the school year I write some 135 to 150 letters, depending upon the quality of the crop, to college coaches all over the country to tell them about the available seniors in our school and our conference," he explained. "I know some of the scholarship offers resulting from these letters have helped more kids go to college because our conference is highly regarded by many college coaches."

Where Freeport fans are concerned, Benefiel says simply:

"Ten percent of them think I'm God. Ten percent hate me, and 80 percent of them come to our games for the sheer pleasure. They like action, and they enjoy watching the kids improve."

Speaking of kids improving, Farrell has proof within his own home.

"Some summers ago our son Terry, enrolled in the northern Wisconsin camp conducted by Ray Meyer, the coach at DePaul. He made excellent progress and was a camp counselor during his fourth summer working with Ray. This instruction helped Terry become an improved player, and he was one of our co-captains before he finished high school."

Turning back the pages of history in the Freeport basketball record book, the saga of Glenn Holmes, Adolph Rupp, Carl Cain, Deacon Davis, and the Hughes twins, Kerry and Kim, provide new dimensions in drama and devastation. And then there is Preston Pearson. Preston was an unsung hero when he was Freeport's leading individual scorer with 419 points playing 27 games in 1963 for a 15.5 point average.

When it was pointed out that Pearson missed one of the Pretzels' 28 games en route to a 22 and 6 record that year, the ever present wag in sports enthused:

"That's the night Preston tested his skills in advance planning to prove he could carry a football as well as shoot a basketball."

Pearson went to the University of Illinois to play football but later decided to try out for Coach Harry Combes' basketball team. He made it, and also made quite an impression in Big Ten games for his aggressive play. Although listed at 5-11, he could rebound with those almost a foot taller, and in many games Pearson was the Illini defender who drew the opposition's "big man". He did not play football his final two years at Illinois, but was drafted by the Baltimore Colts in the annual NFL draft. The Baltimore computers obviously were able to measure what was inside "the Freeport Flash" as well as what Pearson displayed in physical talent.

JOHN THIEL
"Say it like it is . . ."

This is the philosophy of John Thiel, the colorful and capable former basketball coach at Galesburg High School. Early in his career John learned that words spoken off the record frequently find their way into headlines much to the speaker's chagrin. Following a foul-filled loss which ended with a disputed goal tending situation, Thiel said to a group of media representatives:

"Fellows I'm speaking off the record now. Maybe you heard about the Wreck of the Hesperus, and now you just saw the Rape of Champaign."

End of quote. It wasn't, however, the end of the battle of words as one newspaper carried this headline over the story the next day:

"The Rape of Champaign—Thiel"

Thiel produced nine tournament teams in 18 years at Galesburg.

The man they called the "Al McGuire of Illinois basketball" will be the first to admit the breaks always balance out. How else could he explain 15 regional tournament triumphs, and 13 conference championships?

Thiel, who looks like a trim middleweight tuned by full-time enthusiasm, never forgot the first directive he received in Galesburg after leaving the Milwaukee Hawks of the NBA. The message was brief, and to the point: "You're a teacher first, and a coach second, but don't forget you are expected to win." This he did with amazing regularity as evidenced by a record of 396 victories against 90 losses for a .815 percentage.

Despite this outstanding success, there was another State Tournament Week situation Thiel probably never will forget. Lawrence (Bumpy) Nixon, one of the all-time foremost Silver Streaks players, helped Galesburg win the super-sectional on Tuesday, celebrated his 19th birthday on Thursday, and was declared ineligibile for the tournament competition launched on Friday. "Something like this can't happen again," John noted, "because the IHSA has instituted a new rule. It permits players in such situations to finish out the season in the sport they're involved in."

During Thiel's tenure, Galesburg really didn't qualify as a gracious host. The Silver Streaks lost only 21 games on their home court in 18 years, and during this time Galesburg frequently scheduled teams from Chicago and its suburbs.

"Our basketball payed for 75 percent of the school's athletic program," John said, "and that included football. We might have done even better had the school gone through with its original building program. When the new gym was first proposed, the seating capacity was to run between 5,500 and 6,000.

"At the last minute this idea was shelved, and it was decided to put the auditorium where the gym was to be, and put the gym in the first site of the auditorium. This set the gym capacity at 3,800, and I don't mind saying somebody really fouled up. Half the tickets were sold for the season, and it wasn't easy to buy them at anytime."

Thiel didn't believe in holiday tournaments, and always gave his players the week off between Christmas and New Year's while he spent the time on scouting missions. "I always made a point of seeing our possible tournament opponents at least once," John mused, "the better to set up the individual match-ups—the most important part of outlining game plans.

"While we didn't schedule any practice sessions during the holidays, our team didn't lack for exercise. The kids would scrimmage against former Silver Streak players who were home from college to spend the holidays. Due to the emotion and spirit involved in these drills, I felt it was one of our better weeks of the season.

The John Thiel Family could field a three-man team with two cheerleaders among the children. Zack was an All-State player in football for Galesburg, and continued his education at Southern Methodist University. Son Mark was Galesburg's first nine letter winner, winning three as a quarterback in football, three more as a guard on the basketball team, and the final three as a catcher in baseball. He moved from Galesburg to the University of Missouri, and was later drafted by the New York Yankees. The Yankees made Mark their tenth pick, and the first catcher among this group.

"Mark has a tough road ahead," proud Papa John noted, "being on the same club with Thurman Munson, the MVP of the American League. His bonus for signing was big enough so I could scratch his name from my allowance list."

Then there is Eric, a senior at Bloomington H.S. who is the school's top golfer as well as a basketball guard. As a 14-year-old Eric put together 73-77—150 to finish tenth in the state golf tournament. The Thiel cheerleaders are Lisa, a sophomore, and Nancy, a seventh grader. The family moved to Bloomington when John became an advertising sales representative.

Few people have had a more interesting life, and John would be the first to admit it. He launched his Higher education at Carthage College, and finished at the University of Colorado. While still a beardless youth, Thiel joined the House of David, and played both baseball and basketball. "Dutch Witte, who booked the Davids," John recalled, "was a very good friend. He signed me after I finished high school. The first year I made three trips coast to coast before I was 19. Marv Rotblatt, who pitched at the University of Illinois, was my roommate when he joined the baseball club.

"The basketball team used to tour around the country with the Harlem Globetrotters. Some of my teammates were Doc Talley, George Anderson, and Big Johnny Tucker, an outstanding athlete who turned down repeated offers from the New York Giants in baseball."

During his time with the Davids, Thiel saw enough of Sweetwater Clifton to regard him as the strongest hitter ever in baseball. Also he was sitting in the Cleveland Arena one night when he saw a player dribble toward the baseline, stop, and jump up in the air before he shot the ball. "I couldn't believe what I saw," Thiel opted, "until the same player did it two or three more times. Finally I asked the player's name. A young fan sitting behind me said: 'That is Kenny Sailors from the University of Wyoming.' It was an unforgettable game for me. I'd never seen anybody attempt a jump shot. Within a year or two everybody shot in that manner, but I can't forget I saw Kenny Sailors do it first."

Later Thiel signed with the Chicago White Sox, and made a quick tour of the club's farm system. Red Ruffing was his first manager when he played in Muskegon, Michigan. After that John moved on to Hot Springs, Memphis, and Waterloo, but he never got to play in Comiskey Park. Right at that time Thiel probably was the only Cub fan in the Sox system. John was a senior at Beloit High School the last time the Cubs won a pennant. Then the year was 1945.

Thiel is opposed to the elimination of the third place game of the tournament as frequently suggested by some critics across the state. "I don't care when they play it, just as long as they play it, because it is a tremendous achievement just making the final four in a tournament like ours'," the colorful Thiel claimed, adding:

"I've never won the championship, but we've been close enough to find a lot of pleasure in finishing second and third to climax a long, rugged haul."

John never used a whistle during his daily drills because he desires to have his players know his voice at all times—especially when he calls for a special play or has an observation or two about an official's lack of 20-20 eyesight.

The one week in his life that John won't soon forget started with

Galesburg's 23-21 upending of Rock Island and future All-American Don Nelson, and a 61-59 loss to Collinsville three nights later. "After the Rock Island game my wife was feeling sorry for Don Nelson because he was such an outstanding player and suddenly his team has been eliminated," John remembered. "I couldn't say it then, but I can now: we were lucky because Rock Island had a better team than we did."

DUSTER THOMAS

Basketball is a game of three good pivot men; one excellent corner shooter; one outstanding ball handler, and two aggressive and intelligent student managers. Blend this talent with continuity, science, the proper timing, and you can't miss being a winner.

This is the opinion of Duster Thomas, who did more to put Pinckneyville on the map than anybody in history. When he started teaching, his pupils addressed him as Mr. Merrill A. Thomas. When they asked what the A stood for in his middle name he would answer "Algebra."

In many situations this was true because some rival coaches found Thomas as difficult to solve as an advanced algebraic equation.

There are three different stages to Thomas' fabled career. Stage one was the two years he spent at Newton: the first as an assistant, and the second as the head coach. After returning to Pinckneyville— a move which he still brands as moving back home—Duster spent nine years as a head coach who concentrated on the fast break offense.

Then he got an idea. Almost everybody, and certainly most of Pinckneyville's opponents, were going almost full-time with the run and gun game. "I looked around and weighed one situation against the other," Duster recalled, "and decided to go with a deliberate type game. I never switched back, staying with the control style of play for the next nine years.

"We didn't exactly take all the air out of the ball, but we slowed it down enough to bewilder and upset the customary calm of our opponents. The shift in styles couldn't have been too bad. We won 33 of 36 tournament games over a three to four year stretch. Furthermore, there's another statistic which thrills me even more. During one stretch I had 29 of 30 seniors go on to college, and I still have a great deal of regard for the lone boy who didn't make it. He told me something I knew: he was having trouble completing high school, and felt he wasn't qualified to make it through college.

"More than once he told me 'I'm going to be the best shovel miner in the business once I finish high school.' He made good that prom-

SOARING SENATOR—Thornton's Leon Clark (35) grabs a rebound away from Springfield's Tom Frick (40) as Thornton's Renault Banks moves in. (Photo By Champaign News-Gazette)

TALL ITEM—Duane (Skip) Thoren of Rockford (East) soars above Collinsville's Bob Basola (30) and Bobby Meadows (52) for an easy layup in a quarterfinal game of the 1961 State Final. Thoren scored 19 points, but Collinsville rolled to a 71-48 victory. (Photo By Vern Richey, Urbana Courier)

ise. Had it not been for athletics that boy wouldn't have finished high school, but he had the desire and incentive to get his diploma before he went to mining."

He was a disciplinarian as well as a coach. And Duster had a standing rule—and never would he bend it: Athletes earning A's and B's could practice and play fulltime. A C meant adding an hour's daily study time in the library—one hour for each C. Receiving a mark of D, the player was off the squad for a quarter and wasn't allowed to suit up during that time. With a twinkle in his eye, Thomas reacted like a little boy telling a secret: "I started checking the first time period early with the start of school hoping to make sure we were at full strength to start basketball drills."

While he possesses finger tip information in connection with most of his athletes, Thomas can—and does—talk overtime about two of his players. One is Arlen Hill, the other is Rick Talley, whom he still calls Warren Talley.

"Hill had a tremendous sense of humor, and he could express himself excellently. If our defense was clicking, and holding the opponents' big scorer in check, Hill would say nonchalantly but still loudly enough to be heard: 'Hey big guy I see your name in headlines, averaging 35 points a game. You've got only three now, and your teammates aren't giving you the ball. That's going to slice into your average.'

"In due time Arlen would have the guy ready to fight. Then Hill would zing him again with something like this: 'Maybe your teammates won't give you the ball, but we'll make sure you get the last shot of the game.' The guy was so upset he would frequently stumble over his own feet and end up pounding the floor with his fists."

Talley is a globe-trotting Chicago sports columnist who finds time to double in television. In his first season as a Panther, Talley was one of the "Rinky Dinks" who seldom played unless Pinckneyville had the game won, or it was out of reach.

"We had this game with Centralia coming up," Thomas began, "and whenever we played them I always sought to have something new to spring on Arthur Trout, the Centralia coach I admired very much. The one thing Warren could do best was score from out—something I didn't coach too much. You can't play a deliberate game and give the ball away if you shoot and miss from long range. Warren's percentage was pretty good considering he practiced more than he played.

"Going over the game plan with the boys, I told 'em I was going to start Warren Talley because it's impossible for Trout to have a scouting report on him. We go through with the plan, and our man starts hitting bulls-eyes shooting from out. At the finish we have a win, and Warren Talley has 33 points. That particular game was a big boost for his morale when he moved on to play for Southern Illinois University and captained the team one year.

Incidentally, Duster claims a share of the credit for Talley's nickname of Rick. "When he first came out," the Pinckneyville mentor explained, "he was so light and tense and nervous that I called him Ricketts. Some years later he cut his nickname to Rick, and he's never changed it."

Thomas had a way of needling opposing players' egos seeking every possible advantage for his beloved Panthers. Like the night he had the student managers purposely misspell the names of two visiting players. The name of Feizzle came up Fizzle, and Nunberger was Noneberger.

"Pretty soon their teammates noticed the mispelled names on the big scoreboard," Duster recalled, "and they were kidding about Fizzle and Noneberger playing on their side. The joking cut into their concentration, and it helped us win another game. Basketball is a scientific game, but there are many different ways to upset that science. We used everything imaginable.

"Like the night we were playing on the road. The fourth quarter had just started, and we had a six point lead. One of the home team players dives for a loose ball, misses, and crashes head-on into the bleachers. One of my players, Frank Gadson, yells to the referee: 'This man is hurt, we'll take timeout.' All the home team fans hear Gadson, and give us a standing ovation for unusual sportsmanship.

"The injured player is treated, and remained in the game, but the home team has the jitters. We won the game by ten—and we weren't that much better. The home team cheers, I'll always think, sparked a second effort to get us over the hill."

During his youth Thomas played baseball in the Ty Cobb manner: spikes high, mean and aggressive. "Whenever I had an opportunity to see Cobb, and that wasn't too often," Duster explained, "I loved to see him run the bases. Seems like he was always dusting himself off, and that is where I got my nickname of Duster. I attempted to run like Cobb and all my life I've enjoyed winning. Whatever the sport, I was out to win. I played that way, and that's the way I attempted to coach my boys.

"Maybe I waited too long, but I didn't have one tournament team in all the years I used a fast break. After nine years I realized maybe Pinckneyville would prosper with a different type game. Between seasons I decided to shift to the deliberate game, and our fortunes turned around quickly."

Why is the slim, trim mentor so hep about selecting intelligent student managers?

"If a coach desires to prove or sell a particular point," Duster answered, "the best way to do it is with statistics. A coach can preach all night, but he'll never get his point across until he shows a player what he has or hasn't done. Sure my managers kept stats on field goals and free throws, but that wasn't their total job. I wanted figures on playing time, errors and mistakes—they call 'em turnovers now.

"At Pinckneyville I awarded letters based on the team's success. We would limit the letter winners to eight if we lost before reaching a sectional tournament. If we won a game in the sectional, I would up the number to nine. If we went to the state, 10 players would get awards. If we won a game in the state, the number was increased to 11, and 12 if we won a second game.

"Never would I give out more than 12 letters. Many times I've heard kids sitting on the bench yell to the starters: 'Come on you guys, you have to win to help us win our letter.' Often players will listen to other players faster than they will the coach—but not for long if I'm the coach.

"Once a coach has all these statistics timed down to the minute, he can show a player everything he needs to know to prove a point."

Thomas doesn't believe runaway scorers are good for a team's morale and success. Instead he favored having five starters in double digits instead of one having one in 30 to 35 range, and the rest of his players in the 10 to 12 bracket. "It has to be a team game, or you can forget about it," Duster quipped.

When Duster talks about continuity he does so with authority. "We would automatically change our style of attack if we failed to score the first two times we swept down the floor," Thomas stressed. "Also we would do it without taking a time-out. A time-out would give the other coach a chance to sense what we were going to do. I'd rather make him try to adjust after we've made the first move. It's possible we could score two, three or four field goals before the opposition would change its defense. After they switched we frequently went back to our original offense, and hit them with another scoring spree."

Being from the old school, Duster didn't aim for field goals alone. "A basket gives you only two points," Thomas allowed, "and I attempted to teach my players to go for the three or five-point play. We had our own tricks trying to do that. Frequently, one of my players would slap his own wrist while closely guarding an opponent. The referee would hear the slap, and call the opposing player for a foul. Now the innocent opponent is so upset he pops off to the official and is charged with a technical foul. This gives us two free throws and we retain possession. Some of my players would learn to trip themselves in a closely guarded situation, and you would hear the whistle. Another foul on the opposition, and another technical because the opposing player would protest that he didn't trip anybody.

"If these things happened often enough it would be possible to get enough points in the first half to win the game. After that we could play slowdown and force the opposing team to come to us. Nothing illegal. Just a matter of playing heads up basketball."

Not all of Thomas' tricks were saved for the opposing team. Often he would turn out the lights in his team's dressing room during the halftime intermission. Why? "I might have to deliver a lecture about sloppy play, and that way nobody knew who I was talking to. It was an all-for-one speech, and most times we would play better in the second half."

Now that his basketball status has shifted from coach to fan, Thomas continues to enjoy life with a most unusual job situation. Duster works four days a week for the Reynolds Monument Company in DuQuoin, and spends a fifth day working for a men's clothing store in Pinckneyville.

"I sell more good will than monuments or clothing and still have time to play golf and enter a senior's tournament now and then," the astute veteran explained. Merrill Alexander Thomas was born to be different. Rest assured he is whether he's diagramming a basketball play on a blackboard or writing an order for a new headstone or monument.

Even while writing an order he talks basketball, and recalled one of the best one liners of any season. "We had this team beat by 20 with only seven seconds remaining when the opposing coach called time-out," Duster began. "Now he's really berating his players and yells to a bench rider: 'Get in there, and get us some points.' When play was resumed, a fan in the stands yelled out: What did you tell him coach, to play for the win or go for a tie?"

FIZZ WILLS

His nickname is Fizz, and it's a perfect fit for his effervescent personality. Also he considers the "Fizz" billing a blessing compared to what it might have been. During his youth he operated, as well as managed, the soda fountain in his father's drug store. "The kids got to calling me "Fizz," and I loved it," Audrey Addis Wills admitted, "because I realized they could have called me Jerk—and been completely correct inasmuch as jerking sodas took up most of my time. I guess some people have been nicknamed Jerk, but I didn't want any part of it."

So A. A. Wills has been "Fizz" ever since, and he has no desire to change it. What about the Audrey Addis part of his full name? "My grandmother was an English authoress," Wills began, "and she picked out those two names. Ever since I've been old enough to sign official papers I've used the first name of Aubrey because I like it better than Audrey."

Ever since he landed in Joliet originally, Fizz has had only two jobs. He was head basketball coach in the Joliet Junior College and Joliet High School. Would he care to pick the best high school team in Joliet history?

"There can be only one," Fizz started, "and that has to be the High School's team of 1937. It won a state championship. It was our only one, and I don't believe in passing over success or records. Sure it's a matter of record that Joliet has been represented by some outstanding teams, but I've got to go along with the winner.

"The 1937 team had to be a good one when you consider it came down to the Big Four with Decatur, Collinsville, and Pekin. Herm Walser coached that team, and it was an easy winner in the championship game. Decatur was bidding for a second straight title, but it had little chance. Joliet beat Decatur 40-20, and seldom does one team double the score on its opponent playing for the championship.

"Other good teams at both the high school and junior college levels, yes, but. . . .the 1937 club won it all and that is the name of the game. Also there is something else about that team that not everybody remembers. It was Walser's first year as head coach. At the start of the season he replaced Doug Mills, who returned to the University of Illinois to work with G. (George) Huff."

Although Wills isn't one to deal in comparison of teams from one era to another, his own philosophy is different where players are concerned. "I've always felt an outstanding athlete is one who will always be outstanding from the start to the finish of his career," Fizz stressed. "While it's true that I don't think teams of the 1920's and 1930's can compete with teams in the 1960's and 1970's, I do feel differently about players—and their ability to compete successfully from one era to another.

"I'm sure everybody won't agree with my thinking, but it isn't going to change my opinion the least bit."

Armed with information that the heralded Mister Basketball of the Joliet area never had a losing season during his entire coaching career, it isn't easy to take issue with his thinking about comparing athletes instead of teams.

Attempting to stymie coaches who teach and play what he calls "Fraidy Cat" basketball, the slowed down style of offense, Wills favors the installation of the 30-second time clocks for high school basketball. "I've known some coaches who require so many passes and pivots and fakes before they will let one of their boys take a shot," Fizz explained. "I think that is silly. Always I taught my boys to take the open shot when they had the opportunity.

"Some people get the wrong impression of a team playing the open shot style. They claim a team is playing recklessly. How can a team play recklessly when it hits 45 to 52 percent of its shots from the floor? I'm not now pulling these figures out of the air. I've never had a team shoot under 45 percent or over 52 percent for the season. I dare the men who play 'Fraidy' Cat basketball to improve upon those statistics. Maybe they will for a game or two or even three, but never over the entire season—and I'm not forgetting that high school kids are shooting better now than they ever did.

"That is why I favor the clocks. If the fans want action, give it to 'em—and make sure they do it by using the clocks. It doesn't have to be 30 seconds. I'd even consider a 25-second time limit. Once this is done we can forget about raising up the baskets, the zones, the dunk, the widening of the free throw lanes. It will assure action from start to finish.

"My teams used to score 90 to 100 points, and we led the nation a few times offensively. Because of my style of play I detested anybody holding up the ball on us. I've never waited until the last quarter to go out after the ball. If I feel I'm better than they are, I'm going after that ball right now—at the start of the game."

During the time he was a student-athlete at DePauw University in Greencastle, Indiana, Fizz and his teammates enjoyed a very rare achievement in basketball, a tie game. Playing the University of Wisconsin in Madison, DePauw and the Badgers played a triple overtime deadlock. As best he can remember, Fizz is without a reason why the game wasn't played to a decision. "I can remember two things about that game," Wills explained, "because both of them were firsts for me. The tie was 25-25, and after the game Doctor Walter Meanwell, the Wisconsin coach, came onto the court to congratulate me. Why, I'll never know because I didn't think I played any better than anybody else. Still it was a great thrill, a famous coach paying me a compliment."

Selecting standout players of more recent vintage from the Joliet area, Wills picked Jeff Hickman, who played at Lockport (Central) and Roger Powell, formerly of Joliet (Central).

"Both were excellent shooters," Fizz began, "for a very good reason. Every free minute they could find they were in the gym or out on the playground shooting. Practice was their middle name, and they were the type who gave the game third and fourth effort at all times. Hickman enrolled at Houston, but a foot injury cut short his collegiate career.

"Had Lockport and Central both had five Hickmans to play

against five Powells, the two schools would have played the state
championship game three years in a row. No doubt about it in my
book."

Wills' collection of "My boys" in the Joliet area numbered about
35 as he sounded like a depot train-caller running down a list of
civic leaders, professional and business. Later Fizz added the names
of Ken Barone, recently promoted to athletic director at Ventura,
California, Junior College, and Bill Tuffli, an "all everything" in
every sport he played.

The reason for this success? Wills answered, "I demanded that all
my athletes retain a "C" average to assure enrollment at any major
university. Also I stressed "C" for class—the trademark of an outstanding athlete."

Wills regards recognition as the key word in the outstanding
progress of the black athlete in Illinois high school competition,
saying, "Recently, we hear a lot about numbers, the overall increases
of enrollment in the bigger schools, especially in Chicago as well as
the suburbs. Many, many of the black athletes have worked very hard
to obtain success both team-wise and individually. They know this
progress assures them recognition to go on into intercollegiate and
professional basketball. It boils down to this: the opportunity is
there, and the black athlete is taking advantage of it."

Speaking of numbers, Fizz recalls his own situation. He attended
Lewisville, Indiana High School and was one of seven seniors to
graduate from a school with an enrollment of 40. Following graduation from DePauw, Fizz coached for three years in Brook, Indiana,
before moving to Joliet. At the time, due to a teachers' agency based
in Chicago, Wills had his choice: Joliet or Dundee. After a morning
interview in Joliet and an afternoon session in Dundee, he picked
Joliet and has been a fixture there ever since.

Due to the depression Wills missed four pay days for each of his
first five years, losing a total of $1,800 during this time. Now, some-
thing close to 50 years later the loss of the $1,800 makes a good
story as Fizz reviews the reason for the 80 plus trophies on display in
his home.

NORM ZIEBELL

Mention almost any situation in basketball, and the chances are
good Norm Ziebell can top or match it. Did you ever hear of two
principals getting together and deciding they were going to give the
game back to the players by ordering the coaches to watch the action from the stands? Ziebell has. Anybody ever given you a report
on the unethical candidate circulating a petition among the players
trying to get your job two weeks before the season opened? Ziebell
can supply all the details.

Do you know a coach who has supplied back-to-back captains at the University of Illinois, and Northwestern? Ziebell does.

Can you name the coach who devised a T-formation offensive pattern? Ziebell can.

Norm Ziebell is a salty-type guy who speaks his opinions, and did during most of his 18 years coaching in Illinois—15 years at Morton of Cicero, and three more at Moline in the Quad-Cities.

Before he gets around to talking about his 319 career victories, Ziebell stresses the fact he had a junior high school record of 17 and 1 in Rockford to springboard to the varsity plateau. Also, that he was helped out of the starting gate by a coach named Jim Laude, who knows the game from all angles.

Although Alleman of Rock Island, Moline, East Moline, and Rock Island (H.S.) have failed to provide the Quad-Cities with a state championship team, one of Ziebell's Moline teams came close. It was 1951 when Moline settled for second place after a 71-51 loss to Freeport. Two years earlier Moline fielded another tournament team, but it was derailed surprisingly by Nashville.

"I can't understand why the Quad-Cities haven't won at least one championship," Norm noted, "because the competition isn't that rugged, especially when compared with the suburban area around Chicago. I was at Morton long enough to learn that one team will knock you down, and the next one will come along and step on you. It's truly rugged basketball—the type a team has to play to win a tournament.

Harking back to the time when All-American sharpshooter Bill Hapac was playing for Morton, Ziebell observed: "Whatever points Bill scored, he earned. The team was one of the poorest I've ever coached. I just hoped from game to game that the other four players would get the ball and pass it to Bill so we could take advantage of his scoring."

A native of Oshkosh, Wisconsin, Ziebell has a perfect one-for-one record as a forecaster. "Before our game against Centralia in 1941," Norm explained with an added happy lilt in his voice, "I told the newspaper boys we'd (Morton) win if we held Dike Eddleman to 15 points. I knew they didn't believe me, but that was their problem. Not mine. Mister Eddleman scored 15 points, and we won the game, 30-29.

"Inasmuch as this was a four-team field, we had to play only two games to win it. Now we're going to play Urbana, and everybody is saying: 'There's no way Morton can handle Fred Green.' I didn't care what they said because we had a special trap defense designed for Green trying to get him in foul trouble early.

"Don't you know Green fouled out and we won another one

pointer, 32-31, and the championship. A lot of guys said we were lucky, but my kids played two outstanding games. Also, my assistant, George Fencl, had scouted both Eddleman and Green. He designed both defenses and deserves a lot of credit for our success."

When Morton won in 1932, Red Kopecky and Jim Vopicka were the big men for the Cicero machine, a 30-16 winner over Canton. The mention of Vopicka's name triggered another observation from Ziebell, who mused: "We used to have some sayings, funny, but true. I'd tell the kids hold to 'em to 29, and they could win with 30 points. Or, hold 'em to 39, and win with 40. Right in the middle of one of these sessions, Vopicka yelled: 'Hey coach why don't you tell 'em the formula I have with Harry Combes? We say score 59 points, and they have to score 60 to beat you.' It was a pleasure coaching kids like Kopecky and Vopicka."

Ziebell rates the Wharton Fieldhouse in Moline as one of the finest plants in the state. It seats 6,500 persons, and is in the middle of one of the best hotbeds in basketball from an interest standpoint. Almost always adults outnumber kids and students at the average game. "Due to this great interest," Norm claimed, "most of the tickets are sold on a season basis. One year we (Moline) earned $60,000 in basketball at a time when football was just breaking even. You have to love fans like that."

The all-time oddity in Ziebell's career was the timing of what he called a "silly stunt." Minutes away from the tip-off of a suburban league game, the principals of the two schools called the coaches together and said: "We're going to give the game back to the players tonight. You coaches will sit in the stands away from the benches. No orders. No signals. In other words, act like you're scouting instead of coaching."

At first Norm admitted he thought they were playing a little joke, trying to sell some sick humor to offset the tension. "Pretty soon it's obvious they weren't kidding, and I'm asking myself why did I work all week getting the kids up for something like this," Ziebell reasoned. "So I go one way, and the other coach goes in the opposite direction. The game isn't too old when one of my best players, Wilbert Kokes, is hurt and helped off the floor. Kokes is on the bench, and I'm sitting in the stands feeling helpless. .

"Pretty soon Wilbert is back in the game, and I can see he's playing hurt. That boy never did recover fully from that injury, but that was the last time I know of when the principals decided to give the game back to the players."

Ziebell said he felt like he was part of a popularity contest when a bidder for his job asked the players to sign a petition requesting the school officials to name him the new head coach. "They refused, and that situation was settled right away," Norm claimed. "It wasn't, however, the best way to start the season, but we ironed out everything in time. By the way, the board never did hire the guy."

During his tenure at Morton, Ziebell had the distinction of seeing four of his boys become back-to-back captains of their teams at two Big Ten schools: Illinois and Northwestern. First it was John Drish and Bill Hapac at Illinois, and later Chester Strumillo and Chuck Tourek at Northwestern.

In a move to open up the middle, Ziebell sprung what he called a T-formation offense against an unsuspecting opponent. In completing this maneuver the Morton-Moline mentor placed his smallest player under the hoop; stationed his big man at the free throw arc, and spread the remaining three across the floor at the 10 second time line.

"It works," Norm claimed. "I've used it for a couple of quick baskets—and frequently that is enough to decide a close game."

Also Mr. Z has some definite opinions about the discovery of the four corner offense.

"Originally, I heard that Norm Sloan used it first at North Carolina State in recent years. Later Dean Smith was credited with discovering it at North Carolina and making important use of it when the United States won the 1976 Olympic basketball championship.

"That is well and good, but the pattern isn't all that new. I used the four corner offense early in my career at Morton, and later at Moline. Also, other coaches in the state used it then because I've played against it. It matters not who came up with the play first, I'd just like to see some of the old school coaches receive credit along with the current crop."

When it comes to thrills, Ziebell says Bill Seaburg made it all worthwhile, with only six words, the night he was inducted into the Illinois Basketball Hall of Fame. After receiving his plaque, the former Iowa star from Moline came to his table and whispered: "I owe all this to you!" Slightly moist-eyed, Norm admitted: "That was a lifetime of happiness for me."

JIM BROWN

Jim Brown was introduced to the wonderful world of sports in Gary, Indiana, where he was an instant success at Froebel High School.

He started in 1938 in football, playing for John Kyle and ended up as an All-State selection at end. He also had a three-season basketball stint under Coach Hank Mantz. Still, he found time to become one of Indiana's top pole vaulters, and he also had time for baseball. Because high school baseball wasn't approved by the Gary board of education at the time, Jim played in the American Legion program.

This competition was the springboard for the days ahead when Jim would join the New Orleans Crescents and the Chicago Brown Bombers—touring black independent teams tied to "See America First" scheduling. It was not too much later when Jim joined the Navy, and was assigned to Great Lakes. This provided a milestone which Brown never will tire telling. He was the clean-up hitter in the Great Lakes lineup, batting behind longtime major league star, Larry Doby.

At the war's end Jim picked higher education over Doby's bid to join him playing for Newark in black baseball. He entered George Williams college in Chicago, a move which qualified him for teaching and coaching positions. After Brown earned degrees in physical education and recreation he took his first position: a summer teaching job at Dunbar Vocational in 1949.

That fall Jim was offered the basketball coaching job at Southern University in Baton Rouge, Louisiana. Then came the career-changing telephone call which nine out of every 10 successful athletes always receive. The caller was John Meegan, the principal at DuSable High School in Chicago. Meegan, who had gotten to know Jim when he did his practice teaching at DuSable, sought him as the school's new football coach. Brown weighed both offers, and finally decided to remain in Chicago.

One factor was the salary, which was almost double compared to the Southern University offer. Also, Jim was now in position to meet many people and had the opportunity to join several new associations, all stepping stones enabling him to make new contributions to the high school programs within the city and state.

Reviewing his career at DuSable, Brown spends more time retelling about the young people he helped earn scholarships to continue their education than he does his own coaching success.

"Without athletics very few of these youths could afford to attend college," Jim stressed in his typical humble manner. "At least 65 percent of these people earned their degrees. Some became lawyers. Others are doctors, accountants, teachers, and coaches.

"In view of this progress, it thrills me everytime I think back to the decision I made when I weighed the two offers from DuSable and Southern University. It's been a fabulous career."

Brown remained at DuSable until 1968 when he was named a supervisor in the Chicago school system. Another chapter about the fellowship among athletes, past and present, could be written in connection with Jim's promotion. He was recommended by Ernie Leiberson, the man he replaced as supervisor.

When Jim speaks about the Ernie Leibersons and all the other top drawer people he's met among writers, broadcasters, coaches, and athletes, there's a bright new glint in his eyes. He calls Ernie Banks "Mister Cub," and Joe Louis "The Champ," adding: "Nobody will know the many times Ernie Banks has come to my rescue to speak to youth groups when I didn't have a speaker. I hope he always remains with the Cubs' organization because he's every inch a gentleman," Jim noted.

Whenever Jim speaks of Banks, Louis, Jesse Owens and Jackie Robinson and their personalities he labels them "fine men with outstanding charisma."

After finishing his high school eligibility in Gary, Brown enrolled at Michigan State with a combination football-track scholarship. When he was denied an opportunity to play basketball for the Spartans, Jim moved on to Southern University. There he played for A.W. Mumford, Southern's athletic director who also coached football and basketball. "He became one of my very best friends during my two years there when we won everything on the schedule," Jim explained, "including a national tournament for black colleges in Cincinnati."

After he was assigned to Great Lakes, Jim became the recreation director of Unit No. 1911 comprised of black recruits. A short time later he was united with another Garyite: Forddy Anderson. "After we got the basketball program going, Forddy became our coach, and he developed some outstanding teams," Jim said as he reviewed his welcome reunion with Anderson. To this day Jim is irked when he reads where an unhappy player calls football a "torture chamber," or attempts to belittle sports in any manner.

Having been through the mill—some happy and some sad experiences—in the integration of city and state programs, Brown regards improved coaching and the kids' increased interest as the main reasons why Chicago has now won six state championships in basketball. Also he's convinced that 45 should be the cutoff age for high school coaches, noting:

"That is the age level I've found when a coach suddenly becomes an old man to a high school athlete. Sure there are some exceptions, and I don't mean that every 45-year-old coach should be bypassed completely. Instead, I'd like to see him assist the younger coaches by sharing his knowledge and expertise."

While Jim credits the present and more recent black stars for fusing young people's interest in sports, he still rates Joe Louis No. 1 "The Champ," Brown began, "brought new hope to the black youth. He admired him because he was honest and upright. He wasn't flamboyant. Instead he was a new type of talent who produced a different concept within the United States as well as the entire world."

Jim wouldn't buy a win ticket that Chicago will ever again see another Buddy Young considering his size, fortitude, sheer speed, gift of talent, and guts. He regards Cazzie Russell as a natural talent and pure shooter who really didn't develop until he arrived at the University of Michigan to play for Coach Dave Strack.

When anybody mentions the name of Abe Saperstein or the Harlem Globetrotters, Jim reacts like he was the president of the organization's fan club. "Anybody who knocks the Globetrotters," Brown noted, "just doesn't know all the facts. Abe became an ambassador to the world giving the black athlete an opportunity to play. The pay was better. The publicity was tremendous, and the team graduated from the bus to the airplane to tour the world."

Asked if he thought there was too much stress presently placed on high school athletics, Jim answered: "Properly contained, and properly controlled, I don't think athletics ever can be overemphasized. When one looks at central city schools these days he has to shudder wondering where they would be without athletics."

Brown is very proud of his association with the Chicago system, claiming it is the largest conference under one umbrella in the nation. "When I was appointed to the state committee to study the classification situation for the IHSA," Jim observed, "I could speak with experience. Chicago has four classes in high school football, and two in basketball."

Jim, who played in one (Indiana) and coached in the other (Illinois), rates the two states at the top of the list from a caliber of competition standpoint. "If the two state champions played a best-of-seven series each spring, I wouldn't be surprised if it went the limit," he mused. "I don't think there would ever be a sweep because the two states are just that close."

When class basketball was first proposed in Illinois, Brown, just like so many of his coaching counterparts, opposed it. At the outset Jim was a sentimentalist on the issue. He sided with fans and some critics hoping to see more Hebrons and Cobdens. "Finally one had to take a realistic approach, and for the good of our programs the switch was a must," Jim claimed. "It's turned out to be a bonanza. More programs for more people, both boys and girls. For the IHSA it has meant more work and more headaches, but don't forget the other side: more money, more prestige, more publicity."

Considering a question whether the State Tournament has reached its zenith, Brown voted no because he foresees still-rising momentum spiraling to new heights. "I think it may be that within the next 10 years the IHSA might have to restructure its class system with a climb to three divisions," Jim explained. "For the sake of looking into the future with increasing enrollment and the number of competitors, there could be cutoffs at 350—from the present 750—to 900 or 1,000 or even up to 1,500, and the third division over 1,500. In that case we might discover the Assembly Hall may not be big enough for our tournaments. Regardless what figures are used for the cutoffs, I feel the time is coming when we'll have to take grips with the situation."

In connection with high school competition, Brown favors the use of three officials due to the surging up-tempo of the game. Jim bases this opinion on a claim that "it's almost impossible for two officials to keep pace with the young legs of the high school athlete. Also Jim defends the officials, saying:

"Anytime I check a summary and see where 40 to 50 fouls are called in one game, I know two fellows who aren't doing their job. They aren't the officials, they are the two coaches sitting on the bench. Also the use of three officials would enable us to make better and longer use of the older officials whose excellent judgment we value so highly."

During a discussion of the many oddities he encountered during his long association with sports, Brown had an ugly story to tell. It concerned DuSable's 76-70 loss to Mount Vernon in the 1954 championship game. Telling the sad story in detail, Jim said:

"The kids had finished their pre-game meal, and now we were going over the game plan at our motel in Champaign. I had the room door locked by the managers and I'm positive it was locked. Suddenly, some guy walked into the room. I don't know how he got in. I assumed he was a gangster or somebody.

"Then he said: 'You are at 12 to 1 odds to win the game and the state championship.' He also said $1.5 million had been bet on the game, adding: 'Tonight you are going to lose.'

"Then he dropped a package on the floor said to contain $5,000, and that scared the hell out of me. After he left we turned the money over to the police, and sure enough we lost. I'm not going to say the officiating beat us, but it did hurt us.

"Don't forget it was an unusual situation: the first time an all-black team with a black coach ever played for the championship. The loss ended our 31-game winning streak, and that night I learned the value of a good friend.

"I was so upset and dejected I could hardly talk, but Jerry Holtzman (a sports writer for the Chicago Sun-Times) never left my side. He was still with me long after the kids dressed and left. I'll never forget Jerry's friendship because I'll never forget the game or the outcome."

(Editor's Note—The unscheduled visitor to the DuSable meeting room either misspoke or didn't know the difference. Seldom are basketball bets made from an odds standpoint. In the majority of cases basketball wagers are made on point spreads.)

Coach Brown continued his leadership role in behalf of the DuSable players by advising them in the selection of scholarship offers—and there was a flood of them. Paxton Lumpkin and Charlie Brown went to Indiana; Shellie McMillon and Curley Johnson picked Bradley, and Karl Dennis and Bobby Jackson enrolled at Northern Illinois in DeKalb.

JACK BURMASTER

Jack Burmaster was one of the boys during the summer of 1944. Outside of a frequent spin around the front lawn pushing a mower, this Elgin schoolboy's main concern was getting to the radio in time to follow his favorite baseball team, the Chicago White Sox. Jack lived and died with the White Sox—and didn't care who knew it.

Inasmuch as he was ticketed to transfer from Elgin High School to Yale University in the fall, Jack frequently thought about his upcoming transition to Ivy League exposure and tradition. He was confident he would, in time, play basketball for Yale, but he also had another desire. What about an opportunity to play baseball for the Yale Bulldogs?

During one of his mowing sessions, Burmaster noticed a friendly face approaching up the sidewalk. It was Doug Mills, the University of Illinois' athletic director and basketball coach. Nobody had to tell Mills that Burmaster's impressive credentials included selection to the all-Tournament team with the likes of Taylorville's Johnny Orr and Ron Bontemps after the 1944 *Sweet Sixteen.*

Mills also possessed a good book on Burmaster's overall academic and athletic ability and envisioned Jack playing for the Illini. Compared to present day recruiting standards, Mills arrived slightly "light." He offered a state scholarship with a meal job (kitchen duty in exchange for three squares seven days a week) and "possibly a little help" buying the books Jack would need getting his higher education. What about lodging? Jack's family would have to pay for that.

During the visit, Doug noted Jack's deep rooted interest in baseball. Especially the White Sox. Reacting with the speed of Quick Draw McGraw, Doug asked, "How would you like to work out with the Cleveland Indians the next time they come to Chicago?" After Mills explained how he would arrange it with Cleveland Manager-Shortstop Lou Boudreau, two things were definite. Yale had lost one of its blue chip futures, and the University of Illinois had gained one. Because first base was his bag, Jack worked out there. He asked out after Mickey Rocco, the Tribe's regular first baseman, whistled two drives which almost decapitated him. After that Burmaster was content to listen to Boudreau's sales pitch in behalf of the Illini. "If you are interested in basketball," Lou stressed, "there is just one place to play. That is the University of Illinois."

Jack was "sold," and the following September he enrolled at Illinois and completely forgot about Yale.

In this manner Jack was on hand when the famed Whiz Kids returned from service to put the finishing touches on their collegiate careers. When Andy Phillip, Gene Vance, Jack Smiley, and Ken Menke moved on, his teammates included such Illini standouts as Walt Kirk, Fred Greene, Wally Osterkorn, Bill Erickson, and Chick Doster, who arrived on the campus after earning "Mister Everything" status at Decatur.

Following graduation Burmaster switched to professional basketball, joining Oshkosh, Wis. in the old National Basketball League. When Oshkosh folded, Jack moved to Sheboygan and remained with the Redskins until the franchise was shifted to Milwaukee and finally to St. Louis.

"When Milwaukee released me I thought it was the end of the world, and I returned to Elgin to plan my next move," Jack recalled. "The next day Doug Mills called and asked,

"Are you now ready to forget the pros, and settle down in a dependable job? If you are, I can place you in one right now."

With Mills breaking the ice, Burmaster reported immediately to DuPont Manual, one of the bigger high schools in Louisville, Ky., as Dale Barnstable's successor.

Blessed with some outstanding talent, Coach Burmaster's team won 33 and lost only 2 games. The second loss was to upstart Cuba, a small town school with an electrician for a coach, in the 1952 Kentucky State championship game. It was the same year both Illinois and Kentucky had something in common. While Cuba was winning in Kentucky, "Little" Hebron was doing the same thing in Illinois to prove the potentcy of the "Little Davids" in prep play.

There was a second "back home" trip in Burmaster's life following his single successful season in Louisville, where he struck up a friendship with one of the great personalities in basketball: Adolph Rupp. The famous coach at the University of Kentucky followed DuPont Manual at every opportunity in his desire to recruit Phil Grawemeyer to prove anew the claim of "What Rupp wants, Rupp gets."

This time Jack located in Evanston, the big Chicago suburb. The 22-year association of Evanston and Coach Burmaster was spotlighted when the Wildkits made four trips to the *Sweet Sixteen* and won it all in 1968 with 30 victories in 31 games. The critics were quick to label Evanston as the "most physical" team ever to win the Illinois' championship—and not without good reason.

"During my entire career," Jack said, "it was my philosophy to see kids play all sports in season as they desire. Although there are overlaps, I nevertheless like for kids to play football in the fall, basketball in the winter, and baseball or track in the spring.

"The present-day athlete is so well conditioned he can make the transition from football to basketball in about two weeks. During that time he will develop every phase of his game except the shooting finesse he will possess during the second half of the season.

"If I were building strictly a basketball program, I suppose I would want the boy in the gymnasium every possible day. Still I've found that kids who are one-sport conscious are seemingly shell shocked by the end of the season. They are up to here (pointing to his neck) with the sameness of such a rugged program every day, every week.

"I would rather have the well-rounded kid. One who is playing all the different sports as he desires and enjoys. The best recent example is Quinn Buckner, who played both football and basketball for Thornridge of Dolton, before enrolling at Indiana University. There are a lot of people who think he went the wrong way when he dropped football to concentrate on basketball."

Burmaster compared Buckner with Dwight Eddleman, a one-time teammate at Illinois, as a standout in both football and basketball. Starring in more than one sport is Jack's type of a dedicated athlete both at the high school and collegiate plateaus. En route to stardom with the New York Yankees, "Moose" Skowron blended football with baseball first at Weber High School in Chicago and later at Purdue.

And then there's Lou Boudreau, who played both basketball and baseball for the Illini. There would have been another basketballer-baseballer had Burmaster been able to play first base as well as he performed on the hardwood. "I dreamed I was an outstanding first baseman," Jack mused, "but never was I that good playing or batting."

Admitting he was prejudiced in sharing his opinions, Burmaster placed the annual Illinois champion among the first five or six nationally in rating the top powers state by state. "I've watched the scoring, and I do mean outstanding scoring, revolutionize the Illinois tournament. I'm sure Kentucky has improved since I coached there in the early 1950s. Nobody in Indiana would ever admit that their state champion wasn't better than ours."

"Reviewing Johnny Wooden's success at UCLA with mainly California kids proves it is a state to be reckoned with. That's four right there, and maybe there are one or two more to be considered. Still I'd always rate Illinois near the top and never lower than fifth or sixth."

In grading Burmaster's ratings one must remember that they are based on three different levels—player, coach, and television commentator in *Sweet Sixteen* or *Elite Eight* competition spanning more than thirty years.

STANLEY CHANGNON

Prizes and presents for athletic achievement come in many sizes. Maybe it's a gold wrist watch with the numerals set in diamonds. Maybe it's an all-expense trip to an exotic place with a check tossed in for good measure. Maybe it's a special set of golf clubs plus a paid membership in the nearest golf club. And then there's always the possibility of a brand new Cadillac.

When Mount Vernon defeated Hillsboro, 45-39, for the state championship in 1949 only the most optimistic could guess that Coach Stanley Changnon was halfway home to a state basketball tournament record that would be Illinois' first one-school, one-coach two-time consecutive winner. This record was set in 1950 when the Rams roughed up Danville in an 85-61 runaway.

Still, nothing could come close to topping one of the mentor's gifts for that first championship. That would be listing the final score as the new telephone number at the Changnon residence on Mount Vernon's Casey street.

Can you imagine the fun Changnon could have when somebody asked for his home telephone number? If he was so inclined, he could answer:

"You tell me."

"What do you mean?"

"Tell me the score when Mount Vernon won the state championship from Hillsboro in 1949."

"It was 45 to 39."

"That is my telephone number at home."

"What do you mean, that is your home telephone number?"

"Call 242-4539, and see what happens."

"If the line isn't busy, somebody, probably Mrs. Changnon, will answer, and say:

"This is the Changnon residence."

"The town was on its ear, and 'March Madness' was in full bloom after we defeated Hillsboro for the state championship," Mrs. Delphine Changnon recalled. "The celebration was fantastic, and so was the telephone call we received the next day. The caller said he was calling on behalf of the manager of the Mount Vernon telephone company, and the company would like to provide us with a new number, 4539, so we and all Mount Vernon would never forget the game or the score.

"Stanley said he wouldn't object, and within a couple of hours a workman arrived and the Changnons had a memorable new telephone number. We couldn't believe it, but 242-4539 was very busy with calls from friends and fans."

When Coach Changnon moved to Mount Vernon he was best known for the powerful football teams he developed at Johnston City and West Frankfort. He also produced two basketball tournament teams at West Frankfort, but they didn't come close to matching his Mount Vernon powerhouses. And powerhouse teams they were. Especially the 1950 club with Max Hooper fusing the heavy artillery.

Sweeping to nine straight tournament victories with the greatest of ease, the Rams scored 592 points while yielding only 371. Only once Mount Vernon missed coming close to its average. That was in the first round of the regional. The Rams did in Centralia 44-37—and any win over the Orphans then was something akin to doubling a team's and a coach's pleasure.

Long before Hollywood came up with the idea that movies were your best buy, the Changnon mentor was filming his individual gunners to teach them the importance of timing taking one-handed jump shots. Also, the hook shot was a no-no in the Rams' offensive.

The one man with the best book on Changnon is Scott Gill, who first associated himself with basketball in Mount Vernon in 1945 after receiving his discharge from service. During his 30-plus year association with the Rams, Gill served as both head and assistant coach.

"I'm not going to say Changnon discovered the one-handed jump shot," Gill claimed, "but he certainly pioneered it in Southern Illinois. Also he assigned Max Hooper to long sessions of rope jumping to improve his coordination and agility. Max really didn't become interested in the game until he entered junior high school."

Changnon also practiced free speech as a confidence-builder among his players, following the theory that speaking before groups would ease the tension playing before crowds. Especially on the road.

"After almost every practice session," the composed Gill recalled, "Stan would take the boys into the lockerroom and have one or two speak to the squad. They weren't limited to any one subject, and frequently they would review the drill just completed. Right from the outset Hooper took to this special phase of post-practice speaking like he was born to do it.

"He would pinpoint plays and separate subjects then much like he does covering athletic events on both radio and television. Max was the leader, but I remember most of the boys expressed themselves very well by the end of each season."

Mount Vernon is so pro basketball that kids in the grade schools seldom are interested in playing tag or touch football. Some of these youths are such strangers to football that it isn't uncommon for some of them to put on their helmet backwards.

The Rams' famous double in 1949 and 1950 resulted in brisk season ticket sales for choice locations in the school gymnasium which seats 2,400. "I've been told some of these tickets are included in family wills, and passed down to younger generations in this manner," Gill mused.

Mount Vernon won its first state title in 1920, beating Canton 18-14 in the championship game. Then the Rams hit a sudden success jackpot, winning the Changnon-directed double in 1949 and 1950. The Rams showed signs of returning to power with a third place finish in 1952. Coach Changnon retired after the 1953 campaign to devote fulltime to the Rams' athletic directorship, and Harold Hutchins became his successor.

Hutchins became one of the state's first rookie coaches to win a tournament in his first bid when Mount Vernon gained its third championship in six seasons. To do this the Rams took out Chicago (DuSable) 76-70 in a controversial confrontation in 1954.

Typical of coaches in his era, Changnon played a slowed down game, offensively, but he would switch to run and gun when the opportunity presented itself. It was just as Scott Gill observed: "Stan was a master keeping the other guy guessing. He would switch during alternating sweeps down the floor, but he liked the pattern game best."

Changnon completed his school chores in the spring of 1964 when he closed out his athletic directorship. Not too much later the Democrats in Mount Vernon drafted a Republican named Stanley Changnon to run for the clerkship of Mount Vernon Township. He won as easily as most of his basketball teams. Now, after a trio of four-year terms, the man who ran unopposed winning his second and third elections, is retiring from the political arena. This way he will have fulltime to devote to gardening and assisting his wife, a former Latin and English teacher, with her summer canning labors.

RARE COMBINATION—Tom Millikin has both played and coached in the State Tournament. In 1969 he was on the Proviso East bench as his Jim Brewer-led Pirates copped the crown with a 58-51 victory over Peoria (Spalding). Joining Tom on the bench are guard Pete Bouzeos (44), Harvey Roberts and Ralph Sykes. (Photo By United Press International)

Lawrenceville senior Jay Shidler, established the all-time State Basketball Tournament scoring record with a sensational final four-game performance. (Photo By Curt Beamer, Urbana Courier)

TWO-HANDED MAROON—Champaign captain Jesse Clements launches a running two-hander. (Photo By Champaign News-Gazette)

Chapter 4

We're Number 1!
The Teams

COLLINSVILLE

The story is unbelievable. That would be the awesome and completely amazing success story involving basketball at Collinsville High School. This fascinating and victory-packed saga started in 1907 and carried into the United States' bicentennial celebration. Considering the fact no fewer than 14 coaches had a hand—a winning hand in each case—in this success, makes it as American as hot dogs and apple pie.

Even with a two-year time-out from competition, the Kahoks won 1,346 games while losing only 381 when the nation celebrated its 200th birthday. In compiling this super record, Collinsville became the first American school to win 1,000 games, an achievement which was finalized January 14, 1961.

And still there is another interesting story to be told. During all this time Collinsville has managed to win but two state tournaments in the IHSA's post-season series. The Kahoks waited until the 1960s to trigger Operation Title Town. The Kahoks won in 1961 and repeated in 1965 under the direction of Vergil Fletcher. Altogether Fletcher has molded a record 12 tournament series teams.

Fletcher, a 30-year veteran in the coach colony, learned long ago nobody wins without the horses—and Vergil has had more than his share of thoroughbreds. The list starts with Rodger Bohnenstiehl, who went to Kansas, and ends with Fred Riddle, who attended Iowa and wrote a sports love story by marrying the coach's daughter.

In between Fletcher can talk about the Good Ol' Days in recounting the feats of Chuck Kraak and Sammy Miranda, who moved on to

245

Indiana University; Tom Parker, who became one of Coach Adolph Rupp's standouts at Kentucky; Ray Sonnenberg, who attended St. Louis, and Walter "Hoot" Evers.

Evers, a Major League baseball player who became a major league executive for the Detroit Tigers, played at Collinsville before enrolling at the University of Illinois. Hoot advanced from Champaign to the majors and played for the Tigers, Boston Red Sox, Baltimore Orioles, and the Cleveland Indians.

Recalling Evers' accomplishments at Illinois, retired Athletic Director Doug Mills claimed, "If Hoot and his brother Eddie were playing now, they would be super stars. Both were just that outstanding. We've had some great brother acts within the state, but Hoot and Eddie rate among the very best."

Altogether the Kahoks have fielded four All-Americans, and 21 All-Staters. Besides Bohnenstiehl, the All-Americans were Bogie Redmon, Terry Bethel, and Tom Parker.

Collinsville possesses one of the oddest Century Circles in basketball. Six times the Kahoks have won more than 100 games against an individual opponent in this manner:

East St. Louis:	104–25	Alton (Sr.):	112–35
Wood River:	105–21	Belleville (West):	118–21
Granite City (South):	111–37	Edwardsville:	120–34

Coach	Years	Win	Lose
Bliss Dee	1907–1909	18	6
R. C. Sayre	1910	11	2
William Green	1911–1912	28	6
William Street	1913	17	6
William Graham	1914	20	2
T. J. Beck	1915–1916	38	16
M. A. Andreen	1917	7	5
John Hawkins	1920–1924	68	25
W. O. Larson	1925–1937	251	74
Allan Metternick	1938–1942	100	39
James Placek	1943–1944	43	14
D. K. Darling	1945	26	9
Jack Fabri	1946	30	10
Vergil Fletcher	1947–1976	689	167
Totals		1,346	381

While these half dozen opponents were accounting for almost half of Collinsville's total victories, there is ample evidence that the basketball hasn't always bounced in the Kahoks' direction. In Alumni-Varsity competition, the returning Ol' Grads captured six of 11 decisions. Also, it's a matter of record that Collinsville has never beaten Decatur (0-4); trails DuQuoin (3-4); lost six of nine decisions involving Mount Vernon, and played Nashville to a 5-5 standoff.

Collinsville isn't without a "Rags to Riches" story featuring one of its All-Americans, Roger Bohnenstiehl. Roger was cut from the junior high school squad and stayed out during his freshman year. While Tom Parker and Terry Bethel dominate most of the Kahoks' individual scoring records, there is one statistic which stands out beacon bright. That would be Bohnenstiehl's .685 shooting percentage during the 1963-1964 season.

When the Kahoks won their second crown in 1965, there was another touch of baseball attached to this success. One of Coach Fletcher's forwards was Harry Parker, who later became a major league pitcher. Harry won eight of 12 decisions for the pennant-winning New York Mets in 1973.

During a 20-year period in Collinsville, Fletcher also coached football. After winning 100 games, Vergil reasoned it was "too much work," and he quit to devote full time to basketball. Twice during his career Coach Fletcher doubled his pleasure. He had two sons playing for the Kahoks. Mike later attended Memphis State. Marc, an All-Stater in 1974, enrolled at Tulane.

In consideration of his outstanding success—opening the 1971-72 season with his 692nd victory—the Collinsville fans named their 4,000 seat gymnasium in Coach Fletcher's honor. This is nothing short of sensational progress reviewing Fletcher's record dating back to 1945 when he coached the base team at Fort Lewis, Washington.

Has Vergil any particular recipe for basketball success? Yes. He's convinced good athletes build great teams, and Fletcher has the record to prove it.

COBDEN

Every game has a turning point, and so it was with tiny Cobden's Cinderella team in 1964. Playing smaller and faster Pekin for all the marbles in this super schoolboy showdown, the battle of wits started before the two rivals took the floor. With at least 95 percent of the capacity crowd in the Assembly Hall cheering for Cobden, Coach Dawson Hawkins made sure his Pekin Chinks wouldn't be psyched out before the tipoff. If Cobden planned an early entry, Pekin would enter side by side to share the fans' thunderous welcome. If Cobden elected to wait awhile, Pekin would follow suit. Hawkins vowed to make it a two team entry if it meant waiting until midnight.

"I knew Dawdy (Coach Hawkins) was playing games," Cobden Coach Dick Ruggles explained, "and we let him wait. As we stalled I told the kids to let the tension out and relax. We talked about everything but basketball. Finally they said "lets go," and the two teams came out of the tunnel together. The enthusiastic roar of the crowd was deafening—and everybody knew who the fans were cheering."

With the entire season riding on the outcome, another battle of wits developed late in the game. Pekin, owning the ball and a two point lead with slightly more than two minutes remaining, took a time-out. As the two teams went to the sidelines, all the famous generals in history never talked strategy faster and more seriously than Hawkins and Ruggles.

Hawkins' command stressed: "Make them come to you." Ruggles repeated his order: "You have to get the ball." The countdown of slightly more than 120 precious seconds would resume at the end of the time-out.

Quick to size up the situation when the two teams returned to the floor, Ruggles whispered to a friend: "We look like we're going out to pick apples!"

Now, more than 10 years later, Dick admits: "I made a mistake. I should have taken another time-out right then and chewed out some people. Maybe it would have been different; the shock of coming back to the bench to catch a lot of . . . Also such a move might have turned off their (Pekin's) momentum geared for the last big push. "I realize all this is history, but I never cease to wonder what might have happened had I called for another time-out right then."

What did happen was Pekin's 50-45 victory to discount the best small-school success story since 1952 when Hebron won. Hebron beat Quincy by five in overtime. This trip Cobden, the new Hebron, lost by five in regulation time.

The finish, nevertheless, put a damper on the then increasing statewide pressure for two-class basketball to help the smaller schools. It didn't look like Cobden needed any saving as it lost a photo finish in another David & Goliath showdown. Compiling a two-season 58-5 record for an awesome .921 percentage, the big kids from the little school were 26-2 as juniors, and 32-3 as seniors under Ruggles' direction.

"We were disappointed we didn't win in 1963," Ruggles reasoned, "when McLeansboro took us out in the sectional. Bob and Jim Burns were the big guns for McLeansboro then, and they helped to shoot us down."

Oddly enough McLeansboro handed the 1964 club its first loss

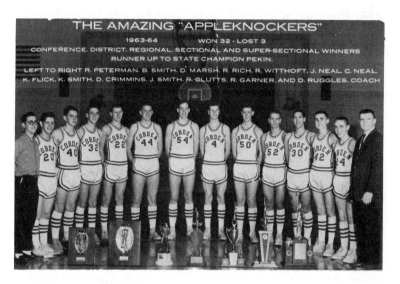

THE AMAZING "APPLEKNOCKERS"

1963-64   WON 32 - LOST 3

CONFERENCE, DISTRICT, REGIONAL, SECTIONAL AND SUPER-SECTIONAL WINNERS
RUNNER UP TO STATE CHAMPION PEKIN.

LEFT TO RIGHT R. PETERMAN, B. SMITH, D. MARSH, R. RICH, R. WITTHOFT, J. NEAL, C. NEAL,
K. FLICK, K. SMITH, D. CRIMMINS, J. SMITH, R. CLUTTS, R. GARNER, AND D. RUGGLES, COACH

MOST REMEMBERED TEAM—Perhaps the team most remembered by the general public, school personnel and the news media was the 1963-64 edition of the Cobden Appleknockers, the gigantic team from the tiny school (enrollment 147) from the little (population 918) Southern Illinois town, which lost the championship game to Pekin 50-45 on Saturday, March 21. Cobden people did not let their friends and relatives forget, either, and this Photo Post Card told the story. The names may be familiar, but the heights of the Appleknockers may not be. Here are both, from the left: Manager Roger Peterman, Bob Smith (5-8), Dan Marsh (6-0), Ralph Rich (6-1), Roy Whitthoft (6-2), Jim Neal (6-5), Chuck Neal (6-6), Ken Flick (6-5), Ken Smith (6-5), Darrell Crimmins (6-1), Jim Smith (6-0), Rodney Clutts (5-11), Roger Garner (5-8) and Coach Dick Ruggles (5-10). The Neals were brothers. The Smiths were all cousins. (Photo Courtesy Dick Ruggles) during a holiday tournament. The Appleknockers didn't lose again until the final game of the regular season. Albion of Edwards County, a 32-point loser in the first game against Cobden, upended the Appleknockers by five.

"I went bananas after this loss," Dick recalled, "but later I had to admit it was the best thing that could have happened to us. We were cocky. We were overconfident. We were lackadaisical. We were everything a team shouldn't be going into the tournament.

"The following week's practice was our best of the season by far, and this is understandable. It was the most intelligent team I ever coached or have been associated with. The senior-class valedictorian and salutorian were regulars. So was the valedictorian of the junior class, and the other two starters ranked high in their classes."

During the dramatic race to the runner-up finish, Cobden played without one of its captains, the result of a tragedy following the 1963 season. Three players went swimming in a near-by lake, and only two returned. Tom Crowell, the captain-elect for 1964, drowned despite the frantic rescue efforts of Ken Smith and Chuck Neal.

When last seen Crowell, a novice swimmer, was walking in chest-high water. Suddenly he faded from view—and was never seen again. Individually, the players dedicated the season to Crowell, vowing to go all the way during a squad meeting before the first practice session.

A staunch booster of team unity, Ruggles used a balanced offense and the Appleknockers ended up with five starters averaging 14-16 points per game through the regular season, and 10 victories in 11 tournament games. "Our kids were very unselfish, and that is the way they played," Ruggles remembered.

Ruggles' move from Massachusetts to Southern Illinois is a typical American sports story. Dick had a friend who knew a friend, and everybody was in the right spot at the right time. Dick's friend was Monroe McLean, his basketball coach at Quincy High School. McLean's friend was Carl Erickson, then the athletic director at SIU. McLean called Erickson with a report on Ruggles. Erickson was interested, and invited Dick to visit the campus. Dick never left outside of holiday and summer vacation visits back home.

He played under Coach Lynn Holder for two years, and spent the next two seasons playing for Harry Gallitan, who left the pro ranks to join the Salukis.

"I had no idea what to expect when I was told to report to Mr. Erickson in Carbondale," Ruggles began. "I loved the Boston area. I loved the ol' Braves, and players like Tommy Holmes, Warren Spahn, Vern Bickford, and Johnny Sain were my heroes. We'd sneak into Braves' field once or twice a week. When the Braves left Boston I was broken-hearted.

"As a National Leaguer I couldn't root for the Red Sox, but I adopted Ted Williams as my hero. Bob Cousy was another of my heroes. As kids we never had enough money to buy tickets to see the Celtics in the Garden, so we'd wait outside for an opportunity to sneak in—and we missed seeing very few games."

Ruggles' first coaching job was at Hurst-Bush, since consolidated with Herrin. Cobden had just finished beating Hurst-Bush by 35 points when a member of the Cobden school board offered him the basketball job. After telling how he took the job on the spot, Dick added: "No coach ever was happier after a 35-point loss than I was that night."

Because word was getting around the state that Cobden could be a factor in tournament play, one of Ruggles' first orders concerned dressing up the Appleknockers with new uniforms. "I called my friend Amos Newlin, an equipment salesman, and told him about the board's order to buy new outfits. He displayed about six different samples, and then showed us the same type uniforms the St. Louis Hawks were wearing. Naturally this made a hit with the kids, and Newlin wrote the order immediately.

"If we weren't the best team in our neck of the woods, we were surely the best dressed."

After the two fabulous seasons with Cobden, Ruggles moved to Nashville as frosh-sophomore coach. Dick arrived in time to start working in Nashville's new gymnasium—a future IHSA tournament site.

Ruggles had another job at Cobden in addition to coaching a tournament team in his fourth year out of SIU. He was in charge of the cheerleaders, and this chore produced a situation Dick hadn't counted upon. Operating on the theory that cheerleaders had to maintain passing grades just like the basketball players, Dick had to: 1) drop two of the cheerleaders, and 2) find replacements. "It wasn't easy, but we got the job done in time to keep everybody happy," Dick recalled.

Following Cobden's advance to the state championship game, the media representatives asked Ruggles to compare two of the state's powerhouse teams: Decatur and Galesburg. Also if Cobden had played its best games in the *Sweet Sixteen* competition?

"Thinking back over the season," Ruggles began, "I said I thought our strongest and best game from start to finish was against Alto Pass. The next day I was embarrassed to read a headline: "Coach Says Cobden Played Better Against Alto Pass."

"The first thing I did was call the coach at Alto Pass and apologize to him and his players after describing the situation. By the way, Alto Pass has since been consolidated with Cobden."

In connection with stepping down from the varsity to the fresh-men-sophomore coach level, Ruggles mused:

"Right now we're going through a period when the coaches are working harder and devoting more time to athletics than the kids. The kids want to compete, but they lack the time to study, practice, watch television, date, and frequently work at a part-time job to earn additional spending-money. There aren't too many around these days who will spend every free minute in the gym shooting or play-ing one on one or two on two like the Eddlemans and Cousys and other outstanding athletes used to do.

"Athletics have become a convenience for them in their search for enough time to touch all the bases."

Meanwhile Ruggles has turned to officiating in his spare time, and he has a milestone he would like to reach. Presently, Dick is work-ing some 40 games a season at both the grade and high school levels trying to improve his status as an official. If the time comes when he is assigned to the championship game in the State Tournament, he will make history. There has never been a coach in the champion-ship game who returned to officiate one.

HEBRON

Little Hebron—with a high school enrollment of 97 and a town pop-ulation of less than eight hundred—was the big team in 1952. Sports writers and sports columnists thrilled at the opportunity to write it like it was: a beautiful blend of Cinderella and David and Goliath. Nevertheless, there were ample other angles such as flexibility and finesse as Hebron raced to 31 victories in the season's first 32 games. Then came the four-game sweep in the *Sweet Sixteen,* with Hebron following Freeport to the throne as the new champion in Illinois high school basketball. In their eagerness to root for the small town favorite, many fans forgot that Hebron was rated No. 1 in the state putting together a fifteen-game winning streak during the season's early play. What was to be Hebron's only loss of the season, a 71-68 setback in Crystal Lake, cost the loss of the top spot in the weekly polls. Hebron, however, regained the top spot going into the *Sweet Sixteen.*

"People, especially people outside our district," Paul Judson, one of the Judson twins, explained, "were surprised that such a small school could be rated so highly. What they apparently didn't know or realize is that we weren't enrolled in any particular conference. We played as many big schools as we played little ones during the regular season.

"Russ Ahearn, our coach, followed one formula from start to fin-ish. He figured our offense was strong enough to average 75 points a game, and our defense—strictly man-to-man—could limit any opponent to 60 or fewer points. Also, he didn't believe in running up the score.

"Anytime the first team scored 50 points, he would start to substitute. If he returned the first team to start the second half, he would start substituting again when he had 65 points on the board."

In the championship test against Quincy, the state's No. 2 team in the polls at the time, Hebron won 64-59 in overtime. It was the only overtime championship game in the "Sweet Sixteen's" long history.

During the Judson twins' (Paul and Phil) four-year tenure at Hebron, the Green Giants won 98 of 113 games for an amazing .865 percentage.

The Hebron record in the Judson era reads:

	W.	L.	Pct.		W.	L.	Pct.
Freshman	14	7	.667	Junior	26	2	.928
Sophomore	23	5	.821	Senior	35	1	.972

	W.	L.	Pct.
Total	98	15	.867

Still the Hebronites probably never will know just how close they came to losing the twins. "Howie, our older brother, played at Hebron for Coach Les Harmon," Paul began, "and he had great respect for him. After our father died, Mom depended on Howie's advice. He was of the opinion that he would like to have us play for Coach Harmon, who had moved from Hebron to Barrington. Most of the arrangements were completed; the family would move to Barrington before we entered high school.

"Then Coach Ahearn moved to Hebron from Elgin, where he had been an assistant under Coach John Kraft. Howie knew Ahearn, and finally it was decided to keep the family home in Hebron. I've often wondered what might have happened had we moved to Barrington."

Hebron's title team was pretty much an ironman machine. Coach Ahearn played just five men against Quincy, and one of these was a six foot, 10-inch center named Bill Schulz. A junior at the time, Bill's teammates called him a "Walking Stepladder." Paul regarded Bill as a "made" player, who developed an effective left-hand hook shot. This shot was so proficient, in fact, that he scored 12 field goals on 16 attempts to pace Hebron's individual scorers against Quincy. The twins didn't have to apologize for their contributions. Paul scored 13 points and Phil 12.

Kenley Spooner and Don Wilbrandt were the two other starters, and game after game they did a lot more than come along for the ride. The summary of the championship games proves that. Wilbrandt scored 10 points and Spooner added five.

Hebron followed pretty much the same offensive pattern during the march to glory. It shot down Champaign in round one 55-46. The Green Giants moved into the semifinals after eliminating Lawrenceville 65-55. Rock Island was the next victim to hit the deck, going down 64-56. Sixty-four was the lucky number again in the championship game with powerhouse Quincy being the victim, this time, as Hebron won 64-59 in overtime.

During the Elgin Regional and the Waukegan Sectional, the Green Giants encountered one very tough and tense game. Recalling host Elgin's all-out effort, Paul Judson explained:

"Elgin led most of the way before we could catch 'em in the last quarter to win 49-47. I do believe that particular win was the second most thrilling of my high school career. Elgin is a big school. It's basketball program is outstanding, and the school is rich in tournament tradition and experience. While we had the feeling, all along, that we could go all the way, I still think that particular game was the clincher. We had the confidence that we could play and beat strong teams."

There is something else about Hebron's success which won't be found studying the summary. That would be the move which sent Schulz to Hebron, the result of a consolidation of Hebron and Alden.

For the Judson twins basketball was a way of life from the time they could handle a basketball. Brother Howie saw to that. Reviewing some of their daily drills, Howie said:

"I can remember times when the twins would practice outside wearing snow suits. It was just that cold, but they seldom missed a practice regardless of the season."

The time he spent helping to bring out the twins' potential ended up costing him a lot of telephone tolls. The White Sox were taking the southern route returning from spring training in Pasadena, California. This meant they were in Arizona, New Mexico, Texas, and finally Louisiana when the state tournament was in progress in Champaign.

Howie would make two or three calls each night to get the score and all the details. The night of the championship game, 'tis said, he called a friend who put the radio next to the telephone to assure him hearing most of the fourth quarter and all of the overtime action.

Following graduation there was talk that the Judson twins would enroll at the University of Wisconsin to assure them being close to the family home and their mother. Then came a switch in plans. They enrolled at the University of Illinois to follow in brother Howie's footsteps. One the their fellow student-athletes was Bruce Brothers, Quincy's best all-around player the previous March when the Green Giants' killer instinct dropped the Blue Devils into second place in a fall heard completely around the state and the far reaches wherever basketball is played.

Chapter 5

Dribble! Pass! Drive! Score!
The Players

DOUG MILLS

When Elgin became the first school to win back-to-back State Tournaments in 1924 and 1925, the Maroons were directed by two different coaches. The record shows Mark Wilson coached in 1924, and Cliff Adams was Elgin's successful mentor in 1925. Recordwise, this information is right as rain, but still there is a catch to it, and no less an authority than Doug Mills has the information to set the situation straight. This is the same Doug Mills who was a regular on both of the title teams.

"The credit for molding and developing our team should go to Otto Vogel, an outfielder who joined the Chicago Cubs in 1923," Mills began. "Elgin was Vogel's first coaching job, and he went there after mid-year graduation from the University of Illinois. Actually Vogel was a replacement when he came to Elgin. Paul Church, an outstanding floor guard at Purdue, was the coach, but he left at the start of the school year to take another job.

"The job was given to Vogel, and he went to work immediately to build the team. Despite the fact we had an excellent record, Vogel quit just before tournament time. He had signed a 1924 contract with the Cubs and left to report for spring training with the team on Catalina Island just off the California coast. We (the team) didn't know it at the time, but baseball was his first love and he was hopeful of becoming a major league outfielder.

"Still, he didn't lose interest in our basketball team. I recall receiving several telephone calls from him checking our progress, and I know he also called some of the other players. After we beat Canton 16-14, he told me Elgin would win it. He was right. We did win, but Wilson was our coach.

"Although 1924 was the last year he played for the Cubs, he didn't return to Elgin. Instead he went to the University of Iowa, replacing Sam Barry as baseball coach in 1925. Otto Vogel was good people, the type who could coach any sport and become a winner. I've often compared Otto with Fritz Crisler and Leo Johnson considering their ability to communicate with their players.

"Due to his vast interest in baseball it's too bad he didn't make it with the Cubs, but he did build some outstanding teams at Iowa. Whenever I went to Iowa City, I'd look up Otto and we would talk about the days when he was building his great team in Elgin, and I was playing with guys like Herb Hill, Harry Long, Louis Semeny, and Andy Solyom. I'll say one thing for Otto: more than once he told me he would make the same move all over again. At least he didn't second guess himself.

"Cliff Adams became our coach in 1925, and I think we won one or two more games than we did the previous year. One thing I'm sure of, we beat Champaign in the finals."

(Mills was pretty close to correct: Elgin had a 24-3 record in 1924, and won 25 of 27 games in 1925.)

Doug also remembers something else: after graduation from the University of Illinois, he coached both football and basketball against Adams when he started at Joliet.

Comparing the 1924 and 1925 Elgin teams, Doug recalled, "There were a few slight changes in personnel. Chapman Wells replaced me at forward when I was shifted to guard, and Andy (Solyom) took over for Harry Lang at center. Gerald Slavic, another newcomer, and Herb (Hill) were the other starters. Having won it once, I think it's a carryover thrill which forces a team to drive and drive. I can't say for sure but I would guess that great Taylorville team (45-0) in 1944 probably wanted a repeat championship more than anything else in 1945. When a team wins once, it's just natural it would like to win two or three in a row. That's competition."

During his first stop at Illinois, Doug won six letters — three in basketball, and three in football. "Funny thing," Mills mused, "nobody ever asks me about my baseball at Illinois. Apparently they knew I was just too tired to play. Still I had some baseball offers when I graduated, and I signed with the St. Louis Cardinals. They sent me through the farm system, and I roomed with Bill Lee at Greensboro, North Carolina. He later pitched for the Cubs, overcoming a sore arm to become an outstanding pitcher. (A total of 169 victories in 14 seasons.)

"Still I had a decision to make: baseball or coaching? I picked coaching, and I've enjoyed every day of it."

Some observations he formulated while playing at Elgin resulted
in Doug accepting the Joliet High School offer instead of collegiate
bids he received from Brown University, the University of Kentucky,
and LaCrosse (Wisconsin) State Teachers' College. "They had many
outstanding athletes in Joliet, and I realized the great potential if a
fellow could get lucky and mold the community's melting pot together. We had one tournament team in basketball, and we took a
squad of four freshmen, one sophomore, and one junior to Champaign.

"Joliet played Moline in the first game of the tournament, one of
those breakfast time matches, and lost. Two years after I left in 1937
these same kids won a state championship for Herm Walser (the
coach)."

Doug's high school coaching career ended when he received a
message from the beloved George Huff, Illinois' fabled athletic director. It read, "We would like to have you return to Illinois." Huff's
timing was all-important because it would assure Doug working for
two coaches for whom he had played: Bob Zuppke in football and
Craig Ruby in basketball.

Doug's return to the Champaign campus came during a mini-
transition period for the Illini. He was the freshmen coach in both
basketball and football. When he was promoted to backfield coach
in football, the famous Mister Z made two other changes in his staff.
Leo Johnson came aboard from Millikin University, and Ralph
Fletcher moved in from Aurora. Although it's impossible to compare recruiting on a then and now basis, Mills knew the way former
day athletes attended college. "The boy either worked his way
through school or depended upon his parents for financial assistance," Doug stressed as he applied new importance to self discipline
in the average athlete's lifestyle.

To this day the former athletic director retains the highest regard
for the high school coaches within the state, saying, "They never attempt to oversell a boy seeking a scholarship or aid. Let me take
Norm Ziebell as an example. During his successful career at Morton
of Cicero, his boys always were basically sound. They were capable
of playing as well as Norm said they could although some would develop faster than others. Never, however, would you have to start at
ground level to teach them fundamentals. They already were well-
schooled."

Proving coaches are really fans when it comes to stressing speed
and action, Doug well remembers one of his summer coaching
school students. That would be Cecil May, who coached at Waterman. "Many coaches have discussed many athletes with me," Doug
explained, "but May is the only one who ever talked more about a

boy's defensive skills than his offensive talents.

"May admired Jack Smiley and he was completely sold on his defensive play. Speaking with complete confidence, he told me: 'Jack will be the best defensive player you ever coached.' He was right. Jack really was the best. Playing head-to-head he could defense an opponent better than anybody I've ever seen."

Enrollment in the Illinois coaching school numbered from 30 to 40 each summer, and this was Doug's way of getting to know the high school coaches. "It wasn't a lark class because the participants received credits," Mills said.

One summer a nun enrolled in the class because she had been appointed to coach the eighth grade boys basketball team at a school in the Peoria area. "She wrote and asked if I could help her learn something about the game. I advised her to enter our school, and she did.

"One of the most interesting letters I've ever received," Doug noted, "came from this nun late the next season. She reported the team's first victory after 13 straight losses. Also she invited me to speak at the team's banquet, and I did."

Mills remains a strong booster of high school coaches, especially in basketball, with full consideration for jobs in the collegiate ranks. Doug feels there is just one difference between the two levels— recruiting. "If a college coach doesn't recruit, he isn't going to win. If he doesn't win, he isn't going to be around too long. I've long felt the high school coach can work successfully with college athletes. He will find a way to communicate and sell his particular philosophy."

"When the athletic director at Illinois decided to fire the basketball coach, he didn't hesitate to hire a high school coach as his successor. I was pleased with the new coach's immediate success. Would I make the same move again? Very definitely."

Mills was named the Illini's AD in 1941. He continued to double as basketball coach until the end of the 1947 season when he reached into Champaign High School to get Harry Combes. "Two checks for two jobs was enjoyable, but I soon learned two jobs for one man was just too rugged," Doug quipped.

The rank and file of Illini fans need just one guess to name the era Mills discovered as the most enjoyable during his entire cage coach role in Champaign. It was the organization and fielding of the Whiz Kids. "It was a pleasure to coach them. They were outstanding athletes and individuals. A person could coach all his life and still never come up with a team like that."

Recalling how he managed to rope the Whiz Kids for the Illini corral, Doug explained: "I saw Gene Vance play just twice in high school. Once in Clinton, and once in a State Tournament game. He fouled out early in the third quarter of the game in Clinton, but I saw enough to convince me that he'd make it. Cecil May's information on Jack Smiley was all I needed. When Granite City won the tournament in 1940, Andy Phillip literally carried the team to victory.

"Andy was such a standout that he was the talk of the tournament. Also Ray Duncan, who was Phillip's junior high school coach, was on our staff at the time and Ray was most helpful selling Illinois to him. Because Ken Menke played at Dundee—not too far from Elgin —I caught him several times. Also, we had a friend in court selling the Illini to Ken in the person of his Dundee coach, Eugene deLacey.

"I was impressed with Menke right from the start. He could play forward or guard, and run all day. deLacey doted on the fast break, and this made Ken even more valuable.

"Art Mathisen was another player I didn't see until he arrived on the campus. Red Pace, who used to do a lot of officiating in the college and professional ranks, was Art's coach at Dwight before he joined our staff. Red's opinion was good enough for me, and Mathisen was the Whiz Kids' first center."

As great as the Whizzers proved to be, Mills is convinced military service calls prevented them from ever reaching their peak due to the long layoff between their junior and senior seasons.

Doug estimated that 80 percent of the tournament players in the 1940s and into the 1950s wanted to attend their state university. He recalled Andy Phillip telling him he didn't know the university was in Champaign until he played in his first tournament at Huff Gym. Mills himself had never been on the campus until he made the first trip with Elgin in 1924.

The man who played, coached, and later became the official host of the tourney after it moved to Champaign cited still another reason besides loyalty for this Illini interest. Most parents favored enrollment at the University of Illinois because it was cheaper compared to out-state schools in tuition and fees. Also closer to home.

Doug pointed to the fellowship attached to Big Ten basketball, explaining, "When I played at Illinois, Bud Foster was playing for Wisconsin, Branch McCracken for Indiana, and Bennie Oosterbaan for Michigan. Later, when we became coaches, we were still playing against each other. We were good friends, but we always went against each other real hard."

Mills admitted he retained his basketball coachship longer than he originally expected because he "hoped for the best, and feared the worst" in connection with the returning Whiz Kids. Due to many upsetting experiences and added responsibilities, the Menke-Phillip-Smiley-Vance foursome never did regain pre-war standards. The best known sixth player for the Whiz Kids was Vic Wukovits from South Bend, Indiana. "Vic walked into my office one day," Doug recalled, "and said he would like to play for Illinois. I asked him if his brother was Tom Wukovits, who played for Notre Dame. He answered "yes", and said his brother suggested that he enter Illinois. All he sought was a meal job, and a second job to help pay part of his room rent. Without a doubt Vic was the best walk-on I ever coached, and he was willing to work for his keep."

During his long association with the university, Doug remembers when the Illini had three of basketball's best quarterbacks: Lou Boudreau, Andy Phillip, and Dike Eddleman. "They could do everything and do it well—the trademark of outstanding leaders," Mills claimed. IHSA boosters need not be told that Lou, Andy, and Dike all played on state championship teams.

Mills had another compliment from his 25 year tenure as athletic director. He has a namesake, Doug Mills from Galesburg. The younger Doug Mills, now an executive in a Champaign bank, played basketball, punted for the football team and pitched so successfully he was a Big Ten leader in 1961 with a 4-0 record with an even 1.00 earned run average spanning 35 innings in five games. And still there hasn't been any mention of his best sport, golf. Doug Mills II, no relation, is one of the leaders in the Champaign-Urbana area going tee to green.

When they write the record on Doug Mills he will be credited with two firsts. 1-He was the father of Saturday afternoon basketball in the Big Ten. 2-He was the state tournament's first official host when the IHSA moved the gala meet to Champaign.

GEORGE KELLER

In 1931 when Coach Gay Kintner was readying Decatur for one of its 11 state tournament appearances, he had a sixth player named George Keller. Considering his many chores and contributions, Keller would be rated a super sub by today's standards. Then he was just an eager handyman, a 5-9 lightweight who would tackle any job including an opportunity to play center.

Now, more than 45 years later, Keller is a youngish senior citizen who hasn't drifted too far away from sports. Unless the weather is too cold for Eskimos, his work week stops at the stroke of 12 noon on Friday and George is headed for his favorite golf course. "I like to be outdoors, and enjoy the competition as well as the walking," Keller explained. "I watch all sports on TV, and follow our high school teams as time permits. Nothing, however, interferes with my golf game."

Keller speaks with tremendous reverence anytime Coach Kintner's name is mentioned. "Our 1931 team was typically Kintner," George began, "because we lost to Springfield twice and dropped three other games during the regular season. These losses seldom upset him because he regarded the state tournament as his foremost goal. He always attached greater importance to his team's tournament record than he did its wins and losses during the season schedule of the Big 12 Conference.

"Coach Kintner stressed defense and ball control. We had tipoff plays and patterns trying to take full advantage of the center jump. Decatur had only one high school at the time, and still most of his players played football and basketball, or basketball and track."

Although Decatur was a five-time loser during the season, Kintner still felt his team reached the zenith when it defeated Galesburg, 30-26, in the championship game for its 29th victory. "After the game we dressed fast to hurry home from Champaign for the victory celebration," Keller recalled. "Most of the townspeople turned out, and I have to think the street car motormen and conductors were the only ones who didn't enjoy all the hoopla.

"Everytime a car would stop, somebody would pull the trolley and street cars were stalled all over town. It wasn't vandalism. Just kids, and frequently their parents, enjoying all the pranks."

After recalling how knee guards and long wool stockings were standard equipment in basketball, Keller called off the names of the starting regulars on Decatur's first championship team. "Because the center was generally the busiest player on the floor," George noted, "I will start with Al Schroeder. He was our center, and a very good one. John Stuckey and Ray Rex were the forwards, and the guards were Kelly Martin and Gene Hagger. When did I play? Not too often. Coach Kintner stayed pretty much with the same lineup for the entire game. This meant mainly the subs would play only if one or two of the regulars fouled out."

The first five starters were seniors, and were graduated before the next season. Being a junior, Keller could have adopted "It's a Lonesome Old Town" for a theme song during the next year as Coach Kintner set out on a new rebuilding program. The next payoff came five years later when Decatur's 1936 team went all the way again. This trip the Reds were an 11-time loser during the season, and still managed to rope unbeaten Danville in the title game 26-22.

In 1937, Decatur returned to the tourney and advanced to the title match, bowing to Joliet, 40-20, to suffer its 12th loss in 35 games during the season as well as the tournament. Kintner's third title team blossomed in 1945, shifting into power drive with a run and gun offensive to trip Champaign, 62-54.

It was after this game that the media changed Decatur's nickname from the Reds to the Runnin' Reds — and with good reason. The 62 points then was an all-time high winning score in tournament history.

Decatur basketball was rocked with tragedy in 1960. Coach Kintner suffered a massive heart attack, stricken seconds after the buzzer sounded to start the second half in Decatur's MacArthur High School gymnasium.

"I talked to him before the game," MacArthur Coach Ray DeMoulin explained, "and he was in good spirits seemingly without an ache or a worry. As our players came to the bench, I looked over and Gay was stretched out on the floor in front of the Red's bench. A total hush came over the crowd as mouth to mouth resuscitation was administered before an ambulance arrived.

Sitting up in the stands watching every move, moist-eyed, was Coach Kintner's handyman sub on the 1931 championship team: George Keller. "I couldn't believe my eyes," Keller claimed, "and it was shocking to even think about. I saw it happen, a man falling over and stretched out on the floor in a matter of seconds.

"My son Doug played in the game for MacArthur, and by the time we returned home the news was announced: Coach Kintner was dead."

Keller, who enrolled at the University of Illinois before dropping out a year later to find a job, officiated in the Decatur area for 27 years. Having started during the depression years of the mid 1930s, George can recall many $5.00 fees for working two games alone. Later he teamed up with Al Unser, who was to become a major league catcher. The Keller-Unser ties from officiating became so strong that George spent one season working as business manager of the Decatur Commodores when Al managed the minor league club.

A typically spirited "let me do it" type, George doesn't cling to any "the good old days were better" claims. "Today's game is many times better than the game we played," George mused, "and I can see even more improvement in the future. I'd favor basketball in high school going to the 30-second clock. Much skill and finesse is involved in the slow-down game, but I feel the fans favor increased scoring and continuous action from start to finish.

"That, however, is the only phase of basketball I would consider changing."

Having been a fan of the Decatur Staleys in the long ago football wars, Keller still follows the fortunes of the Chicago Bears in typical fan manner. He remembers when names like baseball's Chuck Dressen, a Decatur native, and George Halas, who moved the Staleys to Chicago, were at the top of the town's sports news daily when baseball and football were in season.

"And don't forget Millikin," the man said as he rushed away to keep his tee time at the golf course.

LOU BOUDREAU

At fifteen he was a member of Harvey's state championship basketball team and honorary captain of the All-Tournament team. At eighteen he was enrolled at the University of Illinois on a basketball scholarship. At age twenty he was wearing a major league baseball uniform for the Cleveland Indians. Short months after his 24th birthday he became the youngest manager in baseball. In 1948 he was a 30-year-old shortstop-skipper of Cleveland's World Series winning Indians.

This is the bouncy equation Lou Boudreau parlayed into one of sports' most fascinating stories. For the last two of these progressive achievements, Lou deserved credit for triple time in the salary league. As the youngest manager ever, Boudreau received the "Lou Who?" treatment from the Cry Baby Indians—one of pro sports' best band of brawling, rowdy athletes.

During the Indians' twin sweep in 1948—winning the first pennant playoff in American League history and the World Series from the Boston Braves—Lou was working for an owner who sought to unseat him. That would be Bill Veeck, Junior. Veeck admired Shortstop Boudreau, but had little or no time for Manager Boudreau.

In this situation Veeck was over a barrel. He couldn't have one without the other. Thus Veeck learned something that Boudreau knew all the time, and Bill was forced to stick with Lou.

In his typical Friendly Frenchman way, Boudreau had one of his best years ever. He batted .355. He won the American League's Most Valuable Player award, and then anchored Cleveland's 8 to 3 conquest of the Boston Red Sox in the pennant playoff with a perfect four-for-four day at the plate.

This left Veeck with something to do besides going to the bank with Cleveland's all-time home attendance of 2,620,627. Bill also led the league eating "crow" whenever Boudreau's name was mentioned.

For Lucky Louie it was without question one of the greatest One Man Gang jobs by a native from Illinois since Red Grange ran for five touchdowns against Big Ten rival Michigan, or George Halas' leadership in the Bears' 73-0 massacre of the Washington Redskins. Lou was an instant hero, and he deserved every one of his countless accolades. Even the naming of Boudreau Boulevard near the Cleveland Stadium.

It was 1970 when Lou was to enjoy his best day, election to the Baseball Hall of Fame. He was enshrined in Cooperstown, New

York, along with Yankee Great Earle Combs; durable Jesse "Pop" Haines, who won 210 games, and Ford C. Frick, baseball's third commissioner.

Considering the fact basketball was his favorite game as a youth, Lou set new track records finding success in both sports. "I doubt if I would have paid too much attention to baseball," the Harvey hero explained, "if it hadn't been for my father. He envisioned me making greater progress faster in baseball than in basketball. He played baseball, but not basketball. He didn't ask me to quit basketball, but he did suggest that I concentrate more on baseball. He was right. I didn't think so at the time, but, now as I look back, I have to agree with him.

"My first salary in baseball was $325 a month playing for Buffalo, N.Y. in the International League and that was triple A competition. After I moved up to Cleveland with Ray Mack for my first full season, I was paid the minimum salary of $5,000 a year in 1940.

"From a salary standpoint it had to be better than basketball. During parts of two winters I was a player-coach for Hammond, Indiana, in the old National Basketball League. Would you believe that I honestly don't remember what I was paid for this combination job? We played our home games in the Hammond Civic Center, and we drew very well on Sunday afternoons.

"Still, I don't remember what I was paid to both play and coach. This Hammond team was pretty good. I know it wasn't a $100 per game. If I had to venture a guess, maybe it was $50 per game. Really, I can't remember."

There is one thing that Lou doesn't have to guess about. His combined baseball and basketball earnings then wouldn't be tip money for today's money-minded athletes. Reminded of this fact, Lou laughed, and said:

"Yes, but we had more fun in our day. We never had money and it didn't bother us all that much. We made the most of it."

While his father was instrumental in switching him into baseball, Lou never forgot the lessons taught by two of his basketball coaches: Jack Lipe in high school at Harvey, and Doug Mills at the University of Illinois. He admired both Lipe and Mills as outstanding leaders— and still possesses his same high regard for both mentors.

"Coach Lipe was a tremendous organizer," Lou remembered. "He instituted basketball programs in all the grade schools in the Harvey district. He started some players in the sixth grade, and these kids never lacked for coaching or direction."

"Every season after Christmas Coach Lipe would invite all the grade schools in the area to a tournament. Actually it was a clinic as well as a tournament. He would grade the players during the clinic, and seed the teams in the tournament. Once this job was done, he would assign his assistant coaches to direct the instruction. By the time the average athlete finished the eighth grade, Coach knew if he was ready for high school competition. Let me tell you something. He didn't miss on many moving up from grade school to lights and heavies in high school play. I was one of the lucky ones. Normally I would have played with the lights, but he picked me for the heavy-weight squad. Tommie (Nesbit) was another lightweight who played with the heavies."

Lou well remembers the progress the heavyweight team made as freshmen, and how the team jelled as sophomores, saying:

"Most high school teams reach their peak as juniors or seniors. We were ready as sophomores, and most of the credit has to go to Coach Lipe's foresight. He was like a father to us. At least once a week during the season he would invite the entire team to his home for supper, and afterwards we would sit around talking basketball. He would review plays and patterns. Often he would discuss individual mistakes in the previous games, and he would stress ways and means to overcome such errors in future games.

"After that he would send us home to hit the books to make sure everybody remained eligible. Always there was tremendous rapport between Coach Lipe and his players. He was a stickler for extra effort and unselfish team work. He never had time for ball hogs."

Recordwise, the Boudreau-Nesbit-sparked Harvey teams were just the reverse from normal jelling time. Harvey won in 1933 as sophomores and finished second in both 1934 and 1935 as juniors and seniors.

Lou remembers when Lipe pioneered fast break basketball in Illinois high school play. "I think he was the first to teach it," Boudreau explained, "because not too many schools used it at the time. After we won the championship in 1933, a lot of coaches switched to the running game. You didn't hear or read about too many 14 to 13 games after that."

Fourteen to thirteen was the score when Harvey beat Springfield's slow down style of play in the 1933 championship game.

Whether he was first, fifth or tenth in introducing the fast break offensive, Lipe nevertheless got amazing mileage out of the run-gun game. Jack's three straight tournament teams had a three season record of fifty-seven victories in sixty-three games. Four of the six losses came in the team's senior season.

Lou didn't lack for interest in athletics because his father, Lou, Senior, was a better than average third baseman in semi-pro play. He played for teams in Momence, Joliet, and Chicago Heights when the old Trolley League was in operation.

While his baseball and basketball success is an age-old story, it's also a fact that he was an outstanding softball player during a time when the game was also called "Kitten ball." He was an infielder for the Harvey-based Magic Chefs when they won the Chicago Metropolitan softball championship and delivered the game-winning hit in the tenth inning. Lou also played for the Harvey Merchants, and it was through this exposure that major league scouts beat a path to the front door of the Boudreau home.

During his high school days in Harvey, Lou's Number One fan outside of his family was Della DeRuiter. Della, who used to buy a student ticket for fifteen cents to see the Flying Clouds fly past most opponents, also kept a scrapbook of her hero's exceptional achievements. Now her hero is her husband, because Miss DeRuiter is Mrs. Boudreau.

Della well remembers that May day in 1960 when Lou left home to drive to Wrigley Field to double with the late Jack Quinlan telling the Cubs' story on WGN radio. He returned home that night with a new title, Manager of the Cubs. How did that happen? The Cubs switched managers and picked Boudreau to replace Charlie Grimm. Thus, the former Harvey hero moved into the Cubs' dugout as Grimm took possession of his seat in the radio booth.

There have been many oddities in many trades in sports, but whoever heard of swapping a radio announcer for a manager?

It's another first in the life of a good guy named Lou Boudreau.

HOOT EVERS

Hoot Evers said what many million youngsters considered saying at one time or another—he went to high school and college to enjoy athletics. Did he study? Yes. Did he pass? Yes. Was he ever ruled ineligible? Yes, but not for low grades. He cut one too many history classes, and the professor wouldn't permit him to take a make-up examination.

"When this happened, Evers explained, "I left college owing the University of Illinois a year and a half of eligibility."

Before this unscheduled hike, Hoot doubled his pleasure, winning three varsity basketball letters at Collinsville High School, and one at Illinois. He's confident it would have been a 3-3 standoff had he finished college because he regarded himself more proficient at basketball than baseball, football, tennis, or track.

"My first big thrill in sports," the 12-season major league outfielder claimed, "was going to the 1937 State Tournament with Collinsville. We finished third, but I do believe we might have done better had we not encountered one of the smallest jumping jacks I've ever seen. This gutsy guy—Benny Macuk of Joliet (H.S.)—jumped upwards as straight as a string to reach heights our taller players couldn't. I don't remember if Macuk won the tournament's MVP award. If he didn't, he should have."

In his always modest manner, Hoot rated Donnie Ward "our best guard," and credited the outstanding center play of 6-foot-3 Walt Richter as assuring Collinsville's tournament berth. Also he had high praise for Coach W.O. Larson's leadership.

Evers was ticketed to attend high school in St. Louis, where his father was an executive in the mechanical department of the Globe-Democrat. Deciding his family would enjoy life in a small town more than it would in a big city, Dad Evers moved it to Collinsville. This was a good break for Hoot because his new home was next door to a grade school.

"I had two different playgrounds," he enthused. "The school gym was pretty good, and there were two tennis courts just outside the door. I made friends with the school janitor, and he would forget to lock a door and I would practice shooting for an hour or two almost every day. This new life agreed with me. I grew 5½ inches between my freshman and sophomore years.

"Frequently one of my teammates from high school would join me, and we'd play one-on-one. Many fine dribblers and passers have developed their skills playing one-on-one. And, of course, premium shooting was as important then as it is now. Those daily gym sessions taught me something else: a basketball player can go as far as he desires to work. He must dribble, fake shoot, and rebound alone. In trying to play a pickup game in baseball or football, there have to be three or four players on a side to make it interesting. Not so in basketball, and I really worked to improve myself."

Evers was only 15 years old when a man named Vernon Lucas entered his life. He was the coordinator of Collinsville's City League in baseball. Lucas envisioned Hoot as a shortstop for one of the two teams. So did Hoot. Within a few short weeks he was on a team with several players 5 to 10 years older than he was. Still he played, and he played well.

Following graduation from Collinsville, Evers enrolled at the University of Illinois hoping to major in basketball and baseball and minor in whatever was available. As a sophomore Hoot lettered in both sports. Also he noticed some familiar faces in the stands whenever the Illini played. Soon he learned they were scouts, checking basketball as well as baseball prospects.

"I was supposed to have a tryout with the St. Louis pro-basketball team," Hoot recalled, "but it never developed. Some half dozen baseball scouts asked me about my plans for the future, but I couldn't tell them anything definite. I was told Mr. (Branch) Rickey had one of his scouts following me, and I was supposed to go to the Cardinals. Wish Egan of the Tigers talked to me, and I really got to like and enjoy this kind man. He was great.

"Finally I decided I'd go with Egan and the Tigers. When we sat down to talk he took any possible bargaining rights away from me by saying: 'Young man I'm going to give you the same bonus Hank Greenberg received.' " "What was that?" "Five thousand dollars."

"Also, he would make one more consideration. He would give me a major league contract. I signed without ever knowing what size bonus the Cardinals planned to give me."

That one signature turned Evers' life right around. No longer would he spend his summers practicing basketball; playing baseball in the Collinsville town team league; feeding his pet pigeons, and walking his dog.

Looking back on his career now, Evers zeroes in on two thrills. The first was Collinsville's trip to the State Tournament in 1937, and the home run he hit in the 1948 All-Star game with his father and mother sitting in the stands. The American League beat the National League, 5-2, and Hoot didn't lack for famous company in the homer circle. A fellow named Stanley Frank Musial hit one for the National League.

There is still another thrill story attached to the 1937 tournament. It was Joliet's first and only championship in tourney traffic. For Collinsville there was a brand new first—the Kahoks' first finish within the tournament's final four.

DWIGHT "DIKE" EDDLEMAN

One word, versatility, fits hundreds and hundreds of Illinois high school athletes. This skilled field is so well bunched it's entirely possible a statewide election wouldn't establish a clear cut winner. Nevertheless, the extraordinary achievements of a Centralia delegate named Dwight "Dike" Eddleman commands outstanding consideration.

During his playing time as one of Coach Arthur Trout's boys at Centralia, Eddleman won 12 letters before and after delicate surgery on his right knee. Dike's collection of a dozen big C's were earned in this manner: four in basketball; four in track, and two in football. This 4-4-2 ratio adds up to 10, and the Numbers 11 and 12 awards only add to Eddleman's versatility in becoming one of Coach Trout's student managers in football, when he was limited to sideline assistance as the keeper of Centralia's statistics, and notes the coach requested recorded.

With all of his success, and that ranges from Illinois high school competition all the way to the Olympics, Eddleman remembers some of the losses more than he does the outstanding victories. "This particular night Centralia was playing one of Taylorville's great teams at home," Dike began. "When we went back to the dressing room for pre-game instructions, Coach Trout really surprised us when he said: 'I'm going to start four members of the second team with Dike, and the second teamer he replaces will play with the varsity.'

"Everybody was shocked, but didn't say anything. We knew better. Coach Trout was like Notre Dame's Knute Rockne. When he said jump, you asked only: how high? He drew some marks on the blackboard, and then dropped the bombshell about the player shifts.

"I played the first quarter with the second team, and we were down by six points when he played the first team with the lone second teamer in the second quarter. At halftime we trailed by 14 when we returned to the dressing room to await Trout. He didn't show up. Finally he opened the door, looked in, and left without saying a word. Later we found out he was sitting on the bench all by himself.

"As a group of cocky kids we promised we'd show the old man by going out and winning the game. At the start of the third quarter he said: 'Alright you first teamers and Dike, you're going back into the game.' By the end of the third quarter we trailed by 18 points. With about five minutes remaining, Coach Trout called a timeout and told the first team to 'go out, and win the game.'

"Trailing by 22 points we knew we couldn't win if we played all that night, and part of the next day. We ended up losing by 12 or 14 points, and when we returned to the dressing room there wasn't anybody there but the players. The media guys never cover losers, and this night all the sports writers were in the Taylorville dressing room talking to the winners. You know they never show up when you lose. Later, much later, Coach Trout came into the dressing room and sat all of us down on the bench.

"We knew he would have loved to beat Taylorville and Dolph Stanley more than anything else, but he spoke with his customary poise and frankness: 'Boys I wanted you to learn one thing here tonight, that the first team needs Dike just as much as Dike needs the other four players on our first team.'

"He wanted us to learn the value of team unity, and the importance of playing together. That is the way he coached. The boys and the team came first because he was an outstanding builder of men."

Centralia didn't lose again until meeting Morton of Cicero in the first round of the first and only four-team field in the history of the State Tournament. The year was 1941, still a nightmare whenever Dike talks basketball. After beating powerhouse Paris during the season, the Orphans collectively figured they would win the tournament. Especially after drawing a northern team (Morton of Cicero) in the first game. "That was our problem," Eddleman mused, "because we weren't ready to go. We took Morton too lightly, and lost 30-29. Morton beat Urbana in the finals, getting a big break when Fred Green, later a standout player at the University of Illinois, fouled out. We beat Canton to salvage third place."

Eddleman still regards himself as a "lucky guy" because he played in three state tournaments, missing only during his sophomore year at Centralia.

Dike's introduction to big time major track competition came when he was invited to compete in the Big Ten-Pacific Coast Conference meet at Northwestern's Dyche Stadium.

He had won three consecutive state championships in the high jump after finishing second during his freshman season, and this special bid really turned on his adrenalin opposing the collegians. At the finish the talented high school boy from Centralia beat the field with a jump of 6 feet 6 3/4 inches.

What Dike doesn't talk about in connection with this successful exhibition concerns the fact that all but a handful of the assembled 10,000 track buffs had their eyes trained on his winning jump. The crowd cheers, which greeted the announcement of his winning jump, were the loudest of the entire meet, sending most of the fans home asking: "Dike who?" With all his skills, success didn't come easy for Eddleman. He can remember arriving in the Centralia gym at 6:45 a.m. to practice shooting until school started. And the schedule was geared to every day of the year, claiming: "That is the way Coach Trout wanted it in his desire to gain perfection. Now days I doubt if the kids have enough free time to follow such a rugged schedule."

The two most important words in the development of an outstanding athlete in Eddleman's book are speed and finesse. "If a youngster has speed and learns how to handle and pass the ball, he is going to add to his own, as well as his team, value. Never forget the team is the name of the game," Dike stressed.

Eddleman remembers how Coach Trout, an outstanding teacher as well as a coach, always emphasized equal time in the study hall or library. It was Trout's theory that academic excellence and athletic achievement went hand in hand. He took great pride in the vast numbers of "his boys" who continued on to college.

Although Dike received countless scholarship offers and visited several campuses, including Notre Dame's, he decided early in his career at Centralia that he favored enrolling at the University of Illinois. "It wasn't just my desire to attend a state school," Eddleman began, "because I really enjoyed playing in Huff Gym. There was something special attached to playing there that inspired athletes from the smaller schools within the state. Always it was a different kind of a tournament when it was played there."

Dike has good reason for liking Huff Gym. It was there playing against Champaign that he scored a record 24 points as a freshman. It was there he watched Decatur's Eddie Root break his record by scoring 25 points. In the very next game after Root's explosion, Eddleman won back his record with a 26-point spree about an hour later. Still not all of Dike's memories about Huff are linked to victories. One year Salem led Centralia 20-3 at halftime, and Dike accounted for all of his team's points with three free throws.

Also Centralia's 1939 team, when he was a freshman, made it to the State Tournament as a 16-time loser. This trip, the Orphans finished fourth, behind Rockford, Paris, and Wood River.

What was Eddleman's biggest thrill in the schoolboy classic?

"In what was to be my last high school game," the stellar all-around, all-American athlete recalled, "we played Paris for the 1942 championship. Paris was undefeated, having won 39 straight games. With five minutes remaining Paris led us by 13 points. We rallied and pulled out a 35-33 victory in an almost unbelievable finish. Everything we shot had eyes, and bedlam reigned at the game's end. Coach Trout had many, many great games and victories, but I do believe he always considered that one as Centralia's greatest triumphs."

It was a sensational finish for the 135-pound skinny kid, who was 5 feet 11, when it appeared his career might have ended playing only his third football game as a freshman. "We were playing at Johnston City," he remembered, "when the ball had been blown dead and play stopped. I was hit from behind, and went down in a heap when my right leg caved in.

"That ended my football season, and there was some question whether Coach Trout would let me play basketball. They taped me from my thigh to my toes before every game. The next summer I spent most of it in Ann Arbor, Mich., recovering from the operation to correct the injury."

The surgery was successful and so was Eddleman's plea to Coach Trout for permission to return to football in his senior year. Trout wasn't immediately favorable to his star athlete's final-fling requests, and finally left the decision up to Dike. The rest of the story is history: Centralia had an end and exceptional punter back in action on the football field.

Besides his excellent records in football, basketball, and track, Eddleman found new interest in his desire to enter the University of Illinois. He became a fan of the Illini's famous Whiz Kids. Dike marveled at the Whizzers' finesse and teamwork. "I had never seen anything to match their ability to play together with such intensity and perfection," Dike claimed. "Probably present day fans have forgotten the Whiz Kids, but I never will. Whether it was Art Mathieson or Fred Green playing center, it was a great team—one of the all-time greats.

"Had it not been for the war, the Whiz Kids might have reached even greater heights. This much I'm sure about: the Whiz Kids weren't the same team when Philip, Smiley, Menke, and Vance returned from service.

"As underclassmen we played some very outstanding head-to-head practice games against them, but superior team play enabled them to win most of these scrimmages."

For somebody who called any trip outside of Centralia an adventure, Dike stamped himself one of the all-time quick change artists. This particular year he made a holiday trip to the University of Missouri and the University of California at Berkeley with the basketball team. Following the end of the trip in California, Eddleman cut out to join the Illini football team's workouts in Pasadena preparing for the Rose Bowl game against UCLA.

This was the game, January 1, 1946, when West Coasters were clamoring for the Bruins to play Army with Glenn Davis and Doc Blanchard instead of Illinois. Despite the fact they were roasted and belittled by the West coast media daily, the Illini didn't have to make overtime use of Eddleman's excellent punting talents. They buried the Bruins under a 45-14 avalanche of points, power, and panic.

In 1949 Eddleman received the Big Ten's most valuable basketball player award, winning over such outstanding MVPs as Northwestern's Bill Stricklen, Ohio State's Dick Schnittker, Purdue's Howie Williams, Wisconsin's Don Redfeldt, and Indiana's Lou Watson—a later day coach of the Hurryin' Hoosiers. Also Dike was the conference's first MVP from Illinois since Andy Phillip won the award in 1942.

Recognition and talent made Eddleman a ready-made commodity for professional basketball. Finally, he signed with the Tri-City Blackhawks, who later became a portable operation with stops in Milwaukee, St. Louis, and finally Atlanta.

With owner-president Ben Kerner of the Hawks "playing" like baseball's Frank Lane operating with three teams—one coming, one going, and one playing—Dike was sold to the Fort Wayne Pistons. This was a lucky break on two counts. Eddleman became a teammate of Fred Schaus, the present coach at Purdue University. Also he took a summer job with a business firm with headquarters in Decatur, Indiana, working in personnel.

Just in case you are wondering if Eddleman played during the Big Buck era of pro basketball, the answer is a definite no. At the outset

CAN'T BEAR TO LOOK—State Tournament time is a roller coaster for emotions, especially for the cheerleaders. The reaction of Peoria (Spalding) cheerleader Sally Jo Atkins during her team's 77-59 loss to East Moline (United) in 1970 is typical "March Madness". (Photo By Associated Press)

THE LOOK OF 'MARCH MADNESS'—An Aurora (West) rooter, clad in her blue and red T-shirt enscribed "Mac's Pack is Back", in reference to Coach John McDougal, relieves the tension of the title game with a bit of work on the bubble gum. (Photo By Les Sintay, Springfield)

he signed for $7,500 with the Hawks. Eventually his salary advanced to $15,000 with the Pistons, but that was the cutoff point. By present standards of multi-year contracts in the million dollar bonus brackets, some of today's athletes might discover that Dike's two sets of salary figures would hardly qualify for pin or tip money now.

Following retirement from play-for-pay basketball in the NBA, Dike took a full-time personnel position with the company, and moved his new quarters to Gibson City. He remained with this firm, Central Soya, until 1970, returning to the University of Illinois Foundation as director of the grants-in-aid program. Dike's program raises some $400,000 annually for athletic scholarships.

After completing his freshman basketball play in 1942, Eddleman, again, was in the right spot at the right time. He was inducted into the Army at Fort Sheridan one day, and won the high jump in the Chicago Daily News Relays the next. The following week Dike won his specialty event in the Illinois Tech Relays to become Fort Sheridan's only inductee with two firsts in two meets back-to-back.

The University of Illinois later awarded him with his first of 11 varsity letters after the freshmen rule was instituted as a wartime measure for intercollegiate competition. Never did one soldier accomplish so much so rapidly, and still gain deserved recognition.

BILL ERICKSON/VAN ANDERSON

"I was so nervous I couldn't run, talk, or think."

It was Bill Erickson remembering his first state tournament appearance with Rockford (East).

"We walked onto the floor like we owned the place, and right at that time it was the most important thing in my life."

Again it was Bill Erickson speaking. Only this time he was recalling his second and last appearance in the IHSA State Tournament.

"My high school basketball paved the way for me to attend college, and that is something not too many kids got to do in those days."

It was Van Anderson talking about a "Wonderful period of my life" playing for Sullivan.

Both Erickson and Anderson later played for the University of Illinois. Later, much later, they became rivals on the opposite side of the Rock River in Rockford. Rivals doing what? Serving as vice presidents in two Rockford banks. Bill is vice president in charge of publicity at the American National Bank; Van is a senior vice president at the Illinois National Bank & Trust Company.

"Many of my boys ended up in very important positions," former Illinois Coach Harry Combes explained, "but not too many can match Bill and Van. They are bankers in Rockford, rivals in the same city in the same field."

Erickson has good reason for remembering Combes ahead of re-counting his days playing for Harry and the Fightin' Illini. "We won our first two games in the 1946 tournament," Bill began, "getting past Chicago (Tilden Tech) and Collinsville. We weren't cocky, but we were confident we could get to the semi-finals and maybe the finals. To do this we had to play and beat Champaign, the team Harry was coaching. The Maroons beat us, and went on to win the tournament. We played Elgin for third place, and lost again.

"Because I was interested in playing college basketball after high school, I went to the University of Wisconsin to talk to Bud Foster. I also visited Dutch Lonborg at Northwestern. Neither seemed overly interested in me, and I wasn't too sure of my future right then. As a member of the second all-tournament team, I was invited to play in the North-South game later that year.

"As I walked off the floor after the game Doug Mills put his arm over my shoulder, and said he would like to have me enroll at Il-linois. I knew he wanted me from the way he spoke, and right that second I knew I was going to Illinois. The timing of Doug's words was most helpful. I was pretty sure I wasn't going to hear from Fos-ter or Lonborg after my original visits with them."

During his career at Champaign Bill played for both Mills and Harry Combes, who became Doug's successor in 1948 when he switched to devoting fulltime to the athletic directorship. Anderson also played for both Mills and Combes during his divided tenure at Illinois. Seeking ways to add to their financial stability Anderson-Erickson organized their own team following the close of the 1950 season.

The team, named the Illinoisans, was comprised of Rockford's two future bankers, Dike Eddleman, Burdette Thurlby, Jim Marks, and Wally Osterkorn. "We played 31 games all over the state," An-derson explained, "and won 30 of them under very rugged condi-tions. We went to school during the day, and played almost every night. Frequently, some of us had to play hurt because we only had one substitute."

Asked if the players' financial return was worth the demanding and rugged changes in their regular lifestyles, Van said simply: "We did okay."

There was another time in his post-career when Erickson took de-light in his combined social and business world.

"Some years ago I stopped in Denver on a business junket," Bill recalled, "and heard the name of Vince Boryla mentioned. I remem-bered that we were both named to some all-America teams in the 1950s. Although I had never met Vince, I decided to look him up.

Not too much later I was sitting in his home for a delightful visit.

"We replayed a lot of our games at both Illinois and Notre Dame when we were playing—proving to me again the value of athletics all the way from the state tournament to the Big Ten."

Chapter 6

There Is a Lot to Be Said About March Madness

By Pat Harmon

Sports editor, Cincinnati Post

Former sports writer in LaHarpe, Freeport, and Champaign.

Of all the games I saw in the State Tournament, the one I remember most is the 1942 final between Paris and Centralia. Paris led 31-17 with 6½ minutes to play. As basketball was played in those days, 14 points was a lot. No team had ever come from that far behind to win a state championship.

But Centralia won, scoring 18 points in 6½ minutes to make the final score 35-33.

There is a lot of personal history here, because my early career in sports writing involved many State Tournaments.

My first association with a high school basketball team was at LaHarpe, population 1100, located in Hancock County in western Illinois. LaHarpe had a weekly paper, the Quill, and I contributed stories about the high school basketball team.

We had a .500 team but the names are unforgettable. Where else could you think of a lineup of Tub Myers, Rabbit Fowler, Sock Long, Shady Landis, and Hunger Burkhart? Each nickname was honestly earned, a fitting description of the boys' appearance or personality.

The good teams in our territory were at Colusa, Augusta, Dallas City, Good Hope, Bardolph, and Western Academy of Macomb. None of these ever made the State Tournament.

I moved to Freeport in time to witness a changing of high school basketball coaches. Adolph Rupp was leaving for a job at the University of Kentucky, where he would become internationally

famous, and his replacement was George Kloos, who had coached
a state championship team in Iowa. I met both Rupp and Kloos,
and I enrolled at Freeport High School. Soon afterward I was allowed to write some pieces about the team for the Freeport daily,
the Journal-Standard. I saw all the games and also went on scouting
trips with the coaching staff. I met Sam Lifschultz on one of these
trips. Sam is known as the coach of the first good big man, Bob
Gruenig; he coached him at Crane Tech in Chicago. Sam also was
a basketball referee.

In 1932 the Bloomington Pantagraph ran a contest to see who
could pick the most winners of the 64 district tournaments. In those
days that was the first step toward the state. I won the prize, a ticket to the State Tournament in Champaign.

I was 15 years old. I hitch-hiked to Champaign with my ticket
and eight dollars. I ran into Sam Lifschultz at the Bailey Himes
Store, and when he learned I had no place to sleep, he took me to
the fraternity house of his young brother, Sid Lifschultz, and I
stayed there during the tournament.

I saw 16 State Tournaments, from 1932 through 1947, and these
were glory years, because the tournament, for the first time, began
to arouse the kind of interest it has today. I did not see any of the
24 tournaments from 1908 through 1931, but in 1939 I did a research job through old newspapers in order to create records and
history about the event.

Back at Freeport in 1933, I continued to cover our high school
team and also did some writing about teams in other parts of the
state. Freeport was a natural place for this; the school always had
excellent teams and there was great interest in high school basketball. Up to that time, the only All-State teams named were for
players who were in the State Tournament. I decided to name one
for the state at large, and sent copies of my selections to the downstate papers, which printed them.

The 1933 All-State team consisted of Lou Boudreau of Thornton
of Harvey and Lester Tammer of Kankakee, forwards; Bump Jones
of Freeport, center; and Lowell Spurgeon of Centralia and Wilbur
Henry of Benton, guards.

Boudreau was a sophomore. He made my teams again in 1934
and 1935 and was the only three-time All-Stater until Dwight
(Dike) Eddleman of Centralia matched him in 1940, 1941 and
1942.

In the fall of 1934 I enrolled at the University of Illinois and got
a part-time job on the Champaign News Gazette under Eddie Jacquin. I had a tuition scholarship, worth $80 a year, arranged by
Doug Grant, the sports editor of my Freeport paper. The News
Gazette job paid four dollars a week. I also waited tables at Prehn's

Restaurant, and I did a little work for Mike Tobin, the university publicity chief.

These were Depression Years, and there were hundreds, even thousands, perhaps, attending the university under the same conditions. My situation was not unique. We even had guys who worked at jobs, went to class, and played on the football team—guys like Eddie Gryboski, Frank Froschauer and Arvo Antilla. Conditions at the newspaper were so bad the regular staffers had taken three consecutive 10 per cent cuts in salary. I considered myself lucky to have a part-time job.

I wanted to do some previews for the 1935 State Tournament, and the Christmas holiday season was the best time for this. Wayne Eckley at Pontiac had a 16-team invitational tournament. Chick Evans had 16 at DeKalb. A reporter could go to both places and see 32 teams, some of which would be state championship contenders. There also was a big game in Pekin and another in Quincy within the same week.

I went to all these tournaments and all these games. I hitch-hiked. I was on the road a week. Jacquin got me $10 expense money, and I returned $1.25 when I got home. It was the biggest free-load in journalism history. I ate my meals in Pontiac with the teams, and in DeKalb I slept on a cot in the gym, supplied by Chick Evans.

When I got home I wrote a series of articles on the teams who would be state championship contenders, and I picked an All-Star team of the five best players I had seen. In February, Charlie Dunkley, who was the Associated Press sports editor in Chicago, had me do a series of stories on all the good teams in the state. In this series I picked Springfield and Thornton to be the finalists for the state championship; they were.

As the Depression waned, things got better at the paper, and I didn't have to hitch-hike any more. The local high schools, Champaign and Urbana, had good schedules, and often some of the leading teams played there.

In the 1930s the high school teams had styles that reflected their area in the state. Northern Illinois teams, like Freeport, Elgin, Dundee, Streator, and Waukegan, liked to run and shoot. Certain central Illinois teams and almost all southern teams played a deliberate game.

Mark Peterman was the best coach of the slow style. From 1923 through 1935 he was in the State Tournament nine teams in 13 chances, and he won the championship with Canton, in 1928, and Springfield, in 1935.

Gay Kintner also had slow teams in Decatur and won the state with this style in 1931 and 1936. One year he beat another deliberate coach, Joe Axelson of Clinton, 7-6, in the sectional tournament. And that game went to overtime.

The most outrageous example of the slow-down system was a game in 1930 in which Georgetown defeated Homer 1-0. Clarence Stasavich, later a famous football coach at East Carolina University, was the high scorer of the game; he made the free throw.

Peterman and Kintner also were masters of tournament teams. During their regular season they might lose a good many games, but when March 1 came, they were at their peak.

The leading slow-break coaches at the southern end were Hubert Tabor at Benton and Larue Van Meter at Johnston City.

In 1932 the State Tournament did not have a sellout at any of the sessions. In 1933 a new speed team arrived in the midst of the slow-down units. Thornton of Harvey, coached by Jack Lipe, won the championship using a three-lane fast break. Boudreau, Squid Klein, Dar Hutchins, Tommy Nisbet, and Ted Sliwinski were in Thornton's starting lineup.

Thornton was also runnerup in the state in 1934 and 1935. In 1934 the number of teams in the tournament was advanced from eight to the *Sweet Sixteen.*

Teams often reflected the personality and culture of the cities they represented. Everyone knew the Wood River players were from an oil town. Johnston City kids were from a coal-mining center. The Hull boys, who made it to the state in 1936, were farm kids.

As interest increased, the teams began to bring many fans with them. And some became fans of all high school basketball. Rodney Bell of Paris used to see four to six games a week. If there wasn't a game in Paris, he'd drive to Decatur or Springfield for one. Elmer Hazzard of Collinsville went to many games, whether Collinsville was involved or not.

The coaches were terrific. Kintner, after winning with his slow-down offense, switched to the fast-break and won his third state title at Decatur in 1945. Norman Ziebell, a very sound coach for Morton of Cicero, won state titles in 1932 and 1941. Harry Combes at Champaign won the state in 1946 and was runnerup in 1945 and 1947.

Ernest Eveland, who had some good teams at Waterman, switched to Paris and had even better ones. He won his sectional tournament seven straight times, and he won the state in 1943 and 1947.

Eugene deLacey had tremendous fast-breaking teams at Dundee. Dolph Stanley coached at Equality, Mt. Pulaski, and Taylorville and reached the state tournament at least once in all three cities.

Up to 1944 no team had ever gone a full season without losing, although the 1922 Atwood, 1936 Danville, and 1942 Paris teams did not lose until the state championship games. It was considered impossible for a team to win all of its games. Before the 1944 season opened, I asked Stanley what kind of a team he would have at Taylorville. His astonishing reply was, "We won't lose a game." And Taylorville didn't. They played 45 games and became the first undefeated team to win the state tournament.

That same year Mt. Carmel High School won the Chicago championship with an undefeated record in 28 games. Mt. Carmel was not a member of the state association and so did not enter the State Tournament. I tried to arrange a post-season game between unbeaten Mt. Carmel and unbeaten Taylorville in the Chicago Stadium. Both coaches, John Tracy of Mt. Carmel and Stanley of Taylorville, were willing but the state association would not permit the game.

On my All-State team that year—I was now picking them for the Champaign News Gazette—I picked two boys from Taylorville, John Orr and Ron Bontemps, and one from Mt. Carmel, Frank Lake.

My All-State team of 1938 consisted of Otto Graham of Waukegan, Hoot Evers of Collinsville, Don Blanken of Dundee, Frosty Sprowl of Oblong and Bill Hocking of Braidwood. All five of these boys became college stars and three of them were captains of their college teams. Two went to Purdue, two to Illinois and one to Northwestern. It was said afterward that if all of the All-Staters ever went to one school, they would be an unbeatable combination.

This virtually happened with the 1940 All-Staters, who went to Illinois and were named the Whiz Kids. As sophomores they won the Big 10. At that time there was a famous radio program called the Quiz Kids. Grayle Howlett, who wrote sports scripts for the Bob Elson show on WGN, invented the name of Whiz Kids to describe the Illinois sophomores. Ever since then, any young team of championship caliber in any sport is sure to get the name of Whiz Kids. But Howlett was first.

The most remarkable person I met on the high school trail was Arthur Trout, who taught history and coached football and basketball at Centralia. He won state championships in 1918, 1922, and 1942.

Trout could quote brilliant passages from history, and he was a unique coach. His football team had bizarre plays, one of which ended with the center carrying the ball after a lateral pass from the quarterback.

His basketball team used a full-court press on defense and a shoot-and-rebound attack on offense. His players used a two-hand push shot, with their feet and knees together, the whole body cen-

trally balanced, and the ball held against the face just below eye
level.

I named this the "Kiss Shot" because the players seemed to kiss
the ball as they let loose. They shot with a high arch, sending the
ball up among the rafters, and they had instructions to shoot any
time they were past the center line.

Trout, a graduate of Indiana University, used this system when he
began coaching and never changed it. He once told me about his
long tenure at Centralia, "God was good to me. Anytime I'd have a
few bad years and would be wondering if the school board was going to fire me, the Lord would send me a Spurgeon or an Eddleman, and I'd be saved."

He lived in a home on a quiet street in Centralia, with a small
sign in the front yard that read "Coach Trout." He was very calm
at a game, never showing emotion and never, never chewing out a
referee.

His best team, in 1941, was upset by Morton of Cicero in the
state tournament semifinal. That team had four seniors and a junior, Eddleman. Trout regrouped in 1942 with Eddleman and four
subs from the previous year. The team had only fair success in the
regular season, but managed to slip into the state tournament in
March. Then came one of the greatest comebacks of all time. Centralia won four games in the tournament, and three of these were
against teams which had beaten Centralia in the regular season.
Paris, in fact, had beaten Centralia easily and seemed to have the
championship locked up with a 31-17 lead and six and one-half
minutes to play. And then Eddleman, Fred Pearson, Jim Seyler and
Co. scored 18 of the next 20 points and Centralia won the state
championship.

The tournament was a colorful sports event. Teams from all
kinds of cities met to decide the basketball championship. A few
years ago I was invited back to be inducted into the Illinois Basketball Hall of Fame. At the induction I noticed that some of the great
names of the past had not been recognized yet. At the invitation of
the selection committee, I submitted a few recommendations, including Sam Lifschultz, an official and coach, and Lewis Omer,
who, as physical director of the Oak Park YMCA, organized the
first State Tournament in 1908. I had read about Omer in my research.

I have heard some great stories. In 1916 Wayne Gill, playing for
Decatur High in a tournament at Bloomington, scored 12 baskets
in an afternoon game. That night, in another tournament game, the
coach did not use Gill. He explained, "He was so hot this afternoon
I knew he wouldn't be able to hit a thing tonight." Such was the
coaching philosophy 60 years ago.

By Floyd Brown, *Broadcaster*

Provincialism rears its head in basketball probably to a higher degree than in any other sport. Stop any fan on the streets of Ohio, Indiana, New York, California or even Washington, D. C. and they'll tell you these are the spawning grounds of the greatest basketball players in the world. Yes, even little Washington, D. C. compares itself with any state. I know because that's where I was introduced to the game . . . on the hot asphalt playgrounds about a long par five from RFK Stadium.

In my initial years of broadcasting I ran in a kind of fever I had never before experienced, when the little town of Hebron was making the American dream come true . . . the little guy rising to the top; Davids slaying Goliaths; little kids beating up the bullies. How could one not get excited about those six or seven young men hailing from a town located in the middle of nowhere, hardly represented by an appreciable dot on the map?

In those days it was the *Sweet Sixteen* state finals at Champaign, and it was bedlam with people fighting for tickets, meals and hotel accommodations.

The year was 1952 and Hebron did go on to win the state championship (the last little school to win all the marbles) insuring themselves a place in state basketball history.

Not long after the Hebron championship I became a part of the broadcast team covering Elgin High School, noted for its successes when State Tournament time arrived. The conference was the Big Eight. It was fun . . . the competition was keen, the play was excellent and you learned a kind of excitement delivered only by high school basketball. My provincial attitude was under attack.

High school basketball is in a class all to itself. In the pros there is a kind of "monotonous proficiency" by the really great players of the world. To some degree this is also true in college except there the recruiting techniques and massive, on-going publicity of the day make it possible to anticipate a team's performance. Predictability at the high school level? Forget it! Anything can happen on any given night. These kids are 15 to 18 years of age. They aren't sure of their own capabilities, and the coaches always know that at this age there has to be just a little bit more talent still undisplayed.

Their job is to dig it out, and if they do, then they are successful. That's why you see so many teams that are traditionally high performers in state high school competition. In high school, if it isn't there, you must change your strategy and try to con your players into thinking they can go all the way without it. "You've got to believe" . . . the successful coaches sell this and they're back most years, maybe not finishing as high this year as the other, but you'll hear from them in the regionals, sectionals and supersectionals, and many times in the *Elite Eight.*

My first year of play by-play television for the State Basketball Tournament was 1974. Being a regular sportscaster on WGN, Channel 9, Chicago, I was well aware of the "Hawley-Arries" production . . . at least I thought I was. I knew of its reputation as the Number One special statewide TV production each year, but until I became a part of it, I had no idea what a production it really was.

How do you make it successful? Like top high school coaches who get maximum effort from their teams, Rick Hawley and Don Arries developed a formula. Do it over and over again and improve it each time. You get started like the college and pro coaches. You recruit! Call Channel 9 TV and order the finest TV sports camera crew in the country, producers and directors who have great background in TV sports production, a sports editor and his assistant for editing, plus special running statistics and background information, expert engineers and stage hands to build the sets and handle the lighting. Then, bring in knowledgeable people from the University of Illinois Assembly Hall and WCIA-TV in Champaign for further production assistance, and you have the ingredients for good coverage, but it's still "the teams that make the show."

To be selected as one of the play-by-play announcers for the state TV coverage was one of the very high points of my career. I love the sport! I had wanted to do this tournament, but hardly gave a second thought to the possibility of it being a reality. Thanks to people like Jack Jacobsen and other management at WGN along with the Hawley-Arries combination, it happened. Naturally I was jubilant!

Elation is quickly replaced by challenge, however, when you realize that you have to do four games a day (two play-by-play and two color) with eight teams, comprised of 96 players you'll see for the first time on the University of Illinois Assembly Hall floor.

Driving down Highway 47 on the way to the tournament is a pleasant experience with many little towns, beautiful scenery . . . a part of Americana you saw as a kid on the cover of the Saturday Evening Post. However, Champaign-Urbana, home of the THE State Tournament, is much more than a large edition of the smaller towns you've seen along the way. It has a small town warmth about it, but seemingly is replete with big-city conveniences.

The magnificent Assembly Hall, where the finals are held, stands majestically on the campus of the University of Illinois. It's an experience just to enter its steel passageways and steps leading you into the bowels of its huge structure. Underneath are the team dressing rooms located just across the hall from Tournament Central. The treat of a lifetime is yours when you pass through the players' door out into the arena (never call it a gym). When the stands are full, it is overwhelming. You find it necessary to steel yourself to try and remain matter-of-fact, but to no avail. It is really something! It's huge . . . it's expansive . . . it just goes up and out and up! The court seems a mile long and the seats seem endless. You walk onto the court, and you have a sneaking suspicion there's someone hiding under the floor waiting to trip players in front of all those people. This place could overwhelm anyone. It has to be paranoia's playground, and to think about high school kids who are 15 to 18 years old, single elimination, thousands of people in the stands, millions watching on TV and listening to radio, noise, bedlam, pressure . . . more pressure . . . you realize what champions are made of, for they have to produce under these circumstances.

I have always felt that the State Tournament is a special test for coaches. Their efforts must show fruition here if their team is to win. The winning coach has taught his players well, has convinced them that they're the best. He has instilled in them the ability to gain strength and security from their teammates, their coach and the awareness of their individual ability.

On my first tournament Friday, 1974, after a seemingly interminable amount of announcements, color background and up-dated statistics in Tournament Central, the big moment arrived. I headed through the great doors leading to courtside and was greeted by people from around the state yelling "Hi, Floyd . . . WGN . . . Tell 'em, Brown, who number one is!!"

For a moment I reflected on all the little gyms I had done high school games in during the past; driving through blizzards, being engineer, announcer, statistician or whatever.

Then I reflected back on the asphalt courts and gyms and players of Washington, D. C. Suddenly I realized that provincialism can change. Now I really know that these players, coaches, fans and even the playing court at the IHSA State Tournament make up the finest basketball show anywhere!

By JACK PROWELL
Comeback Team Granite City

(Editor's Note: Jack Prowell for many years covered the State Basketball Tournament as sports editor of the News-Gazette in Champaign. The following two brief pieces capture two remarkable segments in the great history of the State Basketball Tournament. The piece on Granite City appeared in the 1952 Official Program, while the piece on the Galesburg-Decatur game was published in the 1954 Official Program.)

The greatest comeback in all state tournament history may have been achieved in 1940 by Granite City High School.

That team, melded into a state champion from a typically American mixture of various nationalities, was able to lose its regional final to Wood River and still—two weeks later—be acclaimed as the finest basketball squad in all of Illinois.

If you recall, both regional winners and runners-up advanced to the sectionals at this time. Thus, given a second chance, Granite City whipped its previous conqueror, Wood River, 36–32 in the sectional.

Granite City never played its best until it was behind. And, it was behind going into the fourth quarter in its last three state tournament games. Only one victory was comparatively easy, that a 45–31 triumph over Streator in the first round of the *Sweet Sixteen.*

Otherwise, Granite City trailed Dundee 28–26 heading into the last eight minutes but won 35–30; lagged behind Moline 29–26 but rallied to win 41–38, and was a point behind Herrin, 16–15, in the finals but came back to capture the championship, 24–22.

Star of this team was Andy Phillip, one of the greatest performers the tournament ever had and later an all-time great at University of Illinois.

Phillip's play in the last two minutes of the Herrin game for the 1940 title is representative. His free throw cut Herrin's lead to 22–18. His basket on an out-of-bounds play made it 22–20. With 30 seconds to play, he out-jumped everyone for a rebound goal that tied the game, 22–all. Then with ten seconds to play, Phillip passed off perfectly to Evon Parsaghian for the winning basket.

No one has ever called Granite City the greatest of Illinois state high school champions, but it surely holds the honor of being the greatest when the chips were down. The pressure was never too great for those sons of Lincoln Place, a foreign settlement in Granite City.

Perhaps their very background, filled with stories of ancestral battles for life in their homelands before migrating to America, had something to do with it. Certainly, Coach Byron Bozarth had molded many nationalities into this great team.

Phillip was the son of a Magyar steel worker, and his real name was Fulop, Dan Eftimoff of Bulgarian descent. Parsaghian, Andy Hagopian, Sam Mauradian, and John Markarian were Armenian, Eddie Muell and Ed Hoff, German. Everett Daniels blended Scotch-Irish stock, and George Gages was a Yugoslav.

All these boys lived in or near Lincoln Place. When the state champions came home, they were paraded through the main part of Granite City, but the parade stopped in Lincoln Place, for there were the boys' homes.

That is where the game was replayed . . . among the Fulops, the Eftimoffs, the Parsaghians, and the Hagopians. It was a state championship, not only for Granite City high school, but for Lincoln Place and America, the land of dreams for the immigrants whose sons played with basketballs instead of guns.

The Most Thrilling Game?

What was the most thrilling game in state tournament history?

Was it the 1942 championship game when Centralia roared from behind to nail undefeated Paris, 35–33? Could it have been Morton's tremendous 30–29 upset of the Orphans of the Storm in the 1941 semifinals? How about Quincy's 39–27 triumph over Lou Boudreau and company of Thornton (Harvey) in 1934 when Quincy's Perry Barclift scored 11 times from the field?

No, it was none of these, if you take the word of observers who have watched state tournaments for years and years. The best of them all, the veterans insist, was Decatur's 73–72 victory over Galesburg in 1945.

This was not the state championship. It was a second round game, played on Friday, March 16,—but what a game it was!

From the very start, fans knew they were about to witness a dandy, because after favored Decatur led at 1–0, Galesburg sped to a 21–12 lead by the end of the first quarter.

Decatur pulled up to 25–24 within three minutes of the second period. After Galesburg moved away, the Reds came back again to tie at 34 and take a 40–39 halftime lead.

Three minutes into the fourth quarter, it was 59-all. Decatur jumped to 63–61, but Galesburg reversed the trend to lead, 66–63.

Galesburg was stalling, out in front, when Ralph Rutherford of the Big 12 champion Reds made a pass at the ball. His arm flicked out, returned with the basketball, and he sped down the floor toward the basket.

If the game were ever replayed, the Galesburg players would choose to let Rutherford score, to get the ball, still holding a one-point lead.

But this was a moment of decision, and Galesburg's decision was wrong. As Rutherford drove to the basket, he was fouled, missed the shot, but was awarded two free throws.

It was a tense situation, but Rutherford's first foul shot was true. Decatur declined the second, taking the ball out of bounds with the score 66–64 against it and nine seconds to play.

What happened next can never be adequately described. Rutherford passed the ball to George Riley, Decatur's giant 6-7½ center, who either fumbled well or passed poorly to Bob Doster under the basket. Doster leaped into the air, scored, and the game was tied, 66–66, with two seconds to play.

That's the way regulation time ended. The overtime was just as hot.

Del Graham scored a free throw for Galesburg with a half a minute gone, but Riley's short basket gave Decatur a 68–67 lead. Jimmy Evans drove under the goal from the side to turn the advantage back to Galesburg, but Riley again came through—with his 13th basket of the game—to return the lead to Decatur at 70–69. Rutherford and Graham traded free throws, and with 1½ minutes left, Decatur led, 71–70.

Big Merle Barstow registered on a push shot from the corner, and Galesburg led, 72–71. Again Decatur was in the shadow of the valley of elimination—and it remained there until only two seconds showed on the big clock at the south end of Huff Gym.

At the finish, it was again Rutherford who got the ball to Doster under the basket for a short shot, a goal, and a 73–72 victory.

When the game ended, the fans were so stunned they sat in silence momentarily, but the scene on the floor was one of wild confusion. Gay Kintner, the Decatur coach, rushed off the bench to give his players big bear-hugs. In the melee, John Malerich of Decatur was knocked to the floor but, fortunately, was uninjured.

When it was all over, and the teams were in their dressing rooms, Jimmy Evans, one of the Galesburg stars, phrased it this way:

"It's just like having two men out in the last of the ninth and the other guy hits a home run with the bases full."

By BERT BERTINE

(Editor's Note: The late Bert Bertine, who personally developed one of the greatest sports sections in the history of Illinois newspapering at the Urbana Courier, wrote the following article, which appeared in the Official Program of the 1949 State Basketball Tournament. Bert's story recalls what at the time were considered his all-time five greatest championship games.)

Recalling the glories and thrills of past state tournaments is a favorite March pastime in Illinois as basketball fans from Hebron to Cairo, from Quincy to Paris turn their eyes and ears towards Huff gym in Champaign-Urbana.

We have been asked to dwell on the five most exciting and memorable championship games during the 41 years of state tourney history. Naturally, we don't expect our choices to coincide or agree with those of all of our readers. We do feel, though, that for thrills-per-minute, for tight, tense basketball—the kind that makes fans' blood race, eyes dilate and voices hoarse—that the five we've selected will measure up against any others. Certainly these five caught all the color, drama and excitement which goes toward the greatest prep event in this hoop-happy state of ours every year.

HERE ARE THE FAMOUS FIVE

The five picked were: Centralia over Paris, 35–33, in 1942; Morton of Cicero over Urbana, 32–31, in 1941; Decatur over Danville, 26–22, in 1936; Thornton of Harvey over Springfield, 14–13, in 1933; and Marion over Rockford, 24–23, in 1921.

Remember, this is no claim that these were the most exciting games in tournament history. No history of the tournament would be complete without complete coverage of such great games as the Decatur-Galesburg 73–72 overtime epic of 1945; or Pekin's two great final-minute wins over Rushville and Woodstock in 1937; and any other number of terrific, no-quarter cage struggles. But we are only attempting to recall a segment of the glory of the past by writing of championship tilts. Oddly enough, showdown games don't always produce top basketball, or necessarily close games. Often Illinois state crowns have been decided by one-sided margins.

Such was not the case, however, in the five years we will cover. Who can forget Dike Eddleman's great one-man rally in 1942 as his underdog Centralians handed Paris its only defeat of a long season to smash Ernie Eveland's dream of producing the first unbeaten state champion in history? Who can forget in a similar case how courageous Decatur, possessing the worst season record of the 16 entrants in 1936, calmly measured undefeated Danville to claim the championship? Who can forget how Fred Green nearly carried a mediocre Urbana team to the 1942 title in what, if his efforts had been successful, probably would have been rated the tournament history's greatest upset? Likewise, those of us who saw the 1933 contest will never forget how Louie Boudreau and his Thornton speed demons finally solved an unyielding Springfield zone to snatch victory in the final minutes. Nor do Marion veterans and other old time Southern Illinois fans cease to speak of Pete Wallace and Norm Belford and their gallant comeback which brought the '21 title.

ORPHANS' STIRRING STRETCH DRIVE

Of the five games, perhaps Centralia made the most stirring stretch drive to capture the state's most coveted prize. Coach Arthur Trout's Orphans of the Storm were just that for three quarters against a poised and polished Paris quintet which had swept 39 straight victories underfoot in its march to the finals. With only eight minutes remaining between them and the championship, the eastern Illinois Tigers owned a handsome 26–16 edge and it appeared only a matter of playing out the clock.

They had not reckoned with the great Eddleman, captain of this year's Illini cagers and captain then of the Orphans, and the greatest player ever to be produced in an Illinois high school. The year before, Centralia and Eddleman had been odds-on favorites to win the state, but a doughty Morton five had come out of nowhere to furnish the state's most amazing upset in the semi-finals.

The 1942 Centralia team was only a remnant of that great 1941 team, but it still had Dike. Winding up the most prolific scoring career in state annals, Eddleman scored 12 points in that final period against Paris. He shot long, he shot short, he rebounded like a demon and almost single-handedly carried his team to the prize it should have won the year before.

EDDLEMAN SHOWS THE WAY

As that fourth quarter opened in 1941 Eddleman had accumulated only four points and it seemed, indeed, that the state's greatest scorer had met his match in a tenacious defense paced by Dick Foley, another player destined for further fame at Illinois. Then Eddleman caught fire, scoring eight points in seven minutes, and, aided by speedy Jim Seyler, the Orphans whittled huge chunks out of Paris' seemingly unsurmountable lead.

Finally with the clock in the red and only 55 seconds left, Dike was fouled as he shot, and tossed in both free throws with his famed kiss shot. That tied it up at 33–33. Seconds later the lad who was to go on to collegiate and Olympic fame leaped high to seize a defensive rebound and dribble the length of the court to lay in a short shot. It missed but Dike grabbed the rebound and put it in—and that did it. Arthur Trout's "po'r little boys" had accomplished what they had failed to do the year before when everything was in their favor.

Another Cinderella team from the southern part of the state was the Marion quintet which copped the 1921 title after winning five tournament games, only one of them with ease. Nineteen teams came to the state that year, and Marion was among those which first had to win its way into the *Sweet Sixteen* by playing an extra game.

OVERTIME VICTORIES PRODUCE

The Wildcats were headed back home in that very first game until a last-minute long shot by Pete Wallace produced a 14–13 triumph over favored Elgin in overtime. Next came Galesburg, another northern power, and again the 'Cats had to take extra time to accomplish a 19–15 verdict. Next one was easy; Marion tripped Macomb by what amounted to a one-sided score in those days, 25–15.

In the semi-finals the eventual champions tangled with a tough

New Trier bunch, and for the third time had to go into overtime to emerge with a 26–24 decision. By the time of the final contest against Rockford it appeared Marion might have shot its wad in the four previous tilts. Rockford had had easier sailing, and besides had had to play only three games to Marion's four to reach the deciding game.

The Rabs of the north quickly went into a lead and with only five minutes left still possessed a comfortable 23–16 edge. Here, Marion's long shot artists went into action like siege guns. First Luke Johnson zeroed in from far out. Norm Belford, a great center, followed with two lengthy shots—both dropped. The score was now 23–22 and Rockford became frantic. Finally Wallace, who had saved two previous overtime tilts, got his hands on the ball, took aim and fired. That shot also went in, and after an amazing exhibition of a dribbling stall the final three minutes, Marion had claimed its first and only state title, 24–23.

A FAVORITE AMERICAN STORY

Americans always have liked the "rags to riches" theme, and that is why tournament old-timers also like to tell about the lightly-regarded 1936 Decatur team which entered the lists with the poorest record of all the entries, but went home with the cup.

Gay Kintner's charges had been beaten 11 times during the regular season, and were ranked, at the very best, a darkhorse. The Reds attained that rating only because they had upset a very good Springfield team, defending state champions, in the sectionals, and because of Kintner's reputation as a tournament coach.

As in the case of Marion in 1921, the Reds' road to glory was a thorny one. Peoria Manual was downed in the opening tilt, 17–13; next came tiny Hull, popular favorite, and Decatur won, 30–27; and in the semi-finals it took a 20–19 game to squeeze by Johnston City.

DANVILLE'S STREAK BROKEN

Decatur's foe in the finals was mighty Danville, unbeaten since the court season began, and victor over strong Centralia, Moline and Mt. Pulaski in its bracket. Danville was a member of the same Big 12 conference to which Decatur belonged, and Ned Whitesell's Maroons had had no trouble running off with the pennant while Decatur trailed.

There was no reason, therefore, to suspect Decatur could handle the unbeaten Maroons. As the game opened, Danville, with Moon Williams and Dick Jones showing the way, waltzed out to quick 6–2 and 11–6 leads, as expected. But Decatur had been behind many times before. The experience didn't bother the Reds.

Paul Weigand, lanky center; Dale Minick, rebounding guard; and clever little Kenny Parks, forward, began clicking, and soon the score became 16–16 in the third quarter as Weigand lofted in a pivot shot. Decatur's sticky defense, backbone of its success, was, slowly but surely, throttling Danville's attack.

From that point on it was nip and tuck. Danville reclaimed the lead at 20–19 but Curly Baker tied it up with a free throw. Then Weigand, the game's leading scorer with 10 points, hooked in two straight baskets. That was the ball game as it turned out, but Danville threw another chill into Decatur hearts when Jack Owens raced in to tally. Decatur stalled it out from there, and, as a final fillip to a great upset, added another goal by Minick seconds before the gun. That cinched the game and the title, 26–22.

BOUDREAU AND THE FLYING CLOUDS

The story of the 1933 championship game, in which a 15-year-old sophomore captain named Louie Boudreau paced his Thornton team to a 14–13 conquest over tall and rock-ribbed Springfield. Here was the story of a great popular favorite staging a desperate final-quarter rally to claim the crown all fans had expected before the tourney began.

Never has a state tournament crowd witnessed a more difficult assignment than Thornton tackled when it attempted to crack the iron wall defense Mark Peterman had erected with his tall Solons. For three tense, but unproductive quarters, the total output of field goals in this strange contest was exactly five. The score, by quarters, until the final canto, was Springfield, 3–3–0; Thornton, 2–2–2.

It wasn't until the final second of the third quarter that the famed Flying Clouds of Thornton, bellwethers of the crowd-pleasing fast break, but unable to get it in gear because of Springfield's chesslike style, were even able to pull up on even terms. During that period the capacity crowd had taken to chanting the number of passes Springfield attempted, without shooting, as it protected its 6–4 lead; once it was 17, again 25 and then 12. But on number 13 of the latter series, Dar Hutchins, of Thornton darted in to intercept and dribble half the court for a short shot and a 6–6 tie.

NISBET'S DRIVE TURNS TIDE

The dam broke in the final quarter, and Thornton's flash flood inundated the Solons. Little Tommy Nisbet, later to share Illini fame with Boudreau, opened the quarter with a lightning field goal, and now Springfield, behind for the first time, had to play Thornton's style. It couldn't, any more than Thornton had been able to score in a slow game before. Nisbet kept driving like a piston and Springfield resorted to fouling. Tom poured through five free throws and a team-mate caged another, and now the score stood 14–9. Two pretty buckets by Capt. Chuck Frazee of the losers went to no avail, and the bizarre but thrilling game ended 14–13.

This was the only championship won by the great Thornton quintet which during Boudreau's three years was the terror of the state. In the two succeeding years the Clouds, coached by Jack Lipe, went all the way to the state finals, a record unequalled in state history at that time. But although it was favored each time, Thornton could not repeat its 1933 title, bowing to Quincy and red-hot Perry Barclift in 1934, and to a vengeance-gaining Springfield quintet in 1935.

FOUR-TEAM TOURNEY THRILLS

Urbana's Tigers, in 1942, came within an ace of turning the same trick Decatur had achieved in 1936. Lew Stephens' charges had had just a so-so season and were the losers of 10 games when tournament time rolled around, but suddenly they got the old tourney fever and began roaring through one opponent after another.

The drive carried them to the four-team tournament, tried only that one year, along with Canton, Morton and heavily-favored Centralia. In the opening games Urbana squeaked by Canton, 39–38, and Morton, as Chet Strumillo turned in a great effort, ousted a Centralia five which had won 41 of 42 games before that meeting. Morton, striking hard and fast while an overconfident Centralia five tried to get its bearings, ran up a 12–2 lead in the opening quarter and doggedly protected it all the way to a 30–29 victory.

Urbana, with 6–6 Fred Green, still another Illini star in the making, who had tallied 22 points against Canton the night before, went into the championship battle a sentimental favorite because of its long climb.

AN IMPORTANT FOURTH FOUL

And with Green wafting in his famous right-handed pivot shots, it appeared the Tigers, indeed, were to be the 1942 state champions. Green, aided by Leal Nelson, paced an attack which by the fourth quarter had produced a 28–24 lead. Then disaster, in the shape of Green's fourth and final foul, struck Urbana. With Green's departure in the first minute the now out-manned Tigers fought desperately but couldn't hold the men of Cicero. In three minutes Morton had gone ahead, 29–28, on Ray Demkovitch's shot. Then Ray Leitner, center, no longer guarded by Green, tipped in a rebound and it was 31–28. Nelson made a free throw, but so did Fred Ploegman, and it was 32–29. In the final seconds Nelson, whose long shot had beaten Canton the night before, sank a similar effort, but it was too little and too late. Morton, conquerors of the stupendous Centralia five, was the state champion, and deservedly so.

Bill Niepoetter
We Won, By Golly We Won!

Sports Editor, Centralia Sentinel

Those words greeted Centralia Sentinel readers in 1918 as their high school basketball team notched the state championship. It was not their last, but possibly the most important for the late Arthur L. Trout, head coach for 37 years before retiring in the 1949–50 season.

King Arthur, a short man with a football background, came to Centralia in 1914–15, and when he finally turned over the reins of Centralia's basketball fortunes to Jimmie Evers during Christmas, 1949, he had registered 809 victories against 334 losses.

Prior to the 1976–77 season Centralia had totaled 1,403 wins while losing 591, 70 per cent, a record any school would be proud of.

Trout was a master of motivation, a psychologist when the word was never heard of. His tricks of the trade were many, but the underlying fact remains, he had great talent and could use it.

King Arthur had an imagination which produced unusual things. State Tournament fans can remember back to the "kiss shot", a patented two-hand set shot that arched into the rafters and came soaring down.

Trout's theory was simple. The basket is only so big and the ball slightly smaller. If the ball was coming downward it had a better chance to go in, rather than at an angle. It also made rebounding a pleasure for jumpers because those missed shots caromed high into the air and the better jumpers got the ball.

He did not believe in one-handed shooters—they were shown the door quickly, and his athletes conformed or got off the team. But one can't argue with success, and Trout's three state championships (1918, 1922, 1942), a second in 1946, and innumerable other trips to Champaign, spell success.

Psychologist Trout had a story for everyone. How the Centralia Cardinals became the Orphans of the Storm was a dandy. He, like Dizzy Dean, gave writers what they wanted—an exclusive. He told one writer the name came from a Chicago writer who wrote of the Centralia team at the Pontiac Tourney, "They looked like orphans in their bedraggled uniforms, tired and dirty from a long trip, but they sure could play basketball."

Later he said the name came to his mind back in the early '20s when he saw Lillian Gish act in the movie "Orphans of Storm."

His showmanship knew no bounds. When "downtown coaches", fans he hassled with annually, thought a freshman cager was not "seasoned" enough to play varsity basketball at Centralia, Trout took the boy to center court wearing a garland of carrots and other vegetables, and sprinkled them with salt. "Now he's seasoned," Trout told the fans.

Trout called most of his players "Mister." And old Orphan players can remember those steely eyes burrowing into anyone doing wrong, and dreaded that next word, "Mister". He would get on his knees in a prayerful position and say, "Mister—please shoot the ball" or "Please don't shoot the ball."

Despite the fact he coached three state champs, the 1941 club, prominently called the Wonder Five, gained most fame. That lineup of Eddleman, Castleman, Klosterman, Wesner and Michael is in the state Hall of Fame and their 42-game win streak in one season is still best at Centralia. They finished third at Champaign, and closed with a 44–2 record.

When Dwight "Dike" Eddleman was grabbing state and national headlines for Centralia, Trout stopped the friction between the other four starters and the Scoring Wonder. He simply played four starters and a reserve one half, then Eddleman and four reserves the next. When the club lost, he pointed out they could not get along without each other and the point was made.

Psychologist Trout was a master of putting reporters in their place. Having coached many all-state basketball players someone was always asking who was best. Lowell Spurgeon? Eddleman? John Scott of Illinois State fame? Or one of the 100 others?

Trout simply asked the age of the player. He had his "best" list according to how old the player was. He rated Colin Anderson of the 1946 club very high because he was just 16. He grew three inches after graduation and was sensational at Georgia Tech.

If success is winning, Trout was a success. In his 37-year reign, King Arthur had only five losing seasons. Fifteen times his clubs recorded 25 or more victories.

If success is producing strong men, the state is full of them and if success is producing good coaches, that list is nearly as long.

Centralia's gymnasium long ago became Trout Gym and a giant portrait of King Arthur greets fans as they arrive. It was painted by a former Trout athlete. His trademarks were a battered hat, which later covered a balding head, and sloppy clothes.

The stories of Trout are many. Everyone has his favorite and as the years go by they have become embellished. But if you hear one, believe, because it is probably true.

Trout was a legend in his own time. More importantly he is still a legend nearly 20 years after his death. Former players speak with respect and he is still called Mister Trout.

His ability to command respect from his players was probably the most important thing in Trout's success. When things were not going well he would take his starters from the court, and, in front of a capacity Trout Gym, march them into the dressing room while the reserves would play.

One former player said it was terrible. "We dreaded going in. He'd keep us there for a quarter and we just knew the second team was getting brained out there. Sometimes he'd blast us for our play—and other times he'd just stand there and look at us. When we finally got to return to the court you could bet we'd be ready to play. The funny part was the reserves usually did a great job and we would have to really go well to beat them."

Legends are made by players, fans, and yes, even writers. Arthur L. Trout was, and is, a legend.

LONG LIVE THE KING!

Forrest R. Kyle
Family Bible Rescues DuQuoin
Sports Editor, Decatur Herald

There is every reason to believe the State Basketball Tournament will start this afternoon at 1:45 o'clock in Huff Gym with a game between Moline and Princeton.

Furthermore, it is expected the remaining 14 teams which won sectional championships last Friday will follow in orderly fashion onto the court until the first round is completed tomorrow night.

There has been no indication that any of the 16 teams, as the result of a star chamber session, will be shipped home without getting to play because of some technicality rendering it ineligible.

The smooth style in which State Tournaments are conducted now is a far cry from the confusion and tangled procedures which marked many of the early tournaments and which caused as much excitement and suspense as the games themselves.

Some of the tournaments held in Decatur were marked by preliminary skirmishes quite unlike the tumult with precedes present-day meets.

Strict eligibility rules now have eliminated what caused most of the trouble in the early days. Then, apparently, no one concerned themselves with the ages of high school athletes until State Tournament time.

The IHSAA Board of Directors had an interesting time of it here in 1916, but it was only a warmup for 1917.

DuQuoin had been declared ineligible for the State Tournament in 1916 because of a player reportedly over 21 years of age. DuQuoin officials declared it wasn't so and started out to prove it.

In the meantime Arthur also was declared ineligible for over-age players and Shelbyville was substituted in the state lineup.

The Board condemned carelessness at Arthur High School after the superintendent of another school produced evidence proving school records had been tampered with and erasures made to cloak absences of three players. Twenty percent of the school year was missed by one player, it was charged.

The DuQuoin affair had all the trappings of an old time silent movie thriller, where Tom Mix gallops up on Tony and lassoes the heroine, pulling her to shore through raging waters just as her careening canoe is about to plunge over a 100-foot waterfall.

"Maybe you think it hasn't been work to gather this proof," one of the DuQuoin officials told a reporter after the Board ruled the player (Ray Harrell) eligible.

"We found that Harrell was born near Harrisburg and we went down there, riding on a passenger and freight train to do it. Then we found that no birth records were available but that the treasurer of Eldorado might know something about the birth.

"We hired a buggy and drove over impossible roads only to have the buggy break down miles from nowhere. We unhitched the horses and rode bareback for some five miles."

Learning that Harrell attended a tiny rural grade school, the intrepid DuQuoin detectives plunged deeper into the boondocks, finally finding a crusty old-fashioned schoolmaster who had records to prove that Harrell graduated from grade school in 1912, but they didn't quite pin down his exact age.

The clincher came when Harrell's aunt was located. She had an old family Bible which registered his birth—November of 1895.

Nearly exhausted after three sleepless days and nights of tracking down the evidence, the DuQuoin faithful hurried back to Decatur to save their team from banishment.

The next year things really were complicated. First, Sullivan proved a Mount Olive player was over-age and ineligible. Mount Olive had won the Charleston District but the Sullivan principal had an affidavit from the player's father saying he was over 21.

Next Arthur filed a protest against Decatur, claiming two players were professionals because they had accepted money to play baseball with a Lovington team.

On top of this Bloomington High officials faced the problem of a small pox quarantine. It finally was decided to keep the players out of school so they wouldn't have to be vaccinated and could play in the tournament.

In the meantime, another protest was filed claiming Belvidere had an over-age player.

The tournament was scheduled to open Thursday night. State

tourney officials met Thursday afternoon to struggle through the documents and affidavits.

The Decatur players were cleared when the Lovington baseball manager said he had paid only $4 expense money for four games. Belvidere was cleared, too, but Mount Olive was ruled out, making it necessary to re-play the Charleston District final with Sullivan opposing Taylorville.

This created the unique situation of starting the State Basketball Tournament before one of the district champs had been determined. (There were no regionals or sectionals in those days).

State tourney games were played Thursday night, then Sullivan and Taylorville played Friday morning for the Charleston District title. Sullivan won, then had to play Belvidere that night and lost.

That was the last year the tournament was held in Decatur. Quite possibly, after the maze of protests officials here had to help arbitrate—one session lasted 15 hours—they were relieved to have it transferred to Springfield the next year.

By the way, Springfield won that 1917 tournament, but only after a pre-tournament protest of its star player, Archie Mann, had been upheld and he had been denied participation in the tournament.

The Springfield coach, Ray Wentz, took it philosophically. "I'll look for another man," he said. "It wouldn't be out of order to say that we've been violating the Mann Act."

(This story appeared in the Decatur Herald March 15, 1953)

John Wasilewski

John Wasilewski was a typical American student-athlete. He mixed studies with sports while attending Athens High School. In pursuit of his higher education, John followed the same lifestyle at Eureka College. Searching for his first post-college job, Wasilewski landed a plum. He was Dolph Stanley's assistant at Taylorville the year the Tornadoes put together their sensational 45–0 record to win the state championship in 1944.

John was a sophomore at Eureka when he received a surprise telephone call. It was H.V. Porter calling from the IHSA office in Chicago. Would John be interested in posing in some basketball-oriented situations? That was like asking the kid next door if he would like a new electric train for Christmas. No one person ever made a faster trip from Eureka to Chicago.

Many different poses were "shot" by photographers assigned to the project by the A.C. Rehberger Company, makers of the IHSA State Basketball Tournament trophies. Two poses were selected after that extended "just one more" photo-shooting session back in 1930. They became the models for the ornaments placed atop the

THE TOP PRIZE—The goal of all young basketball players is to reach Champaign and then take home the top prize. Neither the trophy nor the enthusiasm of the players has changed over the years, as evidenced by the joyous expressions of the 1976 champions: Jeff Anderson, Coach Ed Butkovich and Brad Gibbs of Class A winner Mt. Pulaski in photo at left, and Levi Cobb, Jeff Berry and Laird Smith of Class AA winner Chicago (Morgan Park) in photo at right. (Photos By Thomas Harm, Champaign News-Gazette)

series of trophies, which are still used.

Following his death in July of 1973, four of Wasilewski's former teammates organized a drive to provide aid to students in the field of physical education at Eureka. The foursome was comprised of Marion Loveless, Henry Sand, Harlan Walker, and George Keist. The highspot of Eureka's homecoming ceremonies the following September was a most unusual presentation.

It was a replica of the IHSA championship trophy with John appearing to begin a chest-high pass. The trophy was presented to his widow, Arletta, presently a resident of Riverton. Also, it is the only time a presentation of the exclusive trophy—complete with the ornament depicting the Athens-Eureka standout (a gift from President Avrim Roitmann of the Rehberger company)—has been awarded outside of State Tournament series competition.

By Larry Harnly
Sports Editor, Illinois State Journal

The photo of Springfield High School's 1935 state basketball champions does not include the Senators' coach, Mark Peterman.

There's an interesting reason, according to Herb Scheffler, the standout center on that team. "He wouldn't pose with us," Scheffler said. "That was one of his superstitions. He was real superstitious."

Peterman coached the Senators from 1929 through 1947. He took 11 teams to the state tournament and also directed the 1928 Canton team to the state championship.

Scheffler, now the principal of Franklin Middle School, elaborated on some of Peterman's superstitions. "We played Taylorville in the sectional tournament at Decatur the first night one year. We played at the old gym, which is about half a block from where Kintner gym is now.

"We played the second game that night, and it was crowded when we got there. We had to go past the gym and up a driveway to find a place to park. The next night, even though we were there early, Pete wanted to park in the same place.

"But when we got to the lot, the custodian's car was parked in the place we had parked the night before. Somebody had to go in and get the custodian to move his car even though there were only three cars in the lot,' Scheffler recalled.

"When we won and we were on the road, we had to ride in the same cars and in the same seats."

The 1935 Senators were the second Springfield team to win the state championship, the first coming in 1917 under Roy Wentz.

Springfield won the championship game, 24–19, from Harvey, as

Scheffler scored 13 points.

Springfield's other starters in that game were Emerson Daily and Whitney Sapp at forward and Parry Feaman and Paul Nunes at guard. The other tournament team members were Quenten Engle, Bob Farris, Duane Fultz, Joy Roof and Bob Miller.

Springfield had lost the year before, in the first round of the state tournament, to Chicago Lane Tech in three overtimes. One of the opposing players was Phil Cavarretta, former Chicago Cub player-manager.

Quindy Constantino was on that team and played the first semester the following year before graduating. "The last night he played we were at Collinsville. We gave him a watch chain and told him he'd have a gold basketball to hang on it at the end of the year. He did."

Scheffler recalled some of his state tournament experiences at Champaign. "I remember one time when we played in the state tournament, we stayed at Danville. We'd get on the trolley that ran between Danville and Springfield after the game and go back to Danville.

"He wouldn't let us see anybody else play. I don't think he wanted to scare us."

Scheffler played on "Peterman's Pups" as a freshman and was a varsity regular for 2½ years. He spent one year at Illinois College before transferring to Oklahoma, where he was named to one All-American honor roll.

"Pete was one of those coaches who could look at a boy as a freshman or sophomore and project what he was going to be as a senior," Scheffler said. "I was one of those. My knees acted like a young colt when I was a freshman.

"The thing that impressed me the most about Pete was his dedication, and I never heard him swear at a boy. He was a gentleman. He stood for the things scholarship and athletics should stand for. He had a code of ethics."

Peterman's basketball knowledge also impressed Scheffler. "To me, basketball is like a game of chess. You have to match the other team. You have to maximize the things you can do and minimize your opponent. He was good at this. He could match the other team and take away their real good attack."

Basketball was not much of an offensive game in that era. Scheffler mentioned that the first time he saw a one-handed shot was his senior year.

Scheffler mentioned that Peterman didn't tolerate his players riding a referee during a game. "He'd always tell us, 'I hired them.' He wasn't demonstrative at all during a game—unless an official missed a rule."

Following a professional baseball career in the Boston Red Sox organization and five years in the Air Force, Scheffler succeeded Peterman as coach for the 1947–48 season at age 29. Scheffler took the 1954 Senators to the state tournament and resigned after the following season. Ray Page succeeded him.

"Pete taught me one of the cardinal virtues of basketball," Scheffler said. "That was the value of possessing the ball."

The Capitoline discussed Peterman's slow-break offense. "Ninety percent of the fans were against his style. They wanted fast, breakneck speedy games. The safety and perseverance of the players comes first. There is no sense to run your boys to death."

Times indeed have changed. But the success of Mark and that style is a thing of the past. Peterman should be long remembered.

It was 1959 when Scheffler returned to the tournament, this time to launch a six-season stay as an official. After a three-season wait, he drew the dream game every official desires to work, the 1961 championship game, when Collinsville pushed the speed pedal to run past Thornton of Harvey 84–50.

Scheffler was also involved in the 1966 tourney when son Mark played on the same Springfield team as Dave Robish when the Senators were subjected to a first-round blackout at the hands of Galesburg. The Silver Streaks won a 69–65 pulse-pounder.

Following in his father's footsteps as a player-coach in the classic, Mark showed up for the 1975 meet as coach of Chatham of Glenwood in Class A competition. Chatham won in the Super Sectionals, beating Quincy Catholic 54–51 in overtime. Then Coach Scheffler's team was eliminated in the quarterfinals, bowing to Eldorado 65–60.

Bill is the third Scheffler in the sports' swim, coaching at Grant in Springfield.

And don't for a single second think the men completely rule the Scheffler family roost. Herb's wife, Elaine, placed high up in the national Mothers-Daughters bowling tournament in Chicago in the early 40's.

Coal Chute Ride for Refs
by Eddie Jacquin
Sports Editor, Champaign-Urbana News Gazette; Referee, Announcer

A half-filled University of Illinois Gym Annex for the four-team State Tournament in 1923. It was won by Villa Grove, just a few miles southeast of Urbana.

Ten years later scalpers were asking — and getting — $25 for a season ticket for the *Sweet Sixteen* in George Huff Gymnasium.

Ticket scalpers were the busiest in 1933 when the Purple Flying Clouds of Harvey won the championship. Harvey fielded the amazing Lou Boudreau and was coached by Jack Lipe.

Radio broadcasting of the state finals, over the University of Illinois station, WILL, was at its peak, reaching into every corner of the state. I can still see Captain Boudreau and Coach Lipe climbing up through the bleachers to our booth to say "Hello" to the fans and receive a handful of "best wishes" telegrams.

Pat Harmon, now the esteemed Sports Editor of the Cincinnati Post (then the assistant sports editor of the News Gazette), passed on information that Dick Morgan of Canton played in four state tournaments. One never disputes the Whiz Kid from Freeport who hitchhiked his way around the state picking an All-State Team.

Our first experience officiating basketball was in Longview. Accompanied by Lyle Clarno, one of the nation's top-rated officials, we were rushed down the coal chute into the basement because the gymnasium was so crowded we were unable to get through the fans outside the front door.

The annual "March Madness" in Champaign-Urbana seemed to justify a headline in the News Gazette: "The Greatest Sports Show on Earth."

Fred "Brick" Young, for many years the Sports Editor of the Bloomington Pantagraph, was the pioneer in giving sport-page space to high school games. He gave us this advice: "Write five or six letters a day to high school coaches and they will send you news. "Now well into his 80's, Young writes a daily column for the Pantagraph. He attributes his long life and good health to his many years of officiating after his active participation at Illinois Wesleyan ended.

It was during most of these years that the News Gazette had among its subscribers several hundred high school coaches and principals.

Mike Tobin, the very popular and erudite University of Illinois publicist (he told the world about Red Grange), asked us if we would broadcast the state finals over WILL. We said: "Sure". He added it was worth $50 and that was a lot of money for a young sports editor making only $35 a week.

This meant calling eight games on Thursday of Tournament Week; four on Friday, and four more on Saturday.

Frank Schooley, the director for station WILL, now retired, recalled recently "That you (Jacquin) lost your voice doing the seventh game and I filled in for you." Somebody had to make sure the "show must go on."

Record Unparalleled: Douglas Raymond Mills, guard and captain of two state championship Elgin teams in 1925 and 1925; guard and captain of three University of Illinois basketball teams; half-back on three University of Illinois football teams; coach of out-standing football and basketball teams at Joliet High School. Returning to the University as head basketball coach, he produced an outstanding record and was named athletic director in 1960.

Changing times in lifestyles: motels getting most of the teams, fans and followers, now, who formerly stayed in downtown hotels in Champaign and Urbana.

State classic personal favorites: Andy Phillip, Granite City; Kamp brothers, Mount Carmel; Dike Eddleman, Centralia; Lou Boudreau, Harvey—Coaches we admired: Gay Kintner, Decatur; Harry Combes, Champaign; Vergil Fletcher, Collinsville, and LaRue Van Meter, Johnston City.

When slow motion, hold-the-ball style of basketball was featured in Canton, Athens, and other places in the early 1900s, Bob Zuppke repeated more than once, "You could play that sort of a game in four feet of water." Zup should know. He earned a letter in basketball at Wisconsin.

Dave Manthey
Sports Writer, Chicago Sun-Times

Boosters of Southern and Central Illinois big-school prep basketball have been muffled without a state champion since 1967 when the veteran Dawdy Hawkins coached Pekin to a title.

The string of Chicago-area teams to leave the Assembly Hall in Champaign with a Big Bertha championship trophy now stands at nine.

What were the teams and who were some of the heroes who built this domination? Here's a thumbnail sketch of the recent conquerors of Downstate basketball teams.

● 1968 — Every Evanston starter was in double figures for coach Jack Burmaster, now athletic director at the school. Guard Ron Cooper scored 21 points, 11 of them free throws in a 70–51 title romp over Galesburg. Cooper also grabbed eight rebounds, tying big Bob Lackey who starred in the first two games. Public Leaguer Crane got third place on a big game by Jerome Freeman.

● 1969 — Defensive star Jim Brewer led Proviso East to a 58–51 title victory over Peoria Spalding. Brewer, playing with an ankle sprain, dropped in two free throws with six seconds to play to rally Proviso over Champaign Central 37–36 in the semifinals. Proviso coach Tom Millikin is now principal at the Maywood school.

● 1970 — Owen Brown, who recently died in Virginia, turned in one of the finest individual efforts in a title game 24 points, 24 rebounds — as La Grange beat East Moline 71–52. Coach Ron Nikcevich's Lions went unbeaten in 31 and included standout guard Marc Washington. Joliet Central took third behind Roger Powell.

• 1971 — Thornridge of Dolton started on a record winning string and nipped Oak Lawn 52–50 in an all-South suburb finale for Coach Ron Ferguson, now at Illinois State. Four underclassmen started, including Quinn Buckner. Thornridge committed only four turnovers in the title game against Oak Lawn which paraded C. J. Kupec.

• 1972 — Thornridge returned with Buckner, Bob Batts, Greg Rose and Mike Bonczyk and slammed Quincy 104–69 in a near-perfect championship. The Falcons ran their winning string to 54 with 33 this season. Batts scored 37, Buckner 28 and Rose 26 in the title game when Thornridge shot 62 per cent. East Aurora finished third.

• 1973 — Hirsch of the Public League celebrated the 10th anniversary of the Assembly Hall by downing New Trier East 65–51 for the state title. Rickey Green and John Robinson starred for coach Charles Stimpson's Huskies. New Trier East made only one of 13 shots and was bombed 12–2 in a decisive third period. West Aurora took third on 30 points by Matt Hicks.

• 1974 — Joe Ponsetto muscled up 20 points and 14 rebounds in Proviso East's 61–56 title win over Bloom which had been led by Audie Matthews all year. Proviso coach Glen Wittenberg built a rebounding giant with 6-5 Ponsetto, 6-3, Mike Stockdale and 6-3 Rod Floyd.

• 1975 — The Public League captured its second state title in three years and the fifth in the city's history when Phillips slammed Bloom 76–48. Larry Williams tallied 28 points and 14 rebounds for the Wildcats who finished the season winning 30 straight. Marty Murray also starred.

• 1976 — Another state crown for the Public League as Morgan Park nipped Aurora (West) 45–44 when Larry Smith notched a 22-footer from the right side as time ran out. Morgan Park scored the last five points, including a basket by Levi Cobb who had a game-high 19 points.

Herb Jannusch
Sports Writer, Kankakee Journal

CHAMPAIGN — The stocky, gray-haired man at the next table in the restaurant was immediately recognizable. He was Greg Sloan, whose name may not mean much to a lot of you guys on the younger half of the generation gap but who won't need any introduction to those of you over 40.

The chance meeting started a lot of reminiscing, especially since it was state basketball tournament time and marked the 20th anniversary of Sloan's finest hour.

It was in 1953 that Sloan took his unbeaten LaGrange team into the state finals in old Huff gym, but the tournament was virtually an anti-climax. The Lions had already "won" the championship a week earlier by beating Kankakee in Joliet's old oval gym.

"That," said Sloan who is now an assistant superintendent of the sprawling Rich Township High School district, "had to be the greatest high school basketball game ever played in this state, if not anywhere. There was never anything before or since to equal it in importance, intensity of interest and a match of great talent. It's still a shame that those two teams had to meet then instead of in the finals down here."

"The game," as every middle-aged Kankakeean knows, brought together two undefeated teams which had been ranked one-two in the press ratings from the start of the season. Kankakee was No. 1, mainly because of Harv Schmidt, who had put on a spectacular exhibition the year before, in the state finals, in a losing cause.

Because Earl Jones, the Kankakee coach, had Schmidt and an almost all-veteran squad back for the 1952–53 squad, the Kays grabbed the No. 1 spot and hung onto it rolling roughshod over 26 consecutive foes, most of them in the highly regarded South Suburban League.

The classic, in the first round of the Joliet sectional, might have drawn 50,000 spectators had the the facilities been available. As it was, 5,000 jammed almost every inch of available space and, although all seats had been sold days in advance, hundreds of fans, who had come from far places in the hope of finding scalpers peddling tickets, were left out in the March cold.

The battle turned into a battle of two young giants, the 6-foot, 6-inch Schmidt and LaGrange's 6-8 Ted Caiazza, who were later to be teammates at the University of Illinois. But on that night, at least, Caiazza had the better supporting cast and Schmidt had to try to turn the tide almost alone.

It was LaGrange on top 28–21 at the quarter, but the Kays trailed at halftime only 45–42. The Kays drew even several times and even led briefly but the third quarter was still 62–59.

The Lions came on stronger in the final period and the Kays faded particularly after Schmidt became the third member of his team to foul out, killing off the Kays' last hope. Until he left the game, Harv was superb in trying single-handedly to rally his sagging forces. He was hitting 30 and 35-foot shots with such deadly accuracy that one radio announcer said in awed amazement, "This is the first time I've ever seen a man shoot a basketball that curves."

Schmidt won the scoring battle from Caiazza with 37 points, hitting 16 of his 30 shots, many of them from far out. Big Ted, a 220-pounder whose muscle gave him many a close-in shot, had 31. Chuck Sedgwick scored 20 for LaGrange and Joe McRae 16. The only Kay besides Schmidt to get into double figures was Ed Bertrand, with 10.

The Kays outscored LaGrange from the field, 25–23, but the Lions got a huge total of 52 free throws and hit 37 to win 83–74.

After that, LaGrange swept through the sectional championship game and four foes in the state, with ease, to become one of the few state titleists to boast a perfect season.

For Jones, that was to be his last state tournament team but not for Sloan. Soon after his 1953 triumph, Sloan moved to Rich Township High where two years later he produced another state contender, led by a blond, 6-foot guard named Roger Taylor.

"Taylor was the best shooter I ever coached," Sloan said. "He could kill you from anywhere."

Sloan brought his Rockets to the Kankakee sectional and won to qualify for the Sweet Sixteen, but what happened after that Sloan would rather forget.

When somebody asked who beat him at Champaign, the retired coach grinned wryly.

"I was afraid you were going to ask me ·that," he laughed. "Shawneetown. Remember Shawneetown? I'll bet I am about the only guy around who remembers Shawneetown. They weren't supposed to come close to us but for some reason that day, Taylor couldn't hit anything (he went 8-for-28 from the field). That's one game I'd like to forget."

Taylor subsequently redeemed himself by starring for three years at Illinois and playing for several years in the pro leagues.

By Jack Rosenberg
Sports Editor, WGN

It was March 20, 1976. Levi Cobb controlled the tip. His teammate, Larry Smith, reacted with perfection. He collected the basketball on outstretched fingers and fired from the side. The shot arched through the rim without touching the bottom of the net. It was accompanied by the sounding of the final horn.

Morgan Park had gained instant immortality. The Mustangs of Coach Bill Warden had overcome Aurora (West), 45–44, to capture the state Class AA title in the frenzied atmosphere of the Assembly Hall in Champaign.

March Madness was upon us again in all its glory.

And thus has it ever been since Peoria (Central) won the first state back in 1908.

My own recollections of March Madness cover a broad spectrum, first as 17-year-old sports editor of the Pekin Daily Times prior to entering the Navy in World War II, later with the Peoria Journal, and still later with WGN Television in Chicago.

Random observations:

—Any college coach would have drooled at the thought of keeping the 1976 Class AA all-tournament team intact through four years at a school of higher learning. His inheritance: Levi Cobb of Morgan Park, Ron Hicks of Aurora (West), Chuck Dahms of Oak Park-River Forest and a pair of Decatur (Eisenhower) products, Jeff Roth and Hubert Carter. It's a team that would guarantee to silence the alumni until 1980.

—The greatest individual floor leader I saw over the years at the state was Quinn Buckner of Dolton (Thornridge), who propelled Coach Ron Ferguson's machine to successive titles in 1971–72. Buckner was a wizard even in high school. Small wonder he played key roles in dribbling Indiana University to the national championship and the United States to the Olympic gold medal in 1976.

—The *Sweet Sixteen* tournaments of the old days at Huff Gym developed into an endurance test for all concerned. The eight-game Thursday session began at 10 a.m. and lasted into the night. The current Super-Sectional set-up, as I see it, spreads the great basketball around the state and generates more interest.

—Call it a sign of age, but when I first covered basketball, any player who shot the ball with one hand was considered a showboat.

—I note with glee that Pekin has made 15 tournament appearances.

—Personally, I find third-place games anti-climactic, but maybe it's because I never played on a team which got that far.

—The best advertisement for the Champaign-Urbana area is Chuck Flynn, who was Mr. University of Illinois for so many years before taking over as boss man at the Champaign News - Gazette.

—The Taylorville team that won the state in 1944 with an incredible 45–0 record included Johhny Orr, who gained national basketball fame as head coach at the University of Michigan.

—Jack Burmaster has worn three hats with distinction at the state: as player (Elgin), as coach (Evanston) and as analyst (television). In 1968, his Evanston team won it all. He now is the school's athletic director. There were times during his coaching career that television producers Rick Hawley and Don Arries never knew until the last minute whether Burmaster would appear in Champaign as coach or telecaster. That's because Evanston usually made a run for it in the tournaments and obviously, he took on the television assignment only if his team was out of it.

—Speaking of Hawley and Arries, a man in the television field hasn't lived until he has worked alongside that dynamic duo. They are masters of precision. Their script for each tournament is a year-long labor of love and compares favorably in size with a Sears catalog. They've developed a television feature which has ranked with the finest for a quarter-century. They meet frequently with WGN executives Jack Jacobson and Bill Lotzer thruout the year to make certain that no basketball is left unturned.

—In my teen-age days of the long ago, the No. 1 athlete in the state of Illinois was Dike Eddleman of Centralia, current director of grants-in-aid for the University of Illinois. I still recall the shock created by the semifinal upset of Centralia, 30–29, in 1941, by Cicero (Morton) when only four teams comprised the tournament field. But Eddleman, who scored 2,702 points in his spectacular career, came back as the lone starting holdover in 1942 and Centralia scrambled to the title, overcoming a 13-point deficit in the last five minutes to stop previously-unbeaten Paris, 35–33.

—To hear Eddleman tell it all these years later: "My biggest sports thrill ever was winning that state championship at Centralia." That, it would seem, is an appropriate testimonial to *March Madness.*

Brick Young
Sports Writer and Tournament Official

Many men have had many reasons for becoming a basketball official, but few had a better motive than Fred "Brick" Young. When he started out in 1917 he was looking for a sideline to supplement his salary as an apprentice sports writer. Whatever the fee, a low of $5 to a high of $10, Young always was available. Even if it meant working a 20-hour day to complete all of his chores with a typewriter as well as a whistle.

In the process of a 31-year officiating career in both football and basketball, and a plus 50-year stint on the same newspaper—the Bloomington (Ill.) Pantagraph—Fred Young has become Illinois' best dressed walking encyclopedia of sports. He's been known to change suits before venturing outside his home if only to walk to the post office.

Newspapering, especially in the good old days, ranged from apparel regarded as carelessly casual to rundown heels and million mile sport shirts. Not so with Fred Young. A stranger meeting him for the first time still can't be sure if he's shaking hands with a businessman or a banker or a broker. Always, he's dressed in his Sunday finest seven days a week, looking like he had just stepped out of a bandbox.

In his own quiet way this distinguished graduate of Illinois Wesleyan University has put together a record which probably never will be topped in the history of the Illinois High School Association. Would you believe working 12 straight championship games, from 1918 to 1929? And that isn't all. He also officiated many regionals and sectionals leading up to the Big Apple in Illinois schoolboy basketball.

While calling the championship games, Young had seven different partners, ending up with two newcomers—Lyle "Dutch" Clarno and Carl Johnson. He would later rejoin them in Western Conference (BIG 10) officiating. His parade of firsts also includes the association's move into new Huff gymnasium in Champaign to contest the 1929 tournament. This was something akin to moving from a tent into a penthouse because Huff gym seated 7,000 patrons—and still this wasn't enough room to accommodate all the would-be ticket buyers.

Not all of Young's championship games were cake walks, an official's label for an easy game. During an era when the center jump was in vogue, Young's whistle was heard in such barn-burners as Mount Vernon's 18-14 conquest of Canton in 1919; Marion's 24-23 run past Rockford in 1921; Villa Grove's 32-29 upending of Rockford in 1923, and his final title test in 1929. Then it was Johnston City leading Champaign by a point, 19-18 going into the last quarter. During the final eight minutes, Johnston City literally blew Champaign off the court with an eleven point spree to finalize a 30-21 triumph.

It was a very significant record then. It still is. It's also a tremendous tribute to Brick's courage because it is every official's desire to work at least one state championship game. At last count the association had 5,000 registered officials in Illinois covering both boys basketball and football.

Young was involved in a misnomer when he moved up to the intercollegiate plateau. At that time the Little Nineteen conference was in full bloom. There was just one thing wrong with this count. The conference membership numbered 26 schools and required the services of many more officials.

"I didn't think about it at the time," Brick recalled, "but several coaches accepted me as one of the officials when they played Illinois Wesleyan, my alma mater, either in Bloomington or on the road. This is unthinkable these days, having officials working games where their schools are involved."

Young provided proof that officials have heroes just like fans, players, and coaches. His hero was John Schommer, a standout athlete at the University of Chicago before becoming an outstanding football and basketball official.

Schommer, who desired to enter law and turned to teaching and officiating instead, took Brick under his arm when he was promoted to the Big Ten. His promotion, incidentally, was one of the cheapest ever from a monetary standpoint. He was paid $10 a piece for two Illinois' home games against Michigan and Wisconsin. Also, he received an additional $2 to cover the purchase of two round trip train tickets between Bloomington and Champaign.

"I can't say for sure," Young began, "but I've always felt that the Michigan and Wisconsin victories over Illinois gave me important status with all the other conference coaches."

The fact that he was graduated from a non-conference school added to his credentials along with Schommer's endorsement "that this young man is going to be an outstanding official."

Although he officiated five Notre Dame-Army football games, the one he best remembers was the 21 to 21 tie between Chicago and Illinois during the Red Grange era. "Coach (Alonzo) Stagg had three outstanding fullbacks led by 'Five Yards' McCarthy," Brick recalled, "and they pounded over three touchdowns.

"Then Grange ran for three. He also scored a fourth time, but Illinois was offside. This voided the touchdown, and the game ended in a tie—one of the great games in Big Ten history."

Young always enjoyed Coach Knute Rockne's humor, which he claims was "equal to any occasion."

There is one Nebraska-Notre Dame game that Brick remembers. "The officials were on the field," he began, "when Rockne sent four or five different teams out of the dressing room. The Nebraska coach yelled to Rock, asking which one he planned to start. 'Pick out any one you like, and I'll play it,' Rockne answered, 'because it doesn't make any difference to me.' "

Rockne apparently wasn't kidding because Notre Dame was an easy 34-6 winner over the deflated Cornhuskers.

Brick possesses great admiration for Coach Arthur Trout, who built powerhouse teams in both basketball and football at Centralia. "Trout told me he was so poor that he slept in a barn to assure getting through Indiana. When he went to Centralia he lived in a little cottage on the side of the football field. Trout loved his work, and never did he venture too far away from it."

There are many milestones in Brick's career. Besides Schommer, he also officiated football with Walter Eckersall, another standout when the University of Chicago had Monsters of the Midway billing. In 1944 when Coach Dolph Stanley's Taylorville powerhouse won

45 straight games, Young officiated twelve of them during regular season and tournament competition.

He worked the first and only—to date—Illinois-Indiana All-Star game, in 1941, at Mount Vernon, which cost foxy Doxie Moore his coaching job. "Doxie arranged the game and rented the Mount Vernon gym, which seated about 2,500 persons," Brick remembered. "He hired Abe Martin and myself to officiate it.

"When I arrived at the gym, block long lines of people were trying to get to the ticket office. It was a complete sellout. I'm not sure whether he paid us $25 or $50 a piece. I do recall that Indiana led by 10 points at halftime. Finally the Illinois boys rallied, and won by six (36-30). That sort of debunked Indiana's best label when compared to Illinois high school basketball. A short time later Doxie called me, to report the school board just fired him. 'Don't worry about me. I made a good buck out of the All-Star game, and I'm moving to Indiana to join the governor's official staff. There's one thing I'm sure of, he didn't move out short of money. The gym was filled—every nook and corner, and Doxie was the sole promoter."

Young is Mister Sports wherever he goes in the Bloomington area. Whenever there is a debate about sports, one command leads all others. It's simply: "Check with Brick. He'll have the correct answer." Brick seldom strays too far away from his trusty typewriter because his column, Young's Yarns, is a daily feature in the Pantagraph. It's been said, half in jest and half seriously, that more names appear in Young's Yarns over a year's span than you will find in the Bloomington-Normal telephone directory. Remarkable man, Fred "Brick" Young!

JOY(?) RIDE — Merle Jones, sports editor of the Carbondale Southern Illinoisan, leads the parade through West Frankfort as he said he would — riding a donkey. (Photo Courtesy Southern Illinoisan)

The Historic Battle of West Frankfort

During the 1959–60 season, West Frankfort had just a so-so team while Pinckneyville beat Granite City 66–59 in the championship game of the prestigious Centralia Holiday tourney.

While West Frankfort was beating Mounds (Douglass) and Metropolis by identical 71–69 double overtime scores in the Herrin Sectional, Merle Jones went to the sectional finals at East St. Louis, where Granite City upset Pinckneyville to set up a Granite City vs. West Frankfort Super-Sectional game, with Herschel Wilkinson, a referee who was father of Bryan Wilkinson, a West Frankfort starter.

On the way home from East St. Louis, Wilkinson stopped in Coulterville at a pay station to call home to find out the score of the West Frankfort-Metropolis sectional final game.

"We won 71–69 in two overtimes, Daddy," said Wilkinson's young daughter. "But that was the score last night," said the confused Wilkinson. "Where's your mother?"

"Oh, everybody went downtown to the celebration," said the little girl.

In the Sunday edition of The Southern Illinoisan, Jones wrote that Granite City had the far superior team and that while West Frankfort could go to the State Tournament as guests of the IHSA, the players "would not have to take their uniforms." There was "no chance to beat Granite City."

A West Frankfort fan promptly wrote Jones and challenged him to ride a donkey down Main Street in West Frankfort if the Redbirds won. Jones accepted.

West Frankfort won in East St. Louis, 64–62 in two overtimes on a night so cold and snowy that the team stayed overnight, Tuesday, in East St. Louis.

When the team arrived home at noon the next day, the parade had been arranged with Jones the "marshal" on the donkey.

West Frankfort won its quarterfinal test, 66–65 from Galesburg in the State Tournament, but lost in the semifinals to Bridgeport 74–60. In the third place game Decatur fell 75–53 to assure West Frankfort its best-ever finish.

Chapter 7

The Story in Numbers
From 1908 to the Present

Title Game Recap

YEAR	CHAMPION	COACH	FINAL RECORD	RUNNERUP	FINAL RECORD	TITLE GAME SCORE
1908	Peoria (Central)	Les Straeser	17-1	Rock Island	10-5	48-29
1909	Hinsdale	John Snider	22-2	Washington	27-3	18-13
1910	Bloomington	Tom O'Neill	14-2	Rock Island	14-2	32-25
1911	Rockford	Ralph E. Vennum	22-0	Mt. Carroll		60-15
1912	Batavia	K. C. Merrick	27-2	Galesburg	14-5	28-25
1913	Galesburg	E. W. Hayes	17-1	Peoria (Manual)	17-2	37-37
1914	Hillsboro	D. O. Kime		Freeport	17-1	42-19
1915	Freeport	Dan Daugherty	18-2	Springfield	6-5	27-11
1916	Bloomington	E. W. McClure	13-6	Robinson	21-4	25-16
1917	Springfield	Roy A. Wentz	10-3	Belvidere	11-5	32-11
1918	Centralia	Arthur L. Trout	23-4	Normal (University)	18-7-1	35-29
1919	Rockford	Frank J. Winters	23-1	Springfield	14-10	39-20
1920	Mt. Vernon	Floyd Stables	17-8	Canton	30-4	18-14
1921	Marion	E. H. Schreiber	21-4	Rockford	16-4	24-23
1922	Centralia	Arthur L. Trout	26-4	Atwood	21-1	24-16
1923	Villa Grove	Curtus Pulliam	23-2	Rockford	27-4	32-29
1924	Elgin	Mark Wilson	24-3	Athens	35-2	28-17
1925	Elgin	Clifton E. Adams	25-2	Champaign	21-5	25-17
1926	Freeport	Glenn Holmes	19-2	Canton	24-12	24-13
1927	Mt. Carmel	Cliff Garrett	31-2	Peoria (Central)	30-3	24-18
1928	Canton	Mark A. Peterman	36-6	Aurora (West)	20-5	18-9
1929	Johnston City	Larue Van Meter	29-3	Champaign	28-4	30-21
1930	Peoria (Manual)	Telford Mead	25-5	Bloomington	20-4	38-25
1931	Decatur	Gay A. Kintner	29-5	Galesburg	24-4	30-26
1932	Cicero (Morton)	Norman A. Ziebell	25-4	Canton	27-5	30-16
1933	Harvey (Thornton)	Jack Lipe	13-1	Springfield	8-5	14-13
1934	Quincy	Selmar A. Storby	31-2	Harvey (Thornton)	26-1	39-27
1935	Springfield	Mark A. Peterman	34-3	Harvey (Thornton)	18-4	24-19

YEAR	CHAMPION	COACH	FINAL RECORD	RUNNERUP	FINAL RECORD	TITLE GAME SCORE
1936	Decatur	Gay A. Kintner	24-11	Danville	23-1	26-22
1937	Joliet	Herman Walser	27-4	Decatur	23-12	40-20
1938	Dundee	Eugene de Lacey	36-1	Braidwood	33-3	36-29
1939	Rockford	James Laude	27-2	Paris	37-3	53-44
1940	Granite City	Buron Bozarth	29-5	Herrin	23-8	24-22
1941	Cicero (Morton)	Norman A. Ziebell	23-4	Urbana	22-11	32-31
1942	Centralia	Arthur L. Trout	34-6	Paris	39-1	35-33
1943	Paris	Ernest W. Eveland	37-2	Moline	24-4	46-37
1944	Taylorville	Dolph Stanley	45-0	Elgin	21-4	56-33
1945	Decatur	Gay A. Kintner	39-2	Champaign	34-2	62-54
1946	Champaign	Harry Combes	37-1	Centralia	30-10	54-48
1947	Paris	Ernest W. Eveland	40-2	Champaign	33-4	58-37
1948	Pinckneyville	Merrill Thomas	33-1	Rockford (East)	26-4	65-39
1949	Mt. Vernon	Stanley A. Changnon	30-3	Hillsboro	25-7	45-39
1950	Mt. Vernon	Stanley A. Changnon	33-0	Danville	29-2	85-61
1951	Freeport	Harry Kinert	31-2	Moline	22-9	71-51
1952	Hebron	Russ Ahearn	35-1	Quincy	28-5	64-59
1953	LaGrange (Lyons)	Greg Sloan	29-0	Peoria (Central)	29-4	72-60
1954	Mt. Vernon	Harold Hutchins	29-3	Chicago (DuSable)	31-1	76-70
1955	Rockford (West)	Alex Saudargas	28-1	Elgin	26-4	61-59
1956	Rockford (West)	Alex Saudargas	28-1	Edwardsville	28-6	67-65
1957	Herrin	Earl Lee	31-2	Collinsville	34-1	45-42
1958	Chicago (Marshall)	Isadore Salario	30-0	Rock Falls	32-2	70-64
1959	Springfield	Ray Page	33-1	Aurora (West)	22-7	60-52
1960	Chicago (Marshall)	Isadore Salario	30-2	Bridgeport	33-2	79-55
1961	Collinsville	Vergil Fletcher	32-0	Harvey (Thornton)	27-3	84-50
1962	Decatur	John Schneiter	31-4	Chicago (Carver)	27-5	49-48
1963	Chicago (Carver)	Larry Hawkins	27-5	Centralia	32-3	50-52
1964	Pekin	Dawson Hawkins	30-3	Cobden	32-3	50-45
1965	Collinsville	Vergil Fletcher	30-2	Quincy	26-6	55-52
1966	Harvey (Thornton)	Bob Anderson	30-2	Galesburg	27-3	74-60
1967	Pekin	Dawson Hawkins	31-2	Carbondale	29-3	75-59
1968	Evanston	Jack Burmaster	30-1	Galesburg	27-3	70-51
1969	Maywood (Proviso East)	Tom Millikin	30-1	Peoria (Spalding)	28-4	58-51
1970	LaGrange (Lyons)	Ron Nickcevich	31-0	East Moline	30-3	71-52
1971	Dolton (Thornridge)	Ron Ferguson	31-1	Oak Lawn	30-3	52-60
1972-A	Lawrenceville	Ron Felling	25-8	Mounds (Meridian)	30-2	63-57
AA	Dolton (Thornridge)	Ron Ferguson	33-0	Quincy	28-5	104-69
1973-A	Ridgway	Bob Dallas	32-1	Maple Park (Kaneland)	20-12	54-51
AA	Chicago (Hirsch)	Charles Stimpson	29-2	Winnetka (New Trier East)	23-5	65-51
1974-A	Lawrenceville	Ron Felling	30-3	Ottawa (Marquette)	29-4	54-53
AA	Maywood (Proviso East)	Glenn Whittenberg	29-4	Chicago HTs. (Bloom)	30-3	61-56
1975-A	Venice	Rich Essington	32-2	Elmhurst (Timothy Christian)	27-6	65-46
AA	Chicago (Wendell Phillips)	Herb Brown	32-1	Chicago Hts. (Bloom)	23-10	76-48
1976-A	Mt. Pulaski	Edward Butkovich	29-2	Oneida (ROVA)	28-3	59-58
AA	Chicago (Morgan Park)	Bill Warden	28-5	Aurora (West)	30-3	45-44

Boys State Basketball Tournament Honor Roll

Following is an all-time list of the top-four finishers in every Illinois State Tournament in history. Much of the research is the work of the late Howard V. Millard, former sports editor of the Decatur Herald & Review, and the IHSA is deeply appreciative.

Year	Winner	Second	Third	Fourth
1908	Peoria (Central)	Rock Island	Oak Park	Hinsdale
1909	Hinsdale	Washington	Mount Carroll	Rock Island
1910	Bloomington	Rock Island	Hinsdale	Mount Vernon
1911	Rockford	Mount Carroll	Granite City	Paris
1912	Batavia	Galesburg	Granite City	Decatur
1913	Galesburg	Peoria (Manual)	Hillsboro	Winnetka (New Trier)
1914	Hillsboro	Freeport	Normal (Univ. High)	Evanston (Academy)
1915	Freeport	Springfield	Shelbyville	Carbondale
1916	Bloomington	Robinson	DuQuoin	Springfield
1917	Springfield	Belvidere	Bloomington	Peoria (Manual)
1918	Centralia	Normal (Univ. High)	Canton	Shelbyville
1919	Rockford	Springfield	Peoria (Central)	Herrin
1920	Mount Vernon	Canton	Marion	Olney
1921	Marion	Rockford	Winnetka (New Trier)	Batavia
1922	Centralia	Atwood	Rockford	Peoria (Central)
1923	Villa Grove	Rockford	Canton	Greenville
1924	Elgin	Athens	Canton	West Frankfort
1925	Elgin	Champaign	Canton	Marion
1926	Freeport	Canton	Flora	Athens
1927	Mount Carmel	Peoria (Central)	East St. Louis	Champaign
1928	Canton	Aurora (West)	Witt	Griggsville
1929	Johnston City	Champaign	Freeport	Peoria (Central)
1930	Peoria (Manual)	Bloomington	Olney	Beardstown
1931	Decatur	Galesburg	Chicago (Harrison)	Johnston City
1932	Cicero (Morton)	Canton	Lawrenceville	Kewanee
1933	Harvey (Thornton)	Springfield	Benton	Gillespie
1934	Quincy	Harvey (Thornton)	Equality	Moline
1935	Springfield	Harvey (Thornton)	Pekin	Moline
1936	Decatur	Danville	Johnston City	Mount Pulaski
1937	Joliet	Decatur	Collinsville	Pekin
1938	Dundee	Braidwood	Paris	Chicago (Von Steuben)
1939	Rockford	Paris	Wood River	Centralia
1940	Granite City	Herrin	Moline	Champaign
1941	Cicero (Morton)	Urbana	Centralia	Canton
1942	Centralia	Paris	Freeport	Cicero (Morton)
1943	Paris	Moline	Salem	Elgin
1944	Taylorville	Elgin	Chicago (South Shore)	Champaign
1945	Decatur	Champaign	Quincy	Moline
1946	Champaign	Centralia	Dundee	Rockford (East)
1947	Paris	Champaign	Pinckneyville	Pekin
1948	Pinckneyville	Rockford (East)	Pekin	LaGrange
1949	Mount Vernon	Hillsboro	Aurora (West)	Nashville
1950	Mount Vernon	Danville	Elgin	Collinsville
1951	Freeport	Moline	Quincy	Decatur
1952	Hebron	Quincy	Mount Vernon	Rock Island
1953	LaGrange	Peoria (Central)	Pinckneyville	Danville (Schlarman)
1954	Mount Vernon	Chicago (DuSable)	Pinckneyville	Edwardsville

Year	Winner	Second	Third	Fourth
1955	Rockford (West)	Elgin	Pinckneyville	Princeton
1956	Rockford (West)	Edwardsville	Chicago (Dunbar)	Oak Park
1957	Herrin	Collinsville	Ottawa	Quincy (Notre Dame)
1958	Chicago (Marshall)	Rock Falls	Peoria (Spalding)	Aurora (West)
1959	Springfield	Aurora (West)	Galesburg	Waukegan
1960	Chicago (Marshall)	Bridgeport	West Frankfort	Decatur
1961	Collinsville	Harvey (Thornton)	Chicago (Marshall)	Peoria (Manual)
1962	Decatur	Chicago (Carver)	Quincy	McLeansboro
1963	Chicago (Carver)	Centralia	Springfield (Lanphier)	Peoria (Central)
1964	Pekin	Cobden	Decatur	Rock Island (Alleman)
1965	Collinsville	Quincy	Chicago (Marshall)	Harvey (Thornton)
1966	Harvey (Thornton)	Galesburg	Belleville	Decatur
1967	Pekin	Carbondale	Springfield	Rockford (West)
1968	Evanston	Galesburg	Chicago (Crane Tech)	DeKalb
1969	Maywood (Proviso East)	Peoria (Spalding)	Champaign (Central)	Aurora (East)
1970	LaGrange (Lyons)	East Moline	Joliet (Central)	Peoria (Spalding)
1971	Dolton (Thornridge)	Oak Lawn	Danville	Springfield (Lanphier)
1972A	Lawrenceville	Mounds (Meridian)	Raymond (Lincolnwood)	Thomson
1972AA	Dolton (Thornridge)	Quincy	Aurora (East)	Peoria (Manual)
1973A	Ridgway	Maple Park (Kaneland)	Venice	St. Anne
1973AA	Chicago (Hirsch)	Winnetka (New Trier East)	Aurora (West)	Lockport (Central)
1974A	Lawrenceville	Ottawa (Marquette)	Palos Hts. (Chicago Christian)	Quincy (Catholic Boys)
1974AA	Maywood (Proviso East)	Chicago Hts. (Bloom)	Peoria (Central)	Breese (Mater Dei)
1975A	Venice	Elmhurst (Timothy Christian)	Watseka	Eldorado
1975AA	Chicago (Phillips)	Chicago Hts. (Bloom)	East St. Louis (Sr.)	Peoria (Richwoods)
1976A	Mt. Pulaski	Oneida (ROVA)	Lawrenceville	Buda-Sheffield (Western)
1976AA	Chicago (Morgan Park)	Aurora (West)	Oak Park (O.P.-River Forest)	Decatur (Eisenhower)

All-time Team Data
(Appearances - Records)

Team	Times	First Appearance	Last Appearance	Record	Pct.	Times Placed in Top Four
Abingdon	2	1913	1930	0-2	.000	
Aledo	1	1963	1963	0-1	.000	
Alton (Sr.)	2	1919	1955	0-2	.000	
Anna-Jonesboro	2	1943	1944	1-2	.333	
Arcola	2	1958	1964	0-2	.000	
Arlington Hts. (Hersey)	1	1974AA	1974AA	1-1	.500	
Athens	4	1924	1937	1-5	.170	2
Atwood	3	1919	1930	1-3	.250	
Aurora (East)	6	1916	1972AA	6-7	.460	2
Aurora (Marmion)	1	1976A	1976A	1-1	.500	
Aurora (West)	8	1928	1976AA	16-9	.640	6
Barrington	1	1954	1954	1-1	.500	
Barry	1	1919	1919	0-1	.000	
Batavia	2	1912	1921	6-2	.750	2
Beardstown	3	1930	1947	1-4	.200	1
Belleville	3	1961	1966	3-3	.500	1
Belleville (East)	1	1969	1969	0-1	.000	
Belleville (West)	2	1968	1974AA	0-2	.000	
Belvidere	1	1917	1917	2-1	.667	1
Benton	8	1928	1971	5-8	.385	1
Bloomington	7	1909	1975AA	14-5	.737	4
Bloomington (Catholic)	2	1973A	1976A	2-2	.500	
Bowen	1	1954	1954	0-1	.000	
Breese (Mater Dei)	1	1974AA	1974AA	2-2	.500	1
Bradley-Bourbonnais	5	1939	1973AA	1-5	.167	
Braidwood	2	1938	1963	3-2	.600	
Bridgeport	1	1960	1960	3-1	.750	1
Brooklyn (Lovejoy)	1	1972A	1972A	0-1	.000	
Buda-Sheffield (Western)	2	1975A	1976A	3-3	.500	1
Bushnell-Prairie City	2	1973A	1975A	0-2	.000	
Calumet City (Thornton Fractional)	1	1946	1946	0-1	.000	
Cairo	2	1975A	1976A	0-2	.000	
Canton	17	1912	1953	16-18	.471	9
Carbondale	8	1915	1969	6-9	.400	2
Carmi	1	1975A	1975A	0-1	.000	
Casey	1	1940	1940	0-1	.000	
Centralia	18	1909	1966	21-16	.568	7
Cerro Gordo	2	1973A	1974A	2-2	.500	
Champaign (Central)	23	1918	1969	28-25	.528	9
Charleston	3	1921	1957	1-3	.250	

Team	Times	First Appearance	Last Appearance	Record	Pct.	Times Placed in Top Four
Chatham (Glenwood)	1	1975A	1975A	1-1	.500	
Chicago						
Carver	2	1962	1963	7-1	.875	2
Crane Tech	5	1940	1972AA	4-5	.444	1
Deerfield-Shields	1	1935	1935	0-1	.000	
Dunbar	1	1956	1956	3-1	.750	1
DuSable	2	1953	1954	3-2	.600	1
Harlan	3	1967	1971	0-3	.000	
Harrison	1	1931	1931	2-1	.667	1
Hirsch	2	1969	1973AA	4-1	.800	1
Kelvyn Park	1	1943	1943	1-1	.500	
Lakeview	1	1933	1933	0-1	.000	
Lane Tech.	2	1934	1939	1-2	.333	
Lindblom	1	1942	1942	0-1	.000	
Marshall	10	1934	1972AA	16-8	.667	4
Morgan Park	3	1974AA	1976AA	5-2	.714	1
Phillips	3	1936	1936	0-1	.000	
Parker	2	1951	1973AA	0-2	.000	
Roosevelt	1	1952	1952	0-1	.000	
Senn	1	1945	1945	0-1	.000	
South Shore	2	1944	1947	4-2	.667	1
St. Patrick	1	1962	1962	0-1	.000	
Tilden Tech.	3	1946	1950	2-3	.400	
Vocational	1	1976AA	1976AA	0-1	.000	
Von Steuben	1	1938	1938	2-2	.500	1
Wendell Phillips	2	1974AA	1975AA	4-1	.800	1
Wells	1	1937	1937	1-1	.500	
Chicago Hts. (Bloom)	7	1940	1975AA	6-7	.461	2
Chrisman	1	1972A	1972A	0-1	.000	
Cicero (Morton)	6	1932	1961	8-5	.615	3
Clinton	2	1918	1961	0-2	.000	
Cobden	1	1964	1964	3-1	.750	1
Collinsville	17	1921	1973AA	23-17	.575	5
Crystal Lake	1	1974AA	1974AA	0-1	.000	
Cumberland	1	1954	1954	0-1	.000	
Danville (H.S.)	8	1935	1974AA	10-9	.526	3
Danville (Schlarman)	6	1953	1973A	4-7	.364	1
Decatur (Stephen Decatur)	23	1912	1967	33-23	.589	10
Decatur (Eisenhower)	2	1975AA	1976AA	3-2	.600	1
Decatur (St. Teresa)	1	1953	1953	1-1	.500	
DeKalb	3	1953	1968	2-4	.333	1
Dixon	2	1942	1969	0-2	.000	
Dolton (Thornridge)	3	1971	1976AA	9-1	.900	2
Dundee	6	1919	1947	9-5	.643	2
DuQuoin	4	1916	1972A	5-4	.556	1
Dwight	1	1939	1939	0-1	.000	

Team	Times	First Appearance	Last Appearance	Record	Pct.	Times Placed in Top Four
East Moline (United)	1	1970	1970	3-1	.750	1
East St. Louis (Sr.)	3	1927	1975AA	5-3	.625	2
Edwardsville	4	1951	1976AA	5-5	.500	2
Effingham (H.S.)	2	1967	1968	1-2	.333	
Effingham (St. Anthony)	2	1956	1970	1-2	.333	
Eldorado	2	1975A	1976A	3-3	.500	1
Elgin (H.S.)	18	1918	1976AA	19-17	.583	6
Elgin (Larkin)	1	1971	1971	0-1	.000	
Elgin (St. Edward)	1	1972A	1972A	1-1	.500	
Elmhurst (Timothy Christian)	1	1975A	1975A	3-1	.750	1
Elmhurst (York)	2	1962	1967	2-2	.500	
Equality	1	1934	1934	3-1	.750	1
Evanston	5	1908	1972AA	7-4	.636	1
Evanston (Academy)	1	1914	1914	1-2	.333	1
Fairbury	1	1921	1921	0-1	.000	
Farmington	1	1972A	1972A	0-1	.000	
Flora	6	1919	1947	2-6	.250	1
Franklin	1	1974A	1974A	0-1	.000	
Franklin Park (East Leyden)	2	1965	1975AA	0-2	.000	
Freeport	12	1914	1974AA	17-9	.654	6
Fulton	3	1936	1973A	2-3	.400	
Galesburg	24	1913	1969	25-23	.521	6
Geneva	2	1908	1963	1-2	.333	
Georgetown	1	1955	1955	0-1	.000	
Gibson City	1	1972A	1972A	1-1	.500	
Gillespie	2	1933	1939	1-3	.250	1
Glen Ellyn (Glenbard)	1	1938	1938	0-1	.000	
Granite City	9	1911	1971	7-8	.467	3
Greenville	2	1923	1960	0-3	.000	
Griggsville	1	1928	1928	1-2	.333	1
Harrisburg	1	1938	1938	1-1	.500	
Harvey (Thornton)	13	1917	1969	19-12	.613	6
Havana	1	1976A	1976A	1-1	.500	
Hebron	2	1940	1952	4-1	.800	1
Herrin	6	1919	1963	11-6	.647	3
Highland	2	1953	1958	1-2	.333	
Hillsboro	8	1912	1953	8-9	.471	2
Hinsdale (Central)	5	1909	1972AA	7-5	.583	3
Hoffman Estates (Conant)	1	1972AA	1972AA	0-1	.000	
Homewood-Flossmoor	2	1967	1976AA	1-2	.333	
Hull	1	1936	1936	1-1	.500	
Hume (Shiloh)	1	1975A	1975A	0-1	.000	
Hutsonville	2	1928	1933	0-2	.000	

Team	Times	First Appearance	Last Appearance	Record	Pct.	Times Placed in Top Four
Jacksonville (H.S.)	4	1911	1965	2-4	.333	
Jerseyville	3	1918	1958	0-3	.000	
Johnston City	6	1929	1950	8-6	.571	3
Joliet	7	1909	1943	6-6	.500	1
Joliet (Central)	2	1966	1970	4-2	.667	1
Kankakee	3	1944	1960	0-3	.000	
Kankakee (Eastridge)	1	1972AA	1972AA	0-1	.000	
Kewanee	7	1932	1971	4-8	.333	1
LaGrange (Lyons)	5	1948	1972AA	10-4	.714	3
LaSalle	1	1908	1908	0-1	.000	
LaSalle-Peru	4	1937	1970	2-5	.286	
Lawrenceville	12	1917	1976A	16-10	.615	4
Lebanon	1	1976A	1976A	0-1	.000	
Lemont (Twp.)	1	1975A	1975A	0-1	.000	
Lewistown	1	1940	1940	1-1	.500	
Lexington	1	1974A	1974A	1-1	.500	
Lincoln	6	1929	1973AA	3-6	.333	
Litchfield	1	1954	1954	0-1	.000	
Lockport (Central)	4	1965	1973AA	3-5	.375	1
Lombard (Glenbard East)	1	1964	1964	1-1	.500	
Macomb	2	1921	1959	1-2	.333	
Macomb (Western)	1	1951	1951	0-1	.000	
Madison	2	1952	1959	1-2	.333	
Mahomet	1	1933	1933	0-1	.000	
Maple Park (Kaneland)	1	1973A	1973A	3-1	.750	1
Marion	11	1920	1976AA	13-11	.545	3
Maroa	1	1957	1957	0-1	.000	
Marseilles	2	1944	1947	0-2	.000	
Marshall	1	1973A	1973A	0-1	.000	
Mascoutah	1	1972AA	1972AA	0-1	.000	
Mattoon	1	1969	1969	0-1	.000	
Maywood (Proviso)	1	1936	1936	0-1	.000	
Maywood (Proviso East)	5	1960	1975AA	10-3	.778	2
McHenry	1	1976AA	1976AA	0-1	.000	
McLeansboro	1	1962	1962	2-2	.500	1
Mendon (Unity)	1	1973A	1973A	0-1	.000	
Metropolis	1	1963	1963	1-1	.500	
Milton	1	1938	1938	0-1	.000	
Moline	21	1916	1976AA	22-24	.475	6
Monmouth (H.S.)	4	1950	1974A	1-4	.200	
Morris	1	1919	1919	0-1	.000	
Morrisonville	2	1973A	1975A	0-2	.000	
Mounds (Meridian)	1	1972A	1972A	3-1	.750	1
Mt. Carmel	5	1921	1944	3-4	.429	1

Team	Times	First Appearance	Last Appearance	Record	Pct.	Times Placed in Top Four
Mt. Carroll	3	1908	1911	3-3	.500	2
Mt. Olive	1	1927	1927	0-1	.000	
Mt. Pulaski	2	1936	1976A	6-2	.800	2
Mt. Sterling	1	1910	1910	0-1	.000	
Mt. Vernon	15	1909	1970	20-12	.625	6
Murphysboro	2	1947	1973AA	0-2	.000	
Naperville	1	1915	1915	0-1	.000	
Nashville	2	1949	1971	2-3	.400	1
New Lenox (Lincoln-Way)	1	1975AA	1975AA	0-1	.000	
Nokomis	1	1910	1910	0-1	.000	
Normal (Community)	3	1942	1976A	0-3	.000	
Normal (University)	5	1914	1975A	5-5	.500	2
North Chicago	2	1967	1972AA	0-2	.000	
Oak Park-River Forest	4	1908	1976AA	7-5	.583	3
Oak Lawn	1	1971	1971	3-1	.750	1
Oblong	1	1937	1937	0-1	.000	
Odell (St. Paul)	1	1951	1951	0-1	.000	
Okawville	1	1970	1970	1-1	.500	
Olney	3	1920	1942	5-4	.556	2
Olympia Fields (Rich Central)	1	1974AA	1974AA	0-1	.000	
Oneida (ROVA)	2	1949	1976A	3-2	.600	1
Oswego	1	1974AA	1974AA	1-1	.500	
Ottawa	8	1949	1961	5-8	.385	1
Ottawa (Marquette)	2	1973A	1974A	3-2	.600	1
Palos Hts. (Chicago Christian)	3	1972A	1976A	3-3	.500	1
Pana	1	1946	1946	0-1	.000	
Park Forest (Rich)	1	1955	1955	0-1	.000	
Park Ridge (Maine South)	2	1970	1975AA	0-2	.000	
Paris	12	1911	1971	20-11	.645	6
Pekin	15	1935	1973AA	19-15	.559	6
Peoria (Central)	16	1908	1974AA	21-18	.538	8
Peoria (Manual)	10	1913	1972AA	11-12	.478	5
Peoria (Richwoods)	1	1975AA	1975AA	2-2	.500	1
Peoria (Spalding)	5	1950	1970	8-6	.571	3
Peoria (Woodruff)	3	1939	1951	2-3	.400	
Petersburg (Porta)	1	1973A	1973A	1-1	.500	
Piasa (Southwestern)	1	1972A	1972A	0-1	.000	
Pinckneyville	11	1935	1973A	17-10	.630	5
Pittsfield	2	1921	1970	0-3	.000	
Pleasant Plains	1	1976A	1976A	0-1	.000	
Pontiac	2	1946	1962	0-2	.000	
Port Byron (Riverdale)	2	1975A	1976A	1-2	.333	

Team	Times	First Appearance	Last Appearance	Record	Pct.	Times Placed in Top Four
Princeton	2	1954	1955	2-3	.400	1
Prophetstown	1	1974A	1974A	1-1	.500	
Quincy (H.S.)	22	1934	1974AA	27-21	.563	7
Quincy (Notre Dame/ Catholic Boys)	5	1957	1975A	5-7	.419	2
Rantoul	4	1931	1959	2-4	.333	
Raymond (Lincolnwood)	1	1972A	1972A	3-1	.750	1
Ridgway	2	1973A	1974A	5-1	.833	1
Riverside	1	1908	1908	0-1	.000	
Robinson	5	1916	1951	4-5	.444	1
Rochelle	1	1928	1928	0-1	.000	
Rock Falls	1	1958	1958	3-1	.750	1
Rockford	12	1911	1939	17-9	.654	6
Rockford (Auburn)	5	1962	1975AA	2-5	.286	
Rockford (Boylan)	1	1971	1971	1-1	.500	
Rockford (East)	6	1945	1961	6-7	.462	2
Rockford (West)	9	1943	1973AA	12-8	.600	3
Rock Island (H.S.)	11	1908	1966	9-13	.409	4
Rock Island (Alleman)	2	1964	1972AA	2-3	.400	1
Roodhouse	1	1939	1939	0-1	.000	
Rushville	2	1937	1940	0-2	.000	
St. Anne	1	1973A	1973A	2-2	.500	1
St. Charles	2	1908	1927	0-2	.000	
Salem	2	1940	1943	4-2	750	1
Shabbona	1	1972A	1972A	0-1	.000	
Shawneetown	1	1955	1955	1-1	.500	
Shelbyville	5	1915	1920	4-6	.400	2
Skokie (Niles West)	2	1973AA	1976AA	0-2	.000	
Somonouk	1	1945	1945	1-1	.500	
South Beloit	2	1974A	1975A	0-2	.000	
Springfield (H.S.)	20	1915	1967	24-18	.571	8
Springfield (Cathedral)	3	1942	1948	1-3	.250	
Springfield (Lanphier)	5	1956	1971	5-6	.455	2
Spring Valley (Hall Twp.)	1	1974A	1974A	0-1	.000	
Sterling (Twp.)	3	1950	1975AA	0-3	.000	
Stewardson-Strasburg	1	1974A	1974A	0-1	.000	
Streator (Twp.)	7	1920	1964	2-7	.222	
Streator (Woodland)	1	1972A	1972A	1-1	.500	
Sullivan	1	1917	1917	0-1	.000	
Taylorville	6	1940	1959	5-5	.500	1
Thomson	1	1972A	1972A	2-2	.500	1
Toluca	2	1967	1973A	0-2	.000	
Trenton	1	1921	1921	0-1	.000	
Ullin (Century)	1	1974A	1974A	0-1	.000	

Team	Times	First Appearance	Last Appearance	Record	Pct.	Times Placed in Top Four
Urbana (H.S.)	5	1934	1966	2-5	.286	1
Vandalia	2	1936	1937	2-2	.500	
Venice	3	1973A	1975A	7-2	.778	2
Villa Grove	1	1923	1923	2-0	1.000	1
Washington	3	1909	1962	3-3	.500	1
Waterman	1	1930	1930	0-1	.000	
Watseka	4	1963	1976A	3-4	.428	1
Waukegan	6	1961	1975AA	4-7	.364	1
West Frankfort	9	1924	1960	6-10	.375	2
Westville	1	1976A	1976A	0-1	.000	
Wheaton	2	1908	1929	0-2	.000	
Wheaton (Central)	1	1966	1966	0-1	.000	
Wilmette (Loyola)	1	1976AA	1976AA	1-1	.500	
Winnebago	1	1976A	1976A	0-1	.000	
Winnetka (New Trier East)	8	1913	1973AA	8-8	.500	2
Witt	2	1928	1929	2-2	.500	
Wood River	3	1939	1943	5-3	.625	1
Woodstock	1	1937	1937	1-1	.500	
Zeigler	3	1936	1939	1-3	.250	

ALL-TIME STATE TOURNAMENT DATA

Undefeated teams which have won state championship: (8) — Rockford (22-0), 1911; Taylorville (45), 1944; Mt. Vernon (33), 1950; LaGrange (29), 1953; Chicago (Marshall) (30), 1958; Collinsville (32), 1961; LaGrange (Lyons) (31), 1970; Dolton (Thornridge) (33), 1972AA.

Undefeated teams which were beaten in championship games: (7) — 1914, Freeport, 42-19 by Hillsboro; 1922, Atwood, 24-16 by Centralia; 1934, Harvey (Thornton) 39-27 by Quincy (Sr.); 1936, Danville, 26-22 by Decatur; 1942, Paris, 35-33 by Centralia; 1954, Chicago (DuSable), 76-70 by Mt. Vernon; 1957, Collinsville, 45-42 by Herrin.

Four-time winners of state titles: (2) — Mt. Vernon, 1920-49-50-54; Decatur, 1931-36-45-62.

Three-time winners of state titles: (4) — Rockford, 1911-19-39; Centralia, 1918-22-42; Freeport, 1915-26-51; Springfield, 1917-35-59.

Two-time winners of state titles: (13) — Bloomington, 1910-16; Elgin, 1924-25; Cicero (Morton), 1932-41; Paris, 1943-47; Rockford (West), 1955-56; Chicago (Marshall), 1958-60; Collinsville, 1961-65; Harvey (Thornton), 1933-66; Pekin, 1964-67; LaGrange (Lyons), 1953-70; Dolton (Thornridge), 1971-72AA; Lawrenceville, 1972A-74A; Maywood (Proviso East), 1969-74AA.

Hebron in 1952 was the only district team ever to win the state title since smaller schools were placed in districts in 1938. Braidwood was runnerup to Dundee in 1938, and Cobden was runnerup to Pekin in 1964. (Districts were eliminated in 1972).

Team Records

Most state final tournaments in which team has played: (24) — *Galesburg,* 1912-13-14-18-20-21-31-35-37-38-45-46-47-55-56-57-59-60-63-64-66-68-69-76AA. (23) — *Decatur (Stephen Decatur),* 1912-15-17-20-21-31-36-37-38-42-43-45-46-49-51-55-60-62-63-64-65-66-67; (23) *Champaign (Central),* 1918-19-20-21-25-27-29-34-35-38-39-40-43-44-45-46-47-48-49-52-57-67-69.

Most consecutive tournaments in which team has played: (7) — Champaign, 1943-44-45-46-47-48-49.

Most consecutive times played in state final game: (3) Harvey (Thornton), 1933-34-35; Champaign, 1945-46-47.

SINGLE GAME SCORING,
>> Two Teams — 203, Quincy 107, Aurora (East) 96
Semifinals, 1972 (Class AA).
>> Winning Team — 107, Quincy 107, Aurora
(East) 96 Semifinals, 1972
(Class AA).
>> Losing Team — 96, Aurora (East) 96, Quincy 107
Semifinals, 1972 (Class AA).
>> Margin — 51 Hinsdale 60, Riverside 9, 1908.
Highest total points scored in state tournament, 4 games - 346
(93-83-96-74) Aurora (East) 1972.

Individual Records

SCORING, All Games — 157 (27-37-48-45) Jay Shidler, Law-
renceville, 1976.
>> One Game — 49 (17 FG, 15 FT) Jerry Kuemmerle,
Danville (Schlarman) vs. Rock
Falls, 1958.
>> Championship Game — 37 (14-18 FG, 9-10 FT)
Boyd Batts, Dolton (Thornridge) vs.
Quincy, 1972 (Class AA).

FIELD GOALS, One Game — 19, (31 att.) Dave Robisch,
Springfield vs. Quincy, first round, 1967.
19, (25 att.) Brent Browning, Ridgway vs.
Petersburg (Porta) Quarterfinals, 1973 (Class A).
Championship Game — 16, (28 att.) Max
Hooper, Mt. Vernon vs. Danville, 1950; 16,
(20 att.) Fred Miller, Pekin vs. Carbondale, 1967.

FREE THROWS, One Game — 22, (23 att.) Jim Lazenby,
Pinckneyville vs. Alton, 1955.
>> Championship Game — 13, (attempts unlist-
ed) Torry Foy, Freeport vs. Springfield,
1915.
>> Most Consecutive, One Game — 18 (total for
game, 18 of 21) Terry Bethel, Collinsville vs.
Charleston, 1957.

REBOUNDS, All Games — 77 (20-16-18-23), Dave Robisch,
Springfield, 1967.
>> One Game — 27, Kevin Washington, Petersburg
(Porta) vs. Ridgway, Quarter-
finals, 1973 (Class A).
>> Championship Game — 24, Owen Brown,
LaGrange (Lyons) vs.
East Moline, 1970.

Coaching Records

Three State Champions — Arthur L. Trout, Centralia, 1918-22-42; Gay Kintner, Decatur, 1931-36-45.

Two State Champions — Mark Peterman, Canton, 1928, Springfield, 1935; Norman A. Ziebell, Cicero (Morton), 1932-41; Ernest Eveland, Paris, 1943-47; Stanley Changnon, Mt. Vernon, 1949-50; Alex Saudargas, Rockford (West), 1955-56; Isadore Salario, Chicago (Marshall), 1958-60; Vergil Fletcher, Collinsville, 1961-65; Dawson Hawkins, Pekin, 1964-67; Ron Ferguson, Dolton (Thornridge), 1971-72AA; Ron Felling, Lawrenceville, 1972A-74A.

Most Years in State Tournament — 12, Vergil Fletcher, Collinsville, 1947-48-50-57-61-63-64-65-67-70-72-73AA; 11, Mark Peterman, Canton, 1923-24-25-26-28 and Springfield, 1932-33-34-35-45-47; Gay Kintner, Decatur, 1931-36-37-38-42-43-45-46-49-51-55.

Five Different Teams in State Tournament — Dolph Stanley, Equality, 1934; Mt. Pulaski,1936; Taylorville, 1940-44; Rockford (Auburn), 1962-63-64-68; Rockford (Boylan) 1971.

Most Times Coached Team in State Final Game — 4, Ernest Eveland, Paris, 1939-42-43-47; Mark Peterman, Canton, 1926-28 and Springfield, 1933-35; Gay Kintner, Decatur, 1931-36-37-45; Arthur L. Trout, Centralia, 1918-22-42-46.

All Time State Tournament Data

Most Consecutive Times Coached Team in State Final Game — 3, Jack Lipe, Harvey (Thornton), 1933-34-35; Harry Combes, Champaign (H.S.), 1945-46-47.

ATTENDANCE

Session — 16,310, Saturday afternoon, 1963, Tournament — 123,136 (16 games, eight at eight first-round centers and eight at Assembly Hall), 1967.

All-time Boys Basketball State
Tournament Appearances

Abingdon (2) — 1913 -1930
Aledo (1) — 1963
Alton (2) — 1919 -1955
Anna-Jonesboro (2) — 1943 -1944
Arcola (2) — 1958 -1964
Arlington Heights (Hersey) (1) — 1974AA
Athens (4) — 1924 (2nd) -1926 (4th) -1927 -1937
Atwood (3) — 1919 -1922 (2nd) -1930
Aurora (East) (6) — 1916 -1917 -1947 -1969 (4th) -1970 -
    1972AA (3rd)
Aurora (Marmion) (1) — 1976A
Aurora (West) (8) — 1928 (2nd) -1936 -1949 (3rd) -1958 (4th) -
    1959 (2nd) -1973AA (3rd) -1975AA -1976AA (2nd)
Barrington (1) — 1954
Barry (1) — 1919
Batavia (2) — 1912 (1st) -1921 (4th)
Beardstown (3) — 1930 (4th) -1940 -1947
Belleville (3) — 1961 -1962 -1966 (3rd)
Belleville (East) (1) — 1969
Belleville (West) (2) — 1968 -1974AA
Belvidere (1) — 1917 (2nd)
Benton (8) — 1928 -1932 -1933 (3rd) -1959 -1961 -1966 -1967 -
    1971
Bloomington (7) — 1909 -1910 (1st) -1916 (1st) -1917 (3rd) -
    1920 -1930 (2nd) -1975AA
Bloomington (Central Catholic) (2) — 1973A -1976A
Bowen (1) — 1954
Bradley-Bourbonnais (5) — 1939 -1950 -1958 -1964 -1973AA
Braidwood (2) — 1938 (2nd) -1963
Breese (Mater Dei) (1) — 1974AA (4th)
Bridgeport (1) — 1960 (2nd)
Brooklyn (Lovejoy) (1) — 1972A
Buda-Sheffield (Western) (2) — 1975A -1976A (4th)
Bushnell-Prairie City (2) — 1973A, 1975A
Calumet City (Thornton Fractional) (1) — 1946
Cairo (2) — 1975A -1976A
Canton (17) — 1912 -1916 -1918 (3rd) -1920 (2nd) -1923 (3rd) -
    1924 (3rd) -1925 (3rd) -1926 (2nd) -1928 (1st) -1932 (2nd) -
    1933 -1939 -1941 (4th) -1943 -1944 -1948 -1953

Carbondale (8) — 1915 (4th) -1930 -1937 -1938 -1945 -1967 (2nd) -1968 -1969

Carmi (1) — 1975A

Casey (1) — 1940

Centralia (18) — 1909 -1914 -1917 -1918 (1st) -1920 -1922 (1st) -1934 -1936 -1939 (4th) -1941 (3rd) -1942 (1st) -1946 (2nd) -1959 -1961 -1962 -1963 (2nd) -1964 -1966

Cerro Gordo (2) — 1973A -1974A

Champaign (Central) (23) — 1918 -1919 -1920 -1921 -1925 (2nd) -1927 (4th) -1929 (2nd) -1934 -1935 -1938 -1939 - 1940 (4th) -1943 -1944 (4th) -1945 (2nd) -1946 (1st) -1947 (2nd) -1948 -1949 -1952 -1957 -1967 -1969 (3rd)

Charleston (3) — 1921 -1934 -1957

Chatham (Glenwood) (1) — 1975A

Chicago (Carver) (2) — 1962 (2nd) -1963 (1st)

Chicago (Crane) (5) — 1940 -1957 -1964 -1968 (3rd) -1972AA

Chicago (Deerfield-Shields) (1) — 1935

Chicago (Dunbar) (1) — 1956 (3rd)

Chicago (DuSable) (2) — 1953 -1954 (2nd)

Chicago (Harlan) (3) — 1967 -1970 -1971

Chicago (Harrison) (1) — 1931 (3rd)

Chicago (Hirsch) (2) — 1969 -1973AA (1st)

Chicago (Kelvyn Park) (1) — 1943

Chicago (Lake View) (1) — 1933

Chicago (Lane Tech) (2) — 1934 -1939

Chicago (Lindbloom) (1) — 1942

Chicago (Marshall) (10) — 1934 -1948 -1955 -1958 (1st) -1959 - 1960 (1st) -1961 (3rd) -1965 (3rd) -1966 -1972AA

Chicago (Morgan Park) (3) — 1974AA -1975AA -1976AA (1st)

Chicago (New Phillips) (1) — 1936

Chicago (Parker) (2) — 1951 -1973AA

Chicago (Roosevelt) (1) — 1952

Chicago (Senn) (1) — 1945

Chicago (South Shore) (2) — 1944 (3rd) -1947

Chicago (St. Patrick) (1) — 1962

Chicago (Tilden) (3) — 1946 -1949 -1950

Chicago (Vocational) (1) — 1976AA

Chicago (Von Steuben) (1) — 1938 (4th)

Chicago (Wells) (1) — 1937

Chicago (Wendell Phillips) (2) — 1974AA -1975AA (1st)

Chicago Heights (Bloom) (7) — 1940 -1956 -1957 -1963 - 1973AA -1974AA (2nd) -1975AA (2nd)

Chrisman (1) — 1972A

Cicero (Morton) (6) — 1932 (1st) -1939 -1941 (1st) -1942 (4th) - 1945 -1961

Clinton (2) — 1918 -1961

Cobden (1) — 1964 (2nd)

Crystal Lake (1) — 1974AA

Collinsville (17) — 1921 -1931 -1937 (3rd) -1945 -1946 -1947 - 1948 -1950 (4th) -1957 (2nd) -1961 (1st) -1963 -1964 -1965 (1st) -1967 -1970 -1972AA -1973AA

Cumberland (1) — 1954

Danville (H.S.) (9) — 1935 -1936 (2nd) -1950 (2nd) -1951 -1954 - 1965 -1970 -1971 (3rd) -1974AA

Danville (Schlarman) (6) — 1953 (4th) -1958 -1960 -1961 -1968 - 1973A

Decatur (Stephen Decatur) (23) — 1912 (4th) -1915 -1917 - 1920 -1921 -1931 (1st) -1936 (1st) -1937 (2nd) -1938 -1942 -1943 -1945 (1st) -1946 -1949 -1951 (4th) -1955 -1960 (4th) -1962 (1st) -1963 -1964 (3rd) -1965 -1966 (4th) -1967

Decatur (Eisenhower) (2) — 1975AA -1976AA (3rd)

Decatur (St. Teresa) (1) — 1953

DeKalb (3) — 1953 -1960 -1968 (4th)

Dixon (2) — 1942 -1969

Dolton (Thornridge) (3) — 1971 (1st) -1972AA (1st) -1976AA

Dundee (6) — 1919 -1937 -1938 (1st) -1940 -1946 (3rd) -1947

DuQuoin (4) — 1916 (3rd) -1917 -1918 -1972A

Dwight (1) — 1939

East Moline (United) (1) — 1970 (2nd)

East St. Louis (Sr.) (3) — 1927 (3rd) -1944 -1975AA (3rd)

Edwardsville (4) — 1951 -1954 (4th) -1956 (2nd) -1976AA

Effingham (2) — 1967 -1968

Effingham (St. Anthony) (2) — 1956 -1970

Eldorado (2) — 1975A (4th) -1976A

Elgin (H.S.) (18) — 1918 -1920 -1921 -1924 (1st) -1925 (1st) - 1943 (4th) -1944 (2nd) -1945 -1949 -1950 (3rd) -1953 -1955 (2nd) -1957 -1958 -1960 -1973AA -1974AA -1976AA

Elgin (Larkin) (1) — 1971

Elgin (St. Edward) (1) — 1972A

Elmhurst (Timothy Christian) (1) — 1975A (2nd)

Elmhurst (York) (2) — 1962 -1967

Equality (1) — 1934 (3rd)

Evanston (5) — 1908 -1957 -1964 -1968 (1st) -1972AA

Evanston (Academy) (1) — 1914 (4th)

Fairbury (1) — 1921

Farmington (1) — 1972A

Flora (6) — 1919 -1921 -1926 (3rd) -1939 -1945 -1947

Franklin (1) — 1974A

Franklin Park (East Leyden) (2) — 1965 -1975AA

Freeport (12) — 1914 (2nd) -1915 (1st) -1926 (1st) -1929 (3rd) -
    1934 -1942 (3rd) -1950 -1951 (1st) -1952 -1957 -1965 -
    1974AA

Fulton (3) — 1936 -1958 -1973A

Galesburg (24) — 1921 (2nd) -1913 (1st) -1914 -1918 -1920 -
    1921 -1931 (2nd) -1935 -1937 -1938 -1945 -1946 -1947 -
    1955 -1956 -1957 -1959 (3rd) -1960 -1963 -1964 -1966
    (2nd) -1968 (2nd) -1969 -1976AA

Geneva (2) — 1908 -1963

Georgetown (1) — 1955

Gibson City (1) — 1972A

Gillespie (2) — 1933 (4th) -1939

Glen Ellyn (Glenbard) (1) — 1938

Granite City (9) — 1911 (3rd) -1912 (3rd) -1914 -1915 -1916 -
    1938 -1940 (1st) -1960 -1971

Greenville (2) — 1923 (4th) -1960

Griggsville (1) — 1928 (4th)

Harrisburg (1) — 1938

Harvey (Thornton) (13) — 1917 -1933 (1st) -1934 (2nd) -1935
    (2nd) -1948 -1952 -1954 -1959 -1961 (2nd) -1962 -1965
    (4th) -1966 (1st) -1969

Havana (1) — 1976A

Hebron (2) — 1940 -1952 (1st)

Herrin (6) — 1919 (4th) -1940 (2nd) -1957 (1st) -1958 -1959 -
    1963

Highland (2) — 1953 -1958

Hillsboro (8) — 1912 -1913 -1914 (1st) -1932 -1935 -1948 -1949
    (2nd) -1953

Hinsdale (Central) (5) — 1908 (4th) -1909 (1st) -1910 (3rd) -
    1951 -1972AA

Hoffman Estates (Conant) (1) — 1972AA

Homewood-Flossmoor (2) — 1967 -1976AA

Hull (1) — 1936

Hume (Shiloh) (1) — 1975A

Hutsonville (2) — 1928 -1933
Jacksonville (H.S.) (4) — 1911 -1952 -1953 -1965
Jerseyville (3) — 1918 -1920 -1958
Johnston City (6) — 1929 (1st) -1931 (4th) -1936 (3rd) -1938 -
   1949 -1950
Joliet (7) — 1909 -1916 -1920 -1935 -1936 -1937 (1st) -1943
Joliet (Central) (2) — 1966 -1970 (3rd)
Kankakee (3) — 1944 -1952 -1960
Kankakee (Eastridge) (1) — 1972AA
Kewanee (7) — 1932 (4th) -1943 -1944 -1946 -1947 -1950 -1971
LaGrange (Lyons) (5) — 1948 (4th) -1953 (1st) -1968 -1970 (1st)
   -1972AA
LaSalle (1) — 1908
LaSalle-Peru (5) — 1937 -1948 -1956 -1968 -1970
Lawrenceville (12) — 1917 -1918 -1932 (3rd) -1934 -1950 -1952
   -1953 -1965 -1966 -1972A -1974A (1st) -1976A (3rd)
Lebanon (1) — 1976A
Lemont (Twp.) (1) — 1975A
Lewistown (1) — 1940
Lexington (1) — 1974A
Lincoln (6) — 1929 -1951 -1955 -1969 -1970 -1973AA
Litchfield (1) — 1954
Lockport (Central) (4) — 1965 -1968 -1972AA -1973AA (4th)
Lombard (Glenbard East) (1) — 1964
Macomb (2) — 1921 -1959
Macomb (Western) (1) — 1951
Madison (2) — 1952 -1959
Mahomet (1) — 1933
Marion (11) — 1920 (3rd) -1921 (1st) -1925 (4th) -1934 -1935 -
   1946 -1948 -1951 -1962 -1965 -1976AA
Maroa (1) — 1957
Marseilles (2) — 1944 -1947
Marshall (1) — 1973A
Mascoutah (1) — 1972AA
Mattoon (1) — 1969
Maple Park (Kaneland) (1) — 1973A (2nd)
Maywood (Proviso) (1) — 1936
Maywood (Proviso East) (5) — 1960 -1969 (1st) -1973AA -
   1974AA (1st) -1975AA
McHenry (1) — 1976AA

McLeansboro (1) — 1962 (4th)
Mendon (Unity) (1) — 1973A
Metropolis (1) — 1963
Milton (1) — 1938
Moline (21) — 1916 -1921 -1934 (4th) -1935 (4th) -1936 -1937 -
    1939 -1940 (3rd) -1942 -1943 (2nd) -1945 (4th) -1948 -1949
    -1951 (2nd) -1954 -1955 -1961 -1965 -1967 -1973AA -
    1976AA
Monmouth (H.S.) (4) — 1950 -1960 -1961 -1974A
Morris (1) — 1919
Morrisonville (2) — 1973A -1975A
Mounds (Meridian) (1) — 1972A (2nd)
Mt. Carmel (5) — 1921 -1927 (1st) -1929 -1935 -1944
Mt. Carroll (3) — 1908 -1909 (3rd) -1911 (2nd)
Mt. Olive (1) — 1927
Mt. Pulaski (2) — 1936 (4th), 1976A (1st)
Mt. Sterling (1) — 1910
Mt. Vernon (15) — 1909 -1910 (4th) -1913 -1920 (1st) -1921 -
    1931 -1949 (1st) -1950 (1st) -1952 (3rd) -1954 (1st) -1957 -
    1965 -1968 -1969 -1970
Murphysboro (2) — 1947 -1973AA
Naperville (1) — 1915
Nashville (2) — 1949 (4th) -1971
New Lenox (Lincoln-Way) (1) — 1975AA
Nokomis (1) — 1910
Normal (Community) (3) — 1942 -1969 -1976AA
Normal (University) (5) — 1914 (3rd) -1918 (2nd) -1971 -1972A -
    1975A
North Chicago (2) — 1967 -1972AA
Oak Lawn (Community) (1) — 1971 (2nd)
Oak Park-River Forest (4) — 1908 (3rd) -1951 -1956 (4th) -
    1976AA (3rd)
Okawville (1) — 1970
Oblong (1) — 1937
Odell (St. Paul) (1) — 1951
Olney (East Richland) (4) — 1924 (4th) -1930 (3rd) -1942 -
    1975AA
Olympia Fields (Rich Central) (1) — 1974AA
Oneida (ROVA) (2) — 1949 -1976A (2nd)
Oswego (1) — 1974AA

Ottawa (8) — 1949 -1952 -1953 -1957 (3rd) -1958 -1959 -1960 - 1961

Ottawa (Marquette) (1) — 1974A (2nd)

Palos Heights (Chicago Christian) (3) — 1972A -1974A (3rd) - 1976A

Pana (1) — 1946

Park Forest (Rich Twp.) (1) — 1955

Paris (12) — 1911 -1936 -1938 (3rd) -1939 (2nd) -1940 -1942 (2nd) -1943 (1st) -1944 -1947 (1st) -1950 -1955 -1971

Park Ridge (Maine South) (2) — 1970 -1975AA

Piasa (Southwestern) (1) — 1972A

Pekin (15) — 1935 (3rd) -1937 (4th) -1938 -1943 -1944 -1947 (4th) -1948 (3rd) -1949 -1957 -1960 -1964 (1st) -1965 -1966 -1967 (1st) -1973AA

Peoria (Central) (16) — 1908 (1st) -1919 (3rd) -1921 -1922 (4th) -1927 (2nd) -1929 (4th) -1934 -1935 -1945 -1953 (2nd) - 1954 -1956 -1959 -1963 (4th) -1968 -1974AA (3rd)

Peoria (Manual) (10) — 1913 (2nd) -1914 -1917 (4th) -1920 - 1930 (1st) -1931 -1936 -1952 -1961 (4th) -1972AA (4th)

Peoria (Richwoods) (1) — 1975AA (4th)

Peoria (Spalding) (5) — 1950 -1955 -1958 (3rd) -1969 (2nd) - 1970 (4th)

Peoria (Woodruff) (2) — 1939 -1951

Petersburg (Porta) (1) — 1973A

Pinckneyville (11) — 1935 -1947 (3rd) -1938 (1st) -1951 -1952 - 1953 (3rd) -1954 (3rd) -1955 (3rd) -1956 -1964 -1973A

Pittsfield (3) — 1921 -1949 -1970

Pleasant Plains (1) — 1976A

Pontiac (2) — 1946 -1962

Port Byron (Riverdale) (2) — 1975A -1976A

Princeton (2) — 1954 -1955 (4th)

Quincy (H.S.) (22) — 1934 (1st) -1935 -1942 -1943 -1944 -1945 (3rd) -1946 -1948 -1950 -1951 (3rd) -1952 (2nd) -1954 - 1955 -1956 -1958 -1962 (3rd) -1965 (2nd) -1967 -1968 - 1969 -1972AA (2nd) -1974AA

Quincy (Catholic Boys) (n.e. Notre Dame) (5) — 1957 (4th) -1971 -1972A -1974A (4th) -1975A

Rantoul (4) — 1931 -1932 -1956 -1959

Raymond (Lincolnwood) (1) — 1972A (3rd)

Ridgway (2) — 1973A (1st) -1974A

Riverside (1) — 1908
Robinson (5) — 1916 (2nd) -1946 -1948 -1949 -1951
Rochelle (1) — 1928
Rock Falls (1) — 1958 (2nd)
Rockford (12) — 1911 (1st) -1916 -1918 -1919 (1st) -1920 -1921
    (2nd) -1922 (3rd) -1923 (2nd) -1927 -1935 -1938 -1939 (1st)
Rockford (Auburn) (5) — 1962 -1963 -1964 -1968 -1975AA
Rockford (Boylan) (1) — 1971
Rockford (West) (9) — 1943 -1944 -1949 -1955 (1st) -1956 (1st)
    -1959 -1966 -1967 (4th) -1973AA
Rock Island (11) — 1908 (2nd) -1909 (4th) -1910 (2nd) -1915 -
    1917 -1919 -1938 -1952 (4th) -1953 -1962 -1966
Rock Island (Alleman) (2) — 1964 (4th) -1972AA
Roodhouse (1) — 1939
Rushville (2) — 1937 -1940
St. Anne (1) — 1973 (4th)
St. Charles (2) — 1908 -1927
Salem (2) — 1940 -1943 (3rd)
Shabbona (1) — 1972A
Shawneetown (1) — 1955
Shelbyville (5) — 1915 (3rd) -1916 -1918 (4th) -1919 -1920
Skokie (Niles West) (2) — 1973AA -1976AA
Somonouk (1) — 1945
South Beloit (2) — 1974A -1975A
Springfield (H.S.) (20) — 1915 (2nd) -1916 (4th) -1917 (1st) -
    1919 (2nd) -1921 -1932 -1933 (2nd) -1934 -1935 (1st) -1945
    -1947 -1954 -1957 -1958 -1959 (1st) -1960 -1961 -1962 -
    1966 -1967 (3rd)
Springfield (Cathedral) (3) — 1942 -1946 -1948
Springfield (Lanphier) (5) — 1956 -1963 (3rd) -1964 -1968 -
    1971 (4th)
Spring Valley (Hall) (1) — 1974A
Sterling (3) — 1950 -1970 -1975AA
Stewardson-Strasburg (1) — 1974A
Streator (Twp.) (7) — 1920 -1921 -1928 -1934 -1940 -1942 -
    1964
Streator (Woodland) (1) — 1972A
Sullivan (1) — 1917
Taylorville (6) — 1940 -1944 (1st) -1950 -1952 -1956 -1959
Thomson (1) — 1972A (4th)

Toluca (2) — 1967 -1973A
Trenton (1) — 1921
Ullin (Century) (1) — 1974A
Urbana (5) — 1934 -1941 (2nd) -1942 -1962 -1966
Vandalia (2) — 1936 -1937
Venice (3) — 1973A (3rd) -1974A -1975A (1st)
Villa Grove (1) — 1923 (1st)
Washington (3) — 1909 (2nd) -1911 -1962
Waterman (1) — 1930
Watseka (4) — 1963 -1974A -1975A (3rd) -1976A
Waukegan (6) — 1959 (4th) -1961 -1963 -1969 -1974AA -
    1975AA
West Frankfort (9) — 1924 (4th) -1942 -1943 -1944 -1945 -
    1953 -1956 -1958 -1960 (3rd)
Westville (1) — 1976A
Wheaton (2) — 1908 -1929
Wheaton (Central) (1) — 1966
Wilmette (Loyola) (1) — 1976AA
Winnebago (1) — 1976A
Winnetka (New Trier East) (8) — 1913 -1918 -1921 (3rd) -1956 -
    1965 -1966 -1971 -1973AA (2nd)
Witt (2) -1928 (3rd) -1929
Wood River (3) — 1939 (3rd) -1942 -1943
Woodstock (1) — 1937
Zeigler (3) — 1936 -1937 -1939

All-time State Tournament Leaders

Appearances

1. Galesburg............24
2. Champaign
   (Central) 23
3. Decatur (H.S.).....23
4. Moline.................21
5. Quincy (Sr.).........21
6. Springfield
   (H.S.)..................20
7. Centralia............ 18
8. Canton................ 17
9. Elgin....................17
10. Peoria (Central).. 16
11. Mt. Vernon.........15
12. Pekin..................15
13. Harvey
    (Thornton) 13
14. Freeport.............12
15. Lawrenceville......12
16. Paris...................12
17. Rockford (H.S.)...12
18. Marion................ 11
19. Pinckneyville.......11
20. Rock Island
    (H. S.) 11
21. Chicago
    (Marshall) 10
22. Peoria
    (Manual) 10

Games Won

1. Decatur (H.S.).....33
2. Champaign
   (Central) 28
3. Quincy (Sr.).........27
4. Galesburg...........26
5. Springfield
   (H.S.) 24
6. Collinsville..........23
7. Moline.................22
8. Centralia............21
9. Peoria (Central).. 21
10. Mt. Vernon.........20
11. Paris................... 20
12. Elgin (H.S.)..........19
13. Harvey
    (Thornton) 19
14. Pekin..................19
15. Freeport.............17
16. Pinckneyville.......17
17. Rockford (H.S.)...17
18. Aurora (West)..... 16
19. Lawrenceville......16
20. Canton................16
21. Chicago
    (Marshall) 16

Times Placed Top 4

1. Decatur (H.S.).....10
2. Canton.................9
3. Champaign
   (Central) 9
4. Peoria (Central).... 8
5. Springfield
   (H.S.) 8
6. Centralia...............7
7. Quincy (Sr.)...........7
8. Aurora (West)....... 6
9. Elgin (H.S.)............6
10. Freeport...............6
11. Galesburg.............6
12. Harvey
    (Thornton) 6
13. Moline...................6
14. Mt. Vernon........... 6
15. Paris...................... 6
16. Pekin.....................6
17. Rockford (H.S.).....6
18. Collinsville............ 5
19. Peoria (Manual).... 5
20. Pinckneyville.........5
21. Bloomington
    (H.S.) 4
22. Chicago
    (Marshall) 4
23. Lawrenceville........4
24. Rock Island
    (H.S.) 4

Thornridge High School's
Illinois State High School Record
Winning Streak
(58 Straight)

No.	Date	Site	Opponent	Score	Margin
			1970-71 REGULAR SEASON		
1	1/8/71	A	Chicago Heights (Bloom)	80-69	11
2	1/9/71	H	Racine (Wis.) (Washington Park)	73-61	12
3	1/15/71	H	Arlington Heights (St. Viator)	97-63	34
4	1/22/71	H	Oak Lawn (Richards)	71-44	27
5	1/23/71	A	Olympia Fields (Rich Central)	61-35	26
6	1/29/71	H	Blue Island (Eisenhower)	55-44	11
7	1/30/71	A	Chicago (St. Patrick)	77-67	10
8	2/5/71	A	Harvey (Thornton)	69-51	18
9	2/6/71	A	Flossmoor (Homewood-F.)	73-56	17
10	2/13/71	A	Chicago Heights (Bloom)	84-63	21
11	2/20/71	H	Chicago (St. Ignatius)	80-61	19
12	2/26/71	A	Oak Lawn (Richards)	65-48	17
			1971 Dolton (Thornridge) Regional		
13	3/1/71	H	Chicago (St. Francis de Sales)	86-44	42
14	3/3/71	H	Chicago (Quigley South)	102-41	61
15	3/5/71	H	Harvey (Thornton)	66-58	8
			1971 Joliet (Central) Sectional		
16	3/10/71	N	Chicago (Marist)	66-55	11
17	3/12/71	A	Joliet (Central)	66-63	3
			1971 Crete-Monee Supersectional		
18	3/16/71	N	Chicago (Harlan)	73-63	10
			1971 State Finals in Assembly Hall		
19	3/19/71	N	Kewanee	63-58	5
20	3/20/71	N	Danville	57-47	10
21	3/20/71	N	Oak Lawn (Title Game)	52-50	2
			1971-72 REGULAR SEASON		
22	11/19/71	H	Park Forest (Rich East)	70-52	18
			Rockford Thanksgiving Tournament		
23	11/26/71	N	Batavia	97-71	26
24	11/27/71	N	Peoria (Manual)	107-60	47
25	11/27/71	A	Rockford (Guilford) (Title)	88-57	31
26	12/4/71	H	Waukegan	75-50	25
27	12/10/71	H	Blue Island (Eisenhower)	75-52	23
28	12/17/71	A	Harvey (Thornton)	71-54	17
29	12/18/71	A	Maywood (Proviso East)	89-59	30

No.	Date	Site	Opponent	Score	Margin
			Carbondale Holiday Tourney		
30	12/27/71	N	Chicago Hts. (Marian Catholic)	86-52	34
31	12/28/71	N	Decatur (Eisenhower)	89-63	26
32	12/29/71	N	Peoria (Manual)	92-65	27
33	12/29/71	N	Carbondale	85-47	38
34	1/7/72	H	Chicago Hts. (Bloom)	99-65	34
35	1/8/72	A	Racine (Wis.) (Washington Park)	83-39	44
36	1/14/72	A	Arlington Hts. (St. Viator)	102-64	38
37	1/21/72	A	Oak Lawn (Richards)	95-42	53
38	1/22/72	H	Olympia Fields (Rich Central)	106-68	38
39	1/28/72	A	Blue Island (Eisenhower)	72-42	30
40	1/29/72	A	Chicago (St. Patrick)	70-56	14
41	2/4/72	H	Harvey (Thornton)	73-52	21
42	2/5/72	H	Flossmoor (Homewood-F.)	89-53	36
43	2/17/72	A	Chicago Hts. (Bloom)	90-62	28
44	2/18/72	H	South Holland (Thornwood)	103-57	46
45	2/19/72	A	Chicago (St. Ignatius)	90-52	38
46	2/25/72	H	Oak Lawn (Richards)	90-53	37
			1972 Dolton (Thornridge) Regional		
47	2/29/72	H	Chicago (St. Francis de Sales)	113-59	54
48	3/3/72	H	Calumet City (Thornton Fractional North)	101-68	33
			1972 Chicago Heights (Bloom) Sectional		
49	3/7/72	A	Chicago Hts. (Bloom)	65-42	23
50	3/10/72	N	Harvey (Thornton)	71-43	28
			1972 Crete-Monee Supersectional		
51	3/14/72	N	Lockport (Central)	74-46	28
			1972 Class AA State Finals in Assembly Hall		
52	3/17/72	N	Collinsville	95-66	29
53	3/18/72	N	Peoria (Manual)	71-52	19
54	3/18/72	N	Quincy (H.S.) (Title)	104-69	25
			1972-73 REGULAR SEASON		
			Rockford Turkey Classic		
55	11/24/72	N	Peoria (Manual)	81-59	22
56	11/25/72	N	Batavia	79-33	46
57	11/25/72	N	Rockford (Guilford) (Title)	79-59	20
58	12/1/72	H	Danville (H.S.)	92-44	48
59	12/2/72	A	Waukegan	49-58	9

HUFF GYM—From 1926 until 1962, Huff Gym— the hardwood house named after former Univ. of Illinois coach and athletic director George Huff—was the site of the annual State Basketball Tournament. Legends of what went on in Huff Gym during those 38 years are part of the history of the Golden Era in the tournament series. Huff Gym seated 6,925 for the State Tournament.

HOME OF THE STATE TOURNAMENT—The beautiful Assembly Hall on the campus of the University of Illinois throbs with pressure of "March Madness". Seating capacity for the State Tournament is 15,877. In addition, the television and news media provide the greatest coverage of a high school athletic event in America. As many as 50 radio stations broadcast the games. Fans are seated in theatre-type, padded seats. (Photo By Jim Reiter, Univ. of Illinois)

CLASS AA TEAM DATA
(State Final Tournament Only)
APPEARANCES

School	Year/Place	Won/Loss	Pct.	Times Placed in Top Four
Arlington Heights (Hersey)	1974	0-1	.000	
Aurora (East)	1972 (3rd)	2-1	.667	1
Aurora (West)	1973 (3rd) 1976 (2nd)	4-2	.667	2
Bloomington (H.S.)	1975	0-1	.000	
Breese (Mater Dei)	1974 (4th)	1-2	.333	1
Chicago (Crane)	1972	0-1	.000	
Chicago (Hirsch)	1973 (1st)	3-0	1.000	1
Chicago (Morgan Park)	1974, 1976 (1st)	3-1	.750	1
Chicago (Wendell Phillips)	1975 (1st)	3-0	1.000	1
Chicago Heights (Bloom)	1974 (2nd) 1975 (2nd)	4-2	.667	2
Collinsville	1972-1973	0-2	.000	
Danville (H.S.)	1974	0-1	.000	
Decatur (Eisenhower)	1976 (4th)	1-2	.333	1
Dolton (Thornridge)	1972 (1st), 1976	3-1	.750	1
East St. Louis (Sr.)	1975 (3rd)	2-1	.667	1
Elgin (H.S.)	1973	0-1	.000	
Evanston	1972	0-1	.000	
Galesburg	1976	0-1	.000	
Hinsdale (Central)	1972	0-1	.000	
Lincoln	1973	0-1	.000	
Lockport (Central)	1973 (4th)	1-2	.333	1
Marion	1976	0-1	.000	
Maywood (Proviso East)	1974 (1st), 1975	3-1	.750	1
Moline	1973	0-1	.000	
Oak Park (O.P.-River Forest)	1976 (3rd)	2-1	.667	1
Oswego	1974	0-1	.000	
Peoria (Central)	1974 (3rd)	2-1	.667	1
Peoria (Manual)	1972 (4th)	1-2	.333	1
Peoria (Richwoods)	1975 (4th)	1-2	.333	1
Quincy (Sr.)	1972 (2nd)	2-1	.667	1
Rockford (Auburn)	1975	0-1	.000	
Waukegan	1975	0-1	.000	
Wilmette (Loyola)	1976	0-1	.000	
Winnetka (New Trier East)	1973 (2nd)	2-1	.667	1

CLASS AA TOURNAMENT RECORDS
CHAMPIONSHIP GAME RECORDS

Team

MOST POINTS, 2 Teams — 173, Dolton (Thornridge) (104), Quincy (69), 1972.

        Winning Team — 104, Dolton (Thornridge) vs. Quincy (69), 1972.

        Losing Team — 69, Quincy vs. Dolton (Thornridge) (104), 1972.

POINT MARGIN — 35 Dolton (Thornridge) (104), Quincy (69), 1972.

FIELD GOALS, Number — 43 (of 69), Dolton (Thornridge) vs. Quincy, 1972.

        Percentage — .623 (43-69), Dolton (Thornridge) vs. Quincy, 1972.

FREE THROWS, Number — 23 (of 29), Quincy vs. Dolton (Thornridge), 1972.

        Percentage — .818 (9-11), Chicago (Hirsch) vs. Winnetka (New Trier East), 1973.

REBOUNDS — 52, Chicago (Wendell Phillips) vs. Chicago Hts. (Bloom), 1975.

Individual

POINTS — 37, Boyd Batts (14-18 FG and 9-10 FT), Dolton (Thornridge) vs. Quincy, 1972.

FIELD GOALS — 14 (of 18), Boyd Batts, Dolton (Thornridge) vs. Quincy, 1972.

FREE THROWS — 10 (of 10), Don Sorenson, Quincy vs. Dolton (Thornridge), 1972.

REBOUNDS — 15, Emir Hardy, Chicago Hts. (Bloom) vs. Maywood (Proviso East), 1974.

        15, Boyd Batts, Dolton (Thornridge) vs. Quincy, 1972.

        15, Robert McCoy, Chicago Hts. (Bloom) vs. Chicago (Wendell Phillips), 1975.

ALL-GAME RECORDS
Team

MOST POINTS, All Games — 346 (93-83-96-74), Aurora (East), 1972 (took third place).

2 Teams — 203 Quincy (107), Aurora (East) (96), 1972 Semifinals.

Winning Team — 107, Quincy vs. Aurora (East) (96), 1972 Semifinals.

Losing Team — 96, Aurora (East) vs. Quincy (107), 1972 Semifinals.

FEWEST POINTS, One Game — 30, New Lenox (Lincoln-Way) vs. Chicago Hts. (Bloom) (57),1975 Joliet (Central) Super-Sectional.

2 Teams — 70, Waukegan (31) vs. Arlington Hts. (Hersey) (39), 1974 Evanston Super-Sectional.

BIGGEST MARGIN — 40, Aurora (East) (93), Hoffman Estates (Conant) (53), 1972 DeKalb Super-Sectional.

REBOUNDS, All Games — 197 (45-49-56-47), Maywood (Proviso East), 1974.

One Game — 56, Maywood (Proviso East) vs. Breese (Mater Dei), 1974 Semifinals.

MOST REBOUNDS, 2 Teams — 102, Peoria (Central) (52) vs. Breese (Mater Dei) (50), 1974 (took third place). 102, Maywood (Proviso East) (56) vs. Breese (Mater Dei) (46), 1974, Semifinals.

FEWEST REBOUNDS, One Game — 18, Moline vs. Galesburg, 1976, Peoria Super-Sectional.

MOST FIELD GOALS, All Games — 146, (43-41-27-35), Dolton (Thornridge), 1972.

One Game — 43, Dolton (Thornridge) vs. Quincy, 1972 Championship Game (43 of 69).

2 Teams — 87, Quincy (Sr.) (37) vs. Aurora (East) (40), 1972 Semifinals.

Winning Team — 43, Dolton (Thornridge) vs. Quincy, 1972 Championship Game (43 of 69).

Losing Team — 40, Aurora (East) vs. Quincy, 1972 Semifinals (40 of 65).

FEWEST FIELD GOALS, One Game — 11, Aurora (West) vs. Winnetka (New Trier East), 1973 Semifinals (11 of 41). 11, New Lenox (Lincoln-Way) vs. Chicago Hts. (Bloom), 1975 Joliet (Central) Super-Sectional (11 of 48).

MOST FREE THROWS, All Games — 91, (23-33-13-22),
Quincy (Sr.), 1972.
One Game — 33, Quincy (Sr.) vs. Aurora
(East), 1972 Semifinals. (33 of 45).
2 Teams — 49, Quincy (33 of 45) vs. Aurora
(East) (16 of 27), 1972 Semifinals.
Winning Team — 33, Quincy (Sr.) vs. Aurora
(East), 1972 Semifinals (33 of 45).
Losing Team — 23, Quincy (Sr.) vs.
Dolton (Thornridge), 1972 Cham-
pionship Game (23 of 29). 23,
Decatur (Eisenhower) vs. Aurora
(West), 1976 Semifinals, (23 of 31).
FEWEST FREE THROWS, One Game — 0, Moline (0 for 3) vs.
Chicago (Hirsch), 1973 Quarter-
finals.

Individual

MOST POINTS, All Games —   103 (18-34-14-37), Boyd Batts,
Dolton (Thornridge), 1972.
One Game —   44, Greg Smith (18-25 FG and
8-11 FT), Aurora (East) vs.
Quincy, 1972 Semifinals.
FIELD GOALS, All Games —   47 (of 77), Greg Smith, Aurora
(East), 1972.
One Game —   18 (of 25), Greg Smith, Aurora
(East), 1972.
FREE THROWS, All Games —   23 (of 26), John Robinson,
Chicago (Hirsch), 1973.
One Game —   15 (of 17), Bob Bone, Collins-
ville vs. Winnetka (New Trier
East), 1972 Quarterfinals.
Consecutive — 12, Bob Bone, Collinsville,
1973.
One Game
Consecutive — 12 (15 of 17), Bob Bone,
Collinsville vs. Winnetka (New
Trier East), 1973 Quarterfinals.
REBOUNDS,   All Games —   55 (4 games), Boyd Batts,
Dolton (Thornridge), 1972.
—   55 (4 games), Larry Williams,
Chicago (Wendell Phillips),
1975.
One Game —   21, Norman Cook, Lincoln vs.
Bradley-Bourbonnais, 1973,
Normal Super-Sectional.

Class AA Scoring Leaders

Year	Player/School/Class	Game	FG-FGA	Pct.	FT-FTA	Pct.	TP	Average
1972	Boyd Batts (Sr.) Dolton (Thornridge)	4	41-61	.627	21-29	.755	113	28.1
1973	Mathew Hicks (Sr.) Aurora (West)	4	37-82	.451	13-18	.722	87	21.8
1974	Joe Ponsetto (Sr.) Maywood (Proviso East)	4	37-67	.552	14-19	.737	88	22.0
1975	Hubert Hoosman (Sr.) East St. Louis (Sr.)	4	37-66	.561	13-21	.619	87	21.8
1976	Levi Cobb (Sr.) Chicago (Morgan Park)	4	37-69	.536	10-13	.769	84	21.0

Top Ten Performances
Assembly Hall Only

Class AA - Single Game Points
Individual

1. 44 GREG SMITH, Aurora (East) vs. Quincy (Sr.), Semifinals, 1972.
2. 37 BOYD BATTS, Dolton (Thornridge) vs. Quincy (Sr.), Championship, 1972.
3. 36 LARRY MOORE, Quincy (Sr.) vs. Chicago (Crane), Quarterfinals, 1972.
4. 34 BOYD BATTS, Dolton (Thornridge) vs. Collinsville, Quarterfinals, 1972.
5. 32 LARRY MOORE, Quincy (Sr.) vs. Aurora (East), Semifinals, 1972.
6. 31 KELVIN SMALL, Chicago Heights (Bloom) vs. Maywood (Proviso East), Quarterfinals, 1975.
7. 30 JIM FLYNN, Hinsdale (Central) vs. Aurora (East), Quarterfinals, 1972.
8. 29 KELVIN SMALL, Chicago Heights (Bloom) vs. East St. Louis (Sr.), Semifinals, 1975.

     29   JOE PONSETTO, Maywood (Proviso East) vs.
           Breese (Mater Dei), Semifinals, 1974.

10.   28   MATT HICKS, Aurora (West) vs. Lockport (Central),
           Third Place, 1973.

     28   LARRY WILLIAMS, Chicago (Wendell Phillips) vs.
           Chicago Heights (Bloom), Championship, 1975.

     28   QUINN BUCKNER, Dolton (Thornridge) vs. Quincy
           (Sr.), Championship, 1972.

Team

1. 107   Quincy (Sr.) vs. Aurora (East), Semifinals, 1972.
2. 104   Dolton (Thornridge) vs. Quincy (Sr.), Championship, 1972.
3.   96   Aurora (East) vs. Quincy (Sr.), Semifinals, 1972.
4.   95   Dolton (Thornridge) vs. Collinsville, Quarterfinals, 1972.
5.   87   Quincy (Sr.) vs. Chicago (Crane), Quarterfinals, 1972.
6.   86   Chicago (Wendell Phillips) vs. Peoria (Richwoods), Semifinals, 1975.
7.   83   East St. Louis (Sr.) vs. Peoria (Richwoods), Third Place, 1975.
     83   Chicago (Hirsch) vs. Lockport (Central), Semifinals, 1973.
     83   Aurora (East) vs. Hinsdale (Central), Quarterfinals, 1972.
10. 82   Peoria (Manual) vs. Evanston, Quarterfinals, 1972.
     82   Aurora (West) vs. Dolton (Thornridge), Quarterfinals, 1976.

Tournament Points
Individual

1. 113   BOYD BATTS, Dolton (Thornridge), 1972.
2. 112   GREG SMITH, Aurora (East), 1972.
3. 110   LARRY MOORE, Quincy (Sr.), 1972.
4.   90   MIKE DAVIS, Peoria (Manual), 1972.
5.   88   JOE PONSETTO, Maywood (Proviso East), 1974.
6.   87   MATHEW HICKS, Aurora (West), 1973.
     87   HUBERT HOOSMAN, East St. Louis (Sr.), 1975.
8.   86   AUDIE MATTHEWS, Chicago Heights (Bloom), 1975.
9.   84   LEVI COBB, Chicago (Morgan Park), 1976.
10. 79   KELVIN SMALL, Chicago Heights (Bloom), 1975.
     79   JEFF ROTH, Decatur (Eisenhower), 1976.

Single Game Rebounds
Individual

1. 18 BOYD BATTS, Dolton (Thornridge) vs. Collinsville, Quarterfinals, 1972.
   18 JEFF ROTH, Decatur (Eisenhower) vs. Marion, Quarterfinals, 1976.
3. 16 MIKE DAVIS, Peoria (Manual) vs. Evanston, Quarterfinals, 1972.
   16 JEFF WILKINS, Elgin (H.S.) vs. Aurora (West), Quarterfinals, 1973.
   16 JOE PONSETTO, Maywood (Proviso East) vs. Breese (Mater Dei), Semifinals, 1974.
6. 15 BOYD BATTS, Dolton (Thornridge) vs. Quincy (Sr.), Championship, 1972.
   15 MIKE DAVIS, Peoria (Manual) vs. Dolton (Thornridge), Semifinals, 1972.
   15 JOHN BRYANT, Aurora (West) vs. Elgin (H.S.), Quarterfinals, 1973.
   15 CHRIS WALL, Winnetka (New Trier East) vs. Collinsville, Quarterfinals, 1973.
   15 EMIR HARDY, Chicago Heights (Bloom) vs. Maywood (Proviso East), Championship, 1974.
   15 ROBERT McCOY, Chicago Heights (Bloom) vs. Chicago (Wendell Phillips), Championship, 1975.
   15 LARRY WILLIAMS, Chicago (Wendell Phillips) vs. Waukegan, Quarterfinals, 1975.

Team

1. 56 Maywood (Proviso East) vs. Breese (Mater Dei), Semifinals, 1974.
2. 53 East St. Louis (Sr.) vs. Peoria (Richwoods), Semifinals, 1975.
3. 52 Chicago (Wendell Phillips) vs. Chicago Heights (Bloom), Championship, 1975.
   52 Peoria (Central) vs. Breese (Mater Dei), Third Place, 1974.
   52 Dolton (Thornridge) vs. Peoria (Manual), Semifinals, 1972.
6. 50 Bloomington (H.S.) vs. East St. Louis (Sr.), Quarterfinals, 1975.

<table>
<tbody>
<tr><td></td><td>50</td><td>Breese (Mater Dei) vs. Peoria (Central), Third Place, 1974.</td></tr>
<tr><td></td><td>50</td><td>Evanston vs. Peoria (Manual), Quarterfinals, 1972.</td></tr>
<tr><td>9.</td><td>49</td><td>Rockford (Auburn) vs. Peoria (Richwoods), Quarter-finals, 1975.</td></tr>
<tr><td></td><td>49</td><td>Maywood (Proviso East) vs. Chicago (Morgan Park), Quarterfinals, 1974.</td></tr>
<tr><td></td><td>49</td><td>Peoria (Manual) vs. Evanston, Quarterfinals, 1972.</td></tr>
<tr><td></td><td>49</td><td>Quincy (Sr.) vs. Aurora (West), Semifinals, 1972.</td></tr>
<tr><td></td><td>49</td><td>Dolton (Thornridge) vs. Quincy, Championship, 1972.</td></tr>
</tbody>
</table>

Tournament Rebounds
Individual

1.	55	BOYD BATTS, Dolton (Thornridge), 1972.
	55	LARRY WILLIAMS, Chicago (Wendell Phillips), 1975.
3.	53	JOE PONSETTO, Maywood (Proviso East), 1974.
	53	JEFF ROTH, Decatur (Eisenhower), 1976.
5.	52	ANTHONY WILLIAMS, East St. Louis (Sr.), 1975.
6.	47	MIKE DAVIS, Peoria (Manual), 1972.
	47	AUDIE MATTHEWS, Chicago Heights (Bloom), 1974.
8.	45	LANCE REILMANN, Breese (Mater Dei), 1974.
9.	43	CHARLES ANTHONY, East St. Louis (Sr.), 1975.
10.	42	MICHAEL WHITE, Peoria (Central), 1974.
11.	41	HUBERT HOOSMAN, East St. Louis (Sr.), 1975.
	41	CHRIS WILLIAMS, Peoria (Richwoods), 1975.

Single Game Field Goals
Individual

1.	18	GREG SMITH, Aurora (East) vs Quincy (Sr.), Semi-finals, 1972, 18/25.
2.	16	LARRY MOORE, Quincy (Sr.) vs. Chicago (Crane), Quarterfinals, 1972, 16/31.
3.	15	BOYD BATTS, Dolton (Thornridge) vs. Collinsville, Quarterfinals, 1972, 15/20.
4.	14	BOYD BATTS, Dolton (Thornridge) vs. Quincy (Sr.), Championship, 1972, 14/18.
5.	13	KELVIN SMALL, Chicago Heights (Bloom) vs. East St. Louis (Sr.), Semifinals, 1975, 13/22.

13   JIM FLYNN, Hinsdale (Central) vs. Aurora (East), Quarterfinals, 1972, 13/24.

13   LARRY MOORE, Quincy (Sr.) vs. Aurora (East), Semifinals, 1972, 13/37.

13   GREG ROSE, Dolton (Thornridge) vs. Quincy (Sr.), Championship, 1972, 13/21.

13   JEFF ROTH, Decatur (Eisenhower) vs. Marion, Quarterfinals, 1976, 13/19.

10. 12   KELVIN SMALL, Chicago Heights (Bloom) vs. Maywood (Proviso East), Quarterfinals, 1975, 12/15.

12   LARRY WILLIAMS, Chicago (Wendell Phillips) vs. Chicago Heights (Bloom), Championship, 1975, 12/20.

12   KEVIN WESTERVELT, Peoria (Richwoods) vs. East St. Louis (Sr.), Semifinals, 1975, 12/18.

12   RAYMOND WATSON, Danville (H.S.) vs. Peoria (Central), Quarterfinals, 1974, 12/21.

12   JOE WHARTON, Evanston vs. Peoria (Manual), Quarterfinals, 1972, 12/27.

12   GREG ROSE, Dolton (Thornridge) vs. Collinsville, Quarterfinals, 1972, 12/17.

12   MIKE DAVIS, Peoria, (Manual) vs. Aurora (East), Third Place, 1972, 12/23.

12   LEVI COBB, Chicago (Morgan Park) vs. Oak Park-River Forest, Semifinals, 1976, 12/20.

Tournament Field Goals
Individual

1. 47   GREG SMITH, Aurora (East), 1972, 47/77.
2. 44   LARRY MOORE, Quincy (Sr.), 1972, 44/107.
3. 43   GREG ROSE, Dolton (Thornridge), 1972, 43/67.
4. 41   BOYD BATTS, Dolton (Thornridge), 1972, 41/61.
5. 39   MIKE DAVIS, Peoria (Manual), 1972, 39/82.
6. 37   MATT HICKS, Aurora (West), 1973, 37/82.
37   JOE PONSETTO, Maywood (Proviso East), 1974, 37/67.
37   HUBERT HOOSMAN, East St. Louis (Sr.), 1975, 37/66.
37   LEVI COBB, Chicago (Morgan Park), 1976, 37/69.

10.   35   AUDIE MATTHEWS, Chicago Heights (Bloom), 1974, 35/80.
      35   LARRY WILLIAMS, Chicago (Wendell Phillips), 1975, 35/61.

Single Game Free Throws
Individual

1.   15   BOB BONE, Collinsville vs. Winnetka (New Trier East), Quarterfinals, 1973, 15/17.
2.   11   MARTY MURRAY, Chicago (Wendell Phillips) vs. Peoria (Richwoods), Semifinals, 1975, 11/12.
3.   10   DON SORENSON, Quincy (Sr.) vs. Dolton (Thornridge), Championship, 1972, 10/10.
4.   9   BOYD BATTS, Dolton (Thornridge) vs. Quincy (Sr.), Championship, 1972, 9/10.
5.   8   GREG SMITH, Aurora (East) vs. Quincy (Sr.), Semifinals, 1972, 8/11.
      8   DON SORENSON, Quincy (Sr.) vs. Aurora (East), Semifinals, 1972, 8/11.
      8   JOHN BRYANT, Aurora (West) vs. Elgin (H.S.), Quarterfinals, 1973, 8/9.
      8   TIM BUSHELL, Lincoln vs. Lockport (Central), Quarterfinals, 1973, 8/12.
      8   MIKE GUYER, Oswego vs. Breese (Mater Dei), Quarterfinals, 1974, 8/9.
      8   MARK KRAUSE, Arlington Heights (Hersey) vs. Chicago Heights (Bloom), Quarterfinals, 1974, 8/10.
      8   TOM NORRIS, Oak Park-River Forest vs. Wilmette (Loyola), Quarterfinals, 1976, 8/9.
      8   JAY BRYANT, Aurora (West) vs. Chicago (Morgan Park), Title, 1976, 8/9.

Tournament Free Throws
Individual

1.   22   LARRY MOORE, Quincy, (Sr.) 1972, 22/29.
     22   JOHN ROBINSON, Chicago (Hirsch), 1973, 22/26.
3.   21   BOYD BATTS, Dolton (Thornridge), 1972, 21/29.
     21   DON SORENSON, Quincy (Sr.), 1972, 21/26.
     21   DON SPEAR, Quincy (Sr.), 1972, 21/28.

6.   21   BOB BONE, Collinsville, 1973, 21/25.
      21   MICHAEL WILCOXSIN, Chicago (Morgan Park),
            1974, 21/23.
8.   20   JAY BRYANT, Aurora (West), 1976, 20/25.
9.   18   GREG SMITH, Aurora (East), 1972, 18/22.
      18   ROBERT McCOY, Chicago Heights (Bloom), 1975,
            18/31.

COACHING

MOST TITLES — 1, Ron Ferguson, Dolton (Thornridge), 1972; Charles Stimpson, Chicago (Hirsch), 1973; Glenn Whittenberg, Maywood (Proviso East), 1974; Herb Brown, Chicago (Wendell Phillips), 1975; Bill Warden, Chicago (Morgan Park), 1976.

COACHED IN TITLE GAME — 2, Wes Mason, Chicago Hts. (Bloom), 1974, 1975.

APPEARANCES — 3, John McDougal, Aurora (West), 1973, 1975, 1976.

Class AA Attendance Records

TOURNAMENT (16 games) — 104,362 in 1976.
STATE FINALS AT ASSEMBLY HALL — 60,320 in 1972.
SINGLE SESSION — 15,887 (sellout) twice in 1972; once in 1975 (Session No. 2).
TITLE GAME — 15,214 in 1976.
CLASS AA TOTAL STATE FINAL TO DATE —293,268 (5 years)

1972 —	60,320	1973 —	60,187
1974 —	59,020	1975 —	55,886
1976 —	57,855		

Two generations—dad Shelby and son Don—of the Himes family have devoted many hours to a pictoral display of the championship teams in each and every IHSA State Basketball Tournament. The display is located in the family's Bailey & Himes Sporting Goods, Inc. warehouse in Urbana. Several pictures from the collection were graciously loaned to the Association by the Himes for use in this book. The Himes collection is believed to be the only one of its type in the state.

FIRST AWARD—When Peoria (H.S.) captured the first State Basketball Tournament in 1908, the Lions were presented with this banner, symbolic of the accomplishment. It remains on display today in the trophy case at Peoria (H.S.). (IHSA Photo)

Class A Team Data
(State Final Tournament Only)
Appearances

School	Year/Place	Won/Loss	Pct.	Times Placed in Top Four
Aurora (Marmion)	1976	0-1	.000	
Bloomington (Central Catholic)	1973, 1976	0-2	.000	
Buda-Sheffield (Western)	1975, 1976 (4th)	1-3	.250	1
Cerro Gordo	1973, 1974	0-2	.000	
Chatham (Glenwood)	1975	0-1	.000	
Eldorado	1975 (4th), 1976	1-3	.250	1
Elgin (St. Edward)	1972	0-1	.000	
Elmhurst (Timothy Christian)	1975 (2nd)	2-1	.667	1
Fulton	1973	0-1	.000	
Gibson City	1972	0-1	.000	
Havana	1976	0-1	.000	
Lawrenceville	1972 (1st) 1974 (1st) 1976 (3rd)	8-1	.889	3
Lexington	1974	0-1	.000	
Maple Park (Kaneland)	1973 (2nd)	2-1	.667	1
Morrisonville	1975	0-1	.000	
Mounds (Meridian)	1972 (2nd)	2-1	.667	1
Mt. Pulaski	1976 (1st)	3-0	1.000	1
Oneida (ROVA)	1976 (2nd)	2-1	.667	1
Ottawa (Marquette)	1974 (2nd)	2-1	.667	1
Palos Heights (Chicago Christian)	1974 (3rd)	2-1	.667	1
Petersburg (Porta)	1973	0-1	.000	
Port Byron (Riverdale)	1975	0-1	.000	
Prophetstown	1974	0-1	.000	
Quincy (Catholic Boys Notre Dame)	1972-1974 (4th)	1-3	.250	1
Raymond (Lincolnwood)	1972 (3rd)	2-1	.667	1
Ridgway	1973 (1st), 1974	3-1	.750	1
St. Anne	1973 (4th),	1-2	.333	1
Streator (Woodland)	1972	0-1	.000	
Thomson	1972 (4th)	1-2	.333	1
Venice	1973 (3rd) 1975 (1st)	5-1	.833	2
Watseka	1975 (3rd)	2-1	.667	1

Class A Tournament Records

Championship Game Records

Team Records

MOST POINTS, 2 Teams — 120 Lawrenceville 63, Mounds (Meridian) 57, 1972.

Winning Team — 65 Venice vs. Elmhurst (Timothy Christian) 46, 1975.

Losing Team — 58 Oneida (ROVA) vs. Mt. Pulaski 59, 1976.

POINT MARGIN — 19 Venice 65, Elmhurst (Timothy Christian) 46, 1975.

FIELD GOALS, Number — 28, Mt. Pulaski vs. Oneida (ROVA), 1976. 28, Oneida (ROVA) vs. Mt. Pulaski, 1976.

Percentage — .539 (28 of 52), Oneida (ROVA) vs. Mt. Pulaski, 1976.

FREE THROWS, Number — 19, Venice vs. Elmhurst (Timothy Christian), 1975 (19 of 21).

Percentage — .905 (19 of 21), Venice vs. Elmhurst (Timothy Christian), 1975 (Minimum 4 attempts).

REBOUNDS — 43, Lawrenceville vs. Mounds (Meridian), 1972
43, Mounds (Meridian) vs. Lawrenceville, 1972

Individual Records

POINTS — 32, Mike Lockhart (15-28 FG and 2-2 FT) Lawrenceville vs. Mounds (Meridian), 1972.

FIELD GOALS — 15 (of 28), Mike Lockhart, Lawrenceville vs. Mounds (Meridian), 1972.

FREE THROWS — 6 (of 11), Curtis Bogan, Mounds (Meridian) vs. Lawrenceville, 1972.
6 (of 7), Bill Sambrookes, Maple Park (Kaneland) vs. Ridgway, 1973.

REBOUNDS — 16, Jeff Anderson, Mt. Pulaski vs. Oneida (ROVA), 1976.

All-Game Records

Team

MOST POINTS, All Games — 309 (83-68-68-90), Raymond (Lincolnwood), 1972 (took 3rd place).

2 Teams — 164 Ridgway (85), Petersburg (Porta) (79), 1973 in Quarter-finals.

Winning Team — 90, Raymond (Lincolnwood) vs. Thomson (69), 1972 in 3rd place game.

Losing Team — 79, Petersburg (Porta) vs. Ridgway (85), 1973 in Quarterfinals.

FEWEST POINTS, One Game — 18, Port Byron (Riverdale) vs. Elmhurst (Timothy Christian) (48), 1975 in Quarterfinals.

2 Teams — 66 Elmhurst (Timothy Christian) (48), Port Byron (Riverdale) (18), 1975 in Quarterfinals.

POINT MARGIN — 39 Ottawa (Marquette) (78), South Beloit (39), 1974 at DeKalb Super-Sectional.

REBOUNDS, All Games — 189 (38-62-48-41), St. Anne, 1973.

One Game — 62, St. Anne vs. Cerro Gordo, 1973 in Quarterfinals.

Fewest One Game — 14, Spring Valley (Hall Twp.) vs. Palos Hts. (Chicago Christian), 1974 at Streator Super-Sectional.

2 Teams — 120, Buda (Western) (57) vs. Watseka (63), 1973 in Quarterfinals.

FEWEST FIELD GOALS, One Game — 8, Port Byron (River-dale) (8 of 33) vs. Elmhurst (Timothy Christian), 1975 in Quarterfinals.

MOST FIELD GOALS, All Games — 122 (36-22-28-36), St. Anne, 1973 (took fourth place).

One Game — 36, St. Anne vs. Cerro Gordo, 1973 Quarter-finals (36 of 84). 36, St. Anne vs.

Toluca, 1973 Pontiac Super-
Sectional (36 of 76).
2 Teams — 71, Ridgway (35) vs. Peters-
burg (Porta) (36), 1973
Quarterfinals.
Winning Team — 36, St. Anne vs. Cerro
Gordo, 1973 Quarter-finals
(36 of 84). 36, St. Anne vs.
Toluca, 1973 Pontiac
Super-Sectional (36 of 76).
Losing Team — 36, by Petersburg
(Porta) vs. Ridgway, 1973 in
Quarterfinals (36 of 67).
MOST FREE THROWS, All Games — 99 (20-18-36-25), Ray-
mond (Lincolnwood), 1972.
One Game — 36, Raymond (Lincoln-
wood) vs. Lawrenceville, 1972
Semifinals (36 of 43).
2 Teams — 55, Raymond (Lincoln-
wood) (36 of 43) vs. Lawrence-
ville (19 of 30), 1972 Semifinals.
Winning Team — 26, by Thomson (26 of
33) vs. Farmington (East), 1972
East Moline Super-Sectional.
Losing Team — 36, Raymond (Lin-
colnwood) (36 of 43) vs.
Lawrenceville, 1972 Semifinals.
FEWEST FREE THROWS, One Game — 1, Normal (University)
(1 of 6) vs. Watseka, 1975
Normal Super-Sectional.
1, Cairo (1 of 3) vs. Eldorado,
1975 Carbondale Super-
Sectional.

Individual

MOST POINTS, All Games — 157 (27-37-48-45) Jay Shidler,
Lawrenceville, 1976.
One Game — 48, Jay Shidler, Lawrenceville
(18-35 FG and 12-14 FT) vs.
Oneida (ROVA), Semifinals,
1976.

FIELD GOALS, All Games — 63 (of 129) Jay Shidler, Law-
renceville, 1976.
One Game — 19 (of 25), Brent Browning,
Ridgway vs. Petersburg (Porta),
1973 Quarterfinals.
FREE THROWS, All Games — 43 (of 56), Dave Hobson, Ray-
mond (Lincolnwood), 1972.
One Game — 19 (of 20) Dave Johnson,
Oneida (ROVA) vs. Lawrence-
ville, 1976 Semifinals.
Consecutive — 15 (in one game) Dave John-
son, Oneida (ROVA), 1976.
One Game Consecutive — 15 Dave Johnson,
Oneida (ROVA) vs. Lawrence-
ville, Semifinals, 1976.
REBOUNDS, All Games — 75 (4 games), Bob Klaas, Palos
Hts. (Chicago Christian), 1974.
One Game — 27, Kevin Washington, Peters-
burg (Porta) vs. Ridgway, 1973
Quarterfinals.

Class A Scoring Leaders

Year	Player/School/Class	Games	FG-FGA	Pct.	FT-FTA	Pct.	TP	Average
1972	Don Robinson (Sr.) Thomson	4	46-118	.390	31-37	.838	123	30.7
1973	Brent Browning (Sr.) Ridgway	4	45-73	.616	15-25	.600	105	26.3
1974	Rick Leighty (Sr.) Lawrenceville	4	43-78	.551	13-18	.722	99	24.8
1975	Lyndon Swanson (Sr.) Watseka	4	38-86	.442	19-30	.633	95	23.8
1976	Jay Shidler (Sr.) Lawrenceville	4	63-129	.488	31-35	.885	157	39.2

Top Performances — Assembly Hall Only
Class A -Single Game Points
Individual

1. 48 JAY SHIDLER, Lawrenceville vs. Oneida (ROVA), Semifinal, 1976.
2. 45 BRENT BROWNING, Ridgway vs. Petersburg (Porta), Quarterfinals, 1973.
    45 JAY SHIDLER, Lawrenceville vs. Buda-Sheffield (Western), Third Place, 1976.
4. 38 DAVE HOBSON, Raymond (Lincolnwood) vs. Gibson City, Quarterfinals, 1972.
5. 37 LYNDON SWANSON, Watseka vs. Eldorado, Third Place, 1975.
    37 JAY SHIDLER, Lawrenceville vs. Aurora (Marmion), Quarterfinals, 1976.
7. 36 JACK SIKMA, St. Anne vs. Cerro Gordo, Quarterfinals, 1973.
    36 DON ROBINSON, Thomson vs. Raymond (Lincolnwood), Third Place, 1972.
9. 35 JEFF CLEMENTS, Mt. Pulaski vs. Eldorado, Quarterfinals, 1976.
10. 34 DENNIS GRAFF, Gibson City vs. Raymond (Lincolnwood), Quarterfinals, 1972.
11. 33 DAVE JOHNSON, Oneida (ROVA) vs. Lawrenceville, Semifinals, 1976.
12. 32 MIKE LOCKHART, Lawrenceville vs. Mounds (Meridian), Championship, 1972.
13. 31 RICK LEIGHTY, Lawrenceville vs. Raymond (Lincolnwood), Semifinals, 1972.

Team

1. 90 Raymond (Lincolnwood) vs. Thomson, Third Place, 1972.
2. 88 St. Anne vs. Cerro Gordo, Quarterfinals, 1972.
3. 85 Ridgway vs. Petersburg (Porta), Quarterfinals, 1973.
4. 81 Mounds (Meridian) vs. Thomson, Semifinals, 1972.
5. 79 Petersburg (Porta) vs. Ridgway, Quarterfinals, 1973.
6. 77 Oneida (ROVA) vs. Lawrenceville, Semifinals, 1976.
7. 76 Mt. Pulaski vs. Eldorado, Quarterfinals, 1976.

8. 74 Watseka vs. Eldorado, Third Place, 1975.
   74 Thomson vs. Mounds (Meridian), Semifinals, 1972.
   74 Mt. Pulaski vs. Buda-Sheffield (Western), Semifinals, 1976.
11. 73 Ridgway vs. St. Anne, Semifinals, 1973.
   73 Venice vs. St. Anne, Third Place, 1973.

Tournament Points
Individual

1. 157 JAY SHIDLER, Lawrenceville, 1976.
2. 123 DON ROBINSON, Thomson, 1972.
3. 107 DAVE HOBSON, Raymond (Lincolnwood), 1972.
4. 105 BRENT BROWNING, Ridgway, 1973.
   105 DAVE JOHNSON, Oneida (ROVA), 1976.
6. 100 JACK SIKMA, St. Anne, 1973.
7. 99 RICK LEIGHTY, Lawrenceville, 1974.
8. 95 LYNDON SWANSON, Watseka, 1975.
9. 87 JEFF CLEMENTS, Mt. Pulaski, 1976.
10. 83 RON HENRY, Venice, 1973.
11. 82 MIKE DIXON, Ridgway, 1973.
   82 MIKE LOCKHART, Lawrenceville, 1972.

Single Game Rebounds
Individual

1. 27 KEVIN WASHINGTON, Petersburg (Porta) vs. Ridgway, Quarterfinals, 1973.
2. 24 BOB KLAAS, Palos Heights (Chicago Christian) vs. Lexington, Quarterfinals, 1974.
   24 BOB KLAAS, Palos Heights (Chicago Christian) vs. Lawrenceville, Semifinals, 1974.
   24 JACK SIKMA, St. Anne vs. Cerro Gordo, Quarterfinals, 1973.
5. 22 JOHN MOMPER, Aurora (Marmion) vs. Lawrenceville, Quarterfinals, 1976.
6. 20 LYNDON SWANSON, Watseka vs. Venice, Semifinals, 1975.
7. 17 JACK SIKMA, St. Anne vs. Venice, Third Place, 1973.
   17 RICK LEIGHTY, Lawrenceville vs. Raymond (Lincolnwood), Semifinals, 1972.

9. 16 MIKE MILLER, Fulton vs. Maple Park (Kaneland), Quarterfinals, 1973.

16 JACK SIKMA, St. Anne vs. Ridgway, Semifinals, 1973.

16 JEFF ANDERSON, Mt. Pulaski vs. Oneida (ROVA), Title, 1976.

Team

1. 62 St. Anne vs. Cerro Gordo, Quarterfinals, 1972.
2. 55 Mounds (Meridian) vs. Thomson, Semifinals, 1972.
3. 54 Raymond (Lincolnwood) vs. Thomson, Third Place, 1972.
4. 52 Lexington vs. Palos Heights (Chicago Christian), Quarterfinals, 1974.
5. 50 Thomson vs. Mounds (Meridian), Semifinals, 1972.
   50 Palos Heights (Chicago Christian) vs. Lexington, Quarterfinals, 1974.
7. 49 Aurora (Marmion) vs. Lawrenceville, Quarterfinals, 1976.
8. 48 St. Anne vs. Ridgway, Semifinals, 1972.
   48 Thomson vs. Raymond (Lincolnwood), Third Place, 1972.
10. 46 Ottawa (Marquette) vs. Quincy (Catholic Boys), Semifinals, 1974.
    46 Palos Heights (Chicago Christian) vs. Lawrenceville, Semifinals, 1974.
    46 Buda-Sheffield (Western) vs. Watseka, Quarterfinals, 1975.
    46 Watseka vs. Buda-Sheffield (Western), Quarterfinals, 1975.
    46 Buda-Sheffield (Western) vs. Havana, Quarterfinals, 1976.

Tournament Rebounds
Individual

1. 75 BOB KLAAS, Palos Heights (Chicago Christian), 1974.
2. 73 JACK SIKMA, St. Anne, 1973.
3. 55 LYNDON SWANSON, Watseka, 1975.
4. 53 JEFF ANDERSON, Mt. Pulaski, 1976.
5. 48 DAVE JOHNSON, Oneida (ROVA), 1976.

6. 46 RON HENRY, Venice, 1973.
7. 44 MIKE HILL, Thomson, 1972.
    44 KEITH RENKOSIK, Ottawa (Marquette), 1974.
9. 41 RICK LEIGHTY, Lawrenceville, 1972.
    41 DAVE HOBSON, Raymond (Lincolnwood), 1972.
    41 RICK LEIGHTY, Lawrenceville, 1974.
    41 MIKE HENRY, Venice, 1975.

Single Game Field Goals
Individual

1. 19 BRENT BROWNING, Ridgway vs. Petersburg
        (Porta), Quarterfinals, 1973, 19/25.
2. 18 JAY SHIDLER, Lawrenceville vs. Oneida (ROVA),
        Semifinals, 1976, 18/35.
    18 JAY SHIDLER, Lawrenceville vs. Buda-Sheffield
        (Western), Third Place, 1976, 18/28.
4. 16 JACK SIKMA, St. Anne vs. Cerro Gordo, Quar-
        terfinals, 1973, 16/31.
5. 15 MIKE LOCKHART, Lawrenceville vs. Mounds (Meri-
        dian), Championship, 1972, 15/28.
    15 JAY SHIDLER, Lawrenceville vs. Aurora (Marmion),
        Quarterfinals, 1976, 15/44.
7. 14 LYNDON SWANSON, Watseka vs. Eldorado, Third
        Place, 1975, 14/21.
    14 MIKE DUFF, Eldorado vs. Mt. Pulaski, Quarterfinals,
        1976, 14/22.
9. 13 RON HENRY, Venice vs. Bloomington (Central
        Catholic), Quarterfinals, 1973, 13/25.
    13 DON ROBINSON, Thomson vs. Raymond (Lin-
        colnwood), Third Place, 1972, 13/35.
    13 DENNIS GRAFF, Gibson City vs. Raymond (Lin-
        colnwood), Quarterfinals, 1972, 13/23.
    13 DAVE HOBSON, Raymond (Lincolnwood) vs. Gib-
        son City, Quarterfinals, 1972, 13/31.
    13 DAVE JOHNSON, Oneida (ROVA) vs. Mt. Pulaski,
        Title, 1976, 13/22.

Tournament Field Goals
Individual

1. 63 JAY SHIDLER, Lawrenceville, 1976, 63/129.
2. 46 DON ROBINSON, Thomson, 1972, 46/118.

3. 45 BRENT BROWNING, Ridgway, 1973, 45/73.
4. 43 JACK SIKMA, St. Anne, 1973, 43/95.
    43 RICK LEIGHTY, Lawrenceville, 1974, 43/78.
6. 38 LYNDON SWANSON, Watseka, 1975, 38/86.
    38 DAVE JOHNSON, Oneida (ROVA), 1976, 38/67.
8. 37 MIKE LOCKHART, Lawrenceville, 1972, 37/76.
    37 RON HENRY, Venice, 1973, 37/70.
10. 36 JEFF CLEMENTS, Mt. Pulaski, 1976, 36/69.
11. 35 MIKE DUFF, Eldorado, 1975, 35/56.
12. 34 MIKE DIXON, Ridgway, 1973, 34/60.
13. 32 DAVE HOBSON, Raymond (Lincolnwood), 1972, 32/69.

Single Game Free Throws
Individual

1. 19 DAVE   JOHNSON,   Oneida   (ROVA)   vs.   Lawrenceville, Semifinals, 1976, 19/20.
2. 17 DAVE HOBSON, Raymond (Lincolnwood) vs. Lawrenceville, Semifinals, 1972, 17/19.
3. 12 DAVE HOBSON, Raymond (Lincolnwood) vs. Gibson City, Quarterfinals, 1972, 12/15.
    12 JAY SHIDLER, Lawrenceville vs. Oneida (ROVA), Semifinals, 1976, 12/14.
5. 11 TOM WOLFE, Lawrenceville vs. Quincy (Catholic Boys), Quarterfinals, 1972, 11/11.
6. 10 DON ROBINSON, Thomson vs. Mounds (Meridian), Semifinals, 1972, 10/13.
    10 DON ROBINSON, Thomson vs. Raymond (Lincolnwood), Third Place, 1972, 10/10.
8.   9 JAY SHIDLER, Lawrenceville vs. Buda-Sheffield (Western), Third Place, 1972, 9/9.
     9 LYNDON SWANSON, Watseka vs. Eldorado, Third Place, 1975, 9/15.
     9 JEFF CLEMENTS, Mt. Pulaski vs. Eldorado, Quarterfinals, 1976, 9/9.
11. 8 DENNIS GRAFF, Gibson City vs. Raymond (Lincolnwood), Quarterfinals, 1972, 8/10.
     8 MARK HISKES, Palos Heights (Chicago Christian) vs. Quincy (Catholic Boys), Third Place, 1974, 8/10.
     8 MIKE DIXON, Ridgway vs. St. Anne, Semifinals, 1973, 8/8.

Tournament Free Throws
Individual

1. 43 DAVE HOBSON, Raymond (Lincolnwood), 1972, 43/56.
2. 31 JAY SHIDLER, Lawrenceville, 1976, 31/35.
3. 31 DON ROBINSON, Thomson, 1972, 31/37.
4. 29 DAVE JOHNSON, Oneida (ROVA), 1976, 29/35.
5. 19 LYNDON SWANSON, Watseka, 1975, 19/30.
6. 17 DAN FUCHS, Raymond (Lincolnwood), 1972, 17/23.
7. 17 TOM WOLFE, Lawrenceville, 1972, 17/21.
8. 16 CRAIG FITZGERALD, Mounds (Meridian), 1972, 16/21.
9. 16 BRUCE VANDERSCHAAF, Elmhurst (Timothy Christian), 1975, 16/23.
10. 16 BARRY SMITH, Eldorado, 1975, 16/19.

Coaching

MOST TITLES — 2, Ron Felling, Lawrenceville, 1972 (State Final), 1974.

COACHED IN TITLE GAME — 2, Ron Felling, Lawrenceville, 1972 and 1974.

APPEARANCES — 3, Ron Felling, Lawrenceville, 1972, 1974, 1976.

Class A Attendance

TOURNAMENT (16 games total) — 99,878 in 1976
STATE FINALS AT ASSEMBLY HALL — 56,667 in 1976
SINGLE SESSION — 14,552 at Saturday night session in 1974.
TITLE GAME — 14,552 in 1974.
CLASS A TOTAL STATE FINAL TO DATE — 266,778 (5 years)

1972 — 48,904	1973 — 51,553
1974 — 55,423	1975 — 54,231
1976 — 56,667	

All-Time IHSA State Tournament Officials

(Title Game Officials Only From 1909–1928)

1908—Norton
Harlow
1909—Not Available
1910—G. O. Laustead, St.
Louis
G. E. DeKriuf, Chi-
cago
1911—R. Rutherford, Peoria
Earl Bridge, Gales-
burg
1912—Rufus Gilbert, Peoria
Ted Roe
1913—Musselman
Davis
1914—Ralph Tenney, Deca-
tur
C. E. Howell, Decatur
1915—Gunn
D. V. Shipley, Chi-
cago
1916—William Duerr, Deca-
tur
C. E. Howell, Decatur
1917—Charles P. Lantz,
Charleston
D. V. Shipley, Chi-
cago
1918—Fred "Brick" Young,
Bloomington
D. V. Shipley, Chi-
cago
1919—Fred Young,
Bloomington
Charles P. Lantz,
Charleston
1920—Fred Young,
Bloomington
Charles P. Lantz,
Charleston
1921—Fred Young,
Bloomington
Howard Millard, De-
catur

1922—Fred Young,
Bloomington
M. W. Driggs, Rock
Island
1923—Fred Young,
Bloomington
Sam Barry, Gales-
burg
1924—Fred Young,
Bloomington
Art Swedberg, Rock
Island
1925—Fred Young,
Bloomington
Art Swedberg, Rock
Island
1926—Fred Young,
Bloomington
Art Swedberg, Rock
Island
1927—Leo Johnson, Decatur
Fred Young,
Bloomington
1928—Fred Young,
Bloomington
Lyle Clarno, Batavia
1929—Lyle Clarno, Batavia
Carl Johnson, Ba-
tavia
Fred Young,
Bloomington
1930—Arthur J. Bergstrom,
Casey
Art Cox, Rushville
A. C. Serfling, Oak
Park
1931—Arthur J. Bergstrom,
Casey
Milton Forsyth, Mt.
Vernon
A. C. Serfling, Oak
Park

1932—R. L. Ashley, Riverside
Arthur J. Bergstrom, Casey
Harlow Sutherland, Bloomington
1933—R. L. Ashley, Riverside
Milton Forsyth, Mt. Vernon
Harlow Sutherland, Bloomington
1934—Ralph Albro, Peoria
R. L. Ashley, Riverside
Arnold Beem, Shelbyville
Wendell Williams, Mt. Vernon
1935—R. Wayne Gill, Decatur
John C. Robb, Princeton
J. B. Travnicek, Chicago
Wendell Williams, Mt. Vernon
1936—R. Wayne Gill, Decatur
John C. Hall, Mt. Vernon
John C. Robb, Princeton
J. B. Travnicek, Chicago
1937—R. Wayne Gill, Decatur
Edgar G. Gunderson, Belleville
John C. Hall, Mt. Vernon
Ernest Lieberson, Chicago
1938—A. C. Daugherty, Palestine
Ron J. Gibbs, Springfield
Edgar G. Gunderson,

Belleville
Ernest Lieberson, Chicago
1939—A. C. Daugherty, Palestine
R. H. Elliott, Danville
Ron J. Gibbs, Springfield
Stuart LeGault, Chicago
1940—R. H. Elliott, Danville
Stuart LeGault, Chicago
Edward A. Marfell, Hillsboro
M. S. Vaughn, Rockford
1941—Edward A. Marfell, Hillsboro
M. S. Vaughn, Rockford
Phillip E. Mann, Flora
1942—B. C. Beck, Danville
Carl A. Johnson, Batavia
Phillip E. Mann, Flora
Greg Shoaff, Springfield
1943—B. C. Beck, Danville
Carl A. Johnson, Batavia
R. C. Kaegel, Belleville
Greg Shoaff, Springfield
1944—Ernest A. Driggers, Mt. Vernon
Carl A. Johnson, Batavia
R. C. Kaegel, Belleville
Edward F. Murphy, Peoria
1945—William E. Downes, Chicago
Ernest A. Driggers, Mt. Vernon
Walter Johnson,

Cambridge
Edward F. Murphy,
Peoria
1946—William E. Downes,
Chicago
Sam Gillespie, St.
Elmo
Walter Johnson,
Cambridge
Wilbur Layman, Lin-
coln
1947—William Carlin, Peoria
Sam Gillespie, St.
Elmo
Wilbur Layman, Lin-
coln
Ted Search, Chester
1948—William Carlin, Peoria
Gordon Kickels,
Lemont
Ted Search, Chester
Robert Young, May-
wood
1949—Lynn Gibbs, Rantoul
Harold Inman, Cham-
paign
Gordon Kickels,
Lemont
Robert Young, May-
wood
1950—Lynn Gibbs, Rantoul
Harold Inman, Cham-
paign
Merle Ririe, Kewanee
W. Burdell Smith,
Low Point
1951—Art Bouxsein, Prince-
ton
Frank Falzone, Rock-
ford
L. J. Hackett, Peoria
(To replace
Ririe for 1 year)
Clyde McQueen,
Springfield
J. Russell Shields,
Greenfield
W. Burdell Smith, Pe-
oria

1952—Art Bouxsein, Prince-
ton
Frank Falzone, Rock-
ford
John K. Fraser, Alton
Clyde McQueen,
Springfield
Joe Przada, East St.
Louis
J. Russell Shields,
Greenfield
1953—Art Bouxsein, Prince-
ton
Frank Falzone, Rock-
ford
John K. Fraser, Alton
Tom Kouzmanoff, Ar-
lington Hts.
Jim Paterson, Crete
Joe Przada, East St.
Louis
1954—John K. Fraser, Alton
Tom Kouzmanoff, Ar-
lington Hts.
James McCoskey,
Murphysboro
Jim Paterson, Crete
Joe Przada, East St.
Louis
Claude Rhodes, Ben-
ton
1955—William D. Cox,
Charleston
Tom Kouzmanoff, Ar-
lington Hts.
James McCoskey,
Murphysboro
Jim Paterson, Crete
Claude Rhodes, Ben-
ton
Dwight B. Wilkey,
Monticello
1956—William D. Cox,
Charleston
James McCoskey,
Murphysboro
Claude Rhodes, Ben-
ton
Dwight B. Wilkey,

Monticello
1957—William D. Cox,
Charleston
Max Miller, Macomb
Dan Robbins, Ma-
comb
Dwight Wilkey, Mon-
ticello
1958—Edward C. Bronson,
Evergreen Park
William D. Cox,
Charleston
Joe E. Frank, Cham-
paign
Alvin Gebhardt, East
Peoria
Harold Inman, Cham-
paign
James McCoskey,
Murphysboro
Wayne Nohren,
Longview
Robert Young, May-
wood
1959—Edward C. Bronson,
Evergreen Park
Frank Falzone, Rock-
ford
Joe E. Frank, Cham-
paign
Alvin Gebhardt, Pe-
oria
Harold Inman, Cham-
paign
James McCoskey,
Murphysboro
Wayne Nohren,
Longview
Robert Young, May-
wood
1960—Frank Falzone, Rock-
ford
Joe E. Frank, Cham-
paign
Alvin D. Gebhardt,
Peoria
Harold Inman, Cham-
paign

Wayne Nohren,
Longview
Ernest L. Reynolds,
Carterville
Herbert Scheffler,
Springfield
Robert Young, May-
wood
1961—Robert Brodbeck, Pe-
oria
Joe E. Frank, Cham-
paign
Wayne Nohren,
Longview
Ernest Reynolds,
Carterville
Tony Sacco, Oak
Park
Herbert G. Scheffler,
Springfield
Joseph M. Starcevic,
Peoria
Tony Tortorello, Chi-
cago
1962—Alvin D. Gebhardt,
Peoria
Fred L. Gibson, Cen-
tralia
Wayne E. Nohren,
Longview
Ernest L. Reynolds,
Carterville
Tony Sacco, Oak
Park
Herbert G. Scheffler,
Springfield
Joseph Starcevic, Pe-
oria
Tony Tortorello, Chi-
cago
1963—Robert Brodbeck, Pe-
oria
Fred L. Gibson, Cen-
tralia
Ford Peebles, Mur-
physboro
Ernest Reynolds,
Carterville

Tony Sacco, Oak Park
Herbert Scheffler, Springfield
Joseph Starcevic, Peoria
Tony Tortorello, Chicago
1964—Robert Brodbeck, Peoria
A. Kevin Donlan, Oak Park
Thomas J. Frangella, Chicago
Fred L. Gibson, Centralia
Nick L. Gineris, Kankakee
August H. Jacobs, Elmhurst
Ford Peebles, Murphysboro
Joseph M. Starcevic, Peoria
1965—Jean W. DesMarteau, Kankakee
Thomas J. Frangella, Chicago
Robert Freels, Centralia
Nick L. Gineris, Kankakee
Augie Jacobs, Elmhurst
Wayne E. Nohren, Longview
Keith Parker, Granite City
Tommy Stewart, Champaign
1966—Tom Alexander, East Peoria
Paul W. Blakeman, Pontiac
Robert D. Blondi, Benton
Wayne Bollinger, Carterville

Jean W. DesMarteau, Kankakee
Robert Freels, Centralia
Keith Parker, Granite City
Tommy Stewart, Champaign
1967—Tom Alexander, East Peoria
Paul Blakeman, Pontiac
Robert Blondi, Benton
Wayne Bollinger, Carterville
Raymond Brooks, Oak Park
L. Cal Lepore, Chicago
Kenneth Rodermel, Freeport
Harry Wilcoxen, Peoria
1968—Tom Alexander, East Peoria
Raymond F. Brooks, Oak Park
Fred L. Gibson, Carlyle
Augie Jacobs, Glen Ellyn
L. Cal Lepore, Chicago
Patrick J. McGann, Peoria
Ernest L. Reynolds, Carterville
Kenneth G. Rodermel, Freeport
1969—Henry P. Bowman, Chicago
Jean W. DesMarteau, Kankakee
Richard Henley, Herrin
Patrick J. McGann, Peoria

Keith Parker, Granite
City
Ted Search, Jr.,
Chester
Tommy Stewart,
Champaign
Glen Van Proyen,
Glen Ellyn
1970—Wayne Bollinger, Car-
terville
Henry P. Bowman,
Chicago
Harry C. Forrester,
Champaign
Nick L. Gineris, Kan-
kakee
Richard P. Henley,
Herrin
Otho T. Kortz, Jr.,
Chicago
Ted Search, Jr.,
Chester
Glen Van Proyen,
Glen Ellyn
1971—Henry P. Bowman,
Chicago
Daniel F. Davey, Elgin
Harry C. Forrester,
Champaign
Richard F. Henley,
Herrin
Otho T. Kortz, Jr.,
Chicago
Patrick McGann, Pe-
oria
Ted Search, Jr.,
Chester
Glen Van Proyen,
Glen Ellyn
1972-A—Paul Blakeman,
Pontiac
James Bollinger,
Carterville
Paul Brooks, Rock
Island
Russell Chappell,
Granite City
Harry Forrester,

Champaign
Donald Frits, Port
Byron
James Meyer, New
Athens
Kenneth Rodermel,
Freeport
1972AA—Robert Burson,
Western Springs
Daniel Davey,
Elgin
Rich Dietz,
McLeansboro
Thomas Frangella,
Orland Park
Robert Freels,
Centralia
Otho T. Kortz, Jr.,
Chicago
Richard Leiber,
LaGrange
L. Cal Lepore, Chi-
cago
1973-A—James E. Bollinger,
Carterville
Paul E. Brooks,
Rock Island
Thomas E. Eng-
land, Springfield
William E. England,
Peoria
Donald H. Frits,
Port Byron
Ronald D. Gris-
som, Greenville
Norman D. Kruger,
Rockford
Robert L. Wright,
Champaign
1973AA—Raymond Brooks,
Oak Park
Robert Burson,
Western Springs
Russell Chappell,
Granite City
Daniel Davey,
Elgin
Richard Deitz,

McLeansboro
Richard Leiber,
LaGrange
Larry Leitner,
Pekin
James Meyer,
New Athens
1974-A—Stanley Decker,
Bloomington
William Dickson,
Batavia
Thomas E. England, Springfield
William E. England,
Peoria
Mel Klitzing,
Champaign
Norman D. Kruger,
Rockford
Richard J. Lippert,
Rockford
Robert L. Wright,
Champaign
1974AA—Robert Burson,
Western Springs
Wilton E. Crotz,
West Peoria
Richard T. Deitz,
McLeansboro
Ronald D. Grissom, Greenville
Richard A. Leiber,
LaGrange
Larry G. Leitner,
Pekin
Wayne L. Meece,
Normal
James R. Meyer,
James R. Meyer,
New Athens
1975-A—James Bolinger,
Carterville
Stan Decker, Normal
William Dickson,
Batavia
Ken Hungate, Benton
Mel Klitzing,

Champaign
Rockford
Jack Lulay, Peoria
Richard Thompson, Quincy
1975AA—Paul Brooks, Rock Island
Wilton Crotz, West Peoria
Edward Grams,
Aurora
Phil Robinson,
Midlothian
Russell Chappel,
Granite City
Stan Heth, Moline
Ronald Grissom,
Greenville
Wayne Meece,
Normal
1976A—Wayne Bigham, DuQuoin
Dave Dwyer, Peoria
Tom England,
Springfield
William England,
Peoria
Ken Hungate, Benton
Jack Lulay, Peoria
Del Maroon, Altamont
Richard Thompson,
Quincy
1976AA—Wilton Crotz, West Peoria
Ron Fahnestock,
Canton
Edward Grams,
Aurora
Jim Harmison,
Bradley
Stan Heth, Rock Island
Larry Leitner, Pekin
Wayne Meece,
Normal
Edward Norfleet,
Monticello